# Global
# Economic
# Prospects

*A World Bank Group
Flagship Report*

JANUARY 2024

# Global
# Economic
# Prospects

 **WORLD BANK GROUP**

© 2024 International Bank for Reconstruction and Development / The World Bank
1818 H Street NW, Washington, DC 20433
Telephone: 202-473-1000; Internet: www.worldbank.org

Some rights reserved

1 2 3 4   27 26 25 24

This work is a product of the staff of The World Bank with external contributions. The findings, interpretations, and conclusions expressed in this work do not necessarily reflect the views of The World Bank, its Board of Executive Directors, or the governments they represent. The World Bank does not guarantee the accuracy, completeness, or currency of the data included in this work and does not assume responsibility for any errors, omissions, or discrepancies in the information, or liability with respect to the use of or failure to use the information, methods, processes, or conclusions set forth. The boundaries, colors, denominations, and other information shown on any map in this work do not imply any judgment on the part of The World Bank concerning the legal status of any territory or the endorsement or acceptance of such boundaries.

Nothing herein shall constitute or be construed or considered to be a limitation upon or waiver of the privileges and immunities of The World Bank, all of which are specifically reserved.

**Rights and Permissions**

This work is available under the Creative Commons Attribution 3.0 IGO license (CC BY 3.0 IGO) http://creativecommons.org/licenses/by/3.0/igo. Under the Creative Commons Attribution license, you are free to copy, distribute, transmit, and adapt this work, including for commercial purposes, under the following conditions:

**Attribution**—Please cite the work as follows: World Bank. 2024. *Global Economic Prospects, January 2024.* Washington, DC: World Bank. doi:10.1596/978-1-4648-2017-5. License: Creative Commons Attribution CC BY 3.0 IGO

**Translations**—If you create a translation of this work, please add the following disclaimer along with the attribution: *This translation was not created by The World Bank and should not be considered an official World Bank translation. The World Bank shall not be liable for any content or error in this translation.*

**Adaptations**—If you create an adaptation of this work, please add the following disclaimer along with the attribution: *This is an adaptation of an original work by The World Bank. Views and opinions expressed in the adaptation are the sole responsibility of the author or authors of the adaptation and are not endorsed by The World Bank.*

**Third-party content**—The World Bank does not necessarily own each component of the content contained within the work. The World Bank therefore does not warrant that the use of any third-party-owned individual component or part contained in the work will not infringe on the rights of those third parties. The risk of claims resulting from such infringement rests solely with you. If you wish to reuse a component of the work, it is your responsibility to determine whether permission is needed for that reuse and to obtain permission from the copyright owner. Examples of components can include, but are not limited to, tables, figures, or images.

All queries on rights and licenses should be addressed to World Bank Publications, The World Bank Group, 1818 H Street NW, Washington, DC 20433, USA; e-mail: pubrights@worldbank.org.

ISSN: 1014-8906
ISBN (paper): 978-1-4648-2017-5
ISBN (electronic): 978-1-4648-2018-2
DOI: 10.1596/978-1-4648-2017-5

*Cover design*: Bill Pragluski (Critical Stages)

**Library of Congress Control Number: 2023924021.**

The cutoff date for the data used in the report was December 18, 2023.

# Summary of Contents

# Contents

# Acknowledgments

*This World Bank Flagship Report is a product of the Prospects Group in the Development Economics (DEC) Vice Presidency. The project was managed by M. Ayhan Kose and Carlos Arteta, under the general guidance of Indermit S. Gill.*

The report was prepared by a team that included Marie Albert, Francisco Arroyo Marioli, John Baffes, Bram Gootjes, Jongrim Ha, Samuel Hill, Reina Kawai, Philip Kenworthy, Jeetendra Khadan, Dohan Kim, Emiliano Luttini, Joseph Mawejje, Valerie Mercer-Blackman, Alen Mulabdic, Nikita Perevalov, Dominik Peschel, Kersten Stamm, Naotaka Sugawara, Takuma Tanaka, Garima Vasishtha, Guillermo Verduzco, Collette Wheeler, and Shu Yu.

Research assistance was provided by Guillermo Caballero, Mattia Coppo, Franco Diaz Laura, Jiayue Fan, Maria Hazel Macadangdang, Rafaela Martinho Henriques, Muneeb Ahmad Naseem, Vasiliki Papagianni, Lorëz Qehaja, Juan Felipe Serrano Ariza, Shijie Shi, Kaltrina Temaj, Urja Singh Thapa, and Juncheng Zhou. Modeling and data work was provided by Shijie Shi.

Online products were produced by Graeme Littler, with assistance from the Open Knowledge Repository. Joe Rebello managed communications and media outreach with a team that included Nandita Roy, Kristen Milhollin, and Mariana Lozzi Teixeira, and with extensive support from the World Bank's media and digital communications teams. Graeme Littler provided editorial support, with contributions from Adriana Maximiliano and Michael Harrup.

The print publication was produced by Adriana Maximiliano, in collaboration with Cindy Fisher, Maria Hazel Macadangdang, and Jewel McFadden.

Regional projections and write-ups were produced in coordination with country teams, country directors, and the offices of the regional chief economists.

Many reviewers provided extensive advice and comments. The analysis also benefited from comments and suggestions by staff members from World Bank country teams and other World Bank Vice Presidencies as well as Executive Directors in their discussion of the report on December 14, 2023. However, both forecasts and analysis are those of the World Bank staff and should not be attributed to Executive Directors or their national authorities.

# Foreword

Amid a barrage of shocks during the past four years, the global economy has proved to be surprisingly resilient. Major economies are emerging mostly unscathed after the fastest rise in interest rates in 40 years—without the usual scars of steep unemployment rates or financial crashes. Global inflation is being tamed without tipping the world into a recession. It is rare for countries to bring inflation rates down without triggering a downturn, but this time a "soft landing" seems increasingly possible.

Yet beyond the next two years, the outlook is dark. The end of 2024 will mark the halfway point of what was expected to be a transformative decade for development—when extreme poverty was to be extinguished, when major communicable diseases were to be eradicated, and when greenhouse-gas emissions were to be cut nearly in half. What looms instead is a wretched milestone: the weakest global growth performance of any half-decade since the 1990s, with people in one out of every four developing economies poorer than they were before the pandemic.

The forecasts in *Global Economic Prospects* imply that most economies—advanced as well as developing—are set to grow more slowly in 2024 and 2025 than they did in the decade before COVID-19. Global growth is expected to slow for a third year in a row—to 2.4 percent—before ticking up to 2.7 percent in 2025. Those rates, however, would still be far below the 3.1 percent average of the 2010s. Per-capita investment growth in 2023 and 2024 is expected to average just 3.7 percent—barely half the average of the previous two decades. Without corrective action, global growth will remain well below potential for the remainder of the 2020s.

But while the forecasts in this report are dismal, its policy analysis provides hope.

The report includes the first systematic assessment of what it takes to generate the most desirable kind of investment boom—one that comes with an increase in per-capita income growth, a step-up in productivity, and a reduction in poverty. Since the 1950s, countries across the world have managed to generate nearly 200 windfall-producing investment booms—episodes in which per-capita investment growth accelerated to 4 percent or more and stayed there for more than six years. The secret sauce for sparking such episodes was a comprehensive policy package: consolidation of government finances, expansion of trade and financial flows, stronger fiscal and financial institutions, and a better investment climate for private enterprise.

If each developing economy that engineered such an investment boom in the 2000s and 2010s were to repeat the feat in the 2020s, prospects for developing economies would move a third of the way closer to their full economic potential. If all developing economies also repeated their best 10-year performance to improve health, education, and labor force participation, they would close most of the remaining gap. That is, the potential growth in developing economies in the 2020s would be similar to what it was during the 2010s.

An additional avenue is open to the two-thirds of developing economies that rely on commodity exports. They can do better simply by applying the Hippocratic principle to fiscal policy: first, do no harm. These economies are prone to debilitating boom-and-bust cycles because commodity prices can rise or fall suddenly. Their fiscal policies tend to make matters worse. Fiscal procyclicality is 30 percent stronger in commodity-exporting developing economies than it is in other developing economies. Fiscal spending among commodity exporters also tends to be 40 percent more volatile than in other developing economies.

The result is a chronic drag on their growth prospects. The drag can be reduced by putting in place a fiscal framework to discipline government spending, adopting flexible exchange-rate systems, and avoiding restrictions on international movements of capital, among other things. If instituted as a package, these policy measures could help commodity exporters in developing economies increase per capita GDP growth by 1 percentage point every four or five years.

The 2020s have so far been a period of broken promises. Governments across the world have fallen short of the "unprecedented" goals they promised to meet by 2030: "to end poverty and hunger everywhere; to combat inequalities within and among countries;…and to ensure the lasting protection of the planet and its natural resources." But 2030 is still more than a half-decade away. That is long enough for emerging markets and developing economies to regain some of the lost ground—if their governments act now.

**Indermit S. Gill**
Senior Vice President and Chief Economist
The World Bank Group

# Executive Summary

*Global growth is set to slow further this year, amid the lagged and ongoing effects of tight monetary policy, restrictive financial conditions, and feeble global trade and investment. Downside risks to the outlook include an escalation of the recent conflict in the Middle East and associated commodity market disruptions, financial stress amid elevated debt and high borrowing costs, persistent inflation, weaker-than-expected activity in China, trade fragmentation, and climate-related disasters. Against this backdrop, policy makers around the world face enormous challenges. Even though investment in emerging market and developing economies (EMDEs) is likely to remain subdued, lessons learned from episodes of investment growth acceleration over the past seven decades highlight the importance of macroeconomic and structural policy actions and their interaction with well-functioning institutions in boosting investment and thus long-term growth prospects. Commodity-exporting EMDEs face a unique set of challenges amid fiscal policy procyclicality and volatility. This underscores the need for a properly designed fiscal framework that, combined with a strong institutional environment, can help build buffers during commodity price booms that can be drawn upon during subsequent slumps in prices. At the global level, cooperation needs to be strengthened to provide debt relief, facilitate trade integration, tackle climate change, and alleviate food insecurity.*

**Global outlook.** Global growth is expected to slow to 2.4 percent in 2024—the third consecutive year of deceleration—reflecting the lagged and ongoing effects of tight monetary policies to rein in decades-high inflation, restrictive credit conditions, and anemic global trade and investment. Near-term prospects are diverging, with subdued growth in major economies alongside improving conditions in emerging market and developing economies (EMDEs) with solid fundamentals. Meanwhile, the outlook for EMDEs with pronounced vulnerabilities remains precarious amid elevated debt and financing costs. Downside risks to the outlook predominate. The recent conflict in the Middle East, coming on top of the Russian Federation's invasion of Ukraine, has heightened geopolitical risks. Conflict escalation could lead to surging energy prices, with broader implications for global activity and inflation. Other risks include financial stress related to elevated real interest rates, persistent inflation, weaker-than-expected growth in China, further trade fragmentation, and climate change-related disasters.

Against this backdrop, policy makers face enormous challenges and difficult trade-offs. International cooperation needs to be strengthened to provide debt relief, especially for the poorest countries; tackle climate change and foster the energy transition; facilitate trade flows; and alleviate food insecurity. EMDE central banks need to ensure that inflation expectations remain well anchored and that financial systems are resilient. Elevated public debt and borrowing costs limit fiscal space and pose significant challenges to EMDEs—particularly those with weak credit ratings—seeking to improve fiscal sustainability while meeting investment needs. Commodity exporters face the additional challenge of coping with commodity price fluctuations, underscoring the need for strong policy frameworks. To boost longer-term growth, structural reforms are needed to accelerate investment, improve productivity growth, and close gender gaps in labor markets.

**Regional prospects.** Although some improvements in growth are expected in most EMDE regions, the overall outlook remains subdued. Growth this year is projected to soften in East Asia and Pacific—mainly on account of slower growth in China—Europe and Central Asia, and South Asia. Only a slight improvement in growth, from a weak base in 2023, is expected for Latin America and the Caribbean. More marked pickups in growth are projected for the Middle East and North Africa, supported by increased oil production, and Sub-Saharan Africa, reflecting recovery from recent weakness. In 2025, growth is projected to strengthen in most regions as the global recovery firms.

**The Magic of Investment Accelerations.** Investment powers economic growth, helps drive down poverty, and will be indispensable for tackling climate change and achieving other key development goals in emerging market and developing economies (EMDEs). Without further policy action, investment growth in these economies is likely to remain tepid for the remainder of this decade. But it can be boosted. This chapter offers the first comprehensive analysis of investment accelerations—periods in which there is a sustained increase in investment growth to a relatively rapid rate—in EMDEs. During these episodes over the past seven decades, investment growth typically jumped to more than 10 percent per year, which is more than three times the growth rate in other (non-acceleration) years. Countries that had investment accelerations often reaped an economic windfall: output growth increased by about 2 percentage points and productivity growth increased by 1.3 percentage points per year. Other benefits also materialized in the majority of such episodes: inflation fell, fiscal and external balances improved, and the national poverty rate declined. Most accelerations followed, or were accompanied by, policy shifts intended to improve macroeconomic stability, structural reforms, or both. These policy actions were particularly conducive to sparking investment accelerations when combined with well-functioning institutions. A benign external environment also played a crucial role in catalyzing investment accelerations in many cases.

**Fiscal Policy in Commodity Exporters: An Enduring Challenge.** Fiscal policy has been about 30 percent more procyclical and about 40 percent more volatile in commodity-exporting emerging market and developing economies (EMDEs) than in other EMDEs. Both procyclicality and volatility of fiscal policy—which share some underlying drivers—hurt economic growth because they amplify business cycles. Structural policies, including exchange rate flexibility and the easing of restrictions on international financial transactions, can help reduce both fiscal procyclicality and fiscal volatility. By adopting average advanced-economy policies regarding exchange rate regimes, restrictions on cross-border financial flows, and the use of fiscal rules, commodity-exporting EMDEs can increase their GDP per capita growth by about 1 percentage point every four to five years through the reduction in fiscal policy volatility. Such policies should be supported by sustainable, well-designed, and stability-oriented fiscal institutions that can help build buffers during commodity price booms to prepare for any subsequent slump in prices. A strong commitment to fiscal discipline is critical for these institutions to be effective in achieving their objectives.

# Abbreviations

| | |
|---|---|
| AE | advanced economy |
| CA | Central Asia |
| CE | Central Europe |
| CPI | consumer price index |
| EAP | East Asia and Pacific |
| ECA | Europe and Central Asia |
| ECB | European Central Bank |
| EE | Eastern Europe |
| EMBI | Emerging Market Bond Index (J.P. Morgan) |
| EMDEs | emerging market and developing economies |
| EU | European Union |
| FDI | foreign direct investment |
| FY | fiscal year |
| G20 | Group of Twenty (Argentina, Australia, Brazil, Canada, China, France, Germany, India, Indonesia, Italy, Japan, the Republic of Korea, Mexico, the Russian Federation, Saudi Arabia, South Africa, Türkiye, the United Kingdom, the United States, the European Union, and the African Union) |
| GCC | Gulf Cooperation Council |
| GDP | gross domestic product |
| GEP | *Global Economic Prospects* |
| GFC | global financial crisis |
| GNFS | goods and nonfactor services |
| IMF | International Monetary Fund |
| LAC | Latin America and the Caribbean |
| LIC | low-income country |
| MNA | Middle East and North Africa |
| OECD | Organisation for Economic Co-operation and Development |
| OPEC | Organization of the Petroleum Exporting Countries |
| OPEC+ | OPEC and Azerbaijan, Bahrain, Brunei Darussalam, Kazakhstan, Malaysia, Mexico, Oman, the Russian Federation, South Sudan, and Sudan |
| PMI | purchasing managers' index |
| PPP | purchasing power parity |
| RHS | right-hand scale |
| SAR | South Asia |
| SCC | South Caucasus |
| SOE | state-owned enterprise |
| SSA | Sub-Saharan Africa |
| TFP | total factor productivity |
| WAEMU | West African Economic and Monetary Union |
| WDI | World Development Indicators |

# CHAPTER 1

## GLOBAL OUTLOOK

*Global growth is expected to slow to 2.4 percent in 2024—the third consecutive year of deceleration—reflecting the lagged and ongoing effects of tight monetary policies to rein in decades-high inflation, restrictive credit conditions, and anemic global trade and investment. Near-term prospects are diverging, with subdued growth in major economies alongside improving conditions in emerging market and developing economies (EMDEs) with solid fundamentals. Meanwhile, the outlook for EMDEs with pronounced vulnerabilities remains precarious amid elevated debt and financing costs. Downside risks to the outlook predominate. The recent conflict in the Middle East, coming on top of the Russian Federation's invasion of Ukraine, has heightened geopolitical risks. Conflict escalation could lead to surging energy prices, with broader implications for global activity and inflation. Other risks include financial stress related to elevated real interest rates, persistent inflation, weaker-than-expected growth in China, further trade fragmentation, and climate change-related disasters. Against this backdrop, policy makers face enormous challenges and difficult trade-offs. International cooperation needs to be strengthened to provide debt relief, especially for the poorest countries; tackle climate change and foster the energy transition; facilitate trade flows; and alleviate food insecurity. EMDE central banks need to ensure that inflation expectations remain well anchored and that financial systems are resilient. Elevated public debt and borrowing costs limit fiscal space and pose significant challenges to EMDEs—particularly those with weak credit ratings—seeking to improve fiscal sustainability while meeting investment needs. Commodity exporters face the additional challenge of coping with commodity price fluctuations, underscoring the need for strong policy frameworks. To boost longer-term growth, structural reforms are needed to accelerate investment, improve productivity growth, and close gender gaps in labor markets.*

## Summary

Global economic activity continues to soften, amid the effects of tight monetary policies, restrictive financial conditions, and weak global trade growth. After a sharp slowdown in 2022 and another decline last year, global output growth is set to edge down in 2024, marking the third consecutive year of deceleration. The recent conflict in the Middle East has heightened geopolitical risks and raised uncertainty in commodity markets, with potential adverse implications for global growth. This comes while the world economy is continuing to cope with the lingering effects of the overlapping shocks of the past four years—the COVID-19 pandemic, the Russian Federation's invasion of Ukraine, and the rise in inflation and subsequent sharp tightening of global monetary conditions.

Near-term prospects are diverging (figure 1.1.A). Growth in advanced economies as a whole and in China is projected to slow in 2024 to well below its 2010-19 average pace. Meanwhile, aggregate growth is set to improve in EMDEs with strong

credit ratings, remaining close to pre-pandemic average rates. Although overall growth is also expected to firm somewhat from its 2023 low in EMDEs with weak credit ratings, the outlook for many such countries remains precarious, given elevated debt and financing costs, and idiosyncratic headwinds such as conflict.

Global headline and core inflation have continued to decline from 2022 peaks. Nonetheless, inflation remains above target in most advanced economies and about half of inflation-targeting EMDEs. Global inflation is projected to remain above its 2015-19 average beyond 2024 (figure 1.1.B). Monetary tightening in advanced economies is concluding, but real policy interest rates are expected to remain elevated for some time, as inflation returns to target only gradually. This will keep the stance of advanced-economy monetary policies restrictive in the near-term, following the largest and fastest increase in U.S. real policy rates since the early 1980s (figure 1.1.C).

Long-term yields on advanced-economy government bonds were volatile in 2023, reflecting shifting expectations about the path of future interest rates and sizable movements in term premia. Although yields have retreated from their late-October peaks, they still imply increased fiscal vulnerabilities, given that median global

---

*Note*: This chapter was prepared by Carlos Arteta, Phil Kenworthy, Nikita Perevalov, Garima Vasishtha, and Collette Wheeler, with contributions from John Baffes, Samuel Hill, Alen Mulabdic, Dominik Peschel, and Takuma Tanaka.

## TABLE 1.1 Real GDP[1]

(Percent change from previous year unless indicated otherwise)

Percentage point differences from
June 2023 projections

| | 2021 | 2022 | 2023e | 2024f | 2025f | 2023e | 2024f | 2025f |
|---|---|---|---|---|---|---|---|---|
| **World** | **6.2** | **3.0** | **2.6** | **2.4** | **2.7** | **0.5** | **0.0** | **-0.3** |
| **Advanced economies** | **5.5** | **2.5** | **1.5** | **1.2** | **1.6** | **0.8** | **0.0** | **-0.6** |
| United States | 5.8 | 1.9 | 2.5 | 1.6 | 1.7 | 1.4 | 0.8 | -0.6 |
| Euro area | 5.9 | 3.4 | 0.4 | 0.7 | 1.6 | 0.0 | -0.6 | -0.7 |
| Japan | 2.6 | 1.0 | 1.8 | 0.9 | 0.8 | 1.0 | 0.2 | 0.2 |
| **Emerging market and developing economies** | **7.0** | **3.7** | **4.0** | **3.9** | **4.0** | **0.0** | **0.0** | **0.0** |
| East Asia and Pacific | 7.5 | 3.4 | 5.1 | 4.5 | 4.4 | -0.4 | -0.1 | -0.1 |
| China | 8.4 | 3.0 | 5.2 | 4.5 | 4.3 | -0.4 | -0.1 | -0.1 |
| Indonesia | 3.7 | 5.3 | 5.0 | 4.9 | 4.9 | 0.1 | 0.0 | -0.1 |
| Thailand | 1.5 | 2.6 | 2.5 | 3.2 | 3.1 | -1.4 | -0.4 | -0.3 |
| Europe and Central Asia | 7.1 | 1.2 | 2.7 | 2.4 | 2.7 | 1.3 | -0.3 | 0.0 |
| Russian Federation | 5.6 | -2.1 | 2.6 | 1.3 | 0.9 | 2.8 | 0.1 | 0.1 |
| Türkiye | 11.4 | 5.5 | 4.2 | 3.1 | 3.9 | 1.0 | -1.2 | -0.2 |
| Poland | 6.9 | 5.1 | 0.5 | 2.6 | 3.4 | -0.2 | 0.0 | 0.2 |
| Latin America and the Caribbean | 7.2 | 3.9 | 2.2 | 2.3 | 2.5 | 0.7 | 0.3 | -0.1 |
| Brazil | 5.0 | 2.9 | 3.1 | 1.5 | 2.2 | 1.9 | 0.1 | -0.2 |
| Mexico | 5.8 | 3.9 | 3.6 | 2.6 | 2.1 | 1.1 | 0.7 | 0.1 |
| Argentina | 10.7 | 5.0 | -2.5 | 2.7 | 3.2 | -0.5 | 0.4 | 1.2 |
| Middle East and North Africa | 3.8 | 5.8 | 1.9 | 3.5 | 3.5 | -0.3 | 0.2 | 0.5 |
| Saudi Arabia | 3.9 | 8.7 | -0.5 | 4.1 | 4.2 | -2.7 | 0.8 | 1.7 |
| Iran, Islamic Rep.[2] | 4.7 | 3.8 | 4.2 | 3.7 | 3.2 | 2.0 | 1.7 | 1.3 |
| Egypt, Arab Rep.[2] | 3.3 | 6.6 | 3.8 | 3.5 | 3.9 | -0.2 | -0.5 | -0.8 |
| South Asia | 8.3 | 5.9 | 5.7 | 5.6 | 5.9 | -0.2 | 0.5 | -0.5 |
| India[2] | 9.1 | 7.2 | 6.3 | 6.4 | 6.5 | 0.0 | 0.0 | 0.0 |
| Bangladesh[2] | 6.9 | 7.1 | 6.0 | 5.6 | 5.8 | 0.8 | -0.6 | -0.6 |
| Pakistan[2] | 5.8 | 6.2 | -0.2 | 1.7 | 2.4 | -0.6 | -0.3 | -0.6 |
| Sub-Saharan Africa | 4.4 | 3.7 | 2.9 | 3.8 | 4.1 | -0.3 | -0.1 | 0.1 |
| Nigeria | 3.6 | 3.3 | 2.9 | 3.3 | 3.7 | 0.1 | 0.3 | 0.6 |
| South Africa | 4.7 | 1.9 | 0.7 | 1.3 | 1.5 | 0.4 | -0.2 | -0.1 |
| Angola | 1.2 | 3.0 | 0.5 | 2.8 | 3.1 | -2.1 | -0.5 | 0.0 |
| ***Memorandum items:*** | | | | | | | | |
| **Real GDP[1]** | | | | | | | | |
| High-income countries | 5.5 | 2.8 | 1.5 | 1.3 | 1.8 | 0.7 | 0.0 | -0.5 |
| Middle-income countries | 7.2 | 3.4 | 4.3 | 4.0 | 4.0 | 0.1 | 0.0 | -0.1 |
| Low-income countries | 4.2 | 4.8 | 3.5 | 5.5 | 5.6 | -1.7 | -0.5 | -0.4 |
| EMDEs excluding China | 6.0 | 4.2 | 3.2 | 3.5 | 3.8 | 0.3 | 0.1 | 0.0 |
| Commodity-exporting EMDEs | 5.2 | 3.2 | 2.5 | 2.9 | 3.1 | 0.6 | 0.1 | 0.2 |
| Commodity-importing EMDEs | 7.9 | 3.9 | 4.8 | 4.4 | 4.4 | -0.2 | 0.0 | -0.1 |
| Commodity-importing EMDEs excluding China | 7.2 | 5.3 | 4.2 | 4.2 | 4.5 | 0.0 | 0.0 | -0.3 |
| EM7 | 7.8 | 3.3 | 4.9 | 4.1 | 4.1 | 0.2 | 0.0 | -0.1 |
| World (PPP weights)[3] | 6.4 | 3.3 | 3.0 | 2.9 | 3.1 | 0.3 | 0.0 | -0.3 |
| **World trade volume[4]** | **11.1** | **5.6** | **0.2** | **2.3** | **3.1** | **-1.5** | **-0.5** | **0.1** |

**Commodity prices[5]**

Level differences from
June 2023 projections

| | 2021 | 2022 | 2023e | 2024f | 2025f | 2023e | 2024f | 2025f |
|---|---|---|---|---|---|---|---|---|
| WBG commodity price index | 100.9 | 142.5 | 108.4 | 104.9 | 102.2 | -1.0 | -3.7 | -7.6 |
| Energy index | 95.4 | 152.6 | 107.5 | 103.4 | 100.0 | -1.4 | -5.7 | -11.0 |
| Oil (US$ per barrel) | 70.4 | 99.8 | 83.1 | 81.0 | 78.0 | 3.1 | -1.0 | -6.4 |
| Non-energy index | 112.1 | 122.1 | 110.2 | 107.7 | 106.6 | -0.2 | 0.2 | -0.9 |

*Source:* World Bank.

*Note:* e = estimate; f = forecast. EM7 = Brazil, China, India, Indonesia, Mexico, the Russian Federation, and Türkiye. WBG = World Bank Group. World Bank forecasts are frequently updated based on new information. Consequently, projections presented here may differ from those contained in other World Bank documents, even if basic assessments of countries' prospects do not differ at any given date. For the definition of EMDEs, developing countries, commodity exporters, and commodity importers, please refer to table 1.2. The World Bank is currently not publishing economic output, income, or growth data for Turkmenistan and República Bolivariana de Venezuela owing to lack of reliable data of adequate quality. Turkmenistan and República Bolivariana de Venezuela are excluded from cross-country macroeconomic aggregates.

1. Headline aggregate growth rates are calculated using GDP weights at average 2010-19 prices and market exchange rates.

2. GDP growth rates are on a fiscal year basis. Aggregates that include these countries are calculated using data compiled on a calendar year basis. For India and the Islamic Republic of Iran, the column for 2022 refers to FY2022/23. For Bangladesh, the Arab Republic of Egypt, and Pakistan, the column for 2022 refers to FY2021/22. Pakistan's growth rates are based on GDP at factor cost.

3. World growth rates are calculated using average 2010-19 purchasing power parity (PPP) weights, which attribute a greater share of global GDP to emerging market and developing economies (EMDEs) than market exchange rates.

4. World trade volume of goods and nonfactor services.

5. Indexes are expressed in nominal U.S. dollars (2010 = 100). Oil refers to the Brent crude oil benchmark. The "Level differences from June 2023 projections" (last three columns) are based on an updated non-energy index, which differs slightly from what was reported in the June 2023 edition. For weights and composition of indexes, see https://worldbank.org/commodities.

government debt has risen by 20 percentage points of GDP since 2007, when U.S. yields were last at their current levels. The drag on growth from monetary tightening is expected to peak in 2024 in most major economies, assuming an orderly evolution of broader financial conditions. Thus far, headwinds to growth from elevated interest rates have been offset, to some degree, by households and firms spending out of savings buffers, resilient risk appetite, and extended maturities on stocks of low-cost debt, as well as by expansionary fiscal policy in some cases, most notably the United States.

Global trade growth in 2023 was the slowest outside global recessions in the past 50 years, with goods trade contracting amid anemic global industrial production. Services trade has continued to recover from the effects of the pandemic, but at a slower pace than previously expected. Global trade growth is projected to pick up to 2.3 percent in 2024, partly reflecting a recovery of demand for goods and, more broadly, in advanced-economy trade (figure 1.1.D).

The recent conflict in the Middle East has so far had only a muted impact on commodity prices. In 2023 as a whole, most commodity prices weakened to varying degrees; however, they remain above pre-pandemic levels. Despite recent volatility triggered mainly by the conflict, and assuming hostilities do not escalate, average oil prices in 2024 are projected to edge down as global growth weakens and oil production increases. Metal prices are set to decline again as the slower growth in China further weighs on metal demand. Food prices are expected to soften further this year amid ample supplies for major crops but remain elevated.

Against this backdrop, global growth is estimated to have weakened last year to 2.6 percent (table 1.1). Although this is 0.5 percentage point higher than last June's forecast, it is mainly due to better-than-expected growth in the United States. Global growth is forecast to slow again, to 2.4 percent in 2024. This deceleration reflects softening labor markets, reduced savings buffers, waning pent-up demand for services, the lagged effects of monetary tightening, and fiscal consolidation.

## FIGURE 1.1 Global economic prospects

*Growth rates in advanced economies as a whole and in China are projected to slow in 2024 to well below their 2010-19 average paces. Although growth is forecast to firm slightly in many EMDEs, it will remain below pre-pandemic average rates in countries with weak credit ratings. Global inflation is projected to continue receding only gradually, as demand softens. Advanced-economy monetary policies are expected to remain tight—including in the United States, following the largest and fastest increase in real policy rates since the early 1980s. Global trade, virtually stagnant in 2023, is set to resume slow growth in 2024. In all, 2020-24 marks the weakest start to a decade for global growth since the 1990s. Rising interest rates have driven borrowing costs well above nominal growth rates in many EMDEs, particularly those with weaker creditworthiness, squeezing fiscal space.*

**A. Growth, by economy and EMDE credit rating**

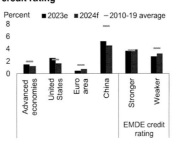

**B. Global consumer price inflation**

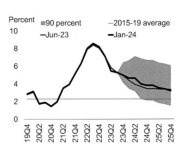

**C. U.S. real interest rate cycles**

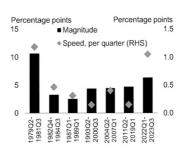

**D. Contributions to global trade growth**

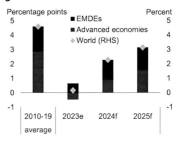

**E. Global growth**

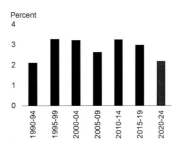

**F. EMDE bond yields minus nominal growth rates**

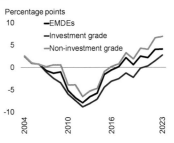

*Sources:* Consensus Economics; Federal Reserve Bank of St. Louis; J.P. Morgan; Moody's Analytics; Oxford Economics; World Bank.
*Note:* e = estimate; f = forecast; CPI = consumer price index; EMBI = Emerging Market Bond Index; EMDEs = emerging market and developing economies. GDP aggregates calculated using real U.S. dollar GDP weights at average 2010-19 prices and market exchange rates. Credit ratings are Moody's sovereign foreign currency ratings.
A. EMDE aggregates show the median. "Stronger" is defined as credit ratings of B and above. "Weaker" is defined as ratings of Caa and below.
B. Model-based GDP-weighted projections of country-level inflation using Oxford Economics' Global Economic Model, using global oil price forecasts from table 1.1. Uncertainty bands are the distribution of forecast errors for total CPI from Consensus Economics for an unbalanced panel of 18 economies.
C. "Magnitude" is the trough-to-peak change and "speed" is the average change per quarter during periods of rising real rates. Real rate is the U.S. policy rate minus one-year-ahead expected inflation from consumer surveys, adjusted for persistent errors.
D. Trade in goods and services is measured as the average of export and import volumes.
F. Lines show medians of annual average U.S. dollar bond yields minus trailing 10-year averages of nominal GDP growth in U.S. dollars. Bond yields are constructed by adding EMBI sovereign spreads to the U.S. 10-year yield. Unbalanced panel of up to 61 EMDEs.

Over 2020-24, the forecast entails the weakest start to a decade for global growth since the 1990s—another period characterized by geopolitical strains and a global recession (figure 1.1.E; Kose, Sugawara, and Terrones 2020). Global growth is projected to pick up to 2.7 percent in 2025, as inflation continues to slow, interest rates decline, and trade growth firms.

Advanced-economy growth is set to bottom out at 1.2 percent in 2024 as growth in the United States slows, while euro area growth, which was feeble last year, picks up slightly as lower inflation boosts real wages. In 2025, growth in advanced economies is forecast to pick up to 1.6 percent as the euro area continues to recover and U.S. growth edges up toward its long-term trend rate amid declining inflation and more supportive monetary policy.

Growth in EMDEs is forecast to average 3.9 percent a year over 2024-25. China's growth is expected to slow notably this year, as tepid consumer sentiment and a continued downturn in the property sector weigh on demand and activity. Excluding China, EMDE growth is set to firm from 3.2 percent in 2023 to 3.5 percent this year and 3.8 percent in 2025. This pickup reflects a rebound in trade and improving domestic demand in several large economies, as inflation continues to recede. Nonetheless, elevated borrowing costs will continue to squeeze fiscal space in EMDEs: U.S. dollar-denominated bond yields are well above the growth rates of nominal GDP in many countries, especially those with weaker creditworthiness (figure 1.1.F). Although growth in low-income countries (LICs) is forecast to firm, this will follow a feeble recovery from 2020, with violence and political instability in some countries curtailing activity last year.

In all, the EMDE recovery from the 2020 pandemic recession remains modest. This reflects the negative effects of headwinds such as tight global financial conditions, a weak recovery in global trade, sharp domestic monetary tightening to tame inflation, the marked slowdown in China, and increased conflict. It also reflects the longer-term downtrend in EMDE potential growth, including in China, due to decelerating invest-

ment and productivity growth, slowing labor force growth amid population aging, and the diminishing growth benefits of improvements in education and health (Kose and Ohnsorge 2023).

Aggregate EMDE output is projected to continue following a lower path than was expected before the pandemic. As such, progress closing the gap in per capita income with advanced economies will remain limited, with EMDEs excluding China and India making no relative gains between 2019 and 2025 (figure 1.2.A). Many vulnerable EMDEs are falling further behind—this year, per capita income is forecast to be below its 2019 level in over one third of LICs and more than half of countries marred by fragility and conflict (figure 1.2.B).

Risks to the outlook remain tilted to the downside, although they have become somewhat more balanced since June, following continued declines in inflation and the stabilization of advanced-economy banking systems after stresses early last year. The recent conflict in the Middle East, coming on top of Russia's invasion of Ukraine, has sharply heightened geopolitical risks (figure 1.2.C). Intensification of these conflicts, or increasing geopolitical tensions elsewhere, could have adverse global repercussions through commodity and financial markets, trade, and confidence. Recent attacks on commercial vessels transiting the Red Sea have already started to disrupt key shipping routes, eroding slack in supply networks and increasing the likelihood of inflationary bottlenecks. In a setting of escalating conflicts, energy supplies could also be substantially disrupted, leading to a spike in energy prices. This would have significant spillovers to other commodity prices and heighten geopolitical and economic uncertainty, which in turn could dampen investment and lead to a further weakening of growth.

Moreover, a range of possible developments—including unexpectedly stubborn inflation in advanced economies requiring higher interest rates than assumed, or rising term premia in bond yields—could precipitate a souring of risk appetite in global financial markets and a sharp tightening of financial conditions, with adverse effects on

EMDEs. Weaker-than-projected growth in China could cause a sharper deceleration in global economic activity than expected. The slowdown in global potential growth could be exacerbated by further increases in trade restrictions and escalating fragmentation of trade and investment networks. Furthermore, the adverse effects of climate change could worsen beyond current expectations, with changing weather patterns contributing to more frequent and severe natural disasters, as well as worsening the incidence of extreme poverty (figure 1.2.D).

On the upside, resilient economic activity and declining inflation in the United States could be sustained, even in the face of substantial headwinds, if aided by further labor supply improvements. There is therefore a possibility that U.S. growth continues to be stronger than projected as price pressures recede and monetary policy is eased, which would bolster global activity.

If any of the aforementioned downside risks were to materialize, they could lead to weaker growth than projected in the baseline. Alternative downside scenarios—including higher oil prices due to an escalation of geopolitical tensions, financial stress in EMDEs that leads to surging sovereign spreads, and weaker growth in China resulting in adverse global spillovers via commodity and other channels—show that in each case global growth in 2024 would be reduced by 0.2 percentage point below the baseline (figure 1.2.E). In contrast, an upside scenario with higher-than-expected U.S. growth due to continuing strong supply conditions could boost global growth by 0.2 percentage point this year.

The weak global growth outlook and the various downside risks highlight the challenges facing policy makers around the world. At the global level, coordinated improvements in debt relief, especially for the poorest countries, will be necessary to free up resources for growth-enhancing investments in human and physical capital. Otherwise, mounting debt-service costs and slow progress in debt restructuring could exacerbate the difficulties facing many EMDEs. Already, about half of LICs and many middle-

## FIGURE 1.2 Global economic prospects (*continued*)

*EMDEs are set to make limited progress catching up to advanced-economy levels of per capita income; excluding China and India, no relative gains are projected between 2019 and 2025. Many vulnerable EMDEs are falling further behind—per capita income is forecast to remain below its 2019 level this year in one-third of LICs and half of economies facing fragile and conflict-affected situations. The recent conflict in the Middle East has heightened geopolitical risks, and an escalation could disrupt goods and commodities trade and global growth. Climate change-related natural disasters could increase extreme poverty. The materialization of downside risks would lead to weaker global growth relative to baseline projections. EMDEs with weak credit ratings have already seen financial pressures crystalize and lack access to international bond markets.*

**A. Change in per capita income relative to advanced economies since 2019**

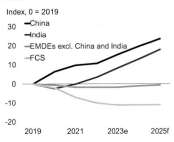

**B. Share of EMDEs with lower GDP per capita in 2024 than in 2019**

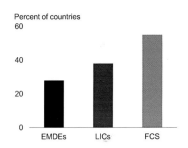

**C. Geopolitical risk index and conflicts**

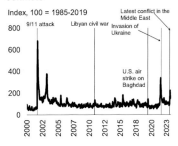

**D. Impact of climate change on extreme poverty by 2030**

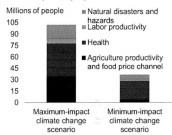

**E. Changes in global growth under alternative scenarios**

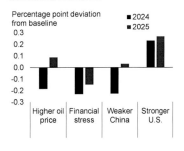

**F. Government bond issuance by non-investment-grade EMDEs**

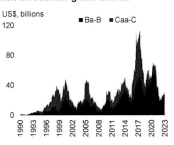

*Sources:* Caldara and Iacoviello (2022); Dealogic; Jafino et al. (2020); Moody's Analytics; Oxford Economics; UN World Population Prospects; World Bank.
*Note:* e = estimate; f = forecast; AEs = advanced economies; EMDEs = emerging market and developing economies; FCS = fragile and conflict-affected situations; LICs = low-income countries. GDP aggregates are calculated using real U.S. dollar GDP weights at average 2010-19 prices and market exchange rates. GDP per capita aggregates are calculated as aggregated GDP divided by the aggregate population.
A. Data show percentage point differences relative to the percent change in GDP per capita in AEs.
C. Geopolitical risk index reflects an automated text-search of electronic articles from 10 newspapers, related to adverse geopolitical events. Last observation is December 11, 2023.
D. Number of additional people in extreme poverty in 2030 due to climate change from Jafino et al. (2020). Climate change is introduced to baseline scenarios, with the minimum and maximum impacts representing the uncertainty surrounding physical impacts and local adaptation policies.
E. Panel shows the deviation in global growth under alternative scenarios relative to the baseline. Scenarios are produced using the Oxford Economics' Global Economic Model.
F. Panel shows rolling 12-month totals for bond issuance by EMDE governments, categorized by Moody's long-term foreign currency sovereign credit ratings. Last observation is November 2023.

income countries are either in, or at high risk of, debt distress. Enhanced international cooperation is also required to tackle the existential threat of climate change, including by accelerating the clean energy transition, helping countries improve energy security and affordability, and incentivizing the investments needed to pursue a path toward resilient, low-carbon growth. In addition, the global community needs to guard against the fragmentation of trade and investment networks, including by prioritizing a rules-based international trading system and expanding trade agreements. Furthermore, global cooperation is critical to address the pressing issues of mounting food insecurity and conflict.

Policy makers at the national level also face formidable challenges, which will require careful calibration of competing priorities. With inflation projected to continue moderating, policy interest rates are set to ease across many EMDEs over 2024 and 2025. However, monetary policy easing in EMDEs could be constrained by narrowing interest rate differentials relative to advanced economies, which could heighten the risk of capital outflows and currency depreciations. Renewed surges in advanced economy yields—driven, for instance, by upside inflation surprises or rising term premia—could also trigger disruptions in EMDE financial markets. Careful attention to risks is therefore required to ensure that monetary policy supports sustainable growth while helping to durably bring down inflation, and to maintain financial stability, particularly in EMDEs with large fiscal and current account deficits.

Fiscal policy space in EMDEs remains narrow amid weak revenues and rising debt-servicing costs. The crises of recent years—particularly the pandemic and the steep rise in living costs resulting partly from the invasion of Ukraine—have seen governments running up public debt and reprioritizing spending away from investment toward shorter-term support for households and firms. Elevated debt, combined with tight financial conditions and tepid growth, is putting further pressure on longer-term fiscal sustainability, while increasing vulnerability to external financial shocks. For EMDEs with weak credit

ratings, these pressures have already crystallized such that international capital markets have effectively been closed to them for two years (figure 1.2.F). In the face of exigent borrowing costs, governments in EMDEs, including LICs, need to scale up revenue mobilization and spending efficiency and bolster debt management. Measures to strengthen government institutions more broadly can support these efforts.

Commodity-exporting EMDEs face particular fiscal challenges from fluctuations in commodity prices (chapter 4). A sustainable, well designed, stability-oriented fiscal framework, combined with strong institutions, can help governments build buffers during commodity price booms that can be drawn upon during subsequent slumps.

Reversing the ongoing weakening of potential growth and its underlying drivers, including investment and productivity growth, will require decisive structural reforms, including measures to promote trade and financial liberalization, develop human capital and infrastructure, close gender gaps, increase labor force participation, and promote innovation. Such reforms—together with policies that ensure macroeconomic stability, including the adoption of inflation targeting where not already credibly in place—can form comprehensive packages of beneficial policies. Implementing these policy packages, with judicious sequencing, can help to spark sustained investment accelerations, which have a strong track record of delivering transformative growth (chapter 3). The presence of well-functioning institutions also raises the chances of igniting an investment acceleration and securing improved long-term growth performance.

## Global context

The global context remains challenging. Global trade growth has been exceptionally weak as a result of subdued global demand, the continued post-pandemic rotation of consumption from goods toward services, and more restrictive trade policies. Notwithstanding recent volatility, prices of most commodities have fallen back from their 2022 peaks but remain above pre-pandemic levels. This moderation has contributed to a decline in global headline inflation. Core inflation, however, has been more persistent, especially in some advanced economies where labor markets remain tight. This suggests that policy interest rates in advanced economies will decline only gradually, contributing to higher longer-term market rates than those that prevailed before the pandemic. EMDE financial conditions remain restrictive, with less creditworthy sovereigns facing greater financial strains, as reflected in sharp currency depreciations and capital outflows.

## Global trade

Global trade in goods and services was virtually flat in 2023, growing by an estimated 0.2 percent—the slowest expansion outside global recessions in the past 50 years. Goods trade contracted last year, reflecting declines in key advanced economies and deceleration in EMDEs, and mirroring the sharp slowdown in the growth of global industrial production. This marked the first sustained contraction in goods trade outside a global recession in the past 20 years (figure 1.3.A). Reflecting stagnant goods trade and fading pandemic-era disruptions, global supply chain pressures have returned to pre-pandemic averages after receding to record lows in mid-2023. Services trade slowed in the second half of 2023, following an initial rebound from the pandemic (figure 1.3.B).

After lagging the pace of global growth in 2023, global trade is projected to pick up to 2.3 percent in 2024, mirroring projected growth in global output (figure 1.3.C). This reflects a partial normalization of trade patterns following exceptional weakness last year (WTO 2023). Goods trade is envisaged to start expanding again, while the contribution of services to total trade growth is expected to decrease, aligning more closely with the trade composition patterns observed before the pandemic. However, in the near term, the responsiveness of global trade to global output is expected to remain lower than before the pandemic, reflecting subdued investment growth. This is because investment tends to be more trade-intensive than other types of expenditures. Global tourist arrivals are expected to return to pre-pandemic levels in 2024,

### FIGURE 1.3 Global trade

*Global goods trade contracted in 2023, marking the first annual decline outside of global recessions in the past 20 years. Services trade growth slowed in the second half of last year, following an initial rebound from the pandemic. After stagnating in 2023, global trade in goods and services is projected to grow by 2.3 percent in 2024. The recovery in global trade in 2021-24 is projected to be the weakest following a global recession in the past half century.*

**A. Growth of global goods trade and industrial production**

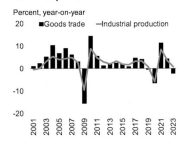

**B. Global PMI new export orders**

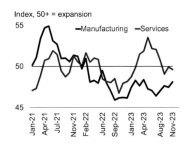

**C. Global trade growth**

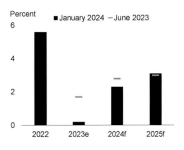

**D. Global trade around global recessions**

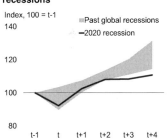

*Sources*: CPB Netherlands Bureau for Economic Policy Analysis; Haver Analytics; World Bank.
*Note*: e = estimate; f = forecast.
A. Panel shows goods trade volumes and industrial production, based on the first 10 months of data in each year for comparability purposes. Last observation is October 2023.
B. Panel shows manufacturing and services subcomponents of the global purchasing managers' index (PMI) new export orders series. PMI readings above (below) 50 indicate expansion (contraction). Last observation is November 2023.
C. Trade in goods and services is measured as the average of export and import volumes. "June 2023" refers to the forecasts presented in the June 2023 edition of the *Global Economic Prospects* report.
D. Panel shows global trade recovery after global recessions. Year "t" denotes the year of the global recessions: 1975, 1982, 1991, 2009, and 2020. Past global recessions show the range for the four global recessions prior to 2020.

although the recovery is set to lag in some countries where reopening was delayed.

The global trade growth forecast for 2024 has been revised down by 0.5 percentage point since June, reflecting weaker-than-expected growth in China and in global investment. As a result, the recovery of trade now projected for 2021-24 is the weakest following a global recession in the past half century (figure 1.3.D).

Geopolitical uncertainty, especially in light of ongoing armed conflicts, and the possibility of a

## FIGURE 1.4 Commodity markets

*Despite the recent conflict in the Middle East, most commodity prices declined in 2023 due to moderating demand, but they remain above pre-pandemic levels. Currently, OPEC+ spare capacity stands at just over 5 mb/d. However, oil prices were highly volatile in the second half of 2023 amid OPEC+ production cuts and the Middle East conflict. Historical precedent suggests that an escalation of the conflict could pose a major upside risk to oil prices. Metal prices fell in 2023, owing to sluggish demand from major economies, notably China. Food commodity prices moderated as well, reflecting improved supplies for major crops. Consumer food price inflation has eased but remains elevated.*

**A. Commodity prices**

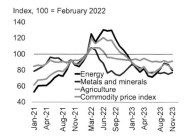

**B. OPEC+ spare capacity**

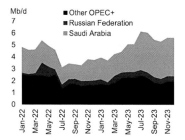

**C. Conflict-driven oil supply disruptions**

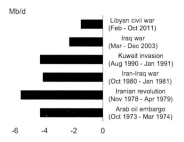

**D. Metals demand growth**

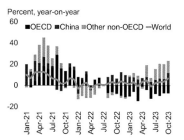

**E. Change in grains supply**

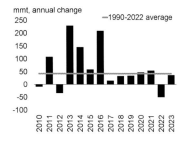

**F. Food price inflation**

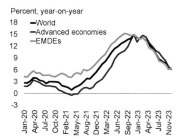

*Sources*: Haver Analytics; IEA (2014, 2023); U.S. Department of Agriculture; World Bank (2023a); World Bureau of Metal Statistics.
*Note*: EMDEs = emerging market and developing economies; OECD = Organisation for Economic Co-operation and Development.
A. Data are measured in U.S. dollars. Last observation is November 2023.
B. Spare capacity for OPEC+ members as reported in IEA (2023), with data extended to December 2023 assuming no change in supply. Other OPEC+ includes Algeria, Angola, Azerbaijan, the Republic of Congo, Equatorial Guinea, Gabon, Iraq, Kazakhstan, Kuwait, Mexico, Nigeria, Oman, the United Arab Emirates, and others.
C. Oil supply disruptions during geopolitical events as defined by IEA (2014).
D. Panel shows year-on-year percent change in metal consumption since January 2021. Last observation is October 2023.
E. mmt = million metric tons. Years represent crop season (for example, 2021 refers to 2021-22). Supply is the sum of beginning stocks and production. Data as of December 2023.
F. Panel shows year-on-year group median inflation for the food component of the consumer price index for up to 117 countries (sample varies across months), of which up to 23 are advanced economies and up to 94 are EMDEs. Last observation is November 2023.

more protracted slowdown in China pose downside risks to the trade outlook. Another downside risk arises from the possibility of further measures to restrict international trade. The recent increase in the use of restrictive trade policies, as well as subsidies and industrial policies aimed at localizing production, has accelerated the reshoring of activities by U.S. and European Union (EU) multinationals, although some of this reflects a desire by firms to diversify sourcing to reduce exposure to adverse shocks (Aiyar, Presbitero, and Ruta 2023; Freund et al. 2023). Continuation of this trend could result in more fragmented supply chains and slower trade growth than projected in the baseline.

## Commodity markets

The average prices of most commodities, in U.S. dollar terms, fell in 2023 amid moderating demand (figure 1.4.A). However, they remain more than 40 percent above pre-pandemic levels. Crude oil prices were volatile last year, including in the wake of the conflict in the Middle East; they averaged $83/bbl, down from $100/bbl in 2022. Production cuts by OPEC+, which were deepened and extended in November 2023, have mostly been offset by robust output elsewhere, including in the Islamic Republic of Iran and the United States. Currently, OPEC+ spare capacity stands at just over 5 mb/d (figure 1.4.B). Oil prices are expected to edge down to $81/bbl in 2024 as global activity slows and China's economy continues to decelerate. An escalation of the conflict in the Middle East is a major upside risk to oil prices. Indeed, since the 1970s, a series of significant geopolitical events, often marked by military conflict, have exerted a pronounced impact on oil supplies (figure 1.4.C). Further extensions of production cuts by OPEC+ (to beyond an expected phase-out of cuts in the first quarter of 2024) and stronger-than-expected demand could also result in higher prices.

Natural gas and coal prices declined considerably in 2023 as countries in Europe reduced energy demand and maintained gas inventories above 90 percent of their storage capacity. Natural gas prices are expected to fall further in 2024 and 2025 as production increases, and as liquefied natural gas exports rise. Key upside risks to gas prices include supply disruptions from the Middle East linked to the conflict and a colder-than-usual winter in Europe.

Metal prices fell by 10 percent in 2023 on account of sluggish demand from major economies—notably China, which accounts for 60 percent of global metal consumption, in the midst of protracted weakness in the country's property sector (figure 1.4.D). Metal prices are expected to fall further in 2024, before picking up in 2025 as China's property sector stabilizes and demand for metals used in the green transition (such as copper and nickel) increases. A greater-than-expected downturn in China's real estate sector is a key downside risk to prices.

Food prices—the biggest component of the agriculture price index—fell by 9 percent in 2023, reflecting ample supplies of major crops, particularly grains (figure 1.4.E). Rice was the exception—its price rose 27 percent in the year amid restrictions on exports of non-basmati rice from India, the world's top rice exporter. Food prices are expected to decline nearly 1 percent in 2024 and 4 percent in 2025. Key upside risks to food prices include increases in energy costs, adverse weather events (possibly as a result of an intensification of the ongoing El Niño), further trade restrictions, and geopolitical uncertainty in the Black Sea region. Longer-term risks include the effects of climate change and the expansion of biofuel mandates.

Food insecurity remains a key challenge amid high, albeit declining, consumer food price inflation (figure 1.4.F). The number of people who are severely food insecure globally is estimated to have risen from 624 million in 2017 to 900 million in 2022 (FAO et al. 2023). The recent surge in rice prices is likely to exacerbate food insecurity as rice is a staple food for over half the world's population, providing more than 20 percent of the calories consumed worldwide.

## Global inflation

Global headline consumer price inflation declined substantially in 2023 (figure 1.5.A). Moderating energy and food price inflation, along with slowing consumer demand for goods and the

## FIGURE 1.5 Global inflation

*Global headline consumer price inflation declined substantially in 2023 but remains above target in most inflation-targeting advanced economies and about half of inflation-targeting EMDEs. In major advanced economies, a notable fall in goods inflation was offset by persistent services inflation. Global headline inflation is projected to moderate further over 2024-25, with core inflation slowing and commodity prices declining, but to remain above its pre-pandemic average beyond 2024. Survey-based inflation expectations are consistent with continued gradual disinflation in 2024-25.*

**A. Headline consumer price inflation**

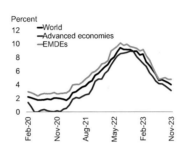

**B. Share of countries with inflation above target**

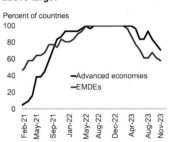

**C. Goods and services inflation**

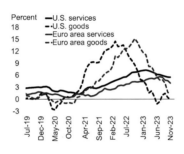

**D. Evolution of headline and core inflation since 2019**

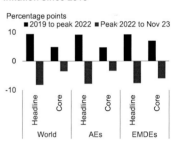

**E. Global consumer price inflation**

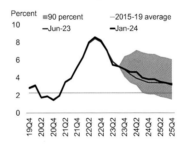

**F. Survey-based inflation expectations**

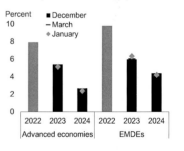

*Sources*: AREAER (database); Consensus Economics; Eurostat; Federal Reserve Bank of St. Louis; Haver Analytics; Oxford Economics; World Bank.
*Note*: AEs = advanced economies; CPI = consumer price index; EMDEs = emerging market and developing economies.
A. Panel shows median year-on-year headline inflation. Sample includes 35 advanced economies and up to 100 EMDEs. Last observation is November 2023.
B. Panel shows the share of economies with inflation-targeting frameworks where year-on-year inflation is more than 0.5 percentage point above target (or the midpoint of the target range). Last observation is November 2023.
C. U.S. goods inflation is the weighted average of durables and non-durables inflation, with their respective shares in the CPI basket as the weights. Last observation is November 2023.
D. Panel shows the percentage point difference in the median 6-month annualized inflation rates from the average 2019 level to the peak in 2022, and from the peak in 2022 to November 2023.
E. Model-based GDP-weighted projections of year-on-year country-level CPI inflation using Oxford Economics' Global Economic Model, using global oil price forecasts from table 1.1. The 90 percent uncertainty bands constructed from the distribution of forecast errors for total CPI from Consensus Economics for an unbalanced panel of 18 economies.
F. Panel shows median headline CPI inflation expectations for 32 advanced economies and 51 EMDEs derived from Consensus Economics surveys in respective months of 2023.

## FIGURE 1.6 Global financial developments

*Advanced-economy monetary policies are expected to remain tight— including in the United States, following the largest and fastest increase in real policy rates since the early 1980s. In October, advanced-economy government bond yields reached their highest levels since the late 2000s, though they have since pulled back. Private sector debt-service ratios remain manageable but have been trending up, particularly in China. Central banks in a growing number of EMDEs have started to cut rates ahead of advanced economies. Financial strains are evident in the one fourth of EMDEs with weak credit ratings: they stopped issuing international bonds two years ago and many have experienced sharp currency depreciation.*

**A. U.S. real interest rate cycles**

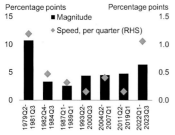

**B. Advanced-economy 10-year bond yields**

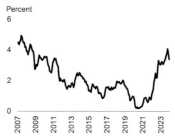

**C. Private sector debt-service ratios**

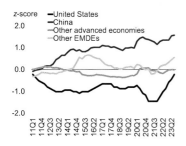

**D. Monetary policy rate changes**

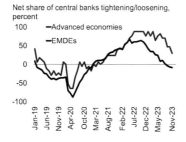

**E. Government bond issuance by non-investment-grade EMDEs**

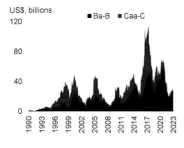

**F. Currency depreciation in EMDEs with weak credit ratings**

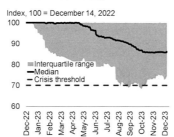

*Sources:* BIS (database); Bloomberg; Dealogic; Federal Reserve Bank of St. Louis; Haver Analytics; Laeven and Valencia (2020); Moody's Analytics; World Bank.
*Note:* AEs = advanced economies; EMDEs = emerging market and developing economies.
A. "Magnitude" is the trough-to-peak change and "speed" is the average change per quarter during periods of rising real rates. Real rate is the U.S. policy rate minus one-year-ahead expected inflation from consumer surveys, adjusted for persistent errors.
B. GDP-weighted average of 10-year government bond yields for the euro area, the United Kingdom, and the United States. Euro area is the 10-year German yield. Last observation is December 18, 2023.
C. Private sector debt-service ratios (z-scores) are defined as the ratio of interest payments plus amortization to income. Lines for "other advanced economies" and "other EMDEs" are GDP-weighted average z-scores of private sector debt-service ratios for the respective country groups.
D. Tightening/loosening is the percentage of central banks raising policy interest rates minus the percentage lowering policy rates in the last three months. Sample includes 17 AEs and 58 EMDEs.
E. Panel shows rolling 12-month totals for bond issuance by EMDE governments, categorized by Moody's long-term foreign currency sovereign credit ratings. Last observation is November 2023.
F. Panel shows the change in the U.S. dollar value of EMDE currencies. Crisis threshold represents a depreciation of 30 percent within one year, the main currency crisis criterion in Laeven and Valencia (2020). Weak credit ratings refer to Moody's sovereign foreign currency ratings of Caa and below. Last observation is December 14, 2023.

recovery of global supply chains, exerted significant downward pressure on goods inflation. Nonetheless, inflation remains above targets in most advanced economies and in about half of inflation-targeting EMDEs (figure 1.5.B). In the major advanced economies, the rotation of demand from goods to services continued. Declining goods inflation amid easing import prices was partly offset, however, by persistent services inflation tied to tight domestic labor markets (figure 1.5.C). As a result, core inflation, which surged less than headline inflation in 2021-22, has also declined less since its 2022 peak (figure 1.5.D).

The decline in core inflation has proceeded under markedly different growth conditions across countries. In the United States, disinflation has occurred alongside resilient activity and low unemployment, thanks partly to increasing labor supply, improving supply chains, and falling oil prices. The decline in the euro area inflation was accompanied by weak growth, reflecting the negative supply shocks from earlier sharp energy price increases. In most EMDEs, headline and core inflation receded last year as growth weakened. Nevertheless, in countries facing financial stress, inflation remained very high, in association with currency depreciations.

In 2024-25, global inflation is expected to decline further, underpinned by the projected weakness in global demand growth and slightly lower commodity prices. Subdued demand reflects the effects of tight monetary and credit conditions and softening labor markets. Thus, global headline inflation, on a year-on-year basis, is forecast to recede to 3.7 percent in 2024 and 3.4 percent in 2025—still above the pre-pandemic (2015-19) average but closer to central bank inflation targets (figure 1.5.E). Surveys of inflation expectations similarly suggest a steady decline in inflation, but to levels in 2024 that are still higher than pre-pandemic averages (figure 1.5.F). In particular, Consensus forecasts indicate lower inflation this year than last in 85 percent of EMDEs.

### Global financial developments

Monetary tightening in advanced economies is concluding, with subsequent easing of policy interest rates likely to proceed at a measured pace. This, alongside softening inflation, could keep real policy rates elevated for an extended period, following the largest and fastest increase in real U.S. policy rates since the early 1980s (figure 1.6.A). In the United States, tight monetary policy reflects better-than-expected growth outturns. In the euro area, persistent core inflation has played a larger role. Reflecting both the outlook for policy rates and volatile term premia, government bond yields in advanced economies in October reached their highest levels since the late 2000s. Although yields have pulled back since then, they remain at levels that will put upward pressure on the cost of capital for governments and firms as debts are rolled over (figure 1.6.B).

High financing costs have been reflected in credit market developments. Advanced-economy banks have been reporting restrictive lending standards, and bank credit growth has slowed sharply. In addition, corporate bankruptcies and credit card delinquencies have picked up. Although private sector debt-service ratios remain generally manageable, reflecting the stock of debt issued at low fixed rates, they have been trending up, most notably in China (figure 1.6.C). Risk appetite in advanced-economy financial markets has nonetheless been resilient, which has somewhat mitigated the tightening effect of higher interest rates on broad financial conditions. Indeed, equity volatility was subdued in the second half of 2023, while corporate credit spreads were generally below 2000-19 median levels.

Across EMDEs, a rising number of central banks have started cutting policy rates, with further reductions expected in the coming months, especially in Europe and Latin America (figure 1.6.D). Most EMDEs have so far exhibited few signs of financial stress, despite higher interest rates. This is likely due to a mix of factors, including better-than-expected growth, limited current account vulnerabilities, and declining inflation following proactive monetary tightening, all of which have helped contain currency depreciation. Unlike other large EMDEs, China has undergone a period of notable financial strain. Subdued growth prospects and upheaval in the property sector have contributed to debt defaults by property developers, net sales of debt and

equity securities by foreign investors, and a decline in the exchange value of the renminbi.

Economies with weak credit ratings—roughly one in four EMDEs—continue to face prohibitively high financing costs. Lacking access to market-based financing, these countries ceased international bond issuance two years ago (figure 1.6.E). In addition, and in contrast to other EMDEs, their currencies depreciated substantially last year—some by as much as 30 percent, a threshold often associated with currency crises (figure 1.6.F).

## Major economies: Recent developments and outlook

### Advanced economies

Aggregate growth in advanced economies was resilient for most of last year, slowing less than previously expected. However, this largely reflected developments in the United States, where consumer spending, in particular, remained robust and fiscal policy was expansionary. Growth in advanced economies is forecast to slow in 2024—for the third year in a row—to 1.2 percent, as domestic demand decelerates (table 1.1). Private consumption growth is set to soften as the boost from one-off factors, such as the stock of excess savings accumulated during the pandemic, gradually fades. Investment growth should also remain subdued as sustained high real interest rates and restrictive credit conditions dampen business investment. Most of the projected slowdown in advanced-economy growth in 2024 is due to a deceleration in the United States; it is only partly offset by an expected pickup in euro area growth as the lingering effects of earlier price shocks dissipate.

In the **United States**, growth was resilient last year, picking up to an estimated 2.5 percent, despite rising borrowing rates and tightening credit conditions. Consumer spending remained solid, supported by accumulated savings, tight labor markets, and a boost to disposable incomes from one-off tax adjustments (figure 1.7.A). Activity was also supported by an expansionary impulse from fiscal policy. Growth appears to have softened in the fourth quarter, with weakness

## FIGURE 1.7 Major economies: Recent developments and outlook

*Consumer spending in the United States was resilient in 2023, reflecting tight labor markets and accumulated household savings. Although U.S. employment growth has slowed gradually, unemployment remains low. Monetary tightening has weighed on credit growth in the United States and the euro area. Economic activity in China was generally weak in 2023, as real estate investment contracted and the growth of infrastructure investment was slower than its pre-pandemic average.*

**A. Annual growth of real consumer spending**

**B. Labor market indicators in the United States**

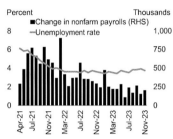

**C. Credit growth**

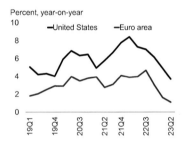

**D. China: Fixed investment growth**

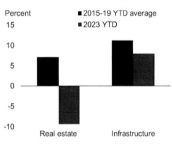

*Sources:* BIS (database); Bureau of Economic Analysis; Bureau of Labor Statistics; European Commission; Federal Reserve Bank of St. Louis; Haver Analytics; World Bank.
*Note:* YTD = year to date.
A. Bars represent year-on-year growth of quarterly real private consumption expenditure. Last observation is 2023Q3.
B. Last observation is November 2023.
C. Panel shows total lending to the private non-financial sector. Last observation is 2023Q2.
D. Blue bars denote the simple average of 2015-19 year-on-year growth of nominal fixed asset investment subcomponents from January to November. Red bars denote year-on-year growth of nominal fixed asset investment subcomponents from January 2023 to November 2023.

set to intensify as the lagged and ongoing effects of tight monetary policy increasingly weigh on household spending, and as temporary factors supporting consumption dissipate. With the household saving rate having fallen far below the pre-pandemic average last year, excess savings accumulated during the pandemic have likely been substantially drawn down (Barbiero and Patki 2023). In addition, the real value of these savings and the growth in real household net worth have been eroded by sharp runups in consumer prices and interest rates.

Tightness in the U.S. labor market has been gradually easing. Job openings have declined,

employment growth has steadily slowed, and wage growth has subsided, despite the unemployment rate remaining near historic lows (figure 1.7.B). Some key drivers of widespread labor shortages, including pent-up demand for labor-intensive services, have been fading. At the same time, labor supply has been rising, with increased prime-age labor force participation partly offsetting the impact of early retirements during the pandemic (Montes, Smith, and Dajon 2022).

In 2024, U.S. growth is expected to slow to 1.6 percent, with high real interest rates restraining activity. Fiscal policy is expected to turn more restrictive, even as elevated interest rates and weakening growth weigh on the federal budget balance (Swagel 2023). A further weakening in consumption growth is projected, amid diminished savings, still-elevated borrowing rates, and easing labor market tightness. Business fixed investment is also set to decelerate further as firms remain cautious, given economic and political uncertainties, and increasingly refinance corporate debt at higher interest rates. Growth is expected to edge up to 1.7 percent in 2025, closer to its trend rate, as the impact of easing monetary policy feeds through the economy.

In the **euro area**, growth slowed sharply in 2023, to an estimated 0.4 percent, as high energy prices—largely related to Russia's invasion of Ukraine—weighed on household spending and firms' activity, particularly in manufacturing. Estimated growth in 2023 is in line with last June's projections, with unexpected resilience in the first half of the year offset by weaker-than-expected activity in the second half. The downturn in late 2023 reflected broadening weakness in the economy, which extended to the services sector. This was partially attributed to the ongoing decline in exports amid deteriorating export price competitiveness and tepid external demand.

Growth in 2024 is forecast to firm to a still-anemic 0.7 percent. Easing price pressures should boost real wages and lift disposable incomes, but the lagged effects of past monetary tightening are expected to keep a lid on domestic demand, especially business investment, partly by reducing credit growth (figure 1.7.C). The forecast for growth in 2024 has been downgraded since June by 0.6 percentage point, largely owing to weaker-than-expected momentum at the start of the year and more adverse credit supply conditions than previously assumed.

Growth is projected to pick up to 1.6 percent in 2025, supported by a recovery in investment growth, especially as the European Union's NextGenerationEU (NGEU) funds lift public investment and help offset modest consolidation of national fiscal balances. Increased absorption of NGEU funds is predicated on reform milestones being met under Recovery and Resilience plans (European Commission 2023). NGEU-related investments and reforms are expected to accelerate the green and digital transitions and address long-standing structural issues, thereby supporting long-term growth (World Bank 2022a).

In **Japan**, growth bounced back to an estimated 1.8 percent in 2023, driven by post-pandemic pent-up demand and a rebound in auto exports and inbound tourism. Despite above-target inflation for over a year, the Bank of Japan continued to maintain accommodative monetary policy, but it gradually relaxed its policy of yield-curve control and allowed longer-term rates to rise. In the forecast horizon, weak growth in major trading partners will weigh on exports, offsetting the support to domestic demand from an expected rebound in real wages amid tight labor markets and slowing inflation. On balance, as the post-pandemic rebound tapers off, growth is forecast to slow to 0.9 percent in 2024 and 0.8 percent in 2025, close to its trend rate.

## China

Growth in China picked up to an estimated 5.2 percent in 2023, 0.4 percentage point below the June forecast. The boost to consumption early in the year from the lifting of pandemic-related restrictions turned out to be unexpectedly short-lived. The downturn in the property sector intensified as property prices and sales fell, and as developers experienced renewed financial pressures. Real estate investment contracted, while the growth of infrastructure investment was slower than pre-pandemic average rates, resulting in lackluster overall fixed investment growth (figure

1.7.D). Private consumption firmed somewhat toward the end of the year, but consumer confidence remained weak, while feeble external demand weighed on exports. The authorities implemented several stimulus measures, including lowering interest rates and deposit requirements for property purchases, while government debt issuance was expanded to support spending.

In 2024, growth is forecast to slow to 4.5 percent—the slowest expansion in over three decades outside the pandemic-affected years of 2020 and 2022, and marginally lower than envisaged in June. Subdued sentiment is expected to weigh on consumption, while persistent strains in the property sector will hold back investment. Soft construction starts in late 2023 signal further weakness in property activity as developers grapple with stressed balance sheets and lackluster demand. While central government support should help boost infrastructure spending, local governments have limited fiscal space for policy maneuvering. Trade growth is also set to remain weak in 2024, with subdued global demand weighing on exports and slower domestic demand growth holding back imports, including of metals.

Growth is expected to edge down further in 2025, to 4.3 percent, amid the continuing slowdown of potential growth. Mounting debt constraining investment, demographic headwinds, and narrowing opportunities for productivity catch-up are all expected to drag on potential growth.

## Emerging market and developing economies

Growth in EMDEs is projected to remain steady at about 3.9 percent a year in the forecast horizon, but with underlying variation across regions (box 1.1). Decelerating activity in China is expected to be offset by firming aggregate growth elsewhere, with improving domestic demand in many countries and a pickup in international trade. Overall, however, the recovery by EMDEs from the pandemic-induced recession of 2020 is expected to remain lackluster, with EMDE growth notably slower than in the recovery from the 2008-09 global financial crisis. Growth is projected to remain weak in EMDEs with low

## BOX 1.1 Regional perspectives: Outlook and risks

*Although some improvements in growth are expected in most emerging market and developing economy (EMDE) regions, the overall outlook remains subdued. Growth this year is projected to soften in East Asia and Pacific—mainly on account of slower growth in China—Europe and Central Asia, and South Asia. Only a slight improvement in growth, from a weak base in 2023, is expected for Latin America and the Caribbean. More marked pickups in growth are projected for the Middle East and North Africa, supported by increased oil production, and Sub-Saharan Africa, reflecting recovery from recent weakness. In 2025, growth is projected to strengthen in most regions as the global recovery firms. Risks to the outlook remain tilted to the downside. An escalation of the conflict in the Middle East could disrupt global oil supplies and cause a surge in prices for energy and food, pushing up inflation in all regions. Other downside risks include further geopolitical and trade tensions, the possibilities of weaker growth in China and weaker external demand, tighter-than-expected financial conditions, and climate-change-related natural disasters.*

### Introduction

Growth prospects for EMDE regions vary in the face of an array of global and domestic currents. Although some improvements in growth are expected in most regions, the overall outlook remains subdued. Projected growth is insufficient to reverse output losses inflicted by the overlapping shocks of the past four years, and implies dim prospects for poverty reduction and catching up to advanced-economy per capita income levels.

A modest improvement in global trade this year is expected to lend some support to activity in EMDE regions, yet overall growth is projected to remain feeble, partly reflecting the slowdown in China. While headline inflation is generally anticipated to continue moderating across regions, it remains elevated in some, limiting the scope for monetary policy easing. Moreover, global financial conditions are envisaged to remain tight, amid elevated real interest rates in the major advanced economies. While risks have become more balanced since June, they remain tilted to the downside. In particular, an escalation of the conflict in the Middle East could disrupt global energy markets, with adverse knock-on effects for some commodity prices, inflation, and food insecurity, and ultimately growth.

In this context, this box considers two questions:

- What are the cross-regional differences in the outlook for growth?

- What are the key risks to the outlook for EMDE regions?

### Outlook

The overall outlook for EMDE regions remains subdued. Assuming the conflict in the Middle East does not escalate, growth in 2024 is projected to decline in East Asia and Pacific (EAP), Europe and Central Asia (ECA), and South Asia (SAR) and somewhat strengthen to varying degrees in other EMDE regions (figure B1.1.1.A). In EAP, the expected slowing mainly reflects declining growth in China in the face of persistent property sector weakness and structural headwinds. In Latin America and the Caribbean (LAC), growth is projected to edge up only slightly, while growth is expected to pick up more markedly from below-trend growth in 2023 in the Middle East and North Africa (MNA)—supported by recoveries in oil-exporting economies—and Sub-Saharan Africa (SSA). In 2025, growth is projected to strengthen in most regions coinciding with an expected step-up in global growth. SAR is projected to remain the fastest-growing EMDE region over the forecast horizon, led by strong growth in India underpinned by resilient domestic demand.

Despite some strengthening, growth in 2024-25 is anticipated to be slower than in the decade preceding the pandemic in some EMDE regions. Projected growth will also be insufficient to reverse the output losses inflicted by the overlapping negative shocks of the pandemic, the Russian Federation's invasion of Ukraine, the sharp tightening of monetary policy, and the conflict in the Middle East, with output set to remain below pre-pandemic trends in 2025 in all regions (figure B1.1.1.B). Particularly in EAP, but also ECA and LAC, output losses relative to pre-pandemic projections are expected to increase in the forecast period. This reflects various headwinds that have weakened growth prospects, including China's slowdown, the impact of Russia's invasion of Ukraine,

---

*Note*: This box was prepared by Samuel Hill.

## BOX 1.1 Regional perspectives: Outlook and risks (*continued*)

### FIGURE B1.1.1 Regional outlooks

*In 2024-25, growth is projected to soften in EAP, reflecting slower growth in China, and to strengthen to varying degrees in most other EMDE regions. Through 2024 and 2025, projected growth will be insufficient to reverse output losses inflicted by the adverse shocks of the past four years in all regions. The pace of catch-up to advanced-economy GDP per capita levels is expected to slow in many EMDE regions compared with the pre-pandemic period, with SSA—the poorest region—set to fall further behind, and at an increased rate.*

**A. Output growth**

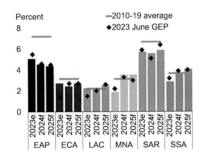

**B. Deviation of output from pre-pandemic trends**

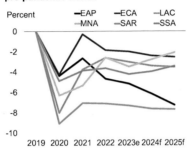

**C. GDP per capita growth relative to AEs**

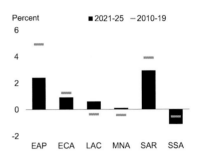

*Source*: World Bank.
*Note*: e = estimate; f = forecast; AEs = advanced economies; EAP = East Asia and Pacific; ECA = Europe and Central Asia; EMDEs = emerging market and developing economies; GEP = *Global Economic Prospects*; LAC = Latin America and the Caribbean; MNA = Middle East and North Africa; SAR = South Asia, SSA = Sub-Saharan Africa.
A. Aggregate growth rates are calculated using GDP weights at average 2010-19 prices and market exchange rates.
B. Panel shows the deviation between current forecasts and January 2020 *Global Economic Prospects*. January 2020 baseline extended to 2025 using projected growth for 2022.
C. Relative GDP per capita growth is calculated as the difference between GDP per capita growth in EMDE regions and advanced economies, expressed in percentage points.

and—particularly in the case of LAC—early and substantial monetary policy tightening in response to rising inflation.

The pace of catch-up to advanced-economy GDP per capita levels is also expected to be slower than in the decade before the pandemic in all EMDE regions except LAC and MNA, where only modest catch-up is expected after a decade of falling behind (figure B1.1.1.C). Worse still, GDP per capita in SSA, which is projected to have the slowest growth among all regions, is set to increasingly lag advanced-economy levels. This decline is occurring in the context of weak institutional quality and flare-ups of conflict and violence, further underscoring the development challenges facing the poorest areas of the world.

After a marked slowdown in global trade last year, an expected modest pickup in 2024 should support output growth in most regions. Many export-oriented economies, including in ECA and LAC, stand to benefit, but in EAP slower growth in China will weigh on regional trade. Tailwinds from the recovery in global

tourism are envisaged to fade through 2024, but to a lesser extent in EAP owing to China's delayed reopening and ongoing recovery in outbound tourism. To varying degrees, over 2024 and 2025 investment is also anticipated to pick up in most regions, supported by lower inflation and easing monetary policy. In energy exporters, particularly in MNA, growth will be supported by elevated energy prices and a ramp-up in oil production. However, continued weakness in metal prices—in part reflecting weaker growth in China, which accounts for most of the global metals demand—is expected to soften growth in metal-exporting countries, especially in LAC and SSA (Baffes and Nagle 2022).

Following a significant decline through 2023, headline consumer price inflation is projected to continue easing across EMDE regions in 2024. However, in ECA, MNA, SAR, and SSA, headline inflation is yet to return to central bank targets in many economies. Moreover, with most commodity prices projected to remain above pre-pandemic levels, households and businesses—particularly in commodity importers—continue to

## BOX 1.1 Regional perspectives: Outlook and risks (*continued*)

### FIGURE B1.1.2 Regional risks

*Risks facing EMDE regions are tilted to the downside, centering on an escalation of the conflict in the Middle East. This would lead to further losses in MNA and could disrupt global energy supply and increase prices, with particularly adverse consequences for net petroleum-importing regions EAP and SAR. Increased uncertainty and weaker-than-expected external demand, including that resulting from a sharper slowdown in China, pose a risk to regions more integrated into global value chains and with closer trade links with that country, including EAP, ECA, LAC, MNA, and SSA. All regions face downside risks from tighter-than-expected financial conditions, particularly given rising indebtedness and widening fiscal deficits. More frequent climate-change-related natural disasters also pose downside risks to all regions.*

A. Net petroleum exports

B. Global value chain output

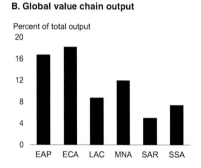

C. China's share of goods exports

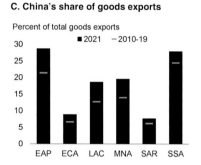

D. Debt

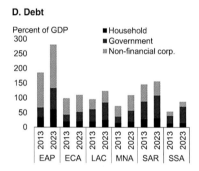

E. Fiscal deficits

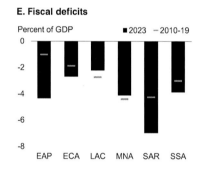

F. Climate-related natural disasters

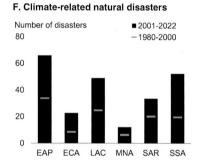

*Sources*: EM-DAT (database); Institute of International Finance; International Monetary Fund; UN Comtrade (database); World Bank.
*Note*: EAP = East Asia and Pacific; ECA = Europe and Central Asia; LAC = Latin America and the Caribbean; MNA = Middle East and North Africa; SAR = South Asia; SSA = Sub-Saharan Africa.
A. Aggregates are GDP-weighted averages of net exports of petroleum products and crude oil as a percent of GDP, between 2018 and 2022.
B. Aggregates are simple averages of global-value chain output as a share of total output, based on Trade in Value Added (TiVA) database. Last observation is 2020.
C. Aggregates are GDP-weighted averages of goods exports to China as a percent of total goods exports. EAP excludes China. Period averages of regional aggregates during 2010-19.
D. Components of regions' total debt as a share of GDP. Aggregates are GDP-weighted averages in percent of GDP. Observation for 2013 is 2013Q2 and for 2023 is 2023Q2. Last observation is 2023Q2.
E. Aggregates are simple averages of the general government fiscal balance as a percent of GDP. Period averages of regional general government fiscal balance during 2010-19. 2023 is estimated.
F. Average annual number of climate-related natural disasters during the period 1980-2000 and 2001-2022. Disasters refer to droughts, floods, extreme temperatures, and storms. Last observation is end-2022.

endure elevated prices. Local food supply shocks—partly due to El Niño conditions—are also contributing to expected persistently high food prices and worsening food insecurity. These challenges are most acute where the food share of household spending is greatest and food supply has been impacted by repeated shocks from conflict and adverse weather, notably in MNA and SSA. The initial rise in oil prices following the conflict in the

Middle East—and the risks associated with an escalation, discussed below—also underscores the significant uncertainty facing commodity markets.

In tandem with easing inflationary pressures, the tightening of monetary policy appears to have generally ended across EMDE regions. In some cases, policy interest rates have recently been reduced, most notably

## BOX 1.1 Regional perspectives: Outlook and risks (*continued*)

in regions where underlying inflationary pressures appear most benign and where central banks began tightening the earliest in response to commodity price shocks through 2022 and 2023. This is particularly evident in LAC and some economies in ECA. While interest rates are expected to decrease further in all EMDE regions this year, the extent of easing may be limited in many instances, partly reflecting continued tight monetary policy in major advanced economies. Given lags in monetary policy transmission, headwinds from the substantial tightening in all EMDE regions through 2022 and much of 2023 will endure in the near term before fading through 2024-25. Moreover, the slowest growth is projected in EMDEs with weaker sovereign credit ratings that have experienced the strongest drags on activity from tight global financial conditions, including in MNA, SAR, and SSA. Fiscal policy is anticipated to exert a broadly neutral influence on activity in the forecast period, though in some regions, including ECA, SAR, and SSA, consolidation is expected to gather momentum, exerting a drag on activity.

### Risks

Risks to the baseline growth projections for EMDE regions remain tilted to the downside, with risks from heightened geopolitical tensions—especially those related to the recent conflict in the Middle East—being particularly salient. As underscored by historical precedent, an escalation in the Middle East conflict could disrupt global energy supplies and cause energy prices to spike (chapter 1; World Bank 2023a). All regions are exposed to the risk of higher energy prices but particularly EAP and SAR, both net petroleum importers (figure B1.1.2.A). By increasing production costs, higher energy prices resulting from the conflict would have adverse knock-on effects for prices of other commodities, including metals and food, pushing up inflation and worsening food security. Higher inflation could force central banks to pause planned easing or even to tighten further, weighing on growth. Moreover, MNA, and other regions directly affected by conflict, including ECA, are exposed to the risk of further losses of human life and destruction of capital, including infrastructure. This could offset any benefit to energy-exporting regions from higher oil prices and significantly weaken productive capacity (Dieppe, Kilic Celik, and Okou 2020).

Heightened geopolitical tensions and trade fragmentation could spur uncertainty and scuttle the projected recoveries in trade and investment growth. In the face of increased trade policy restrictions, firms in EMDEs are contending with mounting trade frictions and higher costs. The near-shoring and friend-shoring of activities in some advanced economies, including in response to domestic content requirements, has strained global supply chains and shifted the global trade and investment landscape (Alfaro and Chor 2023). Regions most reliant on global value chains, especially those with a significant manufacturing sector reliant on intermediate goods trade, including EAP and ECA, are most at risk (figure B1.1.2.B).

All EMDE regions face the risk of weaker-than-expected external demand, including from a sharper slowdown in China. Given China's growing share of global output and trade, it has become a key export market for all EMDE regions, particularly for EAP excluding China and SSA (figure B1.1.2.C). Export-oriented EMDEs with strong direct links to China, notably in EAP, are particularly vulnerable. Exporters of commodities that depend on Chinese demand, notably metals, including those in LAC and SSA, are also vulnerable to the risks associated with a sharper slowdown in China.

Recent bouts of financial stress across EMDEs have generally been confined to a small number of countries with relatively weak credit ratings in MNA, SAR, and SSA. However, there continue to be notable risks of even tighter financial conditions—including associated with currency depreciations—confronting all regions. Overall indebtedness has risen in all regions over the past decade, particularly in EAP and LAC, with mounting public and private debt (figure B1.1.2.D). This magnifies exposure to the risk of higher interest rates than currently anticipated. Moreover, with fiscal deficits estimated to have widened in many EMDEs in 2023—to levels above pre-pandemic averages in most EMDE regions—there is renewed upward pressure on public debt (figure B1.1.2.E).

Climate-change-related extreme weather events, which have become more frequent in all EMDE regions in recent decades, pose a downside risk to growth and poverty alleviation (figure B1.1.2.F; Jafino et al 2020). An elevated risk of El Niño conditions continuing into

**BOX 1.1 Regional perspectives: Outlook and risks (***continued***)**

2024 increases the likelihood of a surge in global temperatures, and of disruptive weather patterns that could damage agricultural output, particularly in EAP, LAC, and SSA (FAO 2023a). Moreover, more frequent storms and floods could damage critical infrastructure, including for transport and energy supplies, with adverse consequences for broader economic activity. Such events can also directly disrupt mining activity, posing a particular threat to ECA, LAC, and SSA. Other types of natural disasters could inflict major costs, as underscored by the devastating earthquakes in MNA and SAR last year.

Finally, growth in the United States was surprisingly resilient in 2023, and the continuation of stronger-than-expected U.S. activity presents an upside risk to the outlook for all EMDE regions. Stronger growth in the United States could be accompanied by declining inflation and easing financial conditions due to further improvements in labor supply or productivity. Export-oriented economies with solid direct trade links to the United States, particularly in EAP and LAC, would benefit most. Other regions would also gain, including through positive spillovers to EMDE commodity exporters from stronger global demand. In such a scenario, improved global sentiment and more favorable financial conditions—including increased global investor risk appetite—could ease financial pressure and borrowing costs in all EMDE regions, thereby supporting demand.

sovereign credit ratings, as they continue to suffer from the tightness of global financial conditions. Growth is forecast to pick up in LICs, but by less than previously expected.

### Recent developments

EMDE growth is estimated to have picked up to 4 percent in 2023—but, excluding China, to have decelerated to 3.2 percent. In many EMDEs, subdued demand for goods in advanced economies weighed on exports, while elevated interest rates dampened domestic demand. Recent business surveys indicate weak expansion in manufacturing and waning growth in services (figure 1.8.A). Reflecting these trends, EMDE growth is estimated to have slowed markedly in the second half of the year (figure 1.8.B).

Shifts in the composition of global demand have led to divergent trade outcomes across countries. Weak global goods trade has weighed on EMDEs with large goods-exporting sectors. Thus, last year, export volumes barely grew in EMDEs in the top quartile for goods exports relative to GDP (figure 1.8.C). Exports held up better among services exporters, which benefited from resilient, albeit slowing, growth of global services activity, including tourism.

Commodity exporters have faced headwinds from subdued growth of global industrial production.

Growth in oil exporters slowed to just 2.1 percent in 2023, amid OPEC+ production cuts. Growth in metals exporters—a group particularly exposed to the slowdown in China—was only 0.7 percent. In all, growth in commodity exporters is estimated to have weakened by about 0.7 percentage point, to 2.5 percent, in 2023.

Commodity importers, excluding China, grew at a more robust pace of 4.2 percent in 2023. This was largely due to continued resilience in India, which is benefiting from increasing public investment and solid services sector growth (World Bank 2023b). Excluding India and China, output in these economies expanded by 3.1 percent. In some commodity importers, severe food and energy price shocks have eroded real wage growth since end-2021, dampening consumption growth.

Growth in LICs in 2023 was particularly disappointing, slowing to 3.5 percent—1.7 percentage points below the June forecast (figure 1.8.D). This downgrade is largely attributed to the economic consequences of renewed civil conflict in Sudan and the coup in Niger. More broadly, the ongoing conflict in the Sahel region has continued to weigh on growth.

### EMDE outlook

Growth in EMDEs is expected to average 3.9 percent per year in 2024-25, broadly in line with estimates of EMDEs' potential growth in the 2020s. Excluding China, EMDE growth is projected to firm from 3.2 percent last year to 3.5 percent in 2024 and 3.8 percent in 2025 (table 1.1). This pickup reflects steady improvements in projected trade growth and expectations for solid domestic demand growth in several large economies, as inflation continues to recede and interest rates decline. The firming outlook for external demand represents a partial normalization of the relationship between global GDP and EMDE goods exports, following an unusually services-intensive expansion last year. Growth is forecast to increase in two-thirds of EMDEs this year.

Despite these improvements, the recovery from the global recession of 2020 over the forecast horizon will remain modest. Overall EMDE growth is projected to be weaker than in the 2010s, partly as a result of the slowing of China's potential growth (figure 1.9.A). Excluding China, EMDE output is set to continue following a lower path than before 2020 (figure 1.9.B). This projected recovery is also substantially weaker than that following the global financial crisis, reflecting the effects of Russia's invasion of Ukraine and the rise in interest rates, as well as longer-term scarring from the pandemic and declining growth in working-age populations (figure 1.9.C).

In commodity exporters, growth is expected to strengthen to 2.9 percent in 2024 and to edge up further to 3.1 percent in 2025 (figure 1.9.D). Much of this projected improvement is due to stronger activity in energy exporters, where energy production is expected to rebound somewhat following large cuts in 2023. Although the forecast assumes modest energy price declines this year and next, projected prices should be sufficient to support investment and fiscal revenues in these economies, which should boost broader economic confidence and non-energy-sector activity.

Growth in metal exporters is forecast to recover somewhat, averaging 2.6 percent over 2024-25, even though growth in both years has been downgraded from June. The slowdown in China's real estate sector, and the structural overcapacity that it reflects, is likely to have enduring

### FIGURE 1.8 Recent developments in emerging market and developing economies

*Recent indicators point to tepid growth in EMDEs, with services activity slowing and manufacturing activity constrained by elevated global interest rates and subdued trade. Growth is estimated to have slowed in the second half of 2023. Weak global trade weighed on growth in EMDEs with large goods-exporting sectors. The largest revisions to 2023 growth forecasts are for LICs, due in part to intensified civil conflicts.*

**A. PMI surveys**

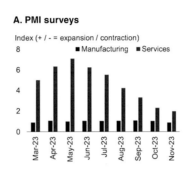

**B. Semi-annual growth in EMDEs**

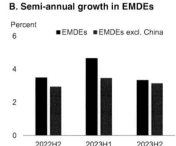

**C. Export growth in goods exporters and services exporters**

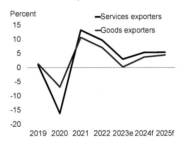

**D. Revisions to 2023 growth, by EMDE group**

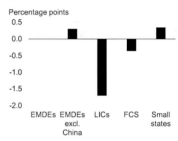

*Sources:* Haver Analytics; World Bank.
*Note:* e = estimate; f = forecast; EMDEs = emerging market and developing economies; FCS = fragile and conflict-affected situations; LICs = low-income countries; PMI = purchasing managers' index.
A. Bars indicate the 3-month moving average of GDP-weighted PMI survey aggregates for EMDEs, minus 50. Values above (below) 0 indicate expanding (contracting) activity.
B. Panel shows annualized 6-month over 6-month growth rates for a sample of 50 EMDEs, comprising 87 percent of estimated 2023 EMDE GDP.
C. Panel shows annual growth in exports. Goods (services) exporters are EMDEs in the top quartile for the ratio of goods (services) exports to GDP, based on average 2015-19 values.
D. Panel shows percentage point changes in growth forecasts relative to the June 2023 edition of the *Global Economic Prospects* report. Small states are EMDEs with populations less than 1.5 million. Sample excludes Guyana.

dampening effects on metals demand. The associated weakness in the export growth and terms of trade of metal exporters is also expected to constrain domestic demand growth, especially in the sizable number of metal exporters (many in Sub-Saharan Africa) facing prohibitive international borrowing costs.

In agricultural exporters, growth is projected to remain stable at 2.6 percent in 2024, before rising to 3.2 percent in 2025. The moderate acceleration next year partly reflects agricultural prices that are high enough to encourage expanded produc-

## FIGURE 1.9 Outlook in emerging market and developing economies

*Growth in EMDEs in 2024-25 is projected at about 3.9 percent per year, close to its estimated potential rate for the 2020s and well below the average growth rate of the 2010s. EMDE output is set to continue on a lower path than expected before the pandemic, even excluding China's slowdown. As such, the recovery from the 2020 recession will remain modest, and weaker than that following the global financial crisis. Growth is envisaged to firm in commodity exporters, while edging down in commodity importers. Fiscal policy is expected to dampen growth somewhat in 2024-25. Growth is forecast to be slowest among EMDEs with weak credit ratings.*

**A. EMDE actual and potential growth**

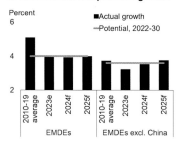

**B. Output in EMDEs excluding China**

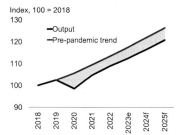

**C. Expansions after 2009 and 2020 in EMDEs excluding China**

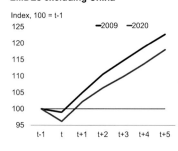

**D. EMDE growth, by commodity exporter status**

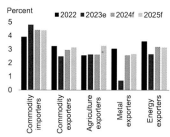

**E. EMDE fiscal impulse and primary deficit**

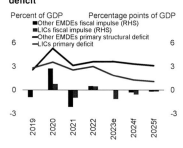

**F. Median growth, by credit rating**

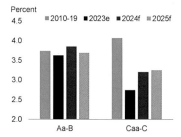

*Sources*: Kose and Ohnsorge (2023); Moody's Analytics; WEO (database); World Bank.
*Note*: e = estimate; f = forecast; EMDEs = emerging market and developing economies; LICs = low-income countries.
A. Potential growth as estimated by the production function approach in Kose and Ohnsorge (2023).
B. Blue line indicates GDP outcomes and current forecasts. Red line indicates the counterfactual had GDP grown in line with the January 2020 *Global Economic Prospects* forecast, extended at constant growth rates beyond 2022.
C. Indices show the evolution of output in EMDEs excluding China around the global recessions of 2009 and 2020. "*t*" represents the year of the global recession. Values for 2024 and 2025 are forecasts.
D. EMDE growth forecast for 56 commodity importers, and for 38 agriculture, 25 metal, and 30 energy exporters.
E. For "Other EMDEs," which are EMDEs excluding LICs, fiscal impulse is calculated as the GDP-weighted inverse of the percentage point change in the primary structural fiscal balance in percent of potential GDP. For LICs, the GDP-weighted fiscal impulse is similarly calculated, but using the simple primary balance in percent of GDP.
F. Panel shows the median growth rate in each year for countries in each credit rating grouping, according to Moody's credit ratings in November 2023. 2010-19 shows the median of country-specific average growth rates within each group.

tion, especially in some large South American economies.

In commodity importers excluding China, growth is forecast to remain at 4.2 percent in 2024, and then increase to 4.5 percent in 2025. Many larger EMDEs in this group have substantial export-oriented manufacturing sectors, which are expected to recover somewhat as goods trade expands after last year's trough. In addition, several economies in Sub-Saharan Africa and East Asia and the Pacific are envisaged to see further recoveries in tourism, which has yet to return to pre-pandemic activity levels. Meanwhile, robust growth in India is mostly due to strong domestic demand: fixed investment is forecast to continue expanding rapidly amid rising public infrastructure spending and strong private-sector credit growth, backed by solid corporate sector balance sheets (World Bank 2023b).

With inflation projected to continue retreating, and policy rates already declining in many EMDEs, monetary policies are expected to be more supportive of EMDE growth in 2024-25 than 2023. Lower domestic interest rates and improving real incomes should start to support consumption and business investment in 2024. A broader easing in global financing conditions is expected to take hold in 2025, as advanced-economy policy rates are further reduced. This, in turn, should translate into a more benign external environment for many EMDEs, as dollar-denominated borrowing costs moderate and firming growth in the United States and euro area supports trade.

Fiscal policies in EMDEs are positioned to dampen growth somewhat this year and next, as governments gradually consolidate budgets following the pandemic-era debt buildup, partly in response to pressures from rising interest rates and debt-service costs (figure 1.9.E). Consolidation is expected to be accomplished mainly through reductions in primary expenditures.

The impact of tight global financial conditions on activity has been most acute in the roughly one-fourth of EMDEs with weak credit ratings (Caa-C). Several have experienced debt or currency crises, necessitating current account adjustments through sharp currency depreciations and import compression. The acute phase of these crises appears to be passing in some countries, helped by the introduction of policy programs supported by multilateral organizations. Overall, growth in EMDEs with weak credit ratings is projected to stabilize somewhat over the next two years, albeit at low rates (figure 1.9.F). Even so, output is set to remain well below pre-crisis paths. In many cases, growth is likely to be too weak to durably resolve the challenge of unsustainable fiscal positions or to repair the deterioration in living standards in recent years.

### LICs outlook

Growth in LICs is projected to pick up from an estimated 3.5 percent rate in 2023 to 5.5 percent this year and 5.6 percent in 2025—about 0.5 percentage point below last June's forecasts in both years (box 1.2). Growth is expected to be relatively strong among some of the largest LICs, including Ethiopia and Uganda, but weaker in fragile LICs. The projected recovery in 2024 is underpinned by a pickup in LIC metal exporters and the stabilization of some economies marred by conflict last year. In particular, Sudan's outlook has improved notably, with household and business spending expected to continue recovering from the sharp conflict-related contraction in 2023.

Many LICs will continue to face daunting challenges, with projected growth insufficient to allow significant progress in reducing poverty. The resources available to LIC governments to support their populations continue to be squeezed by rising debt-service costs. In addition, slow progress in debt restructuring aggravates the situation for many highly indebted LICs, with access to new external financing remaining highly constrained. A surge in political instability poses additional challenges, including to food security, particularly in the Sahel region.

### Per capita income growth

EMDE GDP per capita is projected to grow by 2.9 percent in 2024 and 3 percent in 2025, well below its 2010-19 average annual rate of 3.7 percent. Given subdued projected per capita

growth in advanced economies, averaging 1.2 percent a year in 2024-25, the outlook is for per capita income catch-up by EMDEs at a pace broadly similar to the 2010s. However, excluding China, EMDE per capita growth is forecast to be significantly lower, at 2.2 percent this year and 2.5 percent next year.

Although the projected pace of catch-up is an improvement compared to recent years, it will follow an extended period during which per capita incomes in many EMDEs made little progress toward those in advanced economies. Indeed, excluding China and India, EMDEs in aggregate are projected to make no relative gains on advanced economies between 2019 and 2025 (figure 1.10.A). Some of the most vulnerable EMDEs are falling further behind, with per capita income forecast to remain below its 2019 level this year in over a third of LICs and more than half of economies facing fragile and conflict-affected situations (FCS; figure 1.10.B).

High prices for essential goods remain a major challenge to living standards and, particularly in LICs and FCS economies, to human capital development. Moderate declines in commodity prices since their 2022 peaks have not been fully reflected in consumer prices for food and fuel, and wage rises have generally failed to compensate for earlier runups in these costs (figures 1.10.C and 1.10.D). Thus, although inflation has started to moderate, real incomes remain under pressure. Moreover, the large shocks of the past few years, including the pandemic and the invasion of Ukraine, have tended to hit low-income households disproportionately and exacerbate poverty. This reflects such factors as the unequal labor market impacts of the pandemic and low-income households' high share of spending on food (Adarov et al. 2022; Hoogeveen and Lopez-Acevedo 2021).

## Global outlook and risks

### Summary of global outlook

Global growth is projected to edge down from an estimated 2.6 percent in 2023 to 2.4 percent in 2024, marking the third consecutive year of deceleration (table 1.1; figure 1.11.A). Relative to

## BOX 1.2 Recent developments and outlook for low-income countries

*After slowing to an estimated 3.5 percent in 2023, economic growth in low-income countries (LICs) is projected to recover to about 5.5 percent in both 2024 and 2025—a downward revision from previous projections mainly driven by a deterioration in the outlook for metal-exporting LICs. Additionally, the growth in income per capita in 2024-25 is projected to be lower, at half the rate of gross domestic product (GDP) growth. The number of people struggling with extreme poverty and food insecurity in these countries remains high. Recent flare-ups of political instability and violent conflict have also amplified the challenges faced by some LICs. In many cases, inflation remains elevated, public debt burdens have risen, and activity has been disrupted by extreme weather events. Against this backdrop, risks to the outlook remain tilted to the downside, including those from intensifying insecurity and violent conflict, weaker global growth, higher-than-projected inflation, increased debt distress, and more frequent or intense extreme weather events. An escalation of the conflict in the Middle East could lead to an increase in food price inflation and food insecurity in LICs, especially those highly dependent on food and energy imports.*

### Introduction

Although growth in LICs is expected to improve in 2024 from a weak performance in 2023, the number of people struggling with extreme poverty and food insecurity in these countries will remain high. Sluggish growth last year mainly reflected increased political instability and violent conflict in some fragile LICs, especially Sudan, and weaker outturns in some metal-exporting LICs facing lower global metal prices. Peacebuilding in Ethiopia is gradually yielding dividends, and growth prospects for Niger, South Sudan, and Sudan are improving somewhat.

Nonetheless, many LICs continue to struggle with persistent vulnerabilities and fragility, as the lingering effects of elevated inflation, despite recent declines, still weigh on food affordability for vulnerable populations. Many LICs also continue to face difficult policy trade-offs. Not only has policy space to support the poor been depleted in many of these countries, but high financing needs endanger debt sustainability. Elevated levels of violence and extreme weather events have continued to displace people, disrupt food supplies, and exacerbate poverty.

Multiple downside risks cloud LICs prospects, including a further rise in local or global political instability and violent conflict—especially the conflict in the Middle East, which could exacerbate food insecurity in LICs. Also, the risk of a sharper-than-expected global economic slowdown, especially one emanating from China, or more adverse weather events, could weigh on economic activity. Furthermore, more persistent global inflation could lead to additional monetary tightening, in turn adding pressure on highly indebted countries.

Against this backdrop, this box addresses the following questions.

- What have been the main recent economic developments in LICs?

- What is the baseline outlook for LICs?

- What are the risks to the outlook?

### Recent developments

Growth in LICs slowed from 4.8 percent in 2022 to an estimated 3.5 percent in 2023. The decline was pronounced in Niger, primarily because of the July coup and the subsequent international sanctions. Sudan also faced significant deterioration, with a resumption of conflict damaging the country's industrial base. In about half of the LICs, estimates for growth for 2023 have been downgraded compared with June projections. Pervasive violence and political instability exacerbated the challenging economic and humanitarian situations in many LICs last year—especially in the Sahel region—including Burkina Faso, Mali, Niger, Somalia, South Sudan, and Sudan (figure B.1.2.1.A). While peacebuilding efforts remained fragile in Ethiopia and the Democratic Republic of Congo, growth in these countries, though slowing in 2023, remained above the LIC average.

Output in agricultural commodity exporters grew by 2.9 percent in 2023—below their long-term average but still markedly faster than in their metal-exporting counterparts, where output expanded only marginally as a result of lower global metal prices as well as violent conflict in some of these countries. In Ethiopia, the

*Note*: This box was prepared by Dominik Peschel.

## BOX 1.2 Recent developments and outlook for low-income countries (*continued*)

### FIGURE B1.2.1 LICs: Recent developments

*Challenges in LICs include a large number of violent events, uneven progress with disinflation, and a high level of food insecurity. Violence increased sharply in the Sahel region of northern Africa in 2023, with a number of coups. Progress with disinflation has been uneven, with inflation rising in some countries. Food insecurity leapt in 2022 and remained high in 2023.*

| A. Violent events | B. Consumer price inflation | C. Food insecurity |
|---|---|---|
| 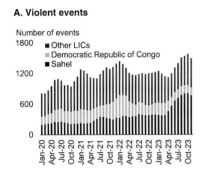 | 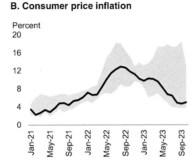 | 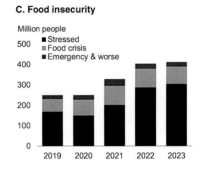 |

*Sources*: ACLED (database); FSIN and GNAFC (2023); Haver Analytics; International Monetary Fund; World Bank.
*Note*: LICs = low-income countries.
A. Three-months moving average; violent events include battles, explosions, violence against civilians, and riots. Last observation is November 2023.
B. Median consumer price inflation, year-on-year. Sample of nine LICs. Shaded area shows the 25 to 75 percentile range of inflation rates among the countries. Last observation is October 2023.
C. Number of people facing food security stress, food security crisis, or emergency and worse. Sample of 24 LICs.

largest agricultural exporter in Sub-Saharan Africa, poultry and fruit production registered sharp increases. In Uganda, increased agricultural production also boosted overall growth. In the Democratic Republic of Congo, the world's largest cobalt producer and a major copper exporter, lower global metal prices and slower growth in domestic metal production contributed to a moderation in activity. Growth in Mozambique picked up as production of liquefied natural gas, coal, and aluminum increased.

While annual consumer price inflation in the median LIC declined in 2023, the progress in achieving disinflation was uneven, with inflation continuing to rise in some countries and remaining in double digits in Ethiopia, The Gambia, Rwanda, and Sierra Leone (figure B.1.2.1.B). In many cases, food price inflation was persistently high (Burundi, Malawi, Sierra Leone, Sudan). High food and energy prices pushed the number of people in LICs facing food security stress or worse circumstances above 400 million in 2022, with some further increase in 2023 (figure B.1.2.1.C). In both the Democratic Republic of Congo and Sudan, more than 20 million people faced high acute food insecurity in August 2023 (FSIN and GNAFC 2023). In some countries, weakening currencies exacerbated inflationary problems (Burundi, Ethiopia, Sudan).

## Outlook

Growth in LICs is projected to increase to 5.5 percent this year and 5.6 percent in 2025, up from 3.5 percent in 2023 (figure B.1.2.2.A). The forecasts assume that the conflict in the Middle East does not escalate, that security challenges in a number of LICs improve, that no debt crises emerge, and that inflation pressures continue to decline.

Despite the expected pickup in aggregate LICs growth in 2024, the forecast has been downgraded by 0.5 percentage point, driven by deterioration in the outlook for metal-exporting LICs. Moreover, projections for growth in 2024 in nearly half of the LICs—fragile and non-fragile alike—have been revised down. Reflecting weaker commodity prices, 2024 growth forecasts have been downgraded for two-thirds of metal-exporting LICs, with downward revisions for the Central African Republic, Democratic Republic of Congo, Mozambique, and Sudan being among the largest.

Growth in fragile LICs is forecast to increase from 3 percent in 2023 to 5.4 percent in 2024 and 5.5 percent in 2025. Growth projections for Sudan have been revised down, as violent conflict has damaged the country's industrial base and education and health

**BOX 1.2 Recent developments and outlook for low-income countries (*continued*)**

### FIGURE B1.2.2 LICs: Outlook and risks

*Growth in LICs is expected to pick up in 2024-25, following a dip in 2023 reflecting weaker performance in several fragile LICs and a slump in growth in metal-exporting LICs. Growth in fragile LICs excluding the two largest economies—Ethiopia and the Democratic Republic of Congo—will remain subdued. As a result, per capita income in this group, on average, is expected to remain markedly below pre-pandemic levels in 2025. Moreover, the share of LICs in debt distress or at high risk thereof has increased significantly.*

A. GDP growth

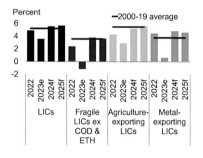

B. Real income per capita in fragile LICs

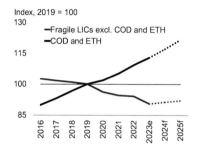

C. Share of LICs in, or at high risk of, debt distress

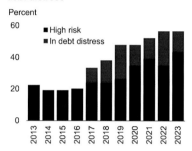

*Sources*: International Monetary Fund; World Bank.
*Note*: e = estimate; f = forecast; COD = Democratic Republic of Congo; ETH = Ethiopia; Fragile LICs = fragile and conflict-affected LICs; LICs = low-income countries.
A. Average GDP growth rates calculated using constant GDP weights at average 2010-19 prices and market exchange rates. Sample comprises 21 LICs, of which 13 are fragile LICs.
B. Fragile LICs exclude the Democratic Republic of Congo and Ethiopia.
C. Panel shows the share of low-income countries eligible to access the IMF's concessional lending facilities by level of debt distress. The sample size varies between 18 and 23 countries. Eritrea and the Syrian Arab Republic are excluded because of lack of adequate data.

facilities, while remaining unchanged for Burkina Faso and South Sudan. Much of the projected strengthening of growth among fragile LICs is accounted for by the two largest economies in the group—Ethiopia and the Democratic Republic of Congo. Assuming that the Ethiopia-Tigray peace agreement of November 2022 holds, continuing recovery in Ethiopia is expected, driven by growth in investment and a recovery in government consumption. In the Democratic Republic of Congo, growth in mining and metal production is expected to be adversely affected by lower prices, but to remain the main driver of growth, albeit with support from expanding services activity.

Growth in non-fragile LICs is forecast to strengthen to 5.8 percent in 2024 and 6.1 percent in 2025. In Uganda, growth is expected to pick up as monetary policy eases amid waning inflation, and as investment supports tourism, export diversification, and agro-industrialization. Firming growth in Rwanda is expected to benefit from increasing tourism revenues and a pickup in construction associated with the new airport, as well as the country's resilient policy framework (World Bank 2023c).

Per capita income growth in LICs is expected to accelerate from an anemic 0.7 percent in 2023 to 2.7 percent in 2024 and 2.8 percent in 2025. However, in fragile LICs, excluding Ethiopia and the Democratic Republic of Congo—the two most populous LICs—per capita income growth will lag significantly behind the LICs' average. As a result, the average per capita income in this subgroup is expected to remain markedly below pre-pandemic levels through 2025 (figure B.1.2.2.B).

Progress in poverty reduction in many LICs is expected to remain slow, with populations still struggling to cope with high costs of living. After current account deficits widened in 2022, primarily driven by surging import bills caused by higher commodity prices, these deficits did not narrow much in 2023 and are not expected to shrink significantly in the forecast horizon. Although government spending, which increased in 2022 to mitigate the cost-of-living increases, came down in 2023, fiscal deficits are expected to remain elevated over the forecast horizon. Debt-service costs and levels of public debt remain high for many LICs, increasing the likelihood of government defaults in the absence of agreements on debt relief (figure B.1.2.2.C).

**BOX 1.2 Recent developments and outlook for low-income countries (*continued*)**

### TABLE B1.2.1 Low-income country forecasts[a]

(Real GDP growth at market prices in percent, unless indicated otherwise)

Percentage point differences from June 2023 projections

| | 2021 | 2022 | 2023e | 2024f | 2025f | 2023e | 2024f | 2025f |
|---|---|---|---|---|---|---|---|---|
| **Low-Income Country, GDP**[b] | **4.2** | **4.8** | **3.5** | **5.5** | **5.6** | **-1.7** | **-0.5** | **-0.4** |
| GDP per capita (U.S. dollars) | 1.3 | 2.0 | 0.7 | 2.7 | 2.8 | -1.6 | -0.4 | -0.4 |
| Afghanistan[c] | -20.7 | .. | .. | .. | .. | .. | .. | .. |
| Burkina Faso | 6.9 | 1.5 | 4.3 | 4.8 | 5.1 | 0.0 | 0.0 | 0.0 |
| Burundi | 3.1 | 1.8 | 2.9 | 4.2 | 4.5 | -0.1 | 0.2 | 0.3 |
| Central African Republic | 1.0 | 0.5 | 1.3 | 1.6 | 3.1 | -1.7 | -2.2 | -0.7 |
| Chad | -1.2 | 2.2 | 3.0 | 2.8 | 2.7 | -0.2 | -0.6 | -0.4 |
| Congo, Dem. Rep. | 6.2 | 8.9 | 6.8 | 6.5 | 6.2 | -0.9 | -1.1 | -1.3 |
| Eritrea | 2.9 | 2.5 | 2.6 | 3.2 | 3.3 | -0.1 | 0.3 | 0.5 |
| Ethiopia[d] | 6.3 | 6.4 | 5.8 | 6.4 | 7.0 | -0.2 | -0.2 | 0.0 |
| Gambia, The | 4.3 | 4.3 | 4.8 | 5.3 | 5.5 | -0.2 | -0.2 | -0.3 |
| Guinea-Bissau | 6.4 | 3.5 | 2.8 | 5.6 | 4.5 | -1.7 | 1.1 | 0.0 |
| Liberia | 5.0 | 4.8 | 4.5 | 5.4 | 6.2 | 0.2 | -0.1 | 0.6 |
| Madagascar | 5.7 | 3.8 | 4.0 | 4.8 | 4.7 | -0.2 | 0.0 | -0.4 |
| Malawi | 2.8 | 0.9 | 1.6 | 2.8 | 3.3 | 0.2 | 0.4 | 0.3 |
| Mali | 3.1 | 3.7 | 4.0 | 4.0 | 5.0 | 0.0 | 0.0 | 0.0 |
| Mozambique | 2.3 | 4.2 | 6.0 | 5.0 | 5.0 | 1.0 | -3.3 | -0.3 |
| Niger | 1.4 | 11.5 | 2.3 | 12.8 | 7.4 | -4.6 | 0.3 | -1.7 |
| Rwanda | 10.9 | 8.2 | 6.9 | 7.5 | 7.8 | 0.7 | 0.0 | 0.3 |
| Sierra Leone | 4.1 | 3.5 | 3.1 | 3.7 | 4.3 | -0.3 | 0.0 | -0.1 |
| South Sudan[d] | -5.1 | -2.3 | -0.4 | 2.3 | 2.4 | 0.0 | 0.0 | 0.0 |
| Sudan | -1.9 | -1.0 | -12.0 | -0.6 | 0.2 | -12.4 | -2.1 | -1.8 |
| Syrian Arab Republic[c] | 1.3 | -3.5 | -5.5 | .. | .. | 0.0 | .. | .. |
| Togo | 6.0 | 5.8 | 5.2 | 5.2 | 5.8 | 0.3 | -0.1 | 0.3 |
| Uganda[d] | 3.4 | 4.7 | 5.3 | 6.0 | 6.6 | -0.4 | -0.2 | -0.1 |
| Yemen, Rep.[c] | -1.0 | 1.5 | -0.5 | 2.0 | .. | 0.0 | 0.0 | .. |

*Source*: World Bank.

*Note*: e = estimate; f = forecast. World Bank forecasts are frequently updated based on new information and changing (global) circumstances. Consequently, projections presented here may differ from those contained in other Bank documents, even if basic assessments of countries' prospects do not significantly differ at any given moment in time.

a. The Democratic People's Republic of Korea and Somalia are not forecast on account of data limitations.

b. Aggregate growth rates are calculated using GDP weights at average 2010-19 prices and market exchange rates.

c. Forecasts for Afghanistan (beyond 2021), the Syrian Arab Republic (beyond 2023), and the Republic of Yemen (beyond 2024) are excluded because of a high degree of uncertainty.

d. GDP growth rates are on a fiscal year basis. For example, the column for 2022 refers to FY2021/22.

## Risks

Risks to the baseline forecast remain tilted to the downside, particularly for countries grappling with fragility, and those susceptible to conflicts and adverse weather events. An escalation of the conflict in the Middle East could exacerbate food insecurity across LICs as many of them are highly dependent on food and energy imports. A conflict-induced sustained oil price spike would not only raise food prices by increasing production and transportation costs but could also

disrupt supply chains, potentially necessitating stronger efforts by the international community to bolster food supplies to LICs with high rates of malnutrition (World Bank 2023a).

Slower-than-expected growth in China could result in lower commodity prices, negatively impacting metal exporters in particular. If inflation retreats more slowly than currently anticipated, central banks might have to maintain elevated interest rates for longer, heightening the risk of debt crises in some LICs. Gross financing

## BOX 1.2 Recent developments and outlook for low-income countries (*continued*)

needs of some LICs have increased substantially since the onset of the pandemic, implying higher risks of debt distress.

Many LICs suffer from fragility stemming from persistent poverty, as well as festering violence and conflict, especially in East Africa and the Sahel (Burkina Faso, Democratic Republic of Congo, Ethiopia, Mali, Somalia, South Sudan, Sudan). While there has been progress with peacemaking efforts in the Democratic Republic of Congo and Ethiopia, there has been increased political instability in several other LICs, with coups d'état in Niger (2023), Burkina Faso (2022), and Chad, Mali, and Sudan (2021). Further violence and conflict would depress growth more severely than in the baseline and result in extended humanitarian crises in these countries that already exhibit an array of macroeconomic vulnerabilities, such as high debt or debt distress, heavy reliance on food or fuel imports, and elevated inflation.

Economic growth and poverty reduction in LICs could slow markedly if the adverse effects of climate change become more severe. Extreme weather events have already had catastrophic consequences in several LICs, especially in the Sahel region, which is warming faster than the global average and is also particularly susceptible to desertification (World Bank 2022b). Additionally, the current El Niño weather pattern could bring further devastation and increase the incidence of vector-borne and waterborne diseases (WHO and WMO 2023). The number of people facing extreme hunger remains high, especially across Eastern Africa. This situation could worsen if global greenhouse gas emissions continue to rise and LICs with substantial adaptation gaps fail to improve their climate resilience because of inadequate financing and support from the international community.

last June's projections, the forecast for 2023 has been revised up by 0.5 percentage point, mainly reflecting the strength of the U.S. economy, whereas that for 2024 is unchanged, with a sizable upgrade to U.S. growth accompanied by a downward revision to euro area activity. Growth is forecast to pick up slightly to 2.7 percent in 2025, owing mainly to firming advanced-economy activity, as inflation continues to soften and interest rates decline. EMDE growth is projected to be virtually unchanged, at about 3.9 percent a year through 2024-25, with growth in China set to slow while that in other EMDEs picks up. EMDE growth is expected to be supported by a modest firming of export and investment growth (figure 1.11.B). However, it is still expected to be weaker than its average pace over the past two decades, though broadly in line with estimated potential growth.

While the moderation in commodity prices in 2023 contributed to a decline in global headline inflation, services inflation has proved more persistent, especially in advanced economies, reflecting still-tight labor markets. As such, the easing of advanced-economy policy interest rates will likely proceed at a measured pace, implying a

continued period of elevated real interest rates. This will be particularly challenging for vulnerable EMDEs with lower sovereign creditworthiness. For most such countries, dollar-denominated bond yields have moved well above nominal GDP growth (in U.S. dollars), squeezing fiscal space (figure 1.11.C).

Notwithstanding the projected firming of global growth, the outlook remains subdued by historical standards: the forecast for global growth over 2024-25, about 2.5 percent a year on average, is 0.6 percentage point below the 2010-19 average rate. This partly reflects the lingering effects of recent shocks, including the pandemic, the invasion of Ukraine, the sharp increase in inflation, and the associated tightening of global financial conditions. Another contributing factor is the weakening of trade growth, partly attributed to more inward-looking policies. However, the subdued expected pace of global growth also reflects a longer-term downtrend in potential growth. The structural slowdown in EMDEs, and especially in China, is due to several forces: labor force growth has slowed because of demographic shifts; productivity growth has weakened as growth dividends from improvements in health and education have diminished, and as some EMDEs have moved closer to productivity frontiers; and the pace of capital accumulation has declined, in part as a result of debt overhangs (figure 1.11.D).

## Risks to the outlook

Risks to the global growth outlook have become somewhat more balanced since last June, as banking system stress in advanced economies has receded and inflation has declined. Nevertheless, risks remain tilted to the downside. The possibility of an intensification of the conflict in the Middle East represents a major downside risk. This, or rising geopolitical tensions elsewhere, could have adverse impacts through commodity markets, trade and financial linkages, uncertainty, and confidence. Weak growth, elevated debt, and still-high interest rates heighten the risk of financial stress, especially in the more vulnerable EMDEs. Higher or more persistent inflation may require a longer-than-assumed period of tight monetary policy. Subdued recent activity in China raises the possibility of slower-than-expected growth, which would have adverse global spillovers. Trade fragmentation and climate-related disasters could also result in weaker growth in the near and longer terms. On the upside, recent surprisingly strong economic activity in the United States, along with declining inflation, points to the possibility that growth may be stronger than projected, perhaps as a result of improved supply conditions.

### *Conflict and geopolitical risks*

Geopolitical risks have increased sharply in the wake of the recent conflict in the Middle East, which comes on top of Russia's invasion of Ukraine (figure 1.12.A). Any escalation of these conflicts could have significant consequences in commodity markets and for economic activity.

While the effects of the conflict in the Middle East on commodity prices have so far been muted, historical precedents suggest that an escalation could lead to significant oil supply disruptions and large spikes in commodity prices, especially if major oil producers became embroiled (figure 1.12.B). At the global level, soaring energy prices could push up inflation, reduce business and

## FIGURE 1.10 Per capita income growth

*EMDEs are set to make limited progress catching up to advanced-economy levels of per capita income; excluding China and India, no relative gains are projected between 2019 and 2025. Many vulnerable EMDEs are falling further behind—per capita income is forecast to remain below its 2019 level this year in one-third of LICs and half of economies facing fragile and conflict-affected situations. High food and fuel prices continue to weigh on real incomes in many EMDEs.*

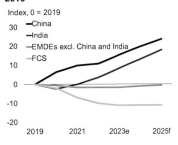

**A. Change in per capita income relative to advanced economies since 2019**

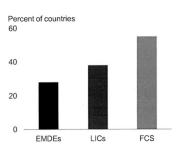

**B. Share of EMDEs with lower GDP per capita in 2024 than in 2019**

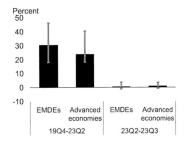

**C. Consumer price inflation, fuel component**

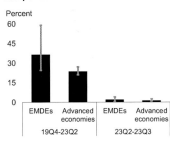

**D. Consumer price inflation, food component**

*Sources:* Haver Analytics; Oxford Economics; UN World Population Prospects; World Bank.
*Note:* e = estimate; f = forecast; CPI = consumer price index; EMDEs = emerging market and developing economies; FCS = fragile and conflict-affected situations; LICs = low-income countries. GDP per capita aggregates are calculated as aggregated GDP divided by the aggregate population. GDP aggregates are calculated using real U.S. dollar GDP weights at average 2010-19 prices and market exchange rates.
A. Panel shows percentage point differences compared with the percent change in GDP per capita in advanced economies.
C. Panel shows percentage changes in the fuel component of the CPI (as presented in the Oxford Economics Model) in the periods shown. Sample includes 35 advanced economies and 30 EMDEs. Orange whiskers show 25th and 75th percentiles.
D. Panel shows percentage changes over 2019Q4-2023Q2 and 2023Q2-2023Q3 in the food component of CPI for up to 25 advanced economies and 94 EMDEs. Orange whiskers show 25th and 75th percentiles.

consumer confidence, and lead to a tightening of financial conditions, dampening investment and overall activity. Indeed, oil price fluctuations have been the predominant driver of global inflation volatility over the last 50 years, especially during the past two decades (Ha et al. 2023).

Heightened uncertainty about the geopolitical environment and conflict outcomes could compound these effects (Caldara et al. 2023). Geopolitical events can prompt a flight to safety in international capital markets, resulting in

## FIGURE 1.11 Global outlook

*Global growth is projected to edge down in 2024, declining for the third consecutive year, before picking up in 2025. Modest recoveries in exports and investment are expected to support EMDE growth in the next two years. Rising interest rates have driven borrowing costs above growth rates in many EMDEs, particularly those with weaker creditworthiness, which has squeezed fiscal space. Subdued EMDE growth partly reflects the downtrend in the drivers of EMDE potential growth.*

**A. Contributions to global growth**

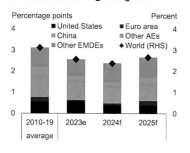

**B. Contributions to EMDE growth**

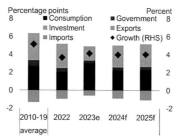

**C. EMDE bond yields minus nominal growth rates**

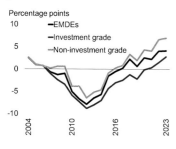

**D. Contributions to EMDE potential growth**

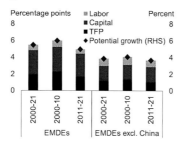

*Sources*: Federal Reserve Bank of St. Louis; J.P. Morgan; Kose and Ohnsorge (2023); Moody's Analytics; World Bank.
*Note*: e = estimate; f = forecast; AEs = advanced economies; EMBI = Emerging Market Bond Index; EMDEs = emerging market and developing economies. Aggregates are calculated using real U.S. dollar GDP weights at average 2010-19 prices and market exchange rates. TFP = total factor productivity.
B. Balanced sample includes 97 EMDEs with data availability for components, and thus may differ from aggregates presented in table 1.1. Components do not add up to headline growth due to statistical discrepancies.
C. Lines show medians of annual average U.S. dollar bond yields minus trailing 10-year averages of nominal GDP growth in U.S. dollars. Bond yields are constructed by adding EMBI sovereign spreads to the U.S. 10-year yield. Unbalanced panel of up to 61 EMDEs.
D. Panel shows GDP-weighted averages of production function-based potential growth estimates. Sample includes 53 EMDEs.

exchange rate depreciations in economies deemed riskier, which can be an important source of inflation in EMDEs (Forbes and Warnock 2012, 2021). Wars can also reduce global supply capacity by diverting international trade and capital flows and disrupting supply chains, including key global shipping routes. Recent attacks on commercial vessels in the Red Sea have prompted the rerouting of much of the freight that usually transits the Suez Canal, lengthening delivery times and increasing costs. These delays

increase the likelihood of inflationary supply bottlenecks, although the extent of this risk will depend on the degree and duration of disruptions, as well as interactions with other supply chain problems such as weather-related capacity reductions in the Panama Canal.

In the regions directly affected—such as the Middle East and Europe and Central Asia—protracted conflict could severely impact growth and development through many channels. The loss of human life, disabling injuries, and the destruction of capital would directly impair the productive capacity of an economy. More precautionary behavior by consumers and businesses would lower demand substantially. Increased debt-financed military spending may offset these negative demand effects in the short term, but it is likely to sap resources from more productive long-term uses (Caldara and Iacoviello 2022).

### Weaker growth in China

A sharper-than-expected slowdown in China would adversely affect global trade as well as commodity and financial markets. The property sector could fail to stabilize if persistent uncertainty holds back prospective buyers, or if mounting financial stress among developers constrain the financing of new projects or force a halt to existing ones. Persistent uncertainty and weak sentiment could hold back household spending and private investment. Against the backdrop of high and rising public and private debt, a sharp slowdown could weaken credit quality and become self-reinforcing, with financial stress exacerbating the challenge of servicing existing debts, generating negative feedback loops to activity.

The international spillovers of a sharp slowdown in China could be severe. China's importance as an export destination has continued to grow in recent decades, especially for EMDEs (figure 1.12.C). At the same time, China has become a much more important source of demand for commodities, notably energy and metals (figure 1.12.D). More recently, the country has emerged as a major consumer of commodities central to the green energy transition (Baffes and Nagle 2022).

The direct spillovers would be most acute for countries deeply engaged in trade with China—particularly those enmeshed in global value chains with China, including many export-oriented economies in the East Asia and Pacific region. In addition, exporters of commodities in Latin America, notably iron ore and copper, would face particularly adverse effects. Weaker activity in China would also weigh on global energy demand and prices, adversely impacting energy exporters.

A slowdown in China could also adversely affect global financial conditions. Although direct linkages between China's economy and global financial markets are limited, the macroeconomic effects of China's credit cycles can drive shifts in investor sentiment. Thus, if the downturn in the real estate sector were to intensify, the resulting increase in non-performing loans could cause domestic lenders to retrench in order to preserve capital and liquidity. The knock-on effects on demand in China and their repercussions could lead market participants to revise global growth expectations down, causing sentiment to weaken and risk aversion to rise, thereby resulting in a tightening of global financial conditions (Ahmed et al. 2019). China's position as a large bilateral creditor to many EMDEs poses a further possible channel for adverse spillovers. Pressure on the balance sheets of domestic lenders could lessen their readiness to extend credit overseas. This, in turn, could exacerbate the already-strained financial positions of some low- and lower-middle-income countries.

### Financial stress

Interest rates in advanced economies have risen markedly over the past couple of years, as central banks have acted to rein in inflation. There have also been occasional surges in long-term bond yields, which have been associated with episodes of financial stress, including instability in U.K. gilt markets in 2022 and the failures of several U.S. banks early last year. These bouts of financial instability were stemmed by timely and extensive policy responses. There remains a risk, however, that renewed increases in market interest rates, or an extended period of elevated real policy rates, could expose latent financial and economic vulnerabilities, precipitating a souring of risk

## FIGURE 1.12 Risks to the outlook

*The ongoing conflict in the Middle East has increased geopolitical risks. Past conflicts in the region have seen oil prices increase considerably. An escalation of the conflict could result in substantial disruptions to global oil supply, which could significantly raise global inflation and dampen activity. Weaker growth in China could have adverse implications for its trading partners, especially commodity exporters.*

**A. Geopolitical risk index and conflicts**

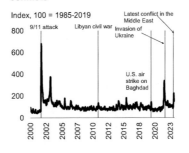

**B. Oil price changes during conflict-related disruptions in the Middle East**

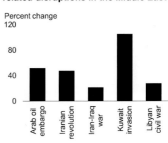

**C. Share of goods exports to China**

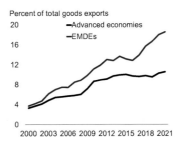

**D. China's share of global commodities consumption**

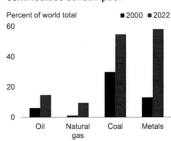

*Sources*: Bloomberg; Caldara and Iacoviello (2022); Energy Institute; UN Comtrade (database); World Bank (2023a); World Bank; World Bureau of Metal Statistics.
*Note*: EMDEs = emerging market and developing economies.
A. Geopolitical risk index reflects an automated text-search of electronic articles from 10 newspapers, related to adverse geopolitical events in each newspaper for each month. A higher index is related to lower investment, stock prices, and employment. Last observation is December 11, 2023. Red vertical lines show adverse geopolitical events.
B. Changes in average monthly oil prices three months after the onset of geopolitical events.
C. Panel shows the share of advanced-economy and EMDE goods exports destined to China. Last observation is 2021.
D. Panel shows China's share of total world consumption of reported commodities.

appetite and a sharp tightening of global financial conditions.

There could be several triggers for such an outcome. Monetary easing in advanced economies could be postponed if progress returning inflation to targets were to slow or if labor markets tightened unexpectedly. Alternatively, a negative supply shock, such as a sizable increase in oil prices related to geopolitical developments, could see inflation resurge. Following a lengthy spell of above-target inflation, central banks might judge that surging non-core prices could raise inflation expectations, necessitating tighter monetary

## FIGURE 1.13 **Risks to the outlook (*continued*)**

*Volatile U.S. term premia point to the persistent risk of financial stress and EMDE capital outflows. Firms in some advanced economies have been reassessing their global supply chain exposures and investing more in their countries or regions. Climate-related natural disasters could increase extreme poverty. In the United States, early retirements have been almost fully offset by rising prime-age labor force participation, potentially supporting both growth and disinflation.*

**A. Average monthly EMDE portfolio flows by change in U.S. term premium, 2010-23**

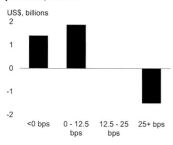

**B. Reshoring by U.S. and EU multinationals**

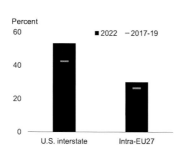

**C. Impact of climate change on extreme poverty by 2030**

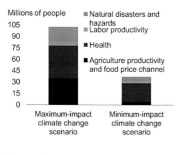

**D. U.S. labor force participation rates**

*Sources*: Federal Reserve Bank of St. Louis; *Financial Times*; Institute of International Finance; Jafino et al. (2020); Kim and Wright (2005); Mulabdic and Nayyar (forthcoming); U.S. Bureau of Labor Statistics; World Bank.

*Note*: EMDEs = emerging market and developing economies; EU = European Union.

A. Panel shows average 4-week net non-resident purchases of EMDE debt and equity securities, categorized by the corresponding 4-week change in the U.S. 10-year term premium, as estimated by Kim and Wright (2005). Unbalanced sample includes up to 20 EMDEs from January 1, 2010, to December 15, 2023.

B. fDi Markets by the *Financial Times*. U.S. values indicate the percentage of total greenfield investment by U.S. companies within the United States; EU-27 values indicate the percentage of greenfield foreign direct investment (FDI) by EU-27 companies in other EU-27 economies. Data are for investment announcements.

C. Number of additional people in extreme poverty in 2030 owing to climate change. Based on Jafino et al. (2020), baseline scenarios are created without accounting for climate change impacts but with factoring in possible changes to demography, education, labor force participation, economic structure, productivity, and redistribution. Then, climate change is introduced in these baselines. The maximum and minimum levels of climate impacts represent the uncertainty on the physical impacts of climate and local adaptation policies.

D. Panel shows difference in percentage points in the 3-month moving average of labor force participation rates since December 2019 for groups 55 and above, 25-54, and all ages. Last observation is November 2023.

policies. In circumstances like these, heightened uncertainty over the path of policy rates, abetted by expansive government borrowing or quantitative tightening, could prompt sharp increases in term premia, driving bond yields higher (Cohen, Hördahl, and Xia 2018). Estimates of U.S. term premia in 2023 exhibited substantial volatility, which could continue into 2024. Sudden moves in

yields could be amplified by the unwinding of the leveraged positions of non-bank financial institutions, including those intended to profit from arbitrage strategies in government bond markets (Avalos and Sushko 2023).

Such developments could drive borrowing rates higher, choke off credit growth, and prompt sharp falls in asset prices. For financial institutions, a sudden and pronounced steepening of the yield curve, driven by a rise in the term premium on long-dated securities, could lead to capital impairment and further exacerbate the credit crunch—a potential outcome made more likely by the lenient regulatory treatment of sovereign risk (BIS 2018). For businesses in interest-sensitive sectors, including commercial real estate, rolling over loans could become challenging. Over time, a rising proportion of households could struggle to service loans, including adjustable-rate mortgages, eroding the quality of bank assets.

EMDEs would be heavily exposed to spillovers from tighter financial conditions caused by higher U.S. interest rates or surging risk aversion. The U.S. dollar would strengthen against EMDE currencies, driving up the cost of servicing dollar-denominated debt and likely exerting a near-term drag on EMDE activity, as well as raising inflation (Boz et al. 2020; Greenwood et al. 2020). EMDEs with twin fiscal and current account deficits would be at particular risk of rapid capital outflows, which tend to accompany sudden increases in U.S. term premia (figure 1.13.A). Inflationary pressures associated with weakening currencies could lead EMDE central banks to delay monetary easing, dampening growth further. The number of EMDEs experiencing debt distress could also increase, raising the probability of a new wave of costly sovereign debt defaults. These dynamics could be exacerbated by negative feedback loops generated by the large exposures of many EMDE banking sectors to local government debt (Feyen and Zuccardi 2019).

### *Trade fragmentation*

Increasing trade restrictions, which have become more common in recent years, present another risk of damage to both near- and long-term global growth prospects. Trade restrictions tend to reduce economic efficiency and often fail to meet their primary objectives because of avoidance efforts. The result may be just a shift in the pattern of interdependence among countries, with increasing indirect linkages through supply chains (Alfaro and Chor 2023; Freund et al. 2023). For instance, following the increases in tariffs imposed by the United States on imports from China in 2018 and 2020, countries that expanded their market shares in the United States also strengthened their trade ties with China. Such tariff increases may therefore not have achieved their primary objective of reducing U.S. economic dependence on China, but they are likely to have led to higher prices of imported goods for U.S. consumers by increasing the length and complexity of supply chains. Other efforts at friend-shoring, near-shoring, or on-shoring, motivated by geopolitical tensions, could have similar results.

Survey data, as well as recent foreign direct investment (FDI) announcements, suggest that firms in some advanced economies have been reassessing global value chain exposures and diverting investment to domestic or regional supply chains to reduce vulnerabilities to geopolitical risks and trade policy shocks (figure 1.13.B; Alicke et al. 2022). However, well-functioning and diversified global value chains are a source of resilience more than vulnerability, and their unraveling could lead to significant welfare losses (Bonadio et al. 2021; di Giovanni and Levchenko 2009; Javorcik et al. 2022).

Global trade growth could also be dampened by other policies, including increases in subsidies for domestic industries in large economies. Over the longer term, the greater fragmentation of investment and trade networks could weaken potential growth by limiting cross-border technological diffusion, reducing efficiency, and raising prices (Branstetter, Glennon, and Jensen 2018; Buera and Oberfield 2020; Góes and Bekkers 2022).

### More frequent natural disasters with worsening impacts

The possibility of increasingly frequent and severe natural disasters resulting from climate change poses a global threat, with the potential to generate significant losses in lives, livelihoods, and output (Casey, Fried, and Goode 2023). Natural disasters, including those linked to climate change, impacted 130 million people and caused more than 40,000 deaths annually, on average, over the past three decades (Song, Hochman, and Timilsina 2023). Climate change-related disasters have caused severe damage to private and public infrastructure, disrupted output, and reduced productivity (Dieppe, Kilic Celik, and Okou 2020; Hallegatte, Jooste, and McIsaac 2022).

The adverse effects of climate change and natural disasters on growth could be amplified by limited fiscal capacity to respond to them, or through their impact on public sector balance sheets (Milivojevic 2023). Natural disasters could also pose risks to the stability of banking sectors by compromising loan collateral and triggering increases in non-performing loans (Nie, Regelink, and Wang 2023). At the same time, the financial sector faces balance sheet risks from the green transition, such as from stranded assets in high-carbon sectors.

Climate change-related natural disasters will likely affect different countries to different extents, depending on their geography and their economic structures. Relative to advanced economies, EMDEs have less capacity to respond to these disasters, while intensive urbanization in some EMDEs may increase vulnerability to such hazards as floods (Rentschler et al. 2022). Moreover, the impacts of natural disasters are likely to be uneven across populations and to increase poverty (Hallegatte and Rozenberg 2017; Jafino et al. 2020).

Climate change and the associated increase in natural disasters can exacerbate poverty through several channels. For example, changing environmental conditions that worsen the spread of disease may result in deteriorating health outcomes for low-income households, including increased prevalence of child stunting (figure 1.13.C). Adverse effects on agricultural yields could also raise food prices, which is especially problematic for poorer households that spend a large share of their income on food. In some countries, poor and vulnerable populations live in informal settlements or may lack access to adequate housing, leaving them more vulnerable to the impacts of extreme weather events, other natural disasters, and associated diseases (Dodman, Archer, and Satterthwaite 2019). Climate change-related and other natural disasters could also disproportionately affect agricultural workers in many EMDEs and increase food insecurity in regions with large numbers of subsistence farmers who lack the resources to maintain consumption in the face of crop failures (Khanal et al. 2021).

### Upside risk: Stronger growth in the United States

Growth in the United States proved more resilient than expected in 2023, with unemployment remaining low, despite the sharpest monetary policy tightening in decades. At the same time, inflation continued to retreat from mid-2022 peaks, partly on account of waning energy and food prices, as well as some moderation in core inflation. These developments—resilient growth, low unemployment, and easing inflation—rarely coincide and represent a break from the generally negative historical relationship between labor market slack and inflation (Hazell et al. 2022). The disinflation is likely attributable to a combination of positive supply developments, including a rebuilding of global supply chains and a gradual post-pandemic recovery in labor supply, and anchored inflation expectations. In addition, a post-pandemic shift of demand, from goods back to services, is likely to have contributed to disinflation in goods prices, with services inflation slower to react.

Looking ahead, further positive developments on the supply side, including continuing increases in labor force participation and efficiency gains in global supply chains, could lift productivity growth (Fernald and Li 2023). This could lead to higher U.S. output growth than projected in the baseline, combined with continued disinflation. The reduction in labor supply caused by the early retirement of older workers during the pandemic has been almost fully offset by increased participation by the prime working-age population (figure 1.13.D). A continuation of this trend would help further boost labor supply and employment; it

could be prompted by abundant job opportunities, a continued recovery in immigration, past wage increases, or depleted savings.

In these conditions, continued employment gains would help support household incomes, while the increased supply of labor, along with productivity gains, would help contain increases in firms' labor costs. Relative to the baseline projection, such a supply gain would allow declining core inflation to be coupled with solid economic growth in the United States, while facilitating the maintenance of healthy household balance sheets. This would generate positive trade spillovers across EMDEs. The impact on global financial conditions would likely also be positive, as prospects for improved growth, lower inflation, and faster easing of U.S. monetary policy would buoy investor risk appetite.

### Growth outcomes under alternative scenarios

If any of the risks discussed above were to materialize, it could likely lead to different growth outcomes from baseline projections. Using a global macroeconomic model, the growth implications of three downside risk scenarios are examined—an increase in oil prices due to a rise in geopolitical tensions, financial stress in EMDEs driven by a reassessment of risk in the context of elevated debt and high borrowing costs, and weaker growth in China because of an intensification of strains in the real estate sector.[1] In addition, one upside scenario is considered, centered on a continuation of robust growth in the United States driven by rising labor supply.[2]

**Higher oil prices.** In the baseline forecast, oil prices are assumed to decline gradually in 2024 and 2025. An alternative scenario envisages oil

---

[1] The scenarios are produced using the Oxford Economics Global Economic Model, a semi-structural macroeconomic projection model that includes 188 individual country blocks in its extended version, available at quarterly or annual frequencies (Oxford Economics 2019). While the risks considered in this section are modeled and presented independently, it is possible that two or more of these shocks could occur together.

[2] The impacts presented in this section are consistent with the existing literature. See Ha et al. (2023) for the effects of oil prices. See Ahmed et al. (2019), Barcelona et al. (2022), Huidrom et al. (2019), and World Bank (2016) for spillovers from China.

prices surging 30 percent above the baseline in the first quarter of 2024 (and 20 percent on average in 2024), driven by disruptions in crude oil supply arising from an escalation of conflict in the Middle East or elsewhere. The initial 30 percent increase is calibrated to mimic price changes seen during similar past episodes (World Bank 2023a). After the first quarter of 2024, oil prices are assumed to gradually return to the baseline. As a result of the jump in oil prices, global consumer price inflation increases by 0.8 percentage point relative to the baseline in 2024, before easing in 2025. Rising gasoline prices reduce real household incomes, while higher input costs drive businesses to curtail investment.[3] As a result, global growth in 2024 is 0.2 percentage point below the baseline. A partial recovery from the oil shock takes hold in 2025, with growth 0.1 percentage point above the baseline (figure 1.14.A).

**Financial stress in EMDEs.** In 2023, financial markets remained generally sanguine about debt-related risks in most EMDEs, despite broadly elevated debt levels and rising advanced-economy bond yields. However, investor risk perceptions, and thus their risk appetite, could deteriorate suddenly, as a result of a wide range of factors. These include the continued buildup of EMDE debt in the context of high global real interest rates, or a surge in term premia on bonds, driven by large fiscal funding requirements in some advanced economies. Such a decline in risk appetite could become self-reinforcing, as currency depreciations and capital outflows put pressure on EMDE balance sheets.

In an EMDE financial stress scenario, spreads on sovereign and corporate debt in EMDEs are assumed to increase by 100-150 basis points in the first quarter of 2024 relative to baseline assumptions, with more vulnerable EMDEs experiencing larger increases. This shock dissipates over the forecast horizon, with spreads gradually returning to baseline levels. As a result, growth in EMDEs in 2024 is 0.6 percentage point below the baseline, as consumers and businesses reduce spending, and global growth is 0.2 percentage point below the

---

[3] This scenario assumes limited reactions from central banks, as the shock does not affect non-oil prices.

**FIGURE 1.14 Growth outcomes under alternative scenarios**

*Alternative downside scenarios include higher oil prices due to an escalation of geopolitical tensions, financial stress in EMDEs leading to surging spreads, and weaker growth in China, resulting in negative spillovers via commodity markets and other channels. In these scenarios, global growth could be up to 0.2 percentage point below the baseline in 2024. An upside scenario envisages higher-than-expected U.S. growth, mainly due to continued strength in supply conditions, which could boost global growth by 0.2 percentage point above the baseline this year.*

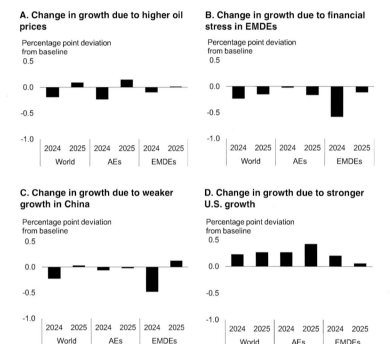

*Sources*: Oxford Economics; World Bank.
*Note*: AEs = advanced economies; EMDEs = emerging market and developing economies.
A.-D. Panels show the impact on growth in alternative scenarios relative to the baseline in percentage points using Oxford Economics' Global Economic Model.

baseline (figure 1.14.B). Advanced economies are initially not significantly affected by the decline in EMDE activity because of the offsetting positive impact of lower commodity prices on domestic demand, but this mitigating factor fades in 2025. Inflation in EMDEs is little changed, with the disinflationary effect of weaker domestic demand offset by the inflationary impact of depreciating currencies. In advanced economies, inflation is reduced significantly in 2024, compared with the baseline, partly on account of weaker commodity prices and appreciating currencies.

**Weaker growth in China.** In the baseline forecast, output in China is projected to grow by 4.5 percent in 2024 and 4.3 percent in 2025.

However, these projections are subject to various downside risks. An alternative scenario envisages China's real estate sector slowing more sharply than expected, with a corresponding decrease in household spending relative to the baseline. The more pronounced slowdown could be driven by tighter credit conditions and weaker confidence. As a result, growth in China is reduced by 1 percentage point in 2024, before recovering in 2025. Other EMDEs are affected by weaker demand from China, particularly for commodities, as well as by increased financial volatility. Thus, aggregate EMDE growth in 2024 is reduced by 0.5 percentage point below the baseline, and global growth by 0.2 percentage point below the baseline, before a rebound in 2025, reflecting the recovery in China (figure 1.14.C).

**Stronger growth in the United States.** The baseline projects that growth in the United States moderates in 2024, partly because some of the supply factors supporting robust growth last year are expected to diminish. Given the possibility of a sustained increase in labor force participation and resilient labor productivity, an alternative scenario is constructed in which the labor force participation rate continues to increase by 0.1 percentage point per quarter—the average pace seen between the fourth quarter of 2020 and the third quarter of 2023—to above pre-pandemic levels. The additional job seekers are absorbed into the labor market with little change in the unemployment rate relative to the baseline. The strong employment growth supports household incomes and spending, raising U.S. growth by 0.5 percentage point in 2024, and 0.7 percentage point in 2025, relative to the baseline. Stronger U.S. activity generates positive spillovers, boosting growth in EMDEs by 0.2 percentage point in 2024. The increase in growth in EMDEs in 2025 is smaller, as monetary policy is adjusted in response to higher demand and inflation.

In all, global growth is 0.2 percentage point higher in 2024 and 0.3 percentage point higher in 2025 than in the baseline (figure 1.14.D). Global inflation is 0.4 percentage point higher in 2024 compared with the baseline, as a result of higher commodity prices and increased activity, before it retreats toward baseline projections in 2025. U.S.

inflation rises by approximately 0.5 percentage point in 2024 above the baseline, before declining in line with lower commodity prices. The Federal Reserve's response to higher inflation is muted given that core prices remain broadly unaffected. Although this leads to no additional increases in U.S. policy rates, the easing path over 2024 is more gradual than in the baseline.

# Policy challenges

Policy makers around the world are facing enormous challenges, many of which pose exacting trade-offs. Global policy efforts are needed to address debt challenges and climate change, and to support populations affected by food insecurity. Boosting international trade is also a key priority given increasing signs of fragmentation and the use of restrictive measures. EMDE policy makers need to strike a difficult balance between ensuring fiscal sustainability and providing targeted support to vulnerable households, while addressing wide investment gaps. This challenge has become harder given weakened fiscal capacity amid higher public debt, increasing debt-servicing costs, and foregone revenues from the persistence of pandemic-related tax cuts. Tight monetary policy or rising bond yields in advanced economies may force EMDEs to delay monetary easing in order to prevent capital outflows and currency pressures. To meet development goals and bolster long-term growth prospects, policy actions to strengthen investment growth are needed.

## Key global challenges

**Elevated debt.** High debt, weak growth, and elevated interest rates pose considerable challenges for many EMDEs, especially the poorest countries, given the resulting increase in debt-servicing burdens (figure 1.15.A). Currently, 13 LICs and 23 middle-income countries have fallen into, or are at high risk of, debt distress. Several countries have entered debt restructuring in the past year, but progress toward adequate resolution has been slow in many cases. The international community needs to pre-emptively address developing risks to avoid the economic costs of debt crises. Crucially, the debt restructuring and relief process, particularly the G20 Common

Framework, needs to be adapted to the changing sovereign debt landscape characterized by more diverse creditors and more complex debt instruments. Greater concessional lending—enabled in part by easier access—and more grants are also needed.

**Climate change.** Bolstering global efforts to address climate change is another critical development challenge. Progress by countries that pledged to cut their greenhouse gas emissions under the 2015 Paris Agreement has fallen short, with vast gaps remaining between the actions needed and those that have been planned and executed (United Nations 2023). Decarbonizing the global economy will require sizable investments and finance—climate finance must increase at least five-fold annually over 2023-50 to contain climate change and avoid its worse effects—at a time when investment growth is set to remain weak (figure 1.15.B; chapter 3; Buchner et al. 2023; World Bank 2022c). Globally, fossil fuel subsidies were 40 percent higher than global investment in climate finance between 2011 and 2020 (Naran et al. 2022). Cutting fossil fuel subsidies can free up significant resources and alleviate the trade-off between financing climate change goals and investing in other longer-term development needs. Moreover, repurposing fossil fuel subsidies toward incentivizing greener production could potentially reduce emissions and pollution while enhancing productivity (Damania et al. 2023).

Upper-middle-income and high-income countries account for nearly three-fourths of greenhouse gas emissions per capita (figure 1.15.C). At the same time, the adverse effects of climate change and natural disasters are disproportionately impacting the poorest, with 40 percent of people affected by disasters living in LICs (Neunuebel 2023). The most vulnerable economies, including LICs and small island developing states, are particularly exposed to droughts, floods, heat waves, rising sea levels, and storms, and often lack the resources to confront these challenges, especially given other pressing development needs (Jafino et al. 2020; Kenworthy, Kirby, and Vorisek 2023). Financing from higher-income economies and the mobilization of private capital will accordingly be needed.

## FIGURE 1.15 Global policy challenges

*Global cooperation is needed to address debt sustainability concerns, particularly in regard to countries already at risk, given record-high debt levels and growing debt-servicing costs. Cooperation is also critical to tackle climate change. Decarbonizing the global economy will require sizable investments at a time when investment growth is set to remain weak. Wealthier countries account for nearly three-fourths of greenhouse gas emissions per capita. Food price inflation is worsening food insecurity and increasing the number of people affected by hunger in many EMDEs, especially those in conflict situations.*

**A. Government net interest payments in EMDEs**

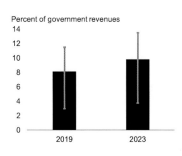

**B. Global investment growth**

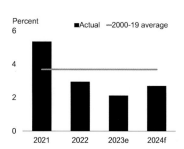

**C. Net greenhouse gas emissions per capita in 2019, by country income group**

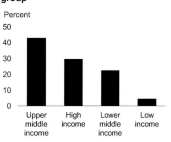

**D. Food insecurity in fragile and conflict-affected situations**

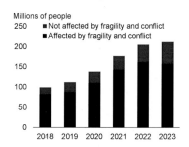

*Sources:* Climate Watch (database); Food and Agriculture Organization of the United Nations; Kose et al. (2022); WEO (database); World Bank (2022c); World Bank; World Food Programme.
*Note:* e = estimate; f = forecast; EMDEs = emerging market and developing economies.
A. Net interest payments are the difference between primary balances and overall fiscal balances. Aggregates computed with government revenues in U.S. dollars as weights, and bars show simple average for 140 EMDEs. Whiskers indicate interquartile range.
B. Investment refers to gross fixed capital formation. The global aggregate is calculated using investment weights at average 2010-19 prices and market exchange rates.
C. Greenhouse gas emissions per capita are defined as tCO2e/person/year. tCO2e = tonnes (metric tons) of carbon dioxide equivalent. Emissions data are from the Climate Watch (database). GDP and population data are from the World Bank.
D. International Food Security Phase Classifications (IPC) include (1) minimal/none, (2) stressed, (3) crisis, (4) emergency, and (5) catastrophe/famine. Bars represent the number of people worldwide that face crisis or more severe (IPC3+) food insecurity. Sample includes 45 economies, of which 19 are economies in fragile and conflict-affected areas.

Decarbonization will require well-targeted regulations that can encourage steps to boost energy efficiency and advance greener technologies (OECD 2023a). As the energy transition will entail substantial redeployments of workers and reallocations of capital from emission-intensive to greener activities, structural reforms and fiscal measures will be needed to reduce labor market

## FIGURE 1.16 **EMDE monetary policy challenges**

*Inflation continues to recede in many EMDEs, allowing central banks to cut policy interest rates. Real and nominal interest rate differentials between EMDEs and the United States have narrowed, which could heighten EMDE vulnerability to capital outflows. EMDE monetary authorities can keep medium-term inflation expectations anchored by signaling readiness to tighten policy again, should inflationary pressures re-emerge.*

**A. Countries with inflation above or below target**

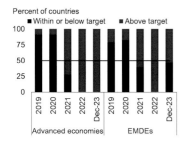

**B. Real policy rate differential between EMDEs and the United States**

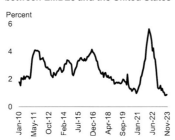

**C. Interest rate differential between EMDEs and the United States**

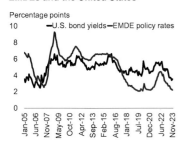

**D. EMDE inflation expectations**

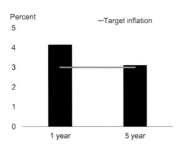

*Sources:* AREAER (database); BIS (database); Bloomberg; Choi et al. (2022); Consensus Economics; Haver Analytics; World Bank.

*Note:* EMDEs = emerging market and developing economies.

A. Share of countries with headline consumer price index (CPI) inflation above or below target. Latest data are based on Consensus Economics forecasts as of December 2023. Sample size includes 11 advanced economies and 28 EMDEs.

B. Line indicates the average differential between U.S. 1-year forward real interest rate and a GDP-weighted average of 1-year forward real interest rate for up to 33 EMDEs. EMDEs exclude Argentina, China, the Russian Federation, and Türkiye.

C. Red line indicates the average differential between U.S. federal funds rate and a GDP-weighted average of policy rates for 18 EMDEs. Blue line indicates the average differential between U.S. 10-year government bond yield and a GDP-weighted average of 10-year government bond yield for up to 14 EMDEs. EMDE sample excludes Argentina, China, the Russian Federation, and Türkiye.

D. Inflation expectations based on Consensus Economics. Line shows median inflation target for 21 EMDEs. 1-year expectations are as of December 2023, and 5-year expectations for 2028 are as of October 2023. Data on inflation expectations are for 33 EMDEs.

frictions and ameliorate uneven distributional impacts across sectors and populations. Sectors such as the mining of fossil fuels and fossil-fuel-intensive industries will face the highest costs of the energy transition, and workers in these sectors lacking the skills needed in greener activities will be at the greatest risk of job losses (OECD 2023a). Cushioning vulnerable groups could increase public support for climate change-mitigation policies (Dechezleprêtre et al. 2022).

Introducing carbon pricing instruments and reducing fuel subsidies could not only help to reduce the carbon intensity of growth but also provide governments with room for transfer payments to vulnerable households (World Bank 2023d).

**Trade fragmentation.** Boosting international trade is another key priority, especially in light of its anemic growth last year and subdued near-term outlook amid the increasing use of restrictions and other signs of fragmentation. Disruptions to global value chains, whether from geopolitical conflict or trade policy restrictions, can lead to significant welfare losses globally. The largest such potential losses are estimated to be in lower-income regions, due to reduced technology spillovers (Eppinger et al. 2021; Góes and Bekker 2022). To guard against the fragmentation of trade and investment networks, the rules-based international order needs to be bolstered, including through improved multilateral cooperation and the expansion of trade agreements. This can be complemented by policies that lower trade costs, encourage the diversification of trade partners and inputs, and attract capital and FDI flows. Such measures include streamlining border procedures with the help of digital technologies and easing other constraints on trade flows, such as uncompetitive logistics sectors. Countries can also invest in modernizing trade information systems, strengthening contract enforcement and addressing market distortions, facilitating trade finance, and promoting competitiveness.

**Food insecurity.** Food price inflation remains elevated, worsening food insecurity and increasing the number of people affected by hunger in many EMDEs, including in FCS economies (figure 1.15.D). Between 691 million and 783 million people are estimated to have gone hungry globally in 2022—122 million more than in 2019—effectively erasing progress made since 2015 (FAO 2023b). The global community can help address food insecurity by avoiding imposing export restrictions, offering technical assistance to strengthen agricultural food systems, and through targeted social protection and cash transfers to poor and vulnerable households. Governments can also shift their focus from costly agricultural subsidies toward measures that sustainably support agricultural producers, such as additional investments in research and development to boost agricultural productivity (World Bank et al. 2023).

## Challenges in emerging market and developing economies

### *EMDE monetary and financial policy challenges*

Global monetary policy tightening is nearing an end, with inflation continuing to decline and the share of EMDEs with above-target inflation falling sharply in recent months (figure 1.16.A). A number of EMDE central banks—some of which were the first, globally, to raise rates in 2021—have already cut policy rates and more are expected to do so in the coming months. In contrast, policy rates are likely to decline more slowly in advanced economies, potentially leading to narrowing differentials between interest rates in advanced economies and EMDEs. In real terms, the policy rate in the United States is already close to parity with the average rate in EMDEs excluding China (on a GDP-weighted basis; figure 1.16.B).

A further shift in real interest rate differentials in favor of advanced economies could increase the risk of EMDE capital outflows, currency depreciations, and resulting surges in inflation (figure 1.16.C). Moreover, a renewed rise in U.S. yields could induce conditions similar to the 2013 "taper tantrum," spurring sudden increases in risk premia and rapid portfolio outflows from EMDEs (Arteta et al. 2015; Sahay et al. 2014). Indeed, there was a marked deterioration in EMDE portfolio flows in September-October last year, when U.S. term premia and longer-term yields increased sharply.

EMDE policy makers can mitigate such risks by indicating their readiness to tighten monetary policy again in response to signs of upward pressure on inflation, including from currency depreciation. This could help keep inflation expectations anchored (figure 1.16.D). More broadly, transparent communication by EMDE monetary authorities, combined with clear and decisive commitment to price stability, can buttress the credibility of their monetary frameworks, thereby lessening long-term inflation pressures (Ha, Kose, and Ohnsorge 2019). In addition, EMDEs can act to conserve or replenish foreign currency reserves, including by demonstrating commitment to policies that boost investor confidence and attract foreign capital.

Heightened volatility in global financial markets could increase liquidity and solvency risks in EMDE financial sectors. In banking sectors, currency and maturity mismatches between assets and liabilities need to be monitored, with prompt action taken to manage emerging issues. The concentration of held-to-maturity securities on the balance sheets of some EMDE banks merits scrutiny, given that carrying values are not marked to market. Highly leveraged non-bank corporations in EMDEs are also vulnerable to rising interest rates (Koh and Yu 2020). Timely and transparent reporting of nonperforming loans is therefore crucial for effective monitoring of banking sector health. Over the medium term, frameworks to address potential banking sector stress in EMDEs could be improved. For example, liquidity requirements could be refined to better address foreign currency liquidity and to ensure assets deemed liquid are of sufficiently high quality (IMF 2023a).

### *EMDE fiscal policy challenges*

Fiscal space in EMDEs remains limited, with median government debt worth 53 percent of GDP in 2023 and debt-to-GDP ratios above pre-pandemic decade averages in more than two-thirds of EMDEs (figure 1.17.A). High debt levels undermine fiscal sustainability, thereby eroding investor sentiment and increasing financing costs. They therefore reduce the effectiveness, as well as the feasibility, of fiscal stimulus measures (figure 1.17.B). The number of EMDEs in sovereign debt distress has risen to its highest level since 2000 (Ohnsorge and Pallan 2023). Past debt defaults suggest that more than one-third of these countries failed to durably reduce their debt or borrowing costs after a default. With global real interest rates expected to remain high, EMDE governments need to prioritize policies that boost growth and safeguard fiscal sustainability.

## FIGURE 1.17 EMDE fiscal policy challenges

*Government debt remains elevated amid tepid revenue collection in many EMDEs. High public debt and spending inefficiencies are dampening the effectiveness of fiscal policy in boosting demand and activity. The persistence of pandemic-related measures, such as tax cuts, has reduced revenues for many EMDEs, including LICs. In most EMDEs, the efficiency of spending on infrastructure, health, and education is lower than in advanced economies. Among EMDE commodity exporters, fiscal policy tends to be more procyclical and volatile than that in non-commodity exporters, amplifying the impact of commodity price cycles on the business cycle.*

### A. Government debt

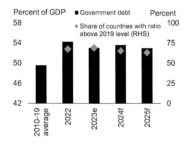

### B. Fiscal multipliers after two years

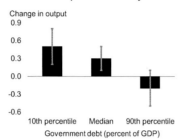

### C. Tax revenues, 2021

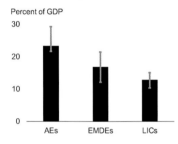

### D. Public spending efficiency score

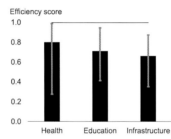

### E. Fiscal policy procyclicality

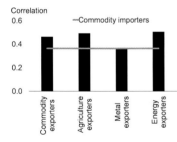

### F. Fiscal policy volatility

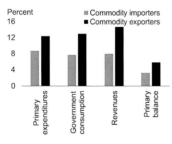

*Sources:* Arroyo Marioli, Fatas, and Vasishtha (2023); Arroyo Marioli and Vegh (2023); Herrera et al. (forthcoming); Huidrom et al. (2019); Kose et al. (2021; 2022); Moody's Analytics; UNU-WIDER (database); WEO (database); World Bank.

Note: e = estimate; f = forecast; AEs = advanced economies; EMDEs = emerging market and developing economies; LICs = low-income countries.

A. Bars show the median value of gross government debt as percent of GDP for 141 EMDEs.

B. Bars show the median conditional fiscal multipliers for different levels of government debt after two years. Fiscal multipliers are defined as cumulative change in output relative to cumulative change in government consumption in response to a 1-unit government consumption shock. They are based on estimates from the interacted panel vector autoregression model, where model coefficients are conditioned only on government debt, as described in Kose et al. (2021). Whiskers show the 16-84 percent confidence bands.

C. GDP-weighted tax revenues for 34 advanced economies, 111 EMDEs, and 14 LICs. Whiskers show the interquartile range.

D. Bars show the average efficiency score, derived from up to five different methodologies, for up to 146 EMDEs for health, education, and infrastructure spending over 2010-20 from Herrera et al. (forthcoming). Whiskers show minimum-maximum values. Horizontal line is the efficiency frontier.

E. Bars show average correlation between the (Hodrick-Prescott-filtered) cyclical components of real GDP and real government spending within groups. The sample period is 1980-2020. Sample includes 38 agricultural, 21 metal, and 31 energy exporters, and 59 commodity importers.

F. Panel shows the unweighted averages, by country group, of the standard deviation of the residuals obtained from regressing four dependent variables—real primary expenditure growth, real government consumption growth, real revenue growth, and change in primary balances (as percent of GDP)—on real GDP growth. Annual data for 148 EMDEs over 1990-2021.

The combination of weak growth, high government debt, and elevated interest rates has contributed to a sharp increase in net interest payments as a share of government revenues in EMDEs. Moreover, the persistence of pandemic-related measures, such as tax cuts, has reduced revenues, compounding the challenges of revenue mobilization for many EMDEs, including LICs (figure 1.17.C). Such measures risk becoming permanent, absent a return to fiscal rules and sunset clauses. Weakened revenue collection also limits the potential redistributive power of taxation and the financing available for social protection systems, thus hindering poverty reduction (Lopez-Acevedo et al. 2023). The erosion of revenue capacity is a particular concern in LICs, where about 10 percent of revenue is spent on servicing external debt and governments are already severely constrained in meeting key development goals (Chuku et al. 2023).

Policy makers face a difficult trade-off between ensuring fiscal sustainability and providing targeted support to vulnerable households. Improving the efficiency of spending can help balance these competing priorities. In most EMDEs, the efficiency of spending on infrastructure, health, and education is lower than in advanced economies (figure 1.17.D; Herrera et al., forthcoming). Spending efficiency in EMDEs with limited fiscal space can be improved by strengthening institutions and governance, bolstering fiscal and public financial management, and improving the effectiveness of fiscal rules and expenditure reviews. Such measures can also support the effective management of debt, especially if complemented with policies that strengthen transparency and legal frameworks (IMF 2023b). Enhancing revenue mobilization is also crucial. Without it, efforts to shore up debt sustainability may be at the expense of critical spending, such as investment in infrastructure and human capital, as has often been the case in EMDEs. Protecting such public investment, while eliminating wasteful spending, is crucial given the projected slowdown in overall investment growth alongside large development needs (chapter 3).

Over the longer term, the trade-off between promoting fiscal sustainability and meeting development needs can be mitigated by market-oriented reforms that both support growth and strengthen fiscal positions by lifting revenues, attracting foreign capital, and lowering borrowing costs. Such reforms can include reductions in barriers to firm entry and trade, measures to bolster financial supervision, and regulatory frameworks that promote competition and contain monopoly power (Aligishiev et al. 2023).

Fiscal space will also be needed to ease the trade-off between responding to climate change challenges and financing other development needs. EMDEs can balance these priorities both by raising revenues through carbon pricing instruments, which have been implemented or scheduled in 14 EMDEs, and by reducing fossil fuel subsidies, which cost 5.6 percent of GDP in EMDEs excluding China in 2022 (Carbon Pricing Dashboard; IEA database). Countries can reprioritize spending on fuel subsidies toward measures that help accelerate the green transition, including by boosting public investment and research and development on low-carbon electricity generation, transport, and technologies.

Commodity-exporting EMDEs face unique fiscal challenges, stemming both from the need to cope with large fluctuations in commodity prices and from the effects of the projected slowdown in China's demand for commodities, notably metals. Declines in commodity prices can trigger procyclical cuts in public expenditures due to reduced revenues, while rising commodity prices can lead to procyclical increases in public spending. As a result, fiscal policy in commodity exporters tends to be more procyclical than in non-commodity exporters, often amplifying the impact of commodity price cycles on economic growth and hence the business cycle (chapter 4; figure 1.17.E). Associated with this issue, fiscal policy tends to be generally more volatile in commodity exporters, adding to the volatility of their economies and thus damaging longer-term growth (figure 1.17.F).

Sustainable, well designed, strong, and stability-oriented fiscal frameworks, such as fiscal rules and sovereign wealth funds, along with strong institutions, can help countries build buffers during commodity price booms to prepare for subsequent slumps. In addition, medium-term expenditure frameworks are vital for strengthening fiscal space, reducing fiscal policy volatility, and supporting countercyclical fiscal policy.

### EMDE structural policy challenges

EMDEs face the difficult challenge of boosting investment to close significant development gaps in an environment of weak growth prospects and limited fiscal resources. Decarbonization alone will require a significant scaling up of investment, combined with structural reforms to promote the green transition. Shoring up food security is also critical, especially given growing trade restrictions. In some countries, closing gender gaps in labor markets could help offset demographic headwinds and bolster longer-term growth prospects.

### Accelerating investment

Continuing a decade of weakness prior to the pandemic, the growth of fixed investment in EMDEs in 2023-24 is expected to average 4.1 percent per year, just over half the average pace over 2000-19. The broad-based investment slowdown has exacerbated large unmet investment needs in many EMDEs (Rozenberg and Fay 2019; World Bank 2022c). Substantial public investment is needed for countries to adapt to, and help contain, climate change; accelerate the digital transition; improve social outcomes; and support long-term growth. At the same time, tight financial conditions, heightened uncertainty, and, in some cases, limited access to international capital markets, continue to weigh on public and business investment, curbing capital deepening and job creation. Given constrained fiscal space for additional public investment and the challenging macroeconomic environment for private investment, there is a clear need for policies that encourage a sustained acceleration of investment in EMDEs (chapter 3).

Investment acceleration episodes have been associated with higher growth, boosted not only by rapid capital accumulation but also by increased growth of employment and productivity, the latter being supported by sectoral shifts of resources facilitated by greater investment (figure

## FIGURE 1.18 EMDE structural policy challenges

*Investment growth acceleration episodes have been associated with higher output growth. The likelihood of an investment acceleration episode occurring is positively related to institutional quality. Food security has worsened in EMDEs, particularly in low-income countries, partly reflecting policies that restrict food exports. The gender gap in labor force participation between EMDEs and advanced economies has widened since the pandemic, underscoring the need for labor and education policy reforms in many EMDEs.*

**A. Output per capita annual growth before and during investment accelerations**

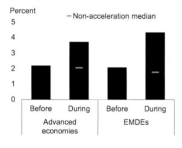

**B. Probability of onset of an investment acceleration, by institutional quality**

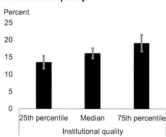

**C. Policies to liberalize or restrict food exports**

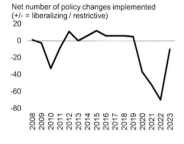

**D. Difference in the ratio of female to male labor force participation rate in advanced economies versus EMDEs**

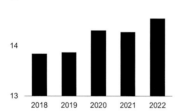

*Sources:* Feenstra, Inklaar, and Timmer (2015); GTA (database); PRS Group (database); WDI (database); World Bank.
*Note:* EMDEs = emerging market and developing economies.
A. Bars show median per capita growth of output in the six years before and during an acceleration. Markers indicate non-acceleration-year medians. See annex 3.1 for the definition and identification of investment accelerations.
B. Bars show the predicted probability of an investment acceleration at different levels of the lagged *International Country Risk Guide* (ICRG) Law and Order index. Whiskers refer to the 90 percent confidence interval. The percentile thresholds of the index are 3, 4, and 5; see column (6) of table A3.2.1. Institutional quality is measured by ICRG's Law and Order index. Sample includes 95 economies.
C. Panel shows net number of policy changes, that is, "liberalizing" changes minus "restrictive" changes. Export policies are those concerning export taxes, export bans, export licensing requirements, export quotas, and export-related non-tariff measures. Data include changes relating to 33 three-figure central product classification codes pertaining to edible agricultural commodities and food items.
D. Panel shows the difference in the average ratio of female to male labor force participation rate between advanced economies and EMDEs. Unbalanced sample includes up to 36 advanced economies and 142 EMDEs.

1.18.A). These episodes have also been frequently accompanied by a range of other economic improvements, such as strengthened fiscal positions, enhanced credit growth, increased trade openness, and greater progress with poverty reduction.

Country case studies of investment accelerations suggest that a wide-ranging package of policies that both ensures macroeconomic stability and promotes private-sector development (for instance, Malaysia in the mid-2000s and India since the 1990s) is more likely to trigger investment accelerations. Empirical cross-country evidence also suggests that improvements in economic policy—such as the strengthening of fiscal positions, the adoption of inflation targeting, and reforms to promote trade and financial integration—have been important drivers of investment growth accelerations, particularly when combined with well-functioning institutions (figure 1.18.B).

### Confronting food insecurity

Food security has deteriorated in recent years, with about 30 percent of the global population facing moderate or severe food insecurity in 2022, up from 25 percent in 2019. Factors contributing to this rise in food insecurity include geopolitical conflict, more adverse weather patterns intensified by climate change, and proliferating food-related trade restrictions (figure 1.18.C). Russia's invasion of Ukraine and the reduction of Ukrainian export capacity, including through the destruction of agricultural land and facilities and the partial blockage of the country's exports, has curtailed an important source of grain supply (Mottaleb, Kruseman, and Snapp 2022). An escalation of the conflict in the Middle East, and the associated disruptions in energy supply and ensuing surge in energy prices, could also substantially exacerbate food insecurity by raising food production costs (World Bank 2023a).

Measures to increase agricultural yields and improve food supply chains in EMDEs could bolster economic resilience while adding to global food supplies. Such policies can include investments in infrastructure to better transport perishables and withstand extreme weather; improvements in market competitiveness, including by reducing barriers to entry; and reforms to formalize and secure land rights, which can incentivize efficient land use and improve access to finance (FAO et al. 2023; Laborde, Lakatos, and Martin 2019; van Berkum 2021). Countries can also improve food security by boosting the technical knowledge of, and advisory services to, those employed in the agriculture sector, including to better monitor weather and flood risks; by enhancing financial support to farmers to cover imports of inputs for planting season; and by encouraging investment in climate-smart technology for agricultural production (Gautam et al. 2022). Repurposing support for fertilizer use could not only free up resources to address food security issues but also support greener production, given that fertilizer is a contributor to nitrogen pollution (Chatterjee et al. 2022; Damania et al. 2023; Ding et al. 2021).

**Closing gender gaps in the labor market**

Improving gender parity in labor markets remains a major challenge, particularly across EMDEs. Barriers to female labor force participation include mismatches in skills; lack of access to child or elderly care; discrimination in hiring and retention; and restrictive policies, laws, and social norms. Globally, average female labor force participation in 2011-22 was 50 percent, compared with 70 percent for men, and the gender participation gap in EMDEs was slightly wider, at 23 percentage points.

The pandemic has resulted in persistent adverse effects in the labor market, particularly for women and vulnerable groups such as the young, low-wage workers, and workers with fewer years of education—a common outcome following large external shocks (Lopez-Acevedo and Robertson 2023). As a result, there has been a widening of gender gaps in labor force participation, and to a greater extent in EMDEs than in advanced economies (figure 1.18.D; WEF 2023). In many EMDEs, women also continue to face higher unemployment rates, lower wages, and more limited access to managerial positions (ILO 2023). While female employment in EMDEs has recovered since the pandemic recession of 2020, it remains lower compared with men, and four-fifths of the jobs created for women in 2022 were in the informal economy compared with two-thirds for men (ILO 2023). Since informal sector jobs tend to be lower paid and less secure, and to provide fewer opportunities for advancement, policies are needed to strengthen inclusion in formal employment (OECD 2023b).

Gender parity in the labor market is particularly lacking in the Middle East and North Africa and South Asia, where female labor force participation is about one-half the EMDE average. If measures were taken in these two regions to gradually raise female participation to the EMDE average by the end of this decade, potential growth in the period could be boosted by about 1.2 percentage points per year (Kose and Ohnsorge 2023). These gains could be amplified by the provision of more and higher-quality education for women. In other regions, particularly East Asia and Pacific and Europe and Central Asia, increasing female labor participation could partly offset the slowing of labor force growth owing to population aging. Female labor force participation can be encouraged by social protection measures that provide adequate social safety nets, access to education, and support for childcare and job re-entry programs. Such policies can be supplemented by investments in safe transport; measures to broaden access to finance, inputs, and markets; information campaigns to address restrictive social norms; and legislative and regulatory changes (Bussolo et al. 2022; World Bank 2022d).

## TABLE 1.2 Emerging market and developing economies[1]

| Commodity exporters[2] | | Commodity importers[3] | |
|---|---|---|---|
| Algeria* | Kyrgyz Republic | Afghanistan | Samoa |
| Angola* | Lao PDR | Albania | Serbia |
| Argentina | Liberia | Antigua and Barbuda | Sri Lanka |
| Armenia | Libya* | Bahamas, The | St. Kitts and Nevis |
| Azerbaijan* | Madagascar | Bangladesh | St. Lucia |
| Bahrain* | Malawi | Barbados | St. Vincent and the Grenadines |
| Belize | Mali | Belarus | Syrian Arab Republic |
| Benin | Mauritania | Bosnia and Herzegovina | Thailand |
| Bhutan* | Mongolia | Bulgaria | Tonga |
| Bolivia* | Mozambique | Cambodia | Tunisia |
| Botswana | Myanmar* | China | Türkiye |
| Brazil | Namibia | Djibouti | Tuvalu |
| Burkina Faso | Nicaragua | Dominica | Vanuatu |
| Burundi | Niger | Dominican Republic | Viet Nam |
| Cabo Verde | Nigeria* | Egypt, Arab Rep. | |
| Cameroon* | Oman* | El Salvador | |
| Central African Republic | Papua New Guinea | Eswatini | |
| Chad* | Paraguay | Georgia | |
| Chile | Peru | Grenada | |
| Colombia* | Qatar* | Haiti | |
| Comoros | Russian Federation* | Hungary | |
| Congo, Dem. Rep. | Rwanda | India | |
| Congo, Rep.* | São Tomé and Príncipe | Jamaica | |
| Costa Rica | Saudi Arabia* | Jordan | |
| Côte d'Ivoire | Senegal | Kiribati | |
| Ecuador* | Seychelles | Lebanon | |
| Equatorial Guinea* | Sierra Leone | Lesotho | |
| Eritrea | Solomon Islands | Malaysia | |
| Ethiopia | South Africa | Maldives | |
| Fiji | South Sudan* | Marshall Islands | |
| Gabon* | Sudan | Mauritius | |
| Gambia, The | Suriname | Mexico | |
| Ghana* | Tajikistan | Micronesia, Fed. Sts. | |
| Guatemala | Tanzania | Moldova | |
| Guinea | Timor-Leste* | Montenegro | |
| Guinea-Bissau | Togo | Morocco | |
| Guyana* | Uganda | Nauru | |
| Honduras | Ukraine | Nepal | |
| Indonesia* | United Arab Emirates* | North Macedonia | |
| Iran, Islamic Rep.* | Uruguay | Pakistan | |
| Iraq* | Uzbekistan | Palau | |
| Kazakhstan* | West Bank and Gaza | Panama | |
| Kenya | Yemen, Rep.* | Philippines | |
| Kosovo | Zambia | Poland | |
| Kuwait* | Zimbabwe | Romania | |

\* Energy exporters.

1. Emerging market and developing economies (EMDEs) include all those that are not classified as advanced economies and for which a forecast is published for this report. Dependent territories are excluded. Advanced economies include Australia; Austria; Belgium; Canada; Cyprus; Czechia; Denmark; Estonia; Finland; France; Germany; Greece; Hong Kong SAR, China; Iceland; Ireland; Israel; Italy; Japan; the Republic of Korea; Latvia; Lithuania; Luxembourg; Malta; the Netherlands; New Zealand; Norway; Portugal; Singapore; the Slovak Republic; Slovenia; Spain; Sweden; Switzerland; the United Kingdom; and the United States. Since Croatia became a member of the euro area on January 1, 2023, it has been removed from the list of EMDEs, and related growth aggregates, to avoid double counting.

2. An economy is defined as commodity exporter when, on average in 2017-19, either (1) total commodities exports accounted for 30 percent or more of total exports or (2) exports of any single commodity accounted for 20 percent or more of total exports. Economies for which these thresholds were met as a result of re-exports were excluded. When data were not available, judgment was used. This taxonomy results in the classification of some well-diversified economies as importers, even if they are exporters of certain commodities (for example, Mexico).

3. Commodity importers are EMDEs not classified as commodity exporters.

# References

ACLED (The Armed Conflict Location & Event Data Project) database. Accessed on December 20, 2023. https://acleddata.com/data-export-tool

Adarov, A., A. Cojocaru, S. Kilic-Celik, and A. Narayan. 2022. "Impact of Covid-19 on Global Income Inequality." In *Global Economic Prospects,* January. Washington DC: World Bank.

Ahmed, S., R. Correa, D. A. Dias, N. Gornemann, J. Hoek, A. Jain, E. Liu, and A. Wong. 2019. "Global Spillovers of a China Hard Landing." International Finance Discussion Paper 1260, Board of Governors of the Federal Reserve System, Washington, DC.

Aiyar, S., A. Presbitero, and M. Ruta, eds. 2023. *Geoeconomic Fragmentation: The Economic Risks from a Fractured World Economy.* Paris and London: Centre for Economic Policy Research Press.

Alfaro, L., and D. Chor. 2023. "Global Supply Chains: The Looming "Great Reallocation." Jackson Hole Symposium, Federal Reserve Bank of Kansas City, Missouri.

Alicke, K., E. Barriball, T. Foster, J. Mauhourat, and V. Trautwein. 2022. "Taking the Pulse of Shifting Supply Chains." McKinsey & Company, Washington, DC.

Aligishiev, Z., G. Cugat, R. A. Duval, D. Furceri, J. T. Jalles, M. MacDonald, G. Melina, et al. 2023. "Market Reforms and Public Debt Dynamics in Emerging Market and Developing Economies." *International Monetary Fund Staff Discussion Notes* 2023 (005): 45.

Arroyo Marioli, F., and C. A. Vegh. 2023. "Fiscal Procyclicality in Commodity Exporting Countries: How Much Does It Pour and Why?" NBER Working Paper 3143, National Bureau of Economic Research, Cambridge, MA.

Arteta, C., M. A. Kose, F. Ohnsorge, and M. Stocker. 2015. "The Coming U.S. Interest Rate Tightening Cycle: Smooth Sailing or Stormy Waters?" Policy Research Note, World Bank, Washington, DC.

Avalos, F., and V. Sushko. 2023. "Margin Leverage and Vulnerabilities in US Treasury Futures." BIS Quarterly Review, Bank for International Settlement, Basel, Switzerland.

Baffes, J., and P. Nagle, eds. 2022. *Commodity Markets Outlook: Evolution, Challenges, and Policies.* Washington, DC: World Bank.

Barbiero, O., and D. Patki. 2023. "Have US Households Depleted All the Excess Savings They Accumulated during the Pandemic?" Current Policy Perspectives, Federal Reserve Bank of Boston, Boston, MA.

Barcelona, W., D. Cascaldi-Garcia, J. Hoek, and E. V. Leemput. 2022. "What Happens in China Does Not Stay in China." International Finance Discussion Paper 1360, Board of Governors of the Federal Reserve System, Washington, DC.

BIS (Bank for International Settlements). 2018. "The Regulatory Treatment of Sovereign Exposures." Discussion Paper, Bank for International Settlements, Basel, Switzerland.

BIS (Bank for International Settlements) database. Accessed on December 15, 2023. https://data.bis.org/

Bonadio, B., Z. Huo, A. A. Levchenko, and N. Pandalai-Nayar. 2021. "Global Supply Chains in the Pandemic." *Journal of International Economics* 133 (November): 103534.

Boz, E., C. Casas, G. Georgiadis, G. Gopinath, H. Le Mezo, A. Mehl, and T. Nguyen. 2020. "Patterns in Invoicing Currency in Global Trade." IMF Working Paper 20/126, International Monetary Fund, Washington, DC.

Branstetter, L., B. Glennon, and J. B. Jensen. 2018. "Knowledge Transfer Abroad: The Role of U.S. Inventors within Global R&D Networks." NBER Working Paper 24453, National Bureau of Economic Research, Cambridge, MA.

Buchner, B., B. Naran, R. Padmanabhi, S. Stout, C. Strinati, D. Wignarajah, G. Miao, J. Connolly, and N. Marini. 2023. "Global Landscape of Climate Finance 2023." Climate Policy Initiative, San Francisco.

Buera, F. J., and E. Oberfield. 2020. "The Global Diffusion of Ideas." *Econometrica* 88 (1): 83-114.

Bussolo, M., J. A. Ezebuihe, A. M. Munoz Boudet, S. Poupakis, T. Rahman, and N. Sarma. 2022. "Social Norms and Gender Equality: A Descriptive Analysis for South Asia." Policy Research Working Paper 10142, World Bank, Washington, DC.

Caldara, D., S. Conlisk, M. Iacoviello, and M. Penn. 2023. "Do Geopolitical Risks Raise or Lower Inflation?" Federal Reserve Board, Washington, DC.

Caldara, D., and M. Iacoviello. 2022. "Measuring Geopolitical Risk." *American Economic Review* 112 (4): 1195-25.

Casey, G., S. Fried, and E. Goode. 2023. "How Long Do Rising Temperatures Affect Economic Growth?" FRBSF Economic Letter, Economic Research, Federal Reserve Bank of San Francisco, San Francisco.

Chatterjee, S., D. Kapur, P. Sekhsaria, and A. Subramanian. 2022. "Agricultural Federalism: New Facts, Constitutional Vision." *Economic & Political Weekly* LVII (36): 1-10.

Choi, J., T. Doh, A. Foerster, and Z. Martinez. 2022. "Monetary Policy Stance Is Tighter than Federal Funds Rate." FRBSF Economic Letter, Federal Reserve Bank of San Francisco, San Francisco.

Chuku, C., P. Samal, J. Saito, D. S. Hakura, M. Chamon, M. D. Cerisola, G. Chabert, and J. Zettelmeyer. 2023. "Are We Heading for Another Debt Crisis in Low-Income Countries? Debt Vulnerabilities: Today vs the Pre-HIPC Era." IMF Working Paper 079/2023, International Monetary Fund, Washington, DC.

Climate Watch (Climate Data for Action) database. 2023. "World Resource Institute." Accessed on December 10, 2023. https://climatewatchdata.org

Cohen, B. H., P. Hördahl, and F. D. Xia. 2018. "Term Premia: Models and Some Stylized Facts." BIS Quarterly Review, Bank for International Settlement, Basel, Switzerland.

Damania, R., E. Balseca, C. de Fontaubert, J. Gill, K. Kim, J. Rentschler, J. Russ, et al. 2023. *Detox Development: Repurposing Environmentally Harmful Subsidies.* Washington, DC: World Bank.

Dechezleprêtre, A., A. Fabre, T. Kruse, B. Planterose, A. S. Chico, and S. Stantcheva. 2022. "Fighting Climate Change: International Attitudes Toward Climate Policies." OECD Working Paper 1714, Organisation for Economic Co-Operation and Development, Paris.

Di Giovanni, J., and A. A. Levchenko. "Trade Openness and Volatility." *Review of Economics and Statistics* 91 (3): 558-85.

Dieppe, A., S. Kilic Celik, and C. Okou. 2020. "Implications of Major Adverse Events on Productivity." Policy Research Working Paper 9411, World Bank, Washington, DC.

Ding, H., A. Markandya, R. Feltran-Barbieri, M. Calmon, M. Cervera, M. Duraisami, R. Singh, J. Warman, and W. Anderson. 2021. "Repurposing Agricultural Subsidies to Restore Degraded Farmland and Grow Rural Prosperity." World Resources Institute, Washington, DC.

Dodman, D., D. Archer, and D. Satterthwaite. 2019. "Responding to Climate Change in Contexts of Urban Poverty and Informality." *International Institute for Environment and Development* 31 (1): 3-368.

EM-DAT (The International Disaster Database) database. Centre for Research on the Epidemiology of Disasters (CRED), UCLouvain, Brussels. Accessed on December 10, 2023. https://www.emdat.be/

Eppinger, P., G. J. Felbermayr, O. Krebs, and B. Kukharskyy. 2021. "Decoupling Global Value Chains." CESifo Working Paper 9079, Center for Economic Studies, ifo Institute, Munich.

European Commission. 2023. "European Economic Forecast." Institutional Paper 258, European Commission, Brussels.

FAO (Food and Agriculture Organization). 2023a. "El Niño: Anticipatory Action and Response Plan, August-December 2023. Mitigating the Expected Impacts of El Niño-Induced Climate Extremes on Agriculture and Food Security." Food and Agriculture Organization of the UN, Rome.

FAO (Food and Agriculture Organization). 2023b. "122 Million More People Pushed into Hunger Since 2019 Due to Multiple Crises, Reveals UN Report." Food and Agriculture Organization, Rome.

FAO (Food and Agriculture Organization), IFAD (International Fund for Agricultural Development), UNICEF (United Nations Children's Fund), WFP (World Food Programme), and WHO (World Health Organization). 2023. *The State of Food Security and Nutrition in the World 2023: Urbanization, Agrifood Systems Transformation and Healthy Diets Across the Rural—Urban Continuum.* Rome, Italy: FAO, IFAD, UNICEF, WFP, WHO.

Feenstra, R. C., R. Inklaar and M. P. Timmer. 2015. "The Next Generation of the Penn World Table." *American Economic Review* 105 (10): 3150-82.

Fernald, J., and H. Li. 2023. "Productivity in the World Economy During and After the Pandemic." Working Paper 2023-29, Federal Reserve Bank of San Francisco, San Francisco.

Feyen, E., and I. Zuccardi. 2019. "The Sovereign-Bank Nexus in EMDEs." Policy Research Working Paper 8950, World Bank, Washington, DC.

Forbes, K. J., and F. E. Warnock. 2012. "Capital Flow Waves: Surges, Stops, Flight, and Retrenchment." *Journal of International Economics* 88 (2): 235-51.

Forbes, K. J., and F. E. Warnock. 2021. "Capital Flow Waves—Or Ripples? Extreme Capital Flow Movements Since the Crisis." *Journal of International Money and Finance, Elsevier* 116 (September): 102394.

Freund, C., A. Mattoo, A. Mulabdic, and M. Ruta. 2023. "Is US Trade Policy Reshaping Global Supply Chains?" Policy Research Working Paper 10593, World Bank, Washington, DC.

FSIN (Food Security Information Network), and GNAFC (Global Network Against Food Crises). 2023. "Global Report on Food Crises: Joint Analysis for Better Decisions." Mid-year update, Food Security Information Network, Rome.

Gautam, M., D. Laborde, A. Mamun, W. Martin, V. Pineiro, and R. Vos. 2022. "Repurposing Agricultural Policies and Support: Options to Transform Agriculture and Food Systems to Better Serve the Health of People, Economies, and the Planet." International Food Policy Research Institute and World Bank, Washington, DC.

Góes, C., and E. Bekkers. 2022. "The Impact of Geopolitical Conflicts on Trade, Growth, and Innovation." WTO Staff Working Papers ERSD-2022-9, Economic Research and Statistics Division, World Trade Organization, Geneva.

Greenwood, R., S. G. Hanson, J. C. Stein, and A. Sunderam. 2020. "A Quantity-Driven Theory of Term Premia and Exchange Rates." NBER Working Paper 27615, National Bureau of Economic Research, Cambridge, MA.

GTA (Global Trade Alert) database. Accessed on December 20, 2023. https://globaltradealert.org/data_extraction

Ha, J., M. A. Kose, and F. Ohnsorge, eds. 2019. *Inflation in Emerging and Developing Economies: Evolution, Drivers, and Policies.* Washington, DC: World Bank.

Ha, J., M. A. Kose, and F. Ohnsorge. 2021. "One Stop Source: A Global Database of Inflation." *Journal of International Money and Finance, Elsevier* 137 (October): 102896.

Ha, J., M. A. Kose, F. Ohnsorge, and H. Yilmazkuday. 2023. "What Explains Global Inflation." Policy Research Working Paper 10648, World Bank, Washington, DC.

Hallegatte, S., C. Jooste, F. J. McIsaac. 2022. "Modeling the Macroeconomic Consequences of Natural Disasters: Capital Stock, Recovery Dynamics, and Monetary Policy." Policy Research Working Paper 9943, World Bank, Washington, DC.

Hallegatte, S., and J. Rozenberg. 2017. "Climate Change Through a Poverty Lens." *Nature Climate Change* 1: 250-56.

Hazell, J., J. Herreño, E. Nakamura, and J. Steinsson. 2022. "The Slope of The Phillips Curve: Evidence from U.S. States." *Quarterly Journal of Economics* 137 (3): 1299-44.

Herrera, S., M. Massimo, J. N. D. Francois, H. Isaka, and H. Sahibzada (database). Forthcoming. "Global Database on Spending Efficiency." Democratic Republic of Congo, Public Finance Review.

Hoogeveen, J. G., and G. Lopez-Acevedo. 2021. "Distributional Impacts of COVID-19 in the Middle East and North Africa Region." MENA Development Report, World Bank. Washington, DC.

Horn, S., B. C. Parks, C. M. Reinhart, and C. Trebesch. 2023. "China as an International Lender of Last Resort." Policy Research Working Paper 10380, World Bank, Washington, DC.

Huidrom, R., M. A. Kose, J. J. Lim, and F. Ohnsorge. 2019. "Why Do Fiscal Multipliers Depend on Fiscal Positions?" *Journal of Monetary Economics* 114 (C): 109-25 .

Huidrom, R., M. A. Kose, H. Matsuoka, and F. Ohnsorge. 2019. "How Important Are Spillovers from Major Emerging Markets?" *International Finance* 23 (1): 47-63.

IEA (International Energy Agency). 2014. *Energy Supply Security: Emergency response of IEA Countries.* Paris: International Energy Agency.

IEA (International Energy Agency). 2023. "Oil Market Report." October. International Energy Agency, Paris.

IEA (International Energy Agency) database. "Fossil Fuel Subsidies Database." Accessed on October 25, 2023. https://iea.org/data-and-statistics/data-product/fossil-fuel-subsidies-database#overview

ILO (International Labour Organization). 2023. "World Employment and Social Outlook; Trends 2023." ILO Flagship Report, Geneva, Switzerland.

IMF-AREAER (International Monetary Fund) database. "Annual Report on Exchange Arrangements and Exchange Restrictions." Accessed on October 5, 2023. https://elibrary-areaer.imf.org/Pages/Home.aspx

IMF-WEO (International Monetary Fund) database. "World Economic Outlook: October 2023." Accessed on October 11, 2023. https://imf.org/en/Publications/WEO/weo-database/2023/October

IMF (International Monetary Fund). 2022. *World Economic Outlook*. Washington, DC: International Monetary Fund.

IMF (International Monetary Fund). 2023a. *Global Financial Stability Report: Financial and Climate Policies for High-Interest-Rate Era*. Washington, DC: International Monetary Fund.

IMF (International Monetary Fund). 2023b. "Making Public Debt Public-Ongoing Initiatives and Reform Options." Policy Paper, International Monetary Fund, Washington, DC.

Jafino, B. A., B. Walsh, J. Rozenberg, and S. Hallegatte. 2020. "Revised Estimates of the Impact of Climate Change on Extreme Poverty by 2030." Policy Research Working Paper 9417, Poverty and Shared Prosperity 2020, World Bank. Washington, DC.

Javorcik, B. S., L. Kitzmueller, H. Schweiger, and M. A. Yıldırım. 2022. "Economic Costs of Friend-Shoring." EBRD Working Paper 274, European Bank for Reconstruction and Development, London.

Kenworthy, P., P. Kirby, and D. Vorisek. 2023. "Small States: Overlapping Crises, Multiple Challenges." In *Global Economic Prospects*, January. Washington, DC: World Bank.

Khanal, U., C. Wilson, S. Rahman, B. L. Lee, and V.-N. Hoang. 2021. "Smallholder Farmers' Adaptation to Climate Change and Its Potential Contribution to UN's Sustainable Development Goals of Zero Hunger and No Poverty." *Journal of Cleaner Production* 281 (January): 124-999.

Kim, D. H., and J. H. Wright. 2005. "An Arbitrage-Free Three-Factor Term Structure Model and the Recent Behavior of Long-Term Yields and Distant-Horizon Forward Rates." Finance and Economics Discussion Series Divisions of Research & Statistics and Monetary Affairs Federal Reserve Board, Washington, DC.

Koh, W. C., and S. Yu. 2020. "A Decade after the 2009 Global Recession: Macroeconomic Developments." Policy Research Working Paper 9290, World Bank, Washington, DC.

Kose, M. A., S. Kurlat, F. Ohnsorge, and N. Sugawara. 2022. "A Cross-Country Database of Fiscal Space."

*Journal of International Money and Finance* 128 (November): 102682.

Kose, M. A., P. Nagle, F. Ohnsorge, and N. Sugawara. 2021. *Global Waves of Debt: Causes and Consequences*. Washington, DC: World Bank.

Kose, M. A., N. Sugawara, and M. E. Terrones. 2020. "Global Recessions." Policy Research Working Paper 9172, World Bank, Washington, DC.

Kose, M. A., and F. Ohnsorge, eds. 2023. *Falling Long-Term Growth Prospects: Trends, Expectations, and Policies*. Washington, DC: World Bank.

Laborde, D., C. Lakatos, and W. Martin. 2019. "Poverty Impacts of Food Price Shocks and Policies." In *Inflation in Emerging and Developing Economies: Evolution, Drivers, and Policies,* edited by J. Ha, M. A. Kose, and F. Ohnsorge, 371-99. Washington, DC: World Bank.

Laeven, L., and F. Valencia. 2020. "Systemic Banking Crises Database: A Timely Update in COVID-19 Times." CEPR Discussion Paper 14569, Center for Economic and Policy Research, Washington, DC.

Lopez-Acevedo, G., M. Ranzani, N. Sinha, and A. Elsheikhi. 2023. "Informality and Inclusive Growth in the Middle East and North Africa." Middle East and North Africa Development Report, World Bank, Washington, DC.

Lopez-Acevedo, G., and R. Robertson, eds. 2023. "Exports to Improve Labor Markets in the Middle East and North Africa." Middle East and North Africa Development Report, World Bank, Washington, DC.

Milivojevic, L. 2023. "Natural Disasters and Fiscal Drought." Policy Research Working Paper 10298, World Bank, Washington, DC.

Montes, J., C. Smith, and J. Dajon. 2022. "'The Great Retirement Boom': The Pandemic-Era Surge in Retirements and Implications for Future Labor Force Participation." Finance and Economics Discussion Series, Federal Reserve Board, Washington, DC.

Mottaleb, K. A., G. Kruseman, and S. Snapp. 2022. "Potential Impacts of Ukraine-Russia Armed Conflict on Global Wheat Food Security: A Quantitative Exploration." *Global Food Security* 35: 12.

Mulabdic, A., and G. Nayyar. Forthcoming. "Friend-shoring, Nearshoring, Reshoring, or Stay-shoring? Evidence from FDI Announcements," World Bank, Washington, DC.

Naran, B., J. Connolly, P. Rosane, D. Wignarajah, G. Wakaba, and B. Buchner. 2022. "Global Landscape of Climate Finance: A Decade of Data." Climate Policy Initiative, San Francisco, California.

Neunuebel, C. 2023. "What the World Bank's Country Climate and Development Reports Tell Us About the Debt-Climate Nexus in Low-income Countries." World Resources Institute, Washington, DC.

Nie, O., M. G. J. Regelink, and D. Wang. 2023. "Banking Sector Risk in the Aftermath of Climate Change and Environmental-Related Natural Disasters." Policy Research Working Paper 10326, World Bank, Washington, DC.

OECD (Organisation for Economic Co-operation and Development). 2023a. *OECD Economic Outlook.* June. Paris, France: Organisation for Economic Co-operation and Development.

OECD (Organisation for Economic Co-operation and Development). 2023b. "SIGI 2023 Global Report: Gender Equality in Times of Crisis." Social Institutions and Gender Index, Organisation for Economic Co-Operation and Development, Paris, France.

Ohnsorge, F., and H. Pallan. 2023. "Spotlight. An Ounce of Prevention, a Pound of Cure: Averting and Dealing with Sovereign Debt Default." In *Toward Faster, Cleaner Growth: South Asia Development Update,* October. Washington, DC: World Bank.

Oxford Economics. 2019. "Global Economic Model." July. Oxford Economics, Oxford, U.K.

PRS Group (Political Risk Services) database. "The International Country Risk Guide (ICRG)." Accessed on November 25, 2023. https://prsgroup.com/explore-our-products/icrg

Rentschler, J., P. Avner, M. Marconcini, R. Su, E. Strano, L. Bernard, C. Riom, and S. Hallegatte. 2022. "Rapid Urban Growth in Flood Zones: Global Evidence since 1985." Policy Research Working Paper 10014, World Bank, Washington, DC.

Rozenberg, J., and M. Fay, eds. 2019. *Beyond the Gap: How Countries Can Afford the Infrastructure They Need While Protecting the Planet.* Washington, DC: World Bank.

Sahay, R., V. Arora, T. Arvanitis, H. Faruqee, P. N'Diaye, and T. Mancini-Griffoli. 2014. "Emerging Markets & Volatility: Lessons from the Taper Tantrum." IMF Staff Discussion Note 14/09, International Monetary Fund, Washington, DC.

Song, Z., G. Hochman, and G. R. Timilsina. 2023. "Natural Disaster, Infrastructure, and Income Distribution: Empirical Evidence from Global Data." Policy Research Working Paper 10504, World bank, Washington, DC.

Swagel, P. L. 2023. "CBO's Current View of the Economy and the Implications for the Federal Budget and for Workers." Congressional Budget Office, US Congress, Washington, DC.

UN Comtrade (United Nations) database. "UN Comtrade." Accessed on October 5, 2023. https://comtradeplus.un.org/

United Nations. 2023. "Technical Dialogue of the First Global Stocktake: Synthesis Report by the Co-facilitators on the Technical Dialogue." Framework Convention on Climate Change, United Nations, Bonn, Germany.

UNU-WIDER (United Nations University World Institute for Development Economics Research) database. "GRD—The Government Revenue Dataset." Accessed on October 19, 2023. https://www.wider.unu.edu/project/grd-government-revenue-dataset

van Barkum, S. 2021. "How Trade Can Drive Inclusive and Sustainable Food System Outcomes in Food Deficit Low-Income Countries." *Food Security* 13: 1541-54.

WEF (World Economic Forum). 2023. "Global Gender Gap Report 2023." Insight Report, World Economic Forum, Cologny, Switzerland.

WHO (World Health Organization) and WMO (World Meteorological Organization). 2023. "Health and the El Niño-Southern Oscillation (ENSO)." Brief, WHO-WMO Climate and Health Office, Geneva.

World Bank. 2016. *Global Economic Prospects: Spillovers amid Weak Growth.* January. Washington, DC: World Bank.

World Bank. 2022a. "Living Up to Potential in the Wake of Adverse Shocks': Growth over the Next Decade." EU Regular Economic Report, Part 2, World Bank, Washington, DC.

World Bank. 2022b. "G5 Sahel Region." Country Climate and Development Report, World Bank, Washington, DC.

World Bank. 2022c. "Climate and Development: An Agenda for Action." Emerging Insights from World Bank Group 2021-22 Country Climate Development Reports, World Bank, Washington, DC.

World Bank. 2022d. *South Asia Economic Focus: Reshaping Norms: A New Way Forward.* Spring. Washington, DC: World Bank.

World Bank. 2023a. *Commodity Markets Outlook: Under the Shadow of Geopolitical Risks.* October. Washington, DC: World Bank.

World Bank. 2023b. *South Asia Development Update: Toward Faster, Cleaner Growth.* October. Washington, DC: World Bank.

World Bank. 2023c. "Inclusiveness of Foreign Direct Investment in Rwanda." Rwanda Economic Update 31, World Bank, Washington, DC.

World Bank. 2023d. *State and Trends of Carbon Pricing 2023.* Washington, DC: World Bank.

World Bank, FAO (Food and Agriculture Organization), IMF (International Monetary Fund), WFP (World Food Programme), and WTO (World Trade Organization). 2023. "Global Food and Nutrition Security Crisis." Statement, Washington, DC.

World Bank—Carbon Pricing Dashboard (World Bank) database. "The World Bank Data Catalog." Accessed on October 27, 2023. https://carbonpricingdashboard.worldbank.org

World Bank - WDI (World Development Indicators) database. "Gender Statistics." Accessed on December 15, 2023. https://databank.worldbank.org/source/world-development-indicators.

WTO (World Trade Organization). 2023. "Global Trade Outlook and Statistics." World Trade Organization, Geneva.

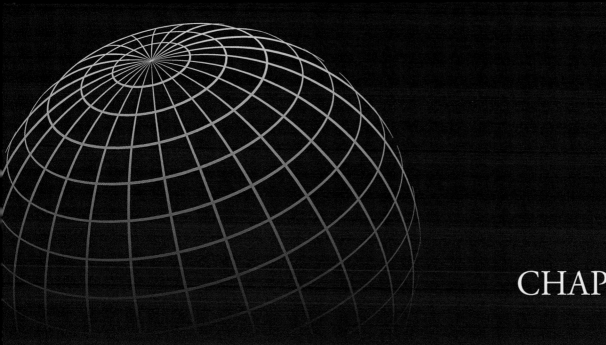

# CHAPTER 2

## REGIONAL OUTLOOKS

# EAST ASIA and PACIFIC

*Growth in the East Asia and Pacific (EAP) region is projected to slow to 4.5 percent in 2024 and to 4.4 percent in 2025, from an estimated 5.1 percent in 2023, mostly owing to an anticipated deceleration in economic activity in China. Amid protracted property sector weakness, growth in China is expected to decline from 5.2 percent in 2023 to 4.5 percent in 2024 and 4.3 percent in 2025. In the rest of the region, growth is projected to edge up from an estimated 4.4 percent in 2023 to 4.7 percent in 2024 and 2025, underpinned by solid domestic demand. Risks to the outlook are skewed to the downside and include a more severe downturn in China, with adverse spillovers to the broader region, and heightened geopolitical tensions—including those from the conflict in the Middle East—which could spur higher energy and food prices and inflation. Weaker-than-expected global demand and trade, as well as climate-change-related extreme weather events, pose further downside risks.*

## Recent developments

Growth in the EAP region rebounded to an estimated 5.1 percent in 2023, mainly reflecting a short-lived activity surge in China early in the year following the reopening from pandemic restrictions (figure 2.1.1.A). In China, the reopening effects faded fast, resulting in a 0.4 percentage point downgrade to estimated growth in 2023 compared with the June forecast. Investment growth in the country was weighed down by continued weakness in the real estate sector, with property developers facing renewed financial pressure amid declining sales and prices (figures 2.1.1.B and 2.1.1.C). Feeble external demand weighed on exports, and while consumption firmed somewhat toward the end of the year, consumer confidence remained well below pre-pandemic levels (figure 2.1.1.D).

In EAP excluding China, growth eased to an estimated 4.4 percent in 2023, as declining international goods trade weighed on activity (figures 2.1.2.A and 2.1.2.B). This was 0.4 percentage point lower than previously projected, partly reflecting spillovers from the surprisingly weak growth in China. In several large economies,

*Note:* This section was prepared by Samuel Hill.

falling goods exports through much of 2023 were partly offset by firming services exports, buoyed by the continued recovery in international tourism. In most economies, goods trade weakness was also offset by robust household consumption, which in many cases continued to be supported by buoyant labor market conditions and cooling inflation.

In 2023, the combined Pacific Island economic output is estimated to have finally exceeded pre-pandemic levels. However, this recovery is not uniform across the subregion, particularly for those economies dependent on tourism, like Palau and Samoa, where recessions were most severe and recoveries slowest. In contrast, in East Asia, output remains below pre-pandemic levels only in Myanmar, reflecting the effects of ongoing conflict and political disruption.

Headline consumer price inflation fell through much of 2023 in most of the region's economies, supported by moderating commodity prices (figure 2.1.2.C). In China, falling food prices and weak demand put further downward pressure on inflation, which was barely positive in the second half of the year. In many economies, headline and core inflation toward the end of the year hovered at about or below central bank targets amid moderate demand pressures, with regulated prices in some cases helping to offset higher oil prices in the second half of the year.

**FIGURE 2.1.1 China: Recent developments**

*Growth in China rebounded in early 2023 following the lifting of pandemic restrictions but slowed through the middle of the year. Slowing growth in 2023 partly reflected a renewed downturn in the property sector, including further declines in sales and prices, which contributed to increased financial stress for developers. Meanwhile, consumer confidence remained weak.*

A. China: GDP growth

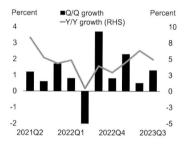

B. China: Property sales growth

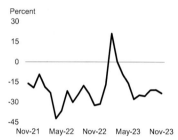

C. China: Property price movements

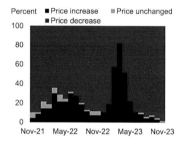

D. China: Consumer confidence

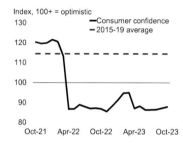

*Sources*: Haver Analytics; National Bureau of Statistics of China.
A. Quarter-on-quarter (Q/Q) and year-on-year (Y/Y) real GDP growth. Last observation is 2023Q3.
B. Year-on-year growth of sales, by volume, of residential building floor space. Last observation is November 2023.
C. Shares of cities with increasing, unchanged, and falling month-on-month existing residential building prices. Sample includes 70 major cities. Last observation is November 2023.
D. Blue line denotes consumer confidence on a scale of 0 to 200, where 200 indicates extreme optimism, 0 extreme pessimism and 100 neutrality. The dotted red line denotes historical average from 2015 to 2019. Last observation is October 2023.

Monetary policy actions across the region diverged somewhat in the second half of 2023. Interest rates were hiked further in Indonesia, the Philippines, and Thailand, reflecting varying factors including currency depreciation in the face of U.S. dollar strength, inflationary pressures and, in the case of Thailand, policy normalization following a period of low interest rates. In Malaysia and Viet Nam, rates were held steady, while in China, weak activity prompted cuts to interest rates and required reserve ratios; in tandem, downpayment requirements for property purchases were lowered to stimulate real estate demand. Easing monetary policy in China widened interest rate spreads with advanced economies, which, together with subdued domestic activity and sentiment, contributed to a

decline in net capital inflows to the country and further depreciation of the renminbi (figure 2.1.2.D). Elsewhere in the region, net capital inflows were generally more resilient, sustained by firmer domestic activity.

# Outlook

Growth in EAP is forecast to decelerate to 4.5 percent in 2024 and to 4.4 percent in 2025, largely reflecting slower growth in China (figure 2.1.3.A). In EAP excluding China, growth is projected to edge up to a solid 4.7 percent in 2024 and 2025, with a more pronounced uptick in Pacific Island economies this year, reflecting continued tourism recoveries (figure 2.1.3.B). Compared with previous projections, growth in EAP is expected to be 0.1 percentage point lower in 2024 and 2025. The projection downgrades mean that EAP output is now expected to fall even further below its pre-pandemic trend over the forecast horizon.

In China, growth is projected to slow to 4.5 percent in 2024, and further to 4.3 percent in 2025. Compared with the June forecasts, growth has been revised down by 0.1 percentage point in 2024 and 2025, primarily as a result of somewhat weaker domestic demand. Consumption is envisaged to slacken sharply amid weak sentiment and heightened economic uncertainty. Investment growth is expected to remain subdued, supported by infrastructure spending but hobbled by continued property sector weakness, after construction starts last year fell to their lowest level since 2006 (figure 2.1.3.C). Over the projection horizon, structural headwinds from rising indebtedness, an aging and shrinking workforce, and narrowing room for productivity catch-up growth are expected to weigh on economic activity (World Bank and DRC 2022).

Elsewhere in the region, solid domestic demand, particularly private consumption, is expected to be the main driver of growth. Modest inflation, and in many cases robust labor markets supported by buoyant services activity, are anticipated to sustain household spending. In some economies, increased government spending, including on social protection and public sector wages, will also support demand. Investment growth is projected to be more subdued, falling short of pre-pandemic averages in most economies through 2024 and 2025. This reflects various headwinds facing private investment, including the lagged effects of monetary policy tightening, policy uncertainty—associated in some countries with government transitions—and rising indebtedness (World Bank 2023a). Elevated public debt and reduced fiscal space are envisaged to constrain public investment growth.

Trade growth is projected to pick up modestly in the near term, supported by a recovery in global trade. Export growth is expected to remain sluggish, falling short of both output growth and pre-pandemic trend rates. Given the high share of intermediate inputs in the region's trade, particularly relating to manufactured goods, weak goods exports are anticipated to also weigh on imports. This will be compounded by soft domestic demand in China, where continued property sector weakness is expected to weigh on global commodities demand, with adverse spillovers to the region's commodity exporters. In contrast, international tourism in the region is envisaged to largely recover from the pandemic in 2024, supported by a continued revival in outbound tourism from China. This will support services exports, particularly in tourism-reliant economies like Cambodia and Thailand.

Headline consumer price inflation is expected to slow slightly in most EAP countries in 2024, aided by moderating global commodity prices, improved food supplies, and well-anchored inflation expectations. However, in some economies, including the Lao People's Democratic Republic, Mongolia, and several Pacific Island states, inflation is expected to remain elevated, reflecting various country-specific factors. These include exchange rate weakness and associated higher import prices, and robust growth. In China, following a temporary decline in food prices, inflation is anticipated to edge up slightly but remain subdued amid weak demand.

With interest rates higher than a year ago in some cases, the lagged effects of monetary policy tightening since 2022 will continue to weigh on economic activity in the near term (figure 2.1.3.D). Despite inflation receding below target

### FIGURE 2.1.2 **EAP excluding China: Recent developments**

*In the East Asia and Pacific region, excluding China, growth mostly slowed in 2023, dampened by shrinking goods exports amid weak global demand. In most economies in the region, headline inflation fell markedly. Capital inflows to China receded, reflecting weak sentiment and activity, as well as widening interest rate spreads with respect to advanced economies. Nevertheless, capital inflows proved more resilient elsewhere in the region.*

**A. Growth in selected EAP economies**

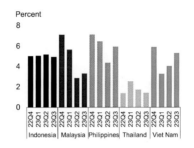

**B. Growth of goods exports**

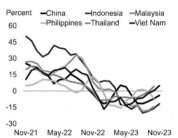

**C. Consumer price inflation**

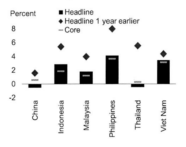

**D. Net capital inflows**

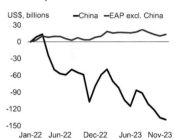

*Sources*: Haver Analytics; Institute of International Finance (database); World Bank.
*Note*: EAP = East Asia and Pacific.
A. Year-on-year real GDP growth. Last observation is 2023Q3.
B. Value of goods exports in U.S. dollars. Three-month moving average of year-on-year change. Last observation is November 2023 for China, Indonesia, and Viet Nam. Last observation is October for Malaysia, the Philippines, and Thailand.
C. Year-on-year headline consumer price inflation and core consumer price inflation. Red diamonds indicate year-on-year headline consumer price inflation one year earlier. Last observation is November 2023 for China, Indonesia, the Philippines, Thailand and Viet Nam. Last observation is October 2023 for Malaysia.
D. Cumulative net portfolio debt and equity inflows since January 2022. Last observation is November 2023.

in many economies, interest rates are expected to remain broadly unchanged in 2024 on account of tight monetary policy in major advanced economies, lingering concerns about weakening exchange rates and capital outflows, and the potential for a resurgence in inflation. With little expected change in nominal interest rates, easing inflation will raise real interest rates through 2024, dampening demand. Moreover, in China, the effectiveness of recent monetary policy easing is likely to remain blunted by high debt, depressed sentiment, and weak credit demand.

In many economies in the region, amid solid government consumption but constrained public

## FIGURE 2.1.3 **EAP: Outlook**

*Growth in China is projected to slow to 4.5 percent in 2024 and to 4.3 percent in 2025. In East Asia and Pacific, excluding China, growth is expected to be broadly stable, except in the Pacific Island economies, in which it will pick up in the near term, reflecting a continued tourism recovery. The slowdown in China's growth partly reflects the persistent weakness in the country's property sector. Monetary policy headwinds are expected to endure, with interest rates higher than a year earlier in some economies.*

**A. China: Contributions to growth**

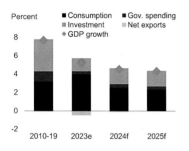

**B. Growth in East Asia and Pacific Island economies**

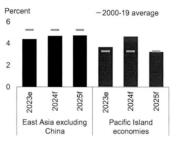

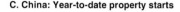

**C. China: Year-to-date property starts**

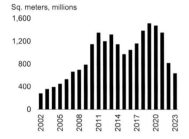

**D. Official interest rates**

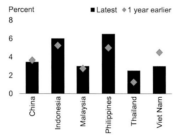

*Sources*: Haver Analytics; World Bank.
*Note*: e = estimate; f = forecast; Gov. = government; Sq. = square.
A. Annual real GDP growth and contributions of expenditure components. Data for 2023 are estimated, while projections for 2024 and 2025 are provided by the World Bank.
B. Annual real GDP growth. Data for 2023 are estimated, while projections for 2024 and 2025 are provided by the World Bank. Aggregate growth rates are calculated using average 2010-19 GDP weights and market exchange rates.
C. Year-to-date volume of residential building floor space construction commenced between January and November. Last observation is November 2023.
D. Main policy interest rate. Orange diamonds refer to the policy rate in the same month one year earlier. Last observation is November 2023.

investment, fiscal policy will overall exert a neutral influence on activity through 2024 and 2025. In China, fiscal policy will provide some demand support, including from a pickup in infrastructure spending in the second half of 2023. However, weakened revenues, mounting debt, and financial pressures will continue to constrain local government spending efforts (World Bank 2023b).

## Risks

Risks to the baseline growth forecast for the region are tilted to the downside and focus on weaker-than-expected growth in China and heightened geopolitical tensions. The conflict in the Middle East could escalate, increasing uncertainty and disrupting energy supply. Other downside risks include prolonged global trade weakness, tighter-than-expected financial conditions, and damaging climate-change-related extreme weather events. Elevated uncertainty or persistent trade weakness could lead to sustained sluggishness in investment growth and harm potential output growth in the region, which is already expected to soften (Kose and Ohnsorge 2023). In contrast, stronger-than-expected growth in the United States poses an upside risk to the forecast.

China could experience a worse-than-expected property sector downturn, with large and protracted falls in prices and activity (chapter 1). Such a scenario would not only lead to a decrease in household wealth but also amplify financial stress on developers, their creditors, and suppliers. Additionally, it could undermine broader demand and squeeze local government revenue. From their peak in mid-2021, existing property prices have fallen by about 6 percent nationally—a smaller decrease and over a shorter period compared to past major property market corrections in other large economies. Protracted weak consumer sentiment, triggered by additional property sector turmoil or broader uncertainty, could spur precautionary saving, dampening consumption growth. Heightened uncertainty could also erode business sentiment, weakening investment and labor market conditions, while high debt and slower growth could lead to a deterioration in credit quality and increased financial pressures.

Given the strong trade links between China and other economies in the region, slower-than-expected growth in China would have negative spillovers to demand and activity across EAP (figure 2.1.4.A). Slower manufacturing growth in China would depress regional processing trade, particularly in economies with large integrated export sectors such as Malaysia and Viet Nam (World Bank 2022a). Commodity exporters in the region, including Indonesia, Mongolia, Myanmar, and the Solomon Islands, would endure reduced demand and prices. Weaker discretionary household spending in China would also spill over to the region, including through dampened demand for international travel, curtailing the tourism recovery in some of the region's economies, including Cambodia and Thailand. Rising global tensions and trade protectionism, could also dampen trade growth, with adverse effects on domestic activity.

An escalation in the conflict in the Middle East also represents a significant downside risk to the outlook. EAP's economies, being generally export-oriented and in many cases dependent on imported energy, particularly petroleum, are especially vulnerable to heightened geopolitical tensions and global energy supply disruptions (figure 2.1.4.B). Escalating conflict in oil-exporting countries in the Middle East or elsewhere could disrupt oil supply, spurring sharp increases in prices for energy and food. This could have broader adverse knock-on effects for prices, stoke inflation, and prompt renewed monetary policy tightening, which could dampen growth.

Global financial conditions could also become tighter than assumed in the baseline, which would weigh on activity and increase risks of financial stress. Borrowing costs could rise if persistently elevated inflation prompts major central banks to pursue tighter-than-expected monetary policy. This would further depress external demand and weaken exports of EAP economies. It would also add downward pressure on exchange rates in the region, making it more difficult for central banks to ease monetary policy to support economic activity. Additionally, the mounting debt levels observed in many EAP economies, with China being a notable example though not the only one, heightens vulnerability to higher borrowing costs (figure 2.1.4.C).

Extreme weather events, the frequency of which has increased in recent decades as a result of climate change, also pose a downside risk to the regional outlook (figure 2.1.4.D). Pacific Island economies are particularly exposed to extreme weather events, notably highly damaging and frequent tropical storms. However, extreme weather events also present a serious threat to larger economies, recently underscored by damaging heatwaves and floods in China, and a cyclone and floods in Myanmar (World Bank 2022b).

## FIGURE 2.1.4 EAP: Risks

*Slower-than-expected growth in China would further weaken activity in the East Asia and Pacific (EAP) region, with more pronounced negative demand spillovers in export-oriented economies, particularly those more reliant on China. A dependence on imported petroleum in many EAP economies exposes them to higher oil prices from escalating conflict in the Middle East, which could disrupt global oil supply. Rising debt leaves the region vulnerable to unexpected tighter financial conditions, while more frequent climate-change-related extreme weather events present further downside risks to the outlook.*

A. Goods exports shares of GDP
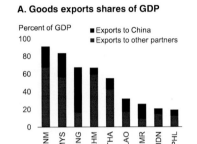

B. Net petroleum imports
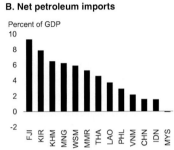

C. Debt
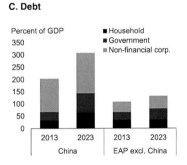

D. Frequency of extreme weather events
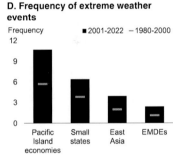

*Sources*: EM-DAT (database); Haver Analytics; Institute of International Finance (database); UN Comtrade (database); World Bank.
*Note*: CHN = China; corp. = corporation; EAP = East Asia and Pacific; EMDEs = emerging market and developing economies; FJI = Fiji; IDN = Indonesia; KHM = Cambodia; KIR = Kiribati; LAO = Lao PDR; MMR = Myanmar; MNG = Mongolia; MYS = Malaysia; PHL = Philippines; THA = Thailand; VNM = Viet Nam; WSM = Samoa.
A. Period averages of goods exports as a share of GDP between 2021 and 2022.
B. Average net imports of petroleum products and crude oil as a percent of GDP between 2018 and 2022.
C. EAP excluding China includes Indonesia, Lao PDR, Malaysia, Mongolia, Papua New Guinea, the Philippines, Thailand, and Viet Nam. The aggregate is calculated as a GDP-weighted average. 2013 refers to 2013Q2 and 2023 refers to 2023Q2. Last observation is 2023Q2.
D. Frequency is calculated based on the annual number of extreme weather events per one million square kilometers of land area. Period averages of frequency for 1980-2000 and 2001-2022. Extreme weather events refer to droughts, extreme temperatures, floods, and storms. Last observation is end-2022.

On the upside, growth in the United States was stronger than expected last year, with resilient labor markets underpinning robust consumption in the face of significant monetary policy tightening. While China's share of exports for most EAP economies has increased markedly in recent decades, the United States remains a key export market for many. Unexpectedly strong growth in the United States would lift external demand in the EAP region, supporting faster exports and output growth.

## TABLE 2.1.1 East Asia and Pacific forecast summary

(Real GDP growth at market prices in percent, unless indicated otherwise)

Percentage point differences from June 2023 projections

| | 2021 | 2022 | 2023e | 2024f | 2025f | 2023e | 2024f | 2025f |
|---|---|---|---|---|---|---|---|---|
| **EMDE EAP, GDP** [1] | **7.5** | **3.4** | **5.1** | **4.5** | **4.4** | **-0.4** | **-0.1** | **-0.1** |
| GDP per capita (U.S. dollars) | 7.2 | 3.2 | 4.8 | 4.3 | 4.1 | -0.4 | -0.1 | -0.1 |
| *(Average including countries that report expenditure components in national accounts)[2]* | | | | | | | | |
| EMDE EAP, GDP [2] | 7.7 | 3.4 | 5.1 | 4.5 | 4.4 | -0.4 | -0.1 | -0.1 |
| PPP GDP | 7.3 | 3.6 | 5.0 | 4.6 | 4.4 | -0.4 | -0.1 | -0.1 |
| Private consumption | 9.5 | 1.9 | 9.2 | 5.9 | 5.4 | -0.4 | 0.5 | 0.1 |
| Public consumption | 3.4 | 4.2 | 2.5 | 3.1 | 2.8 | 0.0 | -0.2 | 0.1 |
| Fixed investment | 3.1 | 3.4 | 3.3 | 4.1 | 4.1 | -0.4 | -0.6 | -0.5 |
| Exports, GNFS [3] | 16.9 | 1.4 | 0.3 | 2.4 | 2.7 | -1.9 | -1.0 | -0.7 |
| Imports, GNFS [3] | 12.3 | -1.3 | 1.9 | 3.0 | 2.9 | -1.1 | -0.9 | -1.0 |
| Net exports, contribution to growth | 1.2 | 0.6 | -0.3 | 0.0 | 0.0 | -0.2 | 0.0 | 0.0 |
| **Memo items: GDP** | | | | | | | | |
| China | 8.4 | 3.0 | 5.2 | 4.5 | 4.3 | -0.4 | -0.1 | -0.1 |
| East Asia and Pacific excluding China | 2.9 | 5.8 | 4.4 | 4.7 | 4.7 | -0.4 | -0.1 | -0.1 |
| Indonesia | 3.7 | 5.3 | 5.0 | 4.9 | 4.9 | 0.1 | 0.0 | -0.1 |
| Thailand | 1.5 | 2.6 | 2.5 | 3.2 | 3.1 | -1.4 | -0.4 | -0.3 |
| Commodity exporters | 2.6 | 5.2 | 4.8 | 4.8 | 4.8 | 0.1 | 0.1 | 0.1 |
| Commodity importers excl. China | 3.2 | 6.3 | 4.1 | 4.6 | 4.7 | -0.8 | -0.2 | -0.1 |
| Pacific Island Economies [4] | -1.5 | 6.0 | 3.7 | 4.6 | 3.2 | -0.1 | 0.4 | 0.0 |

*Source*: World Bank.
*Note*: e = estimate; f = forecast; EAP = East Asia and Pacific; EMDE = emerging market and developing economies; PPP = purchasing power parity. World Bank forecasts are frequently updated based on new information and changing (global) circumstances. Consequently, projections presented here may differ from those contained in other Bank documents, even if basic assessments of countries' prospects do not differ at any given moment in time. 1. GDP and expenditure components are measured in average 2010-19 prices and market exchange rates. Excludes the Democratic People's Republic of Korea and dependent territories.
2. Subregion aggregate excludes the Democratic People's Republic of Korea, dependent territories, Fiji, Kiribati, the Marshall Islands, the Federated States of Micronesia, Myanmar, Palau, Papua New Guinea, Samoa, Timor-Leste, Tonga, Tuvalu, and Vanuatu, for which data limitations prevent the forecasting of GDP components.
3. Exports and imports of goods and nonfactor services (GNFS).
4. Includes Fiji, Kiribati, the Marshall Islands, the Federated States of Micronesia, Nauru, Palau, Papua New Guinea, Samoa, the Solomon Islands, Tonga, Tuvalu, and Vanuatu.


## TABLE 2.1.2 East Asia and Pacific country forecasts [1]

(Real GDP growth at market prices in percent, unless indicated otherwise)

Percentage point differences from June 2023 projections

| | 2021 | 2022 | 2023e | 2024f | 2025f | 2023e | 2024f | 2025f |
|---|---|---|---|---|---|---|---|---|
| Cambodia | 3.0 | 5.2 | 5.4 | 5.8 | 6.1 | -0.1 | -0.3 | -0.2 |
| China | 8.4 | 3.0 | 5.2 | 4.5 | 4.3 | -0.4 | -0.1 | -0.1 |
| Fiji | -5.1 | 20.0 | 7.6 | 4.0 | 3.7 | 2.6 | -0.1 | 0.2 |
| Indonesia | 3.7 | 5.3 | 5.0 | 4.9 | 4.9 | 0.1 | 0.0 | -0.1 |
| Kiribati | 7.9 | 1.2 | 2.5 | 2.4 | 2.3 | 0.0 | 0.0 | 0.0 |
| Lao PDR | 2.5 | 2.7 | 3.7 | 4.1 | 4.3 | -0.2 | -0.1 | -0.1 |
| Malaysia | 3.3 | 8.7 | 3.9 | 4.3 | 4.2 | -0.4 | 0.1 | 0.0 |
| Marshall Islands [2] | 1.0 | -4.5 | 3.0 | 3.0 | 2.0 | 1.1 | 0.9 | -0.3 |
| Micronesia, Fed. Sts. [2] | -3.2 | -0.6 | 2.8 | 2.8 | 1.3 | -0.1 | 0.0 | 0.0 |
| Mongolia | 1.6 | 5.0 | 5.8 | 6.2 | 6.4 | 0.6 | -0.1 | -0.4 |
| Myanmar [2][3] | -12.0 | 4.0 | 1.0 | 2.0 | .. | .. | .. | .. |
| Nauru [2] | 7.2 | 2.8 | 0.6 | 1.4 | 1.2 | -0.4 | -0.6 | -1.3 |
| Palau [2] | -13.4 | -2.0 | 0.8 | 12.4 | 11.9 | -11.5 | 3.3 | 7.2 |
| Papua New Guinea | -0.8 | 5.2 | 3.0 | 5.0 | 3.1 | -0.7 | 0.6 | 0.0 |
| Philippines | 5.7 | 7.6 | 5.6 | 5.8 | 5.8 | -0.4 | -0.1 | -0.1 |
| Samoa [2] | -7.1 | -5.3 | 8.0 | 4.5 | 3.6 | 3.0 | 1.1 | 0.3 |
| Solomon Islands | -0.6 | -4.1 | 1.8 | 2.7 | 3.1 | -0.7 | 0.3 | 0.1 |
| Thailand | 1.5 | 2.6 | 2.5 | 3.2 | 3.1 | -1.4 | -0.4 | -0.3 |
| Timor-Leste | 2.9 | 3.9 | 2.4 | 3.5 | 4.3 | -0.6 | 0.3 | 1.1 |
| Tonga [2] | -2.7 | -2.0 | 2.6 | 2.5 | 2.2 | 0.1 | -0.3 | -0.4 |
| Tuvalu | 1.8 | 0.7 | 3.9 | 3.5 | 2.4 | -0.3 | 0.4 | -0.2 |
| Vanuatu | 0.6 | 1.9 | 1.5 | 2.6 | 3.5 | 1.0 | -1.4 | -0.4 |
| Viet Nam | 2.6 | 8.0 | 4.7 | 5.5 | 6.0 | -1.3 | -0.7 | -0.5 |

Source: World Bank.
Note: e = estimate; f = forecast. World Bank forecasts are frequently updated based on new information and changing (global) circumstances. Consequently, projections presented here may differ from those contained in other Bank documents, even if basic assessments of countries' prospects do not significantly differ at any given moment in time.
1. Data are based on GDP measured in average 2010-19 prices and market exchange rates.
2. Values for Timor-Leste represent non-oil GDP. For the following countries, values correspond to the fiscal year: the Marshall Islands, the Federated States of Micronesia, and Palau (October 1-September 30); Myanmar (April 1-March 31); Nauru, Samoa, and Tonga (July 1-June 30).
3. Data for Myanmar beyond 2024 (which corresponds to the year ending March 2025) are excluded because of a high degree of uncertainty.

# EUROPE and CENTRAL ASIA

*Growth in Europe and Central Asia (ECA) is expected to moderate to 2.4 percent this year, and then firm to 2.7 percent in 2025, supported by strengthening domestic demand and a gradual recovery in the euro area. In the near term, persistently high inflation will prevent a rapid easing of monetary policy in most economies and weigh on private consumption. Projected fiscal consolidation further dampens the outlook. Downside risks continue to predominate. An escalation of the conflict in the Middle East could increase energy prices, tighten financial conditions, and negatively affect confidence. Geopolitical risks in the region, including an escalation of the Russian Federation's invasion of Ukraine, are elevated and could materialize. Higher-than-anticipated inflation or a weaker-than-expected recovery in the euro area would also negatively affect regional activity.*

## Recent developments

Growth in Europe and Central Asia (ECA) is estimated to have picked up to 2.7 percent in 2023 from 1.2 percent in 2022. This recovery primarily reflects firming private consumption, supported by additional fiscal support, robust labor market conditions, and the resumption of growth in Russia and Ukraine. The 1.3 percentage point upward revision from the June 2023 forecast is mainly due to upgrades for these two countries and Türkiye. Excluding them, growth in ECA in 2023 markedly decelerated, to an estimated 1.8 percent, with particularly weak outcomes in Central Europe. Manufacturing activity remained subdued in the second half of the year, while retail sales continued to soften (figure 2.2.1.A).

In Russia, output expanded by an estimated 2.6 percent in 2023. This stronger-than-expected recovery was fueled by substantial fiscal support, including additional military spending. Oil production and exports contracted modestly, and the authorities announced end-2023 an extension of the export curbs of 300,000 barrels per day as well as a deepening by 200,000 barrels per day starting in January 2024. Exchange rate depreciation led to an inflation uptick, prompting

subsequent increases in the policy interest rate. Migration from Central Asia to Russia increased after the invasion, with 43 percent of all entrants migrating for work purposes in 2023 (figure 2.2.1.B).

Growth in Türkiye moderated to an estimated 4.2 percent in 2023. Following the May elections, there were significant hikes in the policy interest rate, from 8.5 percent in May to 42.5 percent in December 2023. Additionally, regulatory changes slowed credit expansion, which started to weigh on growth. Nonetheless, activity expanded more than previously anticipated, thanks to resilient private consumption and substantial post-earthquake fiscal outlays. Inflation exceeded 60 percent in the second half of 2023.

In Ukraine, growth expanded by an estimated 4.8 percent in 2023, following the preceding year's steep contraction. Nonetheless, output remained about 30 percent lower in 2023 than its pre-invasion level (figure 2.2.1.C). Growth was underpinned by improved electricity access, a better harvest, and additional government spending, albeit at the cost of increasing fiscal and current account deficits. While the unraveling of the Black Sea Grain Initiative in July 2023 continues to exert downward pressure on grain exports, Ukraine has successfully identified alternative routes for grain exports that have supported the sector.

*Note:* This section was prepared by Marie Albert.

## FIGURE 2.2.1 ECA: Recent developments

*High-frequency indicators suggest only modest growth in major ECA economies. Following the Russian Federation's invasion of Ukraine, more migrants from Central Asia have entered Russia for work purposes. Ukraine's GDP has declined by about 30 percent since the beginning of the invasion. Tight monetary policies have weighed on regional activity, but several countries have initiated policy interest rates cuts.*

**A. High-frequency indicators for major economies**

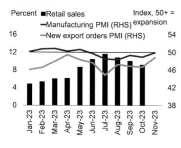

**B. Migration from Central Asia to the Russian Federation, by purpose**

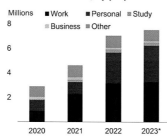

**C. Output in Ukraine**

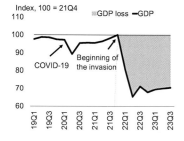

**D. Changes in policy interest rates**

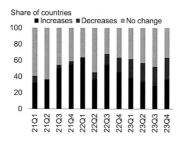

*Sources:* Federal State Statistics Service (Rosstat); Haver Analytics.
*Note:* PMI = purchasing managers' index.
A. Lines show the average value for PMI manufacturing and new export orders. Bars show the average growth in retail sales from a year earlier. Major economies sample comprises Poland, the Russian Federation, and Türkiye.
B. Number of migrant entries by purpose from Central Asia countries into the Russian Federation for each period. * = 2023 data are available until 2023Q3.
C. Blue line shows real GDP level compared to 2021Q4. The yellow-shaded area shows the GDP loss since the start of the invasion of Ukraine.
D. Bars show the shares of countries for which policy rates have increased, decreased, or remained unchanged in the specific quarter. Last data point is November 2023.

Elsewhere in the region, weak external demand from the euro area affected economic activity, especially in Central Europe and the Western Balkans. Remittance flows to ECA supported demand in remittance-intensive countries such as Armenia, Kyrgyz Republic, and Tajikistan. In 2023, remittances declined by 1.4 percent in the region, after an increase of 18.5 percent in 2022, which was a record-high year (World Bank 2023c). Fiscal consolidation efforts were limited due to increasing public sector wages, indexed social benefits, and rising interest payments (World Bank 2023d).

Median headline inflation in the region slowed to 5.4 percent in November, alongside easing energy and food price pressures. Amid subdued activity, policy interest rates have likely peaked in many economies, with several central banks, including Poland, starting to lower rates (figure 2.2.1.D). However, Russia and Türkiye embarked on a tightening cycle.

## Outlook

Economic activity in ECA is projected to moderate to 2.4 percent this year and then firm to 2.7 percent in 2025. The main drivers of growth include private consumption supported by reduced inflationary pressures, and exports boosted by a gradual recovery in the euro area. The 0.3 percentage point downward revision for ECA in 2024 primarily reflects a forecast downgrade in Türkiye due to further monetary policy tightening (figure 2.2.2.A). Uncertainty surrounding the evolution of Russia's invasion of Ukraine plays an important role in shaping the regional outlook. Excluding these two economies, growth in the region is expected to accelerate to 3.1 percent this year and to 3.7 percent in 2025.

Most ECA countries are likely to continue easing monetary policy, as inflation is projected to decline. However, core inflation exceeds the headline inflation, which remains above the targets in most countries. Fiscal consolidation is projected to gather pace in half of the economies in 2024.

Growth in Russia is projected to slow to 1.3 percent in 2024, and then to 0.9 percent in 2025, near its potential rate. Tightening monetary policy is expected to dampen domestic demand. Trade diversion to China, India, and Türkiye is evident for both exports and imports (figure 2.2.2.B). However, for products affected by sanctions in response to the invasion, the increase in imports from China only offsets about a quarter of the decrease in imports from the European Union (EU) in 2022 (Grekou, Mignon, and Ragot 2023). Capacity constraints, including tight labor market conditions and scarcity of domestic labor due to the invasion, will continue to restrict growth.

Growth in Türkiye is forecast to moderate to 3.1 percent in 2024 before picking up to 3.9 percent in 2025. The outlook considers further monetary policy tightening and gradual fiscal consolidation. It also assumes improving financial stability, rising net exports, larger support for exporters, and rebalancing in economic activity. While inflation is expected to remain elevated in the first half of 2024, it is anticipated to gradually ease off starting in the second half of the year, alleviating the negative impact on private consumption.

In Ukraine, the outlook remains highly uncertain. Growth is projected to be 3.2 percent in 2024 and 6.5 percent in 2025. Active hostilities are expected to continue throughout 2024, with base effects and one-off factors including agricultural harvest which should fade. A partial resolution of uncertainty in 2025 would facilitate a resumption of exports and a gradual increase in reconstruction investment.

In Central Europe, the expansion is set to accelerate to 2.8 percent in 2024 and 3.5 percent in 2025. The outlook reflects firming external demand from the euro area, improving domestic demand on the back of a recovery in real wages, and the absorption of EU funds through the Recovery and Resilience Facility.

In the Western Balkans, output is anticipated to rebound by 3 percent in 2024 and 3.5 percent in 2025. Economic activity in the subregion is expected to be underpinned by firming consumption as inflationary pressures ease, a gradual recovery in the euro area, increasing public spending on EU infrastructure projects, and a continuing but slower demand in tourism earnings. Labor markets will continue to be tight and fiscal space will remain limited due to rigidities in non-discretionary spending, such as pensions and wages (World Bank 2023e).

In South Caucasus, growth is projected to hold steady at 3.3 percent a year over 2024-25. While further unwinding in money transfer inflows from Russia is expected, re-exports and tourism will continue to support economic activity. However, long-term growth will remain hampered by commodity dependence, weaknesses in connectivi-

## FIGURE 2.2.2 ECA: Outlook

*Regional growth is projected to pick up modestly in 2024-25. Trade diversion resulting from Russia's invasion of Ukraine and sanctions in response to the invasion has been significant, with increasing exports from China, India, and Türkiye to Central Asia and the Russian Federation. The pace of convergence towards EU per capita incomes is slowing down. Rapid progress on reforms that narrow labor market gender gaps would increase the pace of human capital accumulation, and therefore growth.*

**A. Growth forecasts**

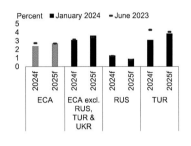

**B. Change in exports to Central Asia and the Russian Federation from 2019 to 2023**

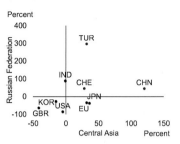

**C. Convergence of GDP per capita with the EU**

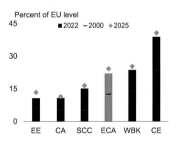

**D. Labor force and gender gap**

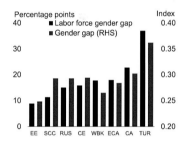

*Sources:* UN Comtrade; World Bank; World Economic Forum.
*Note*: CA = Central Asia; CE = Central Europe; CHE = Switzerland; CHN = China; ECA = Europe and Central Asia; EE = Eastern Europe; EU = European Union; GBR = United Kingdom; IND = India; JPN = Japan; KOR = Korea, Rep.; RUS = Russian Federation; SCC = South Caucasus; TUR = Türkiye; UKR = Ukraine; USA = United States; WBK = Western Balkans.
A. Blue bars show real GDP growth forecasts. Diamonds represent the previous forecasts from the June 2023 edition of *Global Economic Prospects* report. Light blue bars shows the value for ECA region.
B. Each axis shows the percent change of the monthly average exports to the Russian Federation and Central Asia for the first nine months of 2023, or 2022 if 2023 data are not available, compared to the monthly average of the first nine months of 2019. EU is the average of the countries of the European Union. Red dots are for countries showing increase in exports to Central Asia and the Russia Federation since 2019.
C. Bars, red dashes, and orange diamonds show the average (median) share of income per capita compared to the EU income per capita value for each subregion for 2022, 2000, 2025, respectively. Light blue bar shows the value for ECA region.
D. Blue bars denote the difference between male and female labor force participation rates as a percentage of the population age 15+, based on the modeled estimates of the International Labour Organization for 2023. Red bars indicate the complement (1 – the value) of the World Economic Forum's Gender Gap Index for 2023. The index examines the gap between men and women across four fundamental categories: Economic Participation and Opportunity, Educational Attainment, Health and Survival, and Political Empowerment; thus, a higher bar means a higher gender gap.

ty and logistics, and possible continuing geopolitical tensions between Armenia and Azerbaijan.

Growth in Central Asia is forecasted to be broadly stable at about 4.8 percent a year over 2024-25, the highest among subregions. Still-high commodity prices, resilient consumer spending amid cooling inflation, and sustained export growth benefiting from rising oil production capacity in Kazakhstan, are expected to support the activity. Trade diversion triggered by the invasion, leading to increased exports to the region from countries that have reduced their exports to Russia, is expected to persist (figure 2.2.2.B). The flow of remittances from Russia will wind down but remain well above pre-invasion levels.

Regional growth is projected to remain below its pre-pandemic trend, reflecting the lingering effects of the pandemic and Russia's invasion of Ukraine. The pace of income per capita convergence in ECA is expected to remain sluggish, with average income per capita reaching 24 percent of the EU level in 2025 (figure 2.2.2.C). Average income per capita is expected to remain the highest in Central Europe, reaching 41 percent of the EU level in 2025.

Accelerated progress on gender equality could deliver faster and more inclusive growth. Although the ECA region, on average, exhibits a lower gender gap than other EMDE regions, countries in Central Asia and Türkiye still face gender inequality and labor gender gaps. Fast-tracking gender-related reforms could enhance human capital accumulation (figure 2.2.2.D; World Bank 2023f). These reforms involve improving access to quality childcare and safe transport for women, mitigating the double burden of domestic and professional work, and reducing pressure to adhere to traditional gender roles.

## Risks

Risks to the baseline forecast remain tilted to the downside. The ongoing conflict in the Middle East, especially if prolonged or spread, could negatively impact the region (World Bank 2023g). A resurgence in energy prices, particularly European natural gas, would make reducing inflation more challenging, while potential benefits would be limited to energy-exporting economies like Russia and countries in Central Asia. Additionally, elevated uncertainty could

tighten financial conditions, hampering investment and consumption.

Geopolitical tensions continue to pose downside risks. The year-to-October number of political violence events and demonstrations in the region almost trebled between 2021 and 2023, concentrated especially in Russia and Ukraine (figure 2.2.3.A). Intensifying tensions and conflicts could worsen already-heavy human and economic losses. Other geopolitical strains—such as tensions between Armenia and Azerbaijan and between Kosovo and Serbia —could re-emerge. The high number of presidential, parliamentary, and local elections in 2024 also increases uncertainty about future economic policies.

More persistent inflation than currently envisaged could keep monetary policies tighter for longer and weigh on activity. Most of the countries are not likely to reach their inflation targets by the end of 2024 (figure 2.2.3.B). A wage-price spiral in the Western Balkans, Central Europe, and Türkiye, or higher-than-projected commodity prices—potentially driven by an escalation of the conflict in the Middle East—could fuel such inflation. External vulnerabilities are significant in the region, with almost three-fourths of ECA countries having external debt levels exceeding the EMDEs median level in 2022 (figure 2.2.3.C). If global financial conditions tighten, this could trigger capital outflows and increase borrowing costs. Financial stability risks may arise in Central Asia due to underdeveloped banking systems and increasing credit risk. Delayed impacts of sanctions in response to the Russia's invasion of Ukraine could result in higher costs for international payment settlements in the Kyrgyz Republic and Tajikistan.

Weaker-than-expected growth in the euro area, the region's main trading partner, would adversely impact ECA via trade channels. Central Europe, the South Caucasus, and the Western Balkans would be particularly affected, given that half of their goods exports, on average, are destined for the euro area. Increasing trade restrictions could also push further trade fragmentation. Additionally, a more significant slowdown in China or a sharper-than-expected reduction in remittances from Russia would represent external headwinds to Central Asia and the South Caucasus.

Further delays in the disbursement of EU funds pose another downside risk for Central Europe, as do delays in reforms tied to EU accession in the Western Balkans. Concerns about governance have hindered disbursements from the EU to Poland, while political instability has affected Bulgaria (World Bank, forthcoming). In contrast, disbursements to other Central European countries have proceeded, following progress in the implementation of the Recovery and Resilience Facility in the categories of smart, sustainable, and inclusive growth and health, economic, social, and institutional resilience (figure 2.2.3.D).

An ambitious implementation of structural reforms poses an upside risk to the growth outlook. The simultaneous implementation of a large set of reforms (market competition and regulation, taxation, skills, labor market, research and development) among EU's member states could yield substantial GDP gains for Bulgaria and Romania (Pfeiffer, Varga, and in't Veld 2023). Additionally, the EU's new growth plan for the Western Balkans allocates six billion euros in non-repayable support and loans to advance economic integration with the European Union's single market and the Common Regional Market, as well as to accelerate fundamental reforms. Strengthening institutions, especially in Central Asia, would create conditions for promoting investment growth (chapter 3). Reducing the state's presence could increase productivity and financial performance. The green transition would be facilitated through reforms improving the investment climate, encouraging financial sector development, and reducing the carbon footprint of financial flows. The energy sector requires a profound transformation to achieve the net-zero emissions target by 2050, potentially strengthening growth and sustainability (World Bank 2023h, 2023i).

## FIGURE 2.2.3 ECA: Risks

*Risks remain tilted to the downside, with heightened geopolitical tensions. Headline inflation is expected to remain above targets across most of the region, potentially leading to an extended period of higher policy rates. Financial stress could pose notable headwinds, especially for economies with external and fiscal vulnerabilities. In contrast, a faster implementation of structural reforms represents an upside risk. Accelerated disbursement of the EU Recovery and Resilience Facility funds would boost investment.*

**A. Number of violence events and demonstrations**

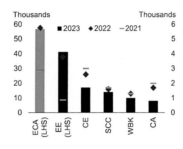

**B. Gaps between inflation and expected inflation, versus inflation targets**

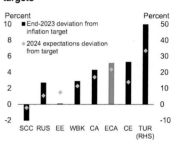

**C. External vulnerabilities**

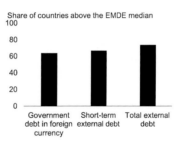

**D. EU Recovery and Resilience Facility allocations and disbursements**

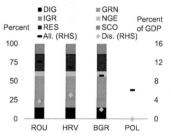

*Sources:* Armed Conflict Location & Event Data Project (ACLED); Consensus Economics; European Commission; Haver Analytics; World Bank.

*Note:* BGR = Bulgaria; CA = Central Asia; CE = Central Europe; ECA = Europe and Central Asia; EE = Eastern Europe; EMDEs = emerging markets and developing economies; EU = European Union; HRV = Croatia; POL = Poland; ROU = Romania; RUS = Russian Federation; SCC = South Caucasus; TUR = Türkiye; WBK = Western Balkans.

A. Cumulative number of political violence events and demonstrations reported across 22 ECA EMDEs. Includes battles, explosions/remote violence, protests, riots, and violence against civilians. Light blue bar shows the value for ECA region. Last observation is December 15, 2023.

B. For each subregion, blue bars show the average difference between the inflation in November 2023 and the target, and the yellow diamonds show the average difference between the expected inflation in 2024 and the target. Light blue bar shows the value for ECA region.

C. Bars show the share of countries in percent for which the indicator is above the EMDE median. General government debt in foreign currency and short-term external debt are as percent of total debt, total external debt is as percent of GDP.

D. All. = Allocation; DIG = digital transformation; Dis. = disbursement; GRN = green transition; IGR = smart, sustainable, and inclusive growth; NGE = policies for the next generation; RES = health and economic, social, and institutional resilience; SCO = social and territorial cohesion. The bars show the breakdown of the current EU Recovery and Resilience Facility disbursements across the six pillars of the regulation—green transition; digital transformation; smart, sustainable, and inclusive growth; social and territorial cohesion; health, and economic, social and institutional resilience; and policies for the next generation—for each country. Purple horizontal bars show the facility allocation, while the yellow diamonds show the current disbursement, both as a percent of the country's GDP.

## TABLE 2.2.1 Europe and Central Asia forecast summary

(Real GDP growth at market prices in percent, unless indicated otherwise)

Percentage point differences
from June 2023 projections

| | 2021 | 2022 | 2023e | 2024f | 2025f | 2023e | 2024f | 2025f |
|---|---|---|---|---|---|---|---|---|
| **EMDE ECA, GDP** [1] | **7.1** | **1.2** | **2.7** | **2.4** | **2.7** | **1.3** | **-0.3** | **0.0** |
| GDP per capita (U.S. dollars) | 7.1 | 1.4 | 2.8 | 2.3 | 2.6 | 1.4 | -0.3 | 0.1 |
| EMDE ECA excl. Russian Federation, Türkiye, and Ukraine, GDP | 6.4 | 4.3 | 1.8 | 3.1 | 3.6 | 0.0 | -0.1 | 0.2 |
| EMDE ECA excl. Russian Federation and Ukraine, GDP | 8.3 | 4.8 | 2.7 | 3.1 | 3.7 | 0.3 | -0.5 | 0.0 |
| EMDE ECA excl. Türkiye, GDP | 5.9 | 0.0 | 2.3 | 2.2 | 2.4 | 1.5 | 0.0 | 0.1 |
| *(Average including countries that report expenditure components in national accounts)* [2] | | | | | | | | |
| EMDE ECA, GDP [2] | 7.3 | 1.0 | 2.6 | 2.3 | 2.5 | 1.4 | -0.3 | -0.1 |
| PPP GDP | 7.2 | 0.3 | 2.7 | 2.3 | 2.6 | 1.5 | -0.4 | 0.0 |
| Private consumption | 10.2 | 4.5 | 4.6 | 2.1 | 2.6 | 3.2 | -0.6 | -0.3 |
| Public consumption | 3.1 | 2.7 | 4.4 | 2.0 | 1.6 | 0.8 | 0.4 | -0.6 |
| Fixed investment | 7.7 | 1.7 | 5.4 | 3.9 | 4.4 | 2.0 | -1.1 | 1.0 |
| Exports, GNFS [3] | 10.2 | -0.8 | -0.8 | 3.2 | 4.1 | -1.3 | -1.3 | -0.9 |
| Imports, GNFS [3] | 12.3 | 0.9 | 2.8 | 3.5 | 5.2 | -1.3 | -2.4 | -0.6 |
| Net exports, contribution to growth | -0.3 | -0.6 | -1.3 | 0.0 | -0.3 | 0.0 | 0.5 | 0.0 |
| **Memo items: GDP** | | | | | | | | |
| Commodity exporters [4] | 5.5 | -2.5 | 3.0 | 1.9 | 1.7 | 2.4 | 0.1 | 0.1 |
| Commodity exporters excl. Russian Federation and Ukraine | 5.5 | 4.5 | 4.4 | 4.3 | 4.4 | 0.6 | 0.2 | 0.4 |
| Commodity importers [5] | 8.8 | 4.8 | 2.5 | 2.9 | 3.6 | 0.3 | -0.6 | 0.0 |
| Central Europe [6] | 6.7 | 4.9 | 0.7 | 2.8 | 3.5 | -0.4 | -0.1 | 0.2 |
| Western Balkans [7] | 7.9 | 3.4 | 2.5 | 3.0 | 3.5 | -0.1 | -0.1 | -0.1 |
| Eastern Europe [8] | 3.6 | -20.2 | 3.9 | 2.4 | 4.2 | 2.4 | -0.4 | -0.3 |
| South Caucasus [9] | 6.7 | 7.1 | 3.5 | 3.3 | 3.3 | 0.5 | -0.1 | -0.3 |
| Central Asia [10] | 5.3 | 4.1 | 4.9 | 4.7 | 4.8 | 0.9 | 0.3 | 0.6 |
| Russian Federation | 5.6 | -2.1 | 2.6 | 1.3 | 0.9 | 2.8 | 0.1 | 0.1 |
| Türkiye | 11.4 | 5.5 | 4.2 | 3.1 | 3.9 | 1.0 | -1.2 | -0.2 |
| Poland | 6.9 | 5.1 | 0.5 | 2.6 | 3.4 | -0.2 | 0.0 | 0.2 |

*Source*: World Bank.

*Note*: e = estimate; f = forecast; PPP = purchasing power parity; EMDE = emerging market and developing economy. World Bank forecasts are frequently updated based on new information and changing (global) circumstances. Consequently, projections presented here may differ from those contained in other Bank documents, even if basic assessments of countries' prospects do not differ at any given moment in time. The World Bank is currently not publishing economic output, income, or growth data for Turkmenistan owing to a lack of reliable data of adequate quality. Turkmenistan is excluded from cross-country macroeconomic aggregates. Since Croatia became a member of the euro area on January 1, 2023, it has been added to the euro area aggregate and removed from the ECA aggregate in all tables to avoid double counting.

1. GDP and expenditure components are measured in average 2010-19 prices and market exchange rates, thus aggregates presented here may differ from other World Bank documents.
2. Aggregates presented here exclude Azerbaijan, Bosnia and Herzegovina, Kazakhstan, Kosovo, the Kyrgyz Republic, Montenegro, Serbia, Tajikistan, Turkmenistan, and Uzbekistan, for which data limitations prevent the forecasting of GDP components.
3. Exports and imports of goods and nonfactor services (GNFS).
4. Includes Armenia, Azerbaijan, Kazakhstan, the Kyrgyz Republic, Kosovo, the Russian Federation, Tajikistan, Ukraine, and Uzbekistan.
5. Includes Albania, Belarus, Bosnia and Herzegovina, Bulgaria, Georgia, Hungary, Moldova, Montenegro, North Macedonia, Poland, Romania, Serbia, and Türkiye.
6. Includes Bulgaria, Hungary, Poland, and Romania.
7. Includes Albania, Bosnia and Herzegovina, Kosovo, Montenegro, North Macedonia, and Serbia.
8. Includes Belarus, Moldova, and Ukraine.
9. Includes Armenia, Azerbaijan, and Georgia.
10. Includes Kazakhstan, the Kyrgyz Republic, Tajikistan, and Uzbekistan.

## TABLE 2.2.2 Europe and Central Asia country forecasts [1]

(Real GDP growth at market prices in percent, unless indicated otherwise)

Percentage point differences from
June 2023 projections

| | 2021 | 2022 | 2023e | 2024f | 2025f | 2023e | 2024f | 2025f |
|---|---|---|---|---|---|---|---|---|
| Albania | 8.9 | 4.8 | 3.6 | 3.2 | 3.2 | 0.8 | -0.1 | -0.1 |
| Armenia | 5.8 | 12.6 | 7.1 | 4.7 | 4.5 | 2.7 | -0.1 | -0.5 |
| Azerbaijan | 5.6 | 4.6 | 1.5 | 2.4 | 2.5 | -0.7 | -0.1 | -0.1 |
| Belarus | 2.4 | -4.7 | 3.0 | 0.8 | 0.8 | 2.4 | -0.6 | -0.5 |
| Bosnia and Herzegovina[2] | 7.4 | 3.9 | 2.2 | 2.8 | 3.4 | -0.3 | -0.2 | -0.1 |
| Bulgaria | 7.7 | 3.9 | 1.7 | 2.4 | 3.3 | 0.2 | -0.4 | 0.3 |
| Croatia | 13.8 | 6.3 | 2.5 | 2.7 | 3.0 | 0.6 | -0.4 | -0.3 |
| Georgia | 10.5 | 10.4 | 6.5 | 4.8 | 4.5 | 2.1 | -0.2 | -0.5 |
| Kazakhstan | 4.3 | 3.2 | 4.5 | 4.3 | 4.5 | 1.0 | 0.3 | 0.9 |
| Kosovo | 10.7 | 5.2 | 3.2 | 3.9 | 4.0 | -0.5 | -0.5 | -0.2 |
| Kyrgyz Republic | 5.5 | 6.3 | 3.5 | 4.0 | 4.0 | 0.0 | 0.0 | 0.0 |
| Moldova | 13.9 | -5.0 | 1.8 | 4.2 | 4.1 | 0.0 | 0.0 | 0.0 |
| Montenegro | 13.0 | 6.4 | 4.8 | 3.2 | 3.1 | 1.4 | 0.1 | 0.2 |
| North Macedonia | 4.5 | 2.2 | 1.8 | 2.5 | 2.9 | -0.6 | -0.2 | 0.0 |
| Poland | 6.9 | 5.1 | 0.5 | 2.6 | 3.4 | -0.2 | 0.0 | 0.2 |
| Romania | 5.7 | 4.6 | 1.8 | 3.3 | 3.8 | -0.8 | -0.6 | -0.3 |
| Russian Federation | 5.6 | -2.1 | 2.6 | 1.3 | 0.9 | 2.8 | 0.1 | 0.1 |
| Serbia | 7.7 | 2.5 | 2.0 | 3.0 | 3.8 | -0.3 | 0.0 | 0.0 |
| Tajikistan | 9.4 | 8.0 | 7.5 | 5.5 | 4.5 | 1.0 | 0.5 | 0.0 |
| Türkiye | 11.4 | 5.5 | 4.2 | 3.1 | 3.9 | 1.0 | -1.2 | -0.2 |
| Ukraine [3] | 3.4 | -29.1 | 4.8 | 3.2 | 6.5 | 2.8 | .. | .. |
| Uzbekistan | 7.4 | 5.7 | 5.5 | 5.5 | 5.5 | 0.4 | 0.1 | -0.3 |

*Source*: World Bank.

*Note*: e = estimate; f = forecast. World Bank forecasts are frequently updated based on new information and changing (global) circumstances. Consequently, projections presented here may differ from those contained in other Bank documents, even if basic assessments of countries' prospects do not significantly differ at any given moment in time. The World Bank is currently not publishing economic output, income, or growth data for Turkmenistan owing to a lack of reliable data of adequate quality. Turkmenistan is excluded from cross-country macroeconomic aggregates.

1. Data are based on GDP measured in average 2010-19 prices and market exchange rates, unless indicated otherwise.
2. GDP growth rate at constant prices is based on production approach.
3. Forecasts beyond 2023 were excluded in the June 2023 edition of *Global Economic Prospects* report.

# LATIN AMERICA and THE CARIBBEAN

*Growth in Latin America and the Caribbean is forecast to edge up from 2.2 percent last year to 2.3 percent in 2024 and then to 2.5 percent in 2025. The drag on economic activity from earlier monetary policy tightening is expected to diminish throughout 2024. Additionally, the expected further easing in policy rates amid moderating inflation is set to bolster growth in 2025. Though commodity prices fell last year, they remain at levels that still support economic activity. Improved prospects among major trading partners will also contribute to growth. Most large regional economies are expected to expand at about their potential rate. Risks to the forecast are tilted to the downside. The conflict in the Middle East could result in higher energy prices, which could alter expected monetary policy paths. In addition, tighter global financial conditions could weigh on private demand and accelerate fiscal consolidation in the region. Extreme El Niño weather events related to climate change pose another downside risk.*

## Recent developments

Growth in Latin America and the Caribbean (LAC) slowed to an estimated 2.2 percent in 2023—about half the growth rate of 2022. In many economies, elevated inflation, tight financial conditions, weak trade, and adverse weather events dampened investment and output growth.

Regional growth in 2023 was 0.7 percentage point higher than previous projections, largely due to upward revisions in the growth forecasts for LAC's two largest economies—Brazil and Mexico. In Brazil, the upward revision to growth in 2023 was mostly due to better-than-expected outturns in agricultural production, private consumption, and exports in the first three quarters of the year. In Mexico, both private consumption and investment growth were stronger than previously envisaged. In contrast, growth was weaker than expected in other large LAC economies, including Argentina, Colombia, and Peru, with recent business surveys pointing to weakening confidence and manufacturing activity (figures 2.3.1.A-C).

Inflation in the region has generally continued to ease, with Argentina being an important exception. Headline consumer price inflation has

recently fallen close to targets of most central banks, in part reflecting moderating energy prices. Core inflation has also continued to moderate but remains slightly above headline inflation (figure 2.3.1.D). Additionally, indicators of inflation expectations have declined in recent months, except in Argentina and Peru. The deceleration in core inflation in most of the region likely reflects the early monetary tightening measures initiated in 2021. As a result, real interest rates have risen over the past year as inflation has fallen.

## Outlook

Growth in LAC is projected to increase slightly in 2024, to 2.3 percent, before firming further to 2.5 percent in 2025. The lagged effects of past monetary tightening will continue to weigh on near-term growth, but with diminishing potency. With inflation in the region anticipated to continue slowing, converging to national targets by late 2024, central banks are expected to continue reducing rates (figure 2.3.2.B). As monetary policy eases, investment growth is expected to pick up in 2024 and 2025. However, fiscal policy is not projected to support growth during this period (figure 2.3.2.A).

The upward revision to LAC's growth forecast in 2024 reflects stronger external demand due to

*Note:* This section was prepared by Francisco Arroyo Marioli.

## FIGURE 2.3.1 **LAC: Recent developments**

*Growth slowed in major LAC countries in the second half of 2023 because of weaker external demand and tight monetary policy. Confidence indicators have been improving for Brazil and Mexico but remain subdued for Chile and Colombia. Purchasing managers' indexes were lower in the second half of 2023 compared with the first half. Headline and core inflation have continued to decline.*

**A. Growth in LAC**

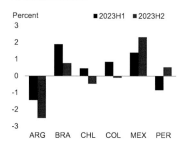

**B. Business confidence indicators**

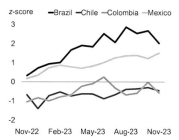

**C. Purchasing managers' indexes**

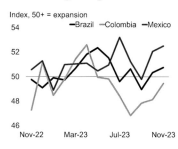

**D. Consumer price inflation**

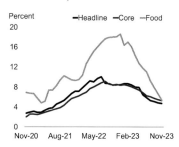

*Sources:* Haver Analytics; World Bank.
*Note:* ARG = Argentina; BRA = Brazil; CHL = Chile; COL = Colombia; LAC = Latin America and the Caribbean; MEX = Mexico; PER = Peru.
A. 2023H1 is seasonally adjusted GDP growth in the first half of 2023 compared with the second half of 2022. 2023H2 is seasonally adjusted GDP growth in the second half of 2023 compared with the first half of 2023. 2023H2 is estimated using the baseline projections in January 2024.
B. Figure shows the z-score for business confidence for Chile and consumer confidence for Brazil, Colombia, and Mexico. Last observation is November 2023.
C. A purchasing managers' index (PMI) of 50 or higher (lower) indicates expansion (contraction). Composite PMI for Brazil and manufacturing PMI for Colombia and Mexico. Last observation is November 2023.
D. Consumer price inflation change from 12 months earlier. Aggregate is median for Brazil, Chile, Colombia, Mexico, and Peru. Last observation is November 2023.

improved U.S. growth expectations, as well as higher-then-expected government spending. The downgrade to China's growth is anticipated to have limited effects on commodity prices, and therefore is not projected to substantially affect LAC. More broadly, commodity price changes over the forecast period are expected to be modest, and not a major driver of regional growth.

Brazil's economy is forecast to grow 1.5 percent in 2024, about half the estimated pace in 2023. The expected decrease in GDP growth reflects both carry-over from the slowdown in the second half of last year and moderating agricultural harvests in

2024. However, a gradual decrease in both headline and core inflation should allow further interest rate cuts, supporting medium-term investment prospects and consumption. Accordingly, output is forecast to increase by 2.2 percent in 2025, even as fiscal support is constrained by the authorities' aim to achieve a primary surplus.

Growth in Mexico is expected to ease to 2.6 percent in 2024 and 2.1 percent in 2025, down from 3.6 percent in 2023. While inflation has fallen, it remains above the central bank's target range. Policy rate cuts are likely to progress gradually, with real interest rates remaining elevated, albeit on a downward path. The antici-pated slowdown in activity in 2024 partly reflects a weakening external environment, mitigated to some degree by increased public investment and fiscal transfers for social programs. Investment is expected to continue to perform well amid increasing nearshoring by firms.

Argentina's economy is projected to rebound, expanding 2.7 percent in 2024 and 3.2 percent in 2025. The pickup reflects a recovery from the drought in 2023, which caused a decline in the country's major commodity exports—maize and soybeans—worth almost 3 percent of GDP. The country is nonetheless facing significant economic and policy uncertainty amid high inflation and steep currency depreciation, which continues to erode consumer confidence. Annual inflation has recently surpassed 150 percent, with no signs of easing. There is also little leeway for fiscal spend-ing to support activity, as the government seeks to address pressing fiscal sustainability issues.

Colombia's growth is expected to increase from 1.2 percent in 2023 to 1.8 percent in 2024 and 3 percent in 2025, close to the economy's potential growth rate. The central bank is expected to cut interest rates later than its regional peers in the face of persistent inflation. As a result, private consumption and investment growth are not expected to gather pace until 2025.

Chile's economy is forecast to expand by 1.8 percent in 2024, after contracting an estimated 0.4 percent in 2023. Growth is expected to further increase to 2.3 percent in 2025. Falling core and headline inflation should allow interest rates to be lowered over the forecast period, gradually unwinding the central bank's restrictive monetary policy stance. The drag on Chile's growth from weak external conditions is also expected to ease as demand for commodities related to green energy continues to expand.

Growth in Peru is projected to rebound to 2.5 percent in 2024 and 2.3 percent in 2025, after contracting 0.4 percent in 2023. Expanding output from major copper mines is expected to contribute to stronger activity. In addition, with inflation on a downward path, further reductions in policy interest rates are likely to support growth over the forecast period. However, political uncertainty continues to affect consumer and business confidence and hinder investment projects. Although the price of copper is expected to decline modestly in 2024, increased mining production will still contribute to overall export growth.

The Caribbean economies are expected to grow 7.6 percent in 2024 and 5.4 percent in 2025, after expanding 4.6 percent in 2023. Excluding Guyana, which remains in a resource-based boom since the discovery of oil in 2015, the region's growth is expected to accelerate to 4.1 percent in 2024 and 3.9 percent in 2025. However, prospects are uneven across the sub-region. The Dominican Republic is forecast to grow by 5.1 percent in 2024 and 5 percent in 2025, amid structural reforms to attract FDI. In contrast, under an optimistic scenario, Haiti's growth is expected to recover slowly, reaching only 1.3 percent in 2024 and 2.2 percent in 2025, following five years of economic contraction. The post-pandemic recovery of tourism in the subregion is incomplete and is expected to continue driving growth (figure 2.3.2.C; Maloney et al. 2023). Remittances into the Caribbean are also expected to continue increasing, albeit at a slower pace (World Bank 2023c).

Growth in Central America is expected to remain broadly steady, at 3.7 percent in 2024 and 3.8 percent in 2025, after an estimated 4.1 percent pace in 2023. As in the Caribbean, moderate remittance growth (except for Costa Rica and Panama) is expected to support activity in 2024.

## FIGURE 2.3.2 **LAC: Outlook**

*Given limited fiscal space, fiscal policy in LAC is generally not expected to support growth over the next two years. At the same time, with core inflation easing across the region, policy rates are expected to be cut over the forecast horizon. Tourism continues to recover toward pre-pandemic levels. Potential output growth in the region is estimated to be lower for the remainder of this decade.*

**A. Fiscal impulse**

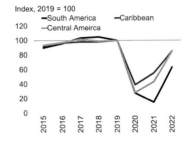

**B. Market-implied real policy rates**

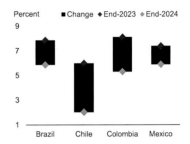

**C. International tourist arrivals**

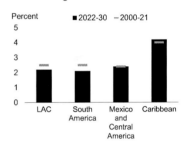

**D. Potential growth**

*Sources*: Bloomberg; Consensus Economics; Haver Analytics; International Monetary Fund; Kose and Ohnsorge (2023); World Bank; World Tourism Organization.
*Note*: e = estimate; f = forecast. LAC = Latin America and the Caribbean.
A. Fiscal impulse is the negative annual change in the structural primary balance for 18 LAC economies, using data from the October 2023 *World Economic Outlook* (database). A positive value indicates fiscal expansion, while a negative value indicates consolidation. Structural primary balance is the general government structural balance excluding net interest costs.
B. Red diamonds denote the policy rate minus the one-year-ahead inflation expectation from Consensus Economics, transformed to a constant time horizon using a weighted average of expectations from 2023 and 2024. Orange diamonds denote the 30-day rolling average of one-year-ahead market implied policy rate, minus the Bloomberg composite consumer price inflation forecast, transformed to a constant time horizon using a weighted average of expectations from 2024 and 2025. Blue bars show the difference between the real interest rates in end-2023 and end-2024. Last observation is December 18, 2023.
C. Last observation is end-2022.
D. Period averages of annual GDP-weighted averages. GDP weights are calculated using average real U.S. dollar GDP (at average 2010-19 prices and market exchange rates) for the period 2000-21. Data for 2022-30 are forecasts. Estimates based on production function approach. South America includes Argentina, Bolivia, Brazil, Chile, Colombia, Ecuador, Peru, Paraguay, and Uruguay. Mexico and Central America includes Costa Rica, Guatemala, Honduras, Mexico, and Nicaragua. Caribbean includes Dominican Republic and Jamaica.

Inflation in Central America has eased but remains high, particularly for food. Within the subregion, growth projections differ. Panama's economy is forecast to expand by 4.6 percent this year, reflecting strong services exports and despite recent shocks from protests, lower copper exports, and the impact of El Niño, while Costa Rica is expected to grow 3.9 percent as domestic demand eases. El Salvador, however, will grow at a more

**FIGURE 2.3.3 LAC: Risks**

*Fiscal deficits are elevated in many LAC countries, exposing them to financial market stress. This stress could be triggered by additional increases in U.S. interest rates or a deterioration in risk appetite. If China's growth softens more than expected, prices of key LAC commodity exports could weaken markedly. LAC has been experiencing frequent extreme weather events, with increasing costs, which is likely to worsen due to climate change.*

A. Commodity trade balances

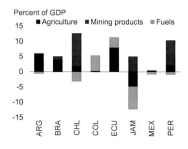

B. Government gross debt and primary balance

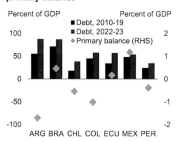

C. LAC good exports

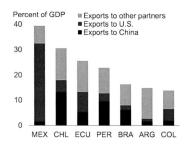

D. Extreme weather events and economic costs

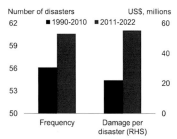

*Sources*: EM-DAT (database); International Monetary Fund; UN Comtrade (database); World Bank.
*Note*: ARG = Argentina; BRA = Brazil; CHL = Chile; COL = Colombia; ECU = Ecuador; JAM = Jamaica; LAC = Latin America and the Caribbean; MEX = Mexico; PER = Peru.
A. Averages of annual commodity trade balances as a percent of GDP between 2015 and 2019.
B. Period averages of government gross debt during 2010-19 and 2022-23. Orange diamonds denote period averages of government primary balance between 2022 and 2023.
C. Period averages of goods export as a share of GDP between 2020 and 2022.
D. Period averages of number of extreme weather events per year and damage per event. Extreme weather events refer to droughts, extreme temperatures, floods, and storms. Last observation is end-2022.

modest 2.3 percent amid slower consumption growth.

Potential economic growth in LAC in 2011-21 is estimated to have declined significantly from the preceding decade (figure 2.3.2.D). Over the remainder of the 2020s, growth of both total factor productivity and the labor force are expected to slow further (Kose and Ohnsorge 2023). In part, this reflects the long-term negative effects of the pandemic, particularly on human capital. Weak potential growth prospects remain a major challenge for the region over the medium term.

# Risks

Risks to the baseline forecast are tilted to the downside (chapter 1). An escalation of the conflict in the Middle East could disrupt energy markets, sending oil prices soaring. Persistent core inflation in advanced economies could lead to higher-than-expected global interest rates and tighter financial conditions, constraining monetary and fiscal policies in LAC. Spillovers from a worse-than-projected slowdown in China could weigh heavily on growth in South America's commodity exporters. Meanwhile, the ongoing El Niño weather pattern heightens the risk of climate-related disruptions and disasters.

The conflict in the Middle East has heightened geopolitical risks globally, with potentially serious implications for commodity markets and growth in LAC. In particular, any further escalation of the conflict that leads to substantial energy market disruptions could send oil prices soaring, dampening confidence and reversing recent disinflation trends in the region (World Bank 2023g). The inflationary effects of rising oil prices would likely be exacerbated by accompanying increases in prices for other energy commodities and fertilizers. Rising inflation could induce central banks in LAC to hold policy rates at levels higher than previously assumed. Falling real incomes and higher borrowing costs could lead to weaker consumption and investment.

Even in the absence of a renewed supply shock, persistent core inflation in advanced economies could result in more restrictive monetary policies than currently priced into financial markets. Consequently, growth in advanced economies could slow more than projected, potentially impacting the prices of commodities exported by LAC (figure 2.3.3.A; Arteta, Kamin, and Ruch 2022). The U.S. dollar is likely to strengthen, with concomitant depreciations of LAC currencies, and hence renewed upward pressure on inflation in the region. This could prompt monetary authorities in LAC to pause interest rate cuts. On the fiscal side, given the context of elevated government debt, the fiscal balances of most LAC economies are insufficient for ensuring debt sustainability (figure 2.3.3.B). Financial stress and high interest rates would exacerbate fiscal challenges by increasing the cost of debt service. This could force governments in LAC to tighten fiscal policy more quickly than currently envisioned, dampening demand.

Growth in China is forecast to slow in 2024-25. Should China's growth prove weaker than projected, there could be substantial external demand spillovers to LAC. In particular, weaker growth of construction and manufacturing in China would translate into softer demand for LAC's key industrial commodity exports, particularly metals. This represents a significant vulnerability for several economies in the region, but particularly to Chile and Peru. Weaker terms of trade would likely result slower income and consumption growth in these economies (figure 2.3.3.C).

Extreme weather events, partly related to climate change, pose an ever-present risk, especially to climate-sensitive sectors like agriculture, energy, and fishing. Climate change can strengthen disruptive El Niño effects, including heavy rains and droughts (figure 2.3.3.D; Cai et al. 2015; Wang et al. 2019). Should weather-related natural disasters intensify in LAC in the coming years, the production of food and other primary goods could be disrupted (Jafino et al. 2020). This, in turn, could affect not only growth, but also the conduct of monetary policy authorities in the region. The adverse effects of disasters on growth would likely be most serious in the region's poorer countries, which tend to have less resilient infrastructure.

### TABLE 2.3.1 Latin America and the Caribbean forecast summary

(Real GDP growth at market prices in percent, unless indicated otherwise)

| | 2021 | 2022 | 2023e | 2024f | 2025f | Percentage point differences from June 2023 projections | | |
| --- | --- | --- | --- | --- | --- | --- | --- | --- |
| | | | | | | 2023e | 2024f | 2025f |
| **EMDE LAC, GDP**[1] | 7.2 | 3.9 | 2.2 | 2.3 | 2.5 | 0.7 | 0.3 | -0.1 |
| GDP per capita (U.S. dollars) | 6.4 | 3.2 | 1.6 | 1.5 | 1.8 | 0.8 | 0.2 | -0.1 |
| (Average including countries that report expenditure components in national accounts)[2] | | | | | | | | |
| EMDE LAC, GDP[2] | 7.2 | 3.8 | 2.2 | 2.1 | 2.5 | 0.8 | 0.1 | 0.0 |
| PPP GDP | 7.4 | 3.9 | 2.1 | 2.2 | 2.5 | 0.6 | 0.2 | 0.0 |
| Private consumption | 7.8 | 5.6 | 2.1 | 1.8 | 2.5 | 0.8 | -0.7 | -0.2 |
| Public consumption | 4.1 | 1.6 | 1.4 | 1.2 | 1.0 | 0.5 | 0.6 | 0.4 |
| Fixed investment | 16.8 | 4.8 | 0.9 | 2.4 | 3.6 | 0.9 | 0.0 | 0.9 |
| Exports, GNFS[3] | 8.3 | 7.7 | 1.1 | 4.5 | 4.0 | -2.0 | 0.1 | -0.5 |
| Imports, GNFS[3] | 17.9 | 7.4 | -0.9 | 3.1 | 3.8 | -2.2 | -1.4 | -0.6 |
| Net exports, contribution to growth | -2.1 | 0.0 | 0.5 | 0.3 | 0.0 | 0.1 | 0.4 | 0.0 |
| **Memo items: GDP** | | | | | | | | |
| South America[4] | 7.3 | 3.6 | 1.6 | 1.8 | 2.4 | 0.8 | 0.0 | -0.1 |
| Central America[5] | 10.5 | 5.5 | 4.1 | 3.7 | 3.8 | 0.5 | -0.1 | -0.1 |
| Caribbean[6] | 9.8 | 8.6 | 4.6 | 7.6 | 5.4 | -0.5 | 2.0 | -1.3 |
| Caribbean excluding Guyana | 9.3 | 5.4 | 2.3 | 4.1 | 3.9 | -1.0 | 0.2 | -0.1 |
| Brazil | 5.0 | 2.9 | 3.1 | 1.5 | 2.2 | 1.9 | 0.1 | -0.2 |
| Mexico | 5.8 | 3.9 | 3.6 | 2.6 | 2.1 | 1.1 | 0.7 | 0.1 |
| Argentina | 10.7 | 5.0 | -2.5 | 2.7 | 3.2 | -0.5 | 0.4 | 1.2 |

*Source*: World Bank.
*Note*: e = estimate; f = forecast; PPP = purchasing power parity; EMDE = emerging market and developing economy. World Bank forecasts are frequently updated based on new information and changing (global) circumstances. Consequently, projections presented here may differ from those contained in other Bank documents, even if basic assessments of countries' prospects do not differ at any given moment in time. The World Bank is currently not publishing economic output, income, or growth data for República Bolivariana de Venezuela owing to a lack of reliable data of adequate quality. República Bolivariana de Venezuela is excluded from cross-country macroeconomic aggregates.
1. GDP and expenditure components are measured in average 2010-19 prices and market exchange rates.
2. Aggregate includes all countries in notes 4, 5, and 6, plus Mexico, but excludes Antigua and Barbuda, Barbados, Dominica, Grenada, Guyana, Haiti, St. Kitts and Nevis, St. Lucia, St. Vincent and the Grenadines, and Suriname.
3. Exports and imports of goods and nonfactor services (GNFS).
4. Includes Argentina, Bolivia, Brazil, Chile, Colombia, Ecuador, Paraguay, Peru, and Uruguay.
5. Includes Costa Rica, El Salvador, Guatemala, Honduras, Nicaragua, and Panama.
6. Includes Antigua and Barbuda, The Bahamas, Barbados, Belize, Dominica, the Dominican Republic, Grenada, Guyana, Haiti, Jamaica, St. Kitts and Nevis, St. Lucia, St. Vincent and the Grenadines, and Suriname.

## TABLE 2.3.2 Latin America and the Caribbean country forecasts [1]

(Real GDP growth at market prices in percent, unless indicated otherwise)

Percentage point differences from June 2023 projections

| | 2021 | 2022 | 2023e | 2024f | 2025f | 2023e | 2024f | 2025f |
|---|---|---|---|---|---|---|---|---|
| Argentina | 10.7 | 5.0 | -2.5 | 2.7 | 3.2 | -0.5 | 0.4 | 1.2 |
| Bahamas, The | 17.0 | 14.4 | 4.3 | 1.8 | 1.6 | 0.0 | -0.2 | -0.3 |
| Barbados | -0.8 | 13.8 | 4.6 | 4.0 | 3.0 | -0.3 | 0.1 | -0.1 |
| Belize | 15.2 | 12.7 | 4.5 | 3.5 | 3.3 | 2.1 | 1.5 | 1.3 |
| Bolivia | 6.1 | 3.5 | 1.9 | 1.5 | 1.5 | -0.6 | -0.5 | -0.5 |
| Brazil | 5.0 | 2.9 | 3.1 | 1.5 | 2.2 | 1.9 | 0.1 | -0.2 |
| Chile | 11.7 | 2.4 | -0.4 | 1.8 | 2.3 | 0.0 | 0.0 | 0.1 |
| Colombia | 11.0 | 7.3 | 1.2 | 1.8 | 3.0 | -0.5 | -0.2 | -0.2 |
| Costa Rica | 7.8 | 4.3 | 5.2 | 3.9 | 3.6 | 2.3 | 0.9 | 0.4 |
| Dominica | 6.9 | 5.9 | 4.9 | 4.6 | 4.0 | 0.2 | 0.0 | -0.2 |
| Dominican Republic | 12.3 | 4.9 | 2.5 | 5.1 | 5.0 | -1.6 | 0.3 | 0.0 |
| Ecuador | 4.2 | 2.9 | 1.3 | 0.7 | 2.0 | -1.3 | -2.1 | -0.8 |
| El Salvador | 11.2 | 2.6 | 2.8 | 2.3 | 2.3 | 0.5 | 0.2 | 0.2 |
| Grenada | 4.7 | 6.4 | 3.9 | 3.8 | 3.5 | 0.3 | 0.5 | 0.4 |
| Guatemala | 8.0 | 4.1 | 3.4 | 3.5 | 3.5 | 0.2 | 0.0 | 0.0 |
| Guyana | 20.1 | 63.4 | 29.0 | 38.2 | 15.2 | 3.8 | 17.0 | -13.0 |
| Haiti [2] | -1.8 | -1.7 | -2.5 | 1.3 | 2.2 | -0.1 | -0.4 | -0.2 |
| Honduras | 12.5 | 4.0 | 3.2 | 3.2 | 3.4 | -0.3 | -0.5 | -0.4 |
| Jamaica | 4.6 | 5.2 | 2.3 | 2.0 | 1.4 | 0.3 | 0.3 | 0.2 |
| Mexico | 5.8 | 3.9 | 3.6 | 2.6 | 2.1 | 1.1 | 0.7 | 0.1 |
| Nicaragua | 10.3 | 3.8 | 3.1 | 3.2 | 3.5 | 0.1 | -0.2 | 0.0 |
| Panama | 15.8 | 10.8 | 4.9 | 4.6 | 5.3 | -0.8 | -1.2 | -0.6 |
| Paraguay | 4.0 | 0.1 | 4.6 | 3.8 | 3.8 | -0.2 | -0.5 | -0.5 |
| Peru | 13.4 | 2.7 | -0.4 | 2.5 | 2.3 | -2.6 | -0.1 | -0.5 |
| St. Lucia | 12.2 | 15.9 | 3.2 | 2.9 | 2.3 | -0.4 | -0.5 | -0.2 |
| St. Vincent and the Grenadines | 0.8 | 4.9 | 6.0 | 4.8 | 3.7 | 0.4 | 0.0 | 0.2 |
| Suriname | -2.4 | 2.4 | 2.0 | 2.6 | 3.0 | -0.4 | -0.6 | -0.1 |
| Uruguay | 5.3 | 4.9 | 1.2 | 3.2 | 2.6 | -0.6 | 0.4 | 0.2 |

*Source*: World Bank.
*Note*: e = estimate; f = forecast. World Bank forecasts are frequently updated based on new information and changing (global) circumstances. Consequently, projections presented here may differ from those contained in other Bank documents, even if basic assessments of countries' prospects do not significantly differ at any given moment in time.
1. Data are based on GDP measured in average 2010-19 prices and market exchange rates.
2. GDP is based on fiscal year, which runs from October to September of next year.

# MIDDLE EAST and NORTH AFRICA

*The ongoing conflict in the Middle East has heightened uncertainty and geopolitical risks in the Middle East and North Africa (MNA) region. Assuming the conflict does not escalate, growth in the region is forecast to reach 3.5 percent in 2024 and 2025—which is stronger than previously envisioned—as oil-exporting economies benefit from the unwinding of oil production cuts. In contrast, the outlook for oil-importing economies has deteriorated on account of weakening domestic conditions, including persistently high inflation. Risks to the outlook are tilted to the downside. Owing to the possibility of escalation in the conflict, potential benefits to oil exporters from higher oil prices, resulting from disruptions in commodity markets, would likely be more than offset by weakened regional activity. Other downside risks include climate-change-related weather shocks and adverse spillovers from further monetary policy tightening in advanced economies and tighter financial conditions.*

## Recent developments

The ongoing conflict has increased geopolitical and policy uncertainty, disrupted financial markets, and damaged investor confidence in MNA (figure 2.4.1.A). It has also dampened tourism-related activity, particularly in neighboring countries. International tourist arrivals in these countries slowed down in late 2023, following robust activity prior to the onset of the conflict. MNA already faced multiple headwinds, including oil production cuts, elevated inflation, and weak private sector activity in oil-importing economies. Accordingly, growth in MNA is estimated to have slowed sharply in 2023, to 1.9 percent, after reaching 5.8 percent in the previous year.

In MNA's oil exporters, while non-oil sector activity was robust, the oil sector weakened markedly as a result of oil production cuts, which dampened growth. Growth in oil importers also slowed somewhat last year, reflecting anemic private sector activity (figure 2.4.1.B).

Oil production in MNA declined in 2023, mainly driven by production cuts in member countries of the Gulf Cooperation Council (GCC), especially

Saudi Arabia, which announced the extension of its voluntary oil production cut until early 2024 (figure 2.4.1.C). Member countries of the Organization of the Petroleum Exporting Countries Plus (OPEC+) also agreed in April on the production cut until the end of 2023. In contrast, oil supply from other economies in the region increased, including the Islamic Republic of Iran, which was exempted from the OPEC+ agreement.

Growth in GCC countries is estimated to have decelerated sharply in 2023 because of the decline in oil production, which more than offset robust non-oil activity driven by strong labor markets, moderating inflation, and supportive fiscal policies. In Saudi Arabia, output is estimated to have fallen by 0.5 percent in 2023, as the contraction in oil activity and exports was dampened somewhat by strong private consumption and public investment. Similarly, Bahrain, Kuwait, Oman, Qatar, and the United Arab Emirates also experienced a downturn in 2023.

In other oil exporters, growth picked up in the Islamic Republic of Iran, as increases in oil production and exports more than offset weak external non-oil demand. In Libya, which was also exempted from the OPEC+ production cut agreement, growth rebounded, as industrial

*Note:* This section was prepared by Naotaka Sugawara.

## FIGURE 2.4.1 MNA: Recent developments

*The onset of the recent conflict in the Middle East disrupted financial markets in the region, raising geopolitical and policy uncertainty. Activity in the private sector remained robust among oil exporters, led by non-oil activity, while activity in oil importers was subdued. Oil production has declined in line with announced production cuts, particularly in GCC countries. In some oil importers, elevated inflation was accompanied by significant depreciation of their currencies.*

**A. Change in stock prices since October 6, 2023**

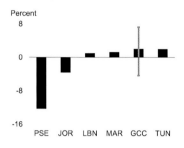

**B. Composite purchasing managers' indexes, 2023**

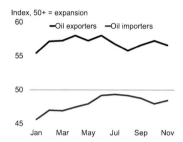

**C. Oil production, 2023**

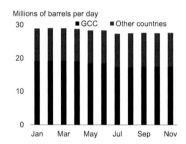

**D. Change in exchange rates and inflation, 2023**

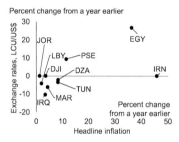

*Sources:* Bloomberg; Haver Analytics; International Energy Agency; World Bank.
*Note:* DJI = Djibouti; DZA = Algeria; EGY = Arab Republic of Egypt; GCC = Gulf Cooperation Council; IRN = Islamic Republic of Iran; IRQ = Iraq; JOR = Jordan; LBN = Lebanon; LBY = Libya; LCU = local currency unit; MAR = Morocco; MNA = Middle East and North Africa; PSE = West Bank and Gaza; TUN = Tunisia.
A. Change in stock price indexes from October 6, 2023 (or closest day before that) to the latest available day with data (December 11-14, 2023). The GCC aggregate is calculated as a weighted average using nominal GDP in U.S. dollars as weights, with the vertical orange line showing the maximum-minimum range among GCC countries.
B. Aggregates are calculated as weighted averages using nominal GDP in U.S. dollars as weights. Sample comprises five countries—three oil exporters and two oil importers.
C. Oil production in MNA, originating from GCC and other countries, which also includes some oil importers.
D. Percent change in nominal exchange rate vis-à-vis U.S. dollars from a year earlier—positive (negative) values showing depreciation (appreciation) against U.S. dollars—on the vertical axis and percent change in headline consumer price index from a year earlier on the horizontal axis. Data are from November 2023 for most countries, except for October 2023 in the cases of Algeria, Libya, and Morocco, September 2023 in the case of the Islamic Republic of Iran, and June 2023 in the case of Iraq. Data are available for Lebanon but excluded from the figure because of scaling: 895.0 percent for change in exchange rates and 215.4 percent for headline inflation in October 2023.

activity was strengthened by oil production, which was unaffected by September's flooding. In contrast, activity in Algeria and Iraq was adversely affected by oil production cuts and declining exports.

In oil-importing economies, growth softened amid elevated macroeconomic imbalances and vulnerabilities. In the Arab Republic of Egypt,

growth is estimated to have slowed to 3.8 percent in fiscal year (FY) 2022/23. Import restrictions constrained access to inputs for domestic production and exports, while declining purchasing power of households and sluggish corporate activity weighed on investment and private consumption. In contrast, growth is estimated to have picked up in Morocco, despite the earthquake in September that caused major humanitarian losses and infrastructure damage. The agricultural sector recovered following a severe drought in 2022.

Inflation was well-contained in GCC countries by late 2023, while it remained elevated in other oil exporters, notably the Islamic Republic of Iran, as well as in some oil importers, despite the decline in oil prices in 2023. In oil importers, food price inflation remained stubbornly high, and elevated headline inflation was often driven by large currency depreciations (figure 2.4.1.D). Consequently, monetary policy was tightened in oil importers; in contrast, policy rates stabilized in GCC countries in late 2023.

## Outlook

The conflict in the Middle East has heightened uncertainty around growth forecasts in the region. Assuming the conflict does not escalate, growth in MNA is expected to pick up to 3.5 percent in 2024 and 2025—0.2 and 0.5 percentage point higher, respectively, than previously projected (figure 2.4.2.A; table 2.4.1). These upward revisions assume improved economic performance among oil exporters, driven by a stronger rebound in oil activity and export growth, following deeper production cuts in 2023 than previously expected. In contrast, the outlook for oil importers appears weaker than previously expected, owing to the adverse impact of the ongoing conflict, including that on tourism, and slower growth in private consumption and investment, as a result of higher inflation and input costs.

Growth in GCC countries is forecast to rise to 3.6 percent in 2024 and 3.8 percent in 2025. In Saudi Arabia, growth is projected to rebound to 4.1 percent in 2024 and 4.2 percent in 2025 (table 2.4.2). The country's oil output and exports are expected to expand, despite an extension of voluntary oil production cuts for early this year. As part of the government's Saudi Vision 2030, investment related to non-oil activity will also be a major driver of growth going forward. An increase in oil production will help boost growth in other GCC countries.

Among other oil exporters, growth is expected to pick up in Algeria and Iraq but to slow in the Islamic Republic of Iran and Libya. In Algeria and Iraq, the expansion of oil production as a result of relaxed production cuts in early 2024 is projected to contribute to faster growth. In contrast, in the Islamic Republic of Iran and Libya, growth is forecast to moderate as oil production stabilizes.

In oil importers, growth is expected to edge up to 3.2 percent this year and 3.7 percent in 2025. In Morocco, the strengthening of growth will be bolstered by a continued recovery in agriculture, an expected rebound in tourism despite the recent earthquake, which is expected to have limited macroeconomic consequences, and fiscal support through the government's reconstruction plan.

In Tunisia, growth is expected to rise to 3 percent in both 2024 and 2025, conditional on the easing of drought conditions and a decrease in inflation. In Djibouti, investment in several large infrastructure projects is expected to boost growth, with increased use of the country's port services by Ethiopia being another positive factor.

In contrast, in Egypt, growth is expected to slow to 3.5 percent in FY2023/24 (July 2023 to June 2024), before rising to 3.9 percent in FY2024/25. The conflict in the Middle East will likely exacerbate the inflation problem, eroding households' purchasing power and constraining activity in the private sector, and intensify pressures on external accounts through implications on tourism, remittances, and oil trade balance. In Jordan, household income growth may be constrained by weak private sector job creation, while the tourism sector will be adversely affected by the conflict in the Middle East. Growth in the Republic of Yemen is expected to be tepid on account of weak governance, political instability, and conflict.

## FIGURE 2.4.2 MNA: Outlook

*Growth in MNA is projected to rise to 3.5 percent in 2024 and 2025, reflecting strong rebounds in growth in oil exporters. In oil importers, weak revenue collection and increased interest payments will widen fiscal deficits, while subdued growth will exacerbate output losses relative to pre-pandemic projections and slow progress in poverty reduction.*

| A. GDP growth | B. Fiscal balances |
|---|---|
| 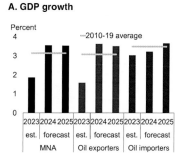 | 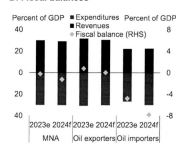 |

| C. GDP forecasts for oil importers | D. Number of poor people in oil importers |
|---|---|
| 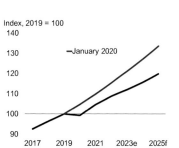 | 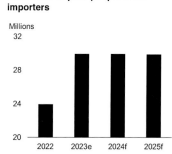 |

*Sources:* International Monetary Fund; World Bank.
*Note:* e = estimate; est. = estimate; f = forecast; MNA = Middle East and North Africa.
A.C. Aggregates are calculated as weighted averages using GDP weights at average 2010-19 prices and market exchange rates.
B. Aggregates are calculated as weighted averages using nominal GDP in U.S. dollars as weights.
C. The line for January 2020 is based on projections in the January 2020 edition of the *Global Economic Prospects* report.
D. The number of poor people is defined by using the lower middle-income poverty threshold of 3.65 international dollars per day in 2017 purchasing power parity. Sample includes five oil importers.

The outlook for West Bank and Gaza is highly uncertain but growth is projected to shrink 6 percent in 2024 after contracting 3.7 percent in 2023. Massive destruction of fixed assets and industrial facilities in Gaza, which represents roughly 16 percent of output in West Bank and Gaza, will cause a significant contraction of economic activity. The ongoing conflict will also exacerbate already-dire economic conditions in West Bank. Heightened restrictions on the free movement of goods and people between and within cities, including access to the Israeli market, will continue to have negative effects on trade and output. Assuming the situation around the conflict cools down, the reconstruction efforts

### FIGURE 2.4.3 MNA: Risks

*The escalation of the recent conflict in the Middle East could cause further damages in growth potential, as historically conflicts in the region have been associated with a huge decline in productivity. The number of refugees in the region has continued to increase, particularly in fragile countries. Deaths from natural disasters, including earthquakes and floods, increased substantially last year. Oil importers in the region are vulnerable to sudden shifts in global financial conditions and risk appetite because of their external financing needs.*

**A. Productivity growth around wars**

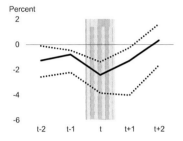

**B. Number of refugees**

**C. Death toll from natural disasters**

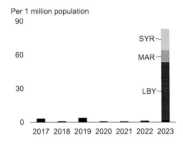

**D. External financing needs**

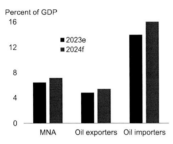

*Sources:* Davies, Pettersson, and Öberg (2023); EM-DAT (database); Feenstra, Inklaar, and Timmer (2015); International Monetary Fund; United Nations High Commissioner for Refugees (UNHCR); World Bank.

*Note:* e = estimate; f = forecast; FCS = fragile and conflict-affected situations; LBY = Libya; MAR = Morocco; MNA = Middle East and North Africa; PSE = West Bank and Gaza; SYR = Syrian Arab Republic.

A. Median total factor productivity growth across nine episodes of wars—defined as those with more than one death per one million population—in MNA. If multiple cases are identified within five years, the one associated with the largest number is chosen. The dotted lines show the interquartile range.

B. The number of refugees in the region under UNHCR's mandate. For West Bank and Gaza, it also includes refugees under the mandate of the United Nations Relief and Works Agency for Palestine Refugees in the Near East.

C. Total number of deaths caused by natural disasters in MNA, divided by population in millions.

D. External financing needs are defined as the sum of amortization of long-term external debt, stock of short-term external debt in the previous year, and current account deficits. Aggregates are calculated as weighted averages using nominal GDP in U.S. dollars as weights.

are expected to contribute to a rebound of growth to 5.4 percent in 2025.

Fiscal deficits are expected to widen in 2024 in MNA, with a notable deterioration in the fiscal positions of oil importers (figure 2.4.2.B). In oil exporters, fiscal surpluses in 2023 will shrink to almost zero, on average, but with diverging trends in GCC and non-GCC oil exporters. Recoveries in oil production are expected to support the improvement of fiscal balances in several GCC

countries, while deficits are projected to widen in some non-GCC oil exporters, as expenditures are likely to outpace revenues. In oil importers, fiscal deficits are expected to widen in 2024, partly reflecting weak revenue, rising debt-service costs, and rising subsidies related to food and energy. In West Bank and Gaza, fiscal deficits are expected to increase significantly in 2024, owing to a decline in both domestically managed tax instruments and the "clearance revenues" transferred from Israel. Additionally, in 2025, the deficits are likely to grow further as a result of expansionary fiscal policy aimed at aiding the recovery from the conflict.

Projected growth in oil importers will be insufficient to return output to its pre-pandemic trend. Output losses relative to the pre-pandemic projections will increase over the forecast period (figure 2.4.2.C). In addition to the ongoing conflict, subdued growth in oil importers—and in some cases persistently high inflation—will also limit progress in reducing poverty and inequality. After experiencing a surge in poverty in 2023, oil importers will likely see elevated poverty rates in the near term (figure 2.4.2.D).

## Risks

A severe downside risk to the baseline growth forecast is the intensification of the ongoing conflict. The escalation of the conflict could result in an increase in energy prices and benefit energy exporters, but this would be more than offset by weakened activity due to a surge in geopolitical tensions in the region. Natural disasters, including climate-change-related weather events, and adverse spillovers from tighter global financial conditions pose further downside risks.

A substantial escalation of the conflict would have significant implications for growth prospects in MNA and increase forecast uncertainty (Gatti et al. 2022). Economies directly affected could see significant declines in investment and productivity growth owing to damage to infrastructure and human losses (figure 2.4.3.A; Dieppe, Kilic Celic, and Okou 2020). Adverse impacts of an escalation of the conflict could spill over into neighboring economies. It could increase uncertainty and dampen investor confidence, reduce tourism, cause capital outflows and instability in financial markets, weigh on investment growth, and subsequently weaken prospects for output and productivity growth in the region. Disruptions in energy markets driven by the escalation of the conflict could lead to increased prices of food and metals by raising production and transportation costs (World Bank 2023g). Such disruptions could also be caused by increased security threats in major shipping lanes in the region. Additionally, the price of gold may rise as the conflict increases uncertainty and reduces investors' risk appetite.

The conflict could be further escalated or protracted because of a surge in refugees or internal displacement of people. It would result in an erosion of human capital via losses of access to essential health and education services (Schady et al. 2023). In MNA, particularly its economies in fragile or conflict-affected situations, the number of refugees has already been increasing (figure 2.4.3.B). As the number of affected people increases, social tensions could rise. Increased violence driven by elevated social tensions could spur greater food insecurity, exacerbated by a rise in food prices. Heightened food insecurity could worsen poverty and inequality outcomes in the region.

MNA is vulnerable to natural disasters, which, apart from their humanitarian toll, can cause severe damage to infrastructure and reduce output, incomes, and productivity. Total deaths from natural disasters rose significantly last year (figure 2.4.3.C). As climate change continues to increase the frequency and severity of adverse weather events, the lack of weather-resilient buildings and infrastructure, along with inadequate maintenance of existing structures and mitigation facilities, could amplify damage (OECD 2018). The impact of extreme weather events tends to be particularly large and persistent in countries without fiscal buffers to enable adequate responses (Pigato 2019). Access to basic services, especially among the vulnerable, could be constrained, further increasing poverty and inequality.

Oil exporters are typically heavily dependent on a single commodity for their output, exports, and government revenues. Weaker global demand relative to the baseline forecast—for example, owing to softer growth in China—would put downward pressure on global oil prices and on growth in MNA's oil exporters. Should oil prices fall or demand weaken, oil production might be curtailed or prolonged in several oil exporters, negatively impacting growth prospects in MNA. In commodity-exporting economies, fiscal policy tends to be more volatile than in other economies, and volatility is negatively associated with economic growth (chapter 4; Arroyo Marioli, Fatás, and Vasishtha 2023). Furthermore, the volatility of terms of trade has been consistently higher in oil exporters in MNA than in other economies and elevated particularly in GCC countries (Gatti et al. 2023).

In advanced economies, interest rates might need to be raised further, given still-elevated inflation. Larger-than-anticipated increases in interest rates, or an extended period of elevated rates, could expose latent economic and financial vulnerabilities and tighten global financial conditions. Such tightening, relative to the baseline forecast, could increase financial instability and lead to capital outflows and currency depreciations, particularly in oil importers. External financing needs are expected to increase in both oil exporters and importers in 2024, but to be more elevated in the latter (figure 2.4.3.D). Given the large external deficits in many oil importers and their limited access to external financing sources, tighter financial conditions would further weaken growth.

## TABLE 2.4.1 Middle East and North Africa forecast summary

(Real GDP growth at market prices in percent, unless indicated otherwise)

Percentage point differences from
June 2023 projections

| | 2021 | 2022 | 2023e | 2024f | 2025f | 2023e | 2024f | 2025f |
|---|---|---|---|---|---|---|---|---|
| **EMDE MNA, GDP[1]** | **3.8** | **5.8** | **1.9** | **3.5** | **3.5** | **-0.3** | **0.2** | **0.5** |
| GDP per capita (U.S. dollars) | 2.6 | 4.4 | 0.5 | 2.2 | 2.2 | -0.4 | 0.2 | 0.5 |
| *(Average including countries that report expenditure components in national accounts)[2]* | | | | | | | | |
| EMDE MNA, GDP[2] | 4.1 | 5.9 | 2.1 | 3.6 | 3.6 | -0.4 | 0.5 | 0.7 |
| PPP GDP | 4.3 | 5.6 | 2.3 | 3.6 | 3.6 | -0.3 | 0.5 | 0.6 |
| Private consumption | 5.8 | 4.5 | 3.2 | 3.0 | 2.9 | -0.1 | -0.1 | -0.1 |
| Public consumption | 2.6 | 3.5 | 4.1 | 2.9 | 2.8 | 1.2 | 0.1 | 0.2 |
| Fixed investment | 5.7 | 10.3 | 4.8 | 3.8 | 3.6 | 0.1 | 0.3 | -0.3 |
| Exports, GNFS[3] | 7.1 | 14.2 | 4.1 | 6.6 | 6.5 | 0.1 | 2.1 | 2.6 |
| Imports, GNFS[3] | 9.2 | 9.9 | 7.3 | 5.6 | 5.3 | 1.3 | 0.9 | 0.9 |
| Net exports, contribution to growth | 0.1 | 3.0 | -0.6 | 1.2 | 1.3 | -0.2 | 0.9 | 1.2 |
| **Memo items: GDP** | | | | | | | | |
| Oil exporters[4] | 3.4 | 6.2 | 1.6 | 3.6 | 3.5 | -0.4 | 0.4 | 0.8 |
| GCC countries[5] | 3.3 | 7.4 | 1.1 | 3.6 | 3.8 | -1.3 | 0.4 | 1.0 |
| Saudi Arabia | 3.9 | 8.7 | -0.5 | 4.1 | 4.2 | -2.7 | 0.8 | 1.7 |
| Iran, Islamic Rep.[6] | 4.7 | 3.8 | 4.2 | 3.7 | 3.2 | 2.0 | 1.7 | 1.3 |
| Oil importers[7] | 5.5 | 3.9 | 3.0 | 3.2 | 3.7 | -0.4 | -0.7 | -0.4 |
| Egypt, Arab Rep.[6] | 3.3 | 6.6 | 3.8 | 3.5 | 3.9 | -0.2 | -0.5 | -0.8 |

*Source*: World Bank.

*Note*: e = estimate; f = forecast; EMDE = emerging market and developing economy; MNA = Middle East and North Africa; PPP = purchasing power parity. World Bank forecasts are frequently updated based on new information and changing (global) circumstances. Consequently, projections presented here may differ from those contained in other Bank documents, even if basic assessments of countries' prospects do not differ at any given moment in time.

1. GDP and expenditure components are measured in average 2010-19 prices and market exchange rates. Excludes Lebanon, the Syrian Arab Republic, and the Republic of Yemen as a result of the high degree of uncertainty.

2. Aggregate includes all economies in notes 4 and 7 except Djibouti, Iraq, Jordan, Qatar, and West Bank and Gaza, for which data limitations prevent the forecasting of GDP components.

3. GNFS refers to goods and non-factor services.

4. Oil exporters include Algeria, Bahrain, the Islamic Republic of Iran, Iraq, Kuwait, Libya, Oman, Qatar, Saudi Arabia, and the United Arab Emirates.

5. The Gulf Cooperation Council (GCC) includes Bahrain, Kuwait, Oman, Qatar, Saudi Arabia, and the United Arab Emirates.

6. Fiscal-year-based numbers. The fiscal year (FY) runs from July 1 to June 30 in the Arab Republic of Egypt, with the column for 2021 reflecting FY2020/21. For the Islamic Republic of Iran, it runs from March 21 through March 20, with the column for 2021 reflecting FY2021/22.

7. Oil importers include Djibouti, Egypt, Jordan, Morocco, Tunisia, and West Bank and Gaza.

## TABLE 2.4.2 Middle East and North Africa economy forecasts[1]

(Real GDP growth at market prices in percent, unless indicated otherwise)

Percentage point differences from June 2023 projections

| | 2021 | 2022 | 2023e | 2024f | 2025f | 2023e | 2024f | 2025f |
|---|---|---|---|---|---|---|---|---|
| Algeria | 3.4 | 3.2 | 2.5 | 2.6 | 2.6 | 0.8 | 0.2 | 0.5 |
| Bahrain | 2.7 | 4.9 | 2.8 | 3.3 | 3.2 | 0.1 | 0.1 | 0.1 |
| Djibouti | 4.5 | 3.1 | 4.7 | 5.1 | 5.7 | 0.3 | -0.3 | -0.2 |
| Egypt, Arab Rep.[2] | 3.3 | 6.6 | 3.8 | 3.5 | 3.9 | -0.2 | -0.5 | -0.8 |
| Iran, Islamic Rep.[2] | 4.7 | 3.8 | 4.2 | 3.7 | 3.2 | 2.0 | 1.7 | 1.3 |
| Iraq | -2.1 | 7.0 | -2.9 | 4.2 | 2.9 | -1.8 | -1.8 | -0.8 |
| Jordan | 3.7 | 2.4 | 2.6 | 2.5 | 2.6 | 0.2 | 0.1 | 0.2 |
| Kuwait | 1.3 | 7.9 | 0.8 | 2.6 | 2.7 | -0.5 | 0.0 | 0.3 |
| Lebanon[3] | -7.0 | -0.6 | 0.2 | .. | .. | 0.7 | .. | .. |
| Libya[3] | 31.4 | -1.2 | 14.1 | 4.1 | 4.3 | .. | .. | .. |
| Morocco | 8.0 | 1.3 | 2.8 | 3.1 | 3.3 | 0.3 | -0.2 | -0.2 |
| Oman | 3.1 | 4.3 | 1.4 | 2.7 | 2.9 | -0.1 | -0.1 | 0.3 |
| Qatar | 1.5 | 4.9 | 2.8 | 2.5 | 3.1 | -0.5 | -0.4 | 0.0 |
| Saudi Arabia | 3.9 | 8.7 | -0.5 | 4.1 | 4.2 | -2.7 | 0.8 | 1.7 |
| Syrian Arab Republic[3] | 1.3 | -3.5 | -5.5 | .. | .. | 0.0 | .. | .. |
| Tunisia | 4.4 | 2.4 | 1.2 | 3.0 | 3.0 | -1.1 | 0.0 | 0.0 |
| United Arab Emirates | 3.5 | 6.6 | 3.4 | 3.7 | 3.8 | 0.6 | 0.3 | 0.4 |
| West Bank and Gaza | 7.0 | 3.9 | -3.7 | -6.0 | 5.4 | -6.7 | -9.0 | 2.4 |
| Yemen, Rep.[3] | -1.0 | 1.5 | -0.5 | 2.0 | .. | 0.0 | 0.0 | .. |

*Source*: World Bank.

*Note*: e = estimate; f = forecast. World Bank forecasts are frequently updated based on new information and changing (global) circumstances. Consequently, projections presented here may differ from those contained in other Bank documents, even if basic assessments of economies' prospects do not significantly differ at any given moment in time.

1. Data are based on GDP measured in average 2010-19 prices and market exchange rates.

2. Fiscal-year-based numbers. The fiscal year (FY) runs from July 1 to June 30 in the Arab Republic of Egypt, with 2021 reflecting FY2020/21. For the Islamic Republic of Iran, it runs from March 21 through March 20, with 2021 reflecting FY2021/22.

3. Forecasts for Lebanon (beyond 2023), the Syrian Arab Republic (beyond 2023), and the Republic of Yemen (beyond 2024) are excluded because of a high degree of uncertainty. Forecasts for Libya beyond 2022 were excluded in the June 2023 edition of the *Global Economic Prospects* report because of a high degree of uncertainty.

# SOUTH ASIA

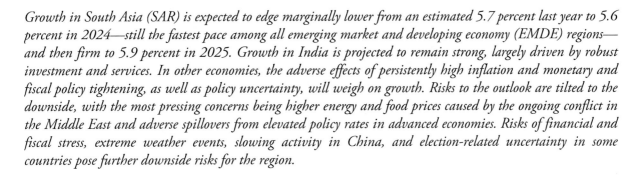

*Growth in South Asia (SAR) is expected to edge marginally lower from an estimated 5.7 percent last year to 5.6 percent in 2024—still the fastest pace among all emerging market and developing economy (EMDE) regions—and then firm to 5.9 percent in 2025. Growth in India is projected to remain strong, largely driven by robust investment and services. In other economies, the adverse effects of persistently high inflation and monetary and fiscal policy tightening, as well as policy uncertainty, will weigh on growth. Risks to the outlook are tilted to the downside, with the most pressing concerns being higher energy and food prices caused by the ongoing conflict in the Middle East and adverse spillovers from elevated policy rates in advanced economies. Risks of financial and fiscal stress, extreme weather events, slowing activity in China, and election-related uncertainty in some countries pose further downside risks for the region.*

## Recent developments

Growth in SAR is estimated to have slowed slightly, from 5.9 percent in 2022 to a still-strong 5.7 percent in 2023—still the fastest of all EMDE regions. This primarily reflected a robust expansion in India, which accounted for more than three-fourths of regional output in 2023 (figure 2.5.1.A). Excluding that in India, however, activity was more subdued.

In India, the slowdown in growth to 7.2 percent in fiscal year (FY) 2022/23, which ended in March 2023, was primarily due to a weakening post-pandemic rebound, particularly in private investment and consumption. However, a strong performance in 2023 was underpinned by robust public investment growth and vibrant services activity, thanks to resilient domestic demand for consumer services and exports of business services. In contrast, merchandise exports slowed, reflecting weak external demand. Headline consumer price inflation remained within monetary authorities' target band of 2-6 percent throughout most of 2023, with policy rates being kept unchanged since February 2023.

In Bangladesh, growth is estimated to have slowed to 6 percent in FY2022/23, as activity was

hampered by import restrictions and rising material and energy costs, as well as mounting external and financial pressures. Headline consumer price inflation increased in 2023, mainly driven by rising food prices and currency depreciation, resulting in tighter monetary policy (figure 2.5.1.B). Balance of payments deteriorated, along with a decline in foreign exchange reserves. Financial sector vulnerabilities rose, as non-performing and other stressed loans increased (World Bank 2023j).

In Pakistan, output contracted an estimated 0.2 percent in FY2022/23 as a result of the effects of damage from the 2022 floods and increased political uncertainty. Consumer price inflation remained elevated, partly reflecting currency depreciation in early 2023 (figure 2.5.1.C). However, by late 2023, the rupee showed signs of stabilization, driven by a variety of factors. These included increased liquidity in the foreign exchange market due to tighter enforcement of regulations, a shrinking money supply, a balance-of-payments surplus on account of low import demand, and a moratorium on Chinese debt repayments.

In Sri Lanka, the economy contracted an estimated 3.8 percent in 2023. Credit to the private sector remained subdued throughout last year, adversely affecting activity. With weaker demand, consumer

*Note:* This section was prepared by Naotaka Sugawara.

## FIGURE 2.5.1 SAR: Recent developments

*Growth has remained strong in the region. Monetary policy was tightened in half of the region's economies in 2023, owing to high inflation, currency depreciation, or both. A solid recovery in international tourism has benefited the region.*

**A. Industrial production growth, 2023**

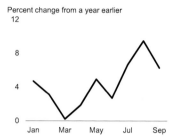

**B. Policy interest rates, 2023**

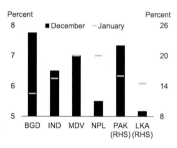

**C. Change in exchange rates and inflation, 2023**

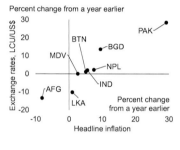

**D. International tourist arrivals**

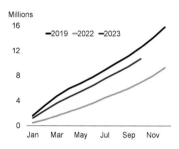

*Sources:* Haver Analytics; World Bank.
*Note:* AFG = Afghanistan; BGD = Bangladesh; BTN = Bhutan; IND = India; LCU = local currency unit; LKA = Sri Lanka; MDV = Maldives; NPL = Nepal; PAK = Pakistan; SAR = South Asia.
A. Aggregates are calculated as weighted averages, with value added by industry at 2015 prices and market exchange rates as weights. Sample includes up to four countries (Bangladesh, India, Pakistan, and Sri Lanka).
B. Nominal policy rates at the beginning of January 2023 and as of December 15, 2023.
C. Percent change in nominal exchange rate vis-à-vis U.S. dollars from a year earlier—positive (negative) values showing depreciation (appreciation) against U.S. dollars—on the vertical axis and percent change in headline consumer price index from a year earlier on the horizontal axis. Data are from November 2023 for most countries, except for October 2023 in the cases of Afghanistan, Bhutan, Maldives, and Nepal.
D. Cumulative number of tourist arrivals in SAR since January of each year. Last observation for 2023 is October. Sample includes up to five countries (Bhutan [for 2019 only], India, Maldives, Nepal, and Sri Lanka).

price inflation declined, and the central bank started to reduce policy rates from mid-2023. Progress was also made in sovereign debt restructuring, as the authorities reached agreements with major official creditors, including China and the Paris Club, as well as the implementation of a domestic debt optimization plan.

In Nepal, growth is estimated to have slowed markedly in FY2022/23, partly reflecting earlier monetary policy tightening to curb credit growth. Import restrictions also weighed on growth, though they were lifted in January 2023 (World

Bank 2023k). Inflation remained high, partly driven by an increase in food price inflation.

For Afghanistan, economic data are sparse. Despite declining food prices in 2023, poverty rates remained high, exacerbated by strong earthquakes in October 2023. The country also faced an increase in unemployment and underemployment, as the rise in the labor supply outpaced the subdued demand (World Bank 2023l).

The recovery in global tourism continued to benefit the region, including Bhutan and Maldives (figure 2.5.1.D). The number of tourist arrivals in Maldives increased by 13 percent in the first ten months of 2023, relative to the same period of 2022. In Bhutan, tourism-related fees were reduced to attract more tourists in September 2023.

## Outlook

Economic growth in SAR is expected to edge slightly lower to a still-robust 5.6 percent pace in 2024, and then strengthen to 5.9 percent in the following year (figure 2.5.2.A; table 2.5.1). Domestic demand, including public consumption and investment, will remain major drivers of economic growth. A pickup in external demand, albeit still subdued, is also expected to contribute to growth. Excluding that in India, output in the region is projected to expand by 3.8 percent in 2024 and 4.1 percent in 2025.

India is anticipated to maintain the fastest growth rate among the world's largest economies, but its post-pandemic recovery is expected to slow, with estimated growth of 6.3 percent in FY2023/24 (April 2023 to March 2024; table 1.1). Growth is then expected to recover gradually, edging up to 6.4 percent in FY2024/25 and 6.5 percent in FY2025/26 (table 2.5.2). Investment is envisaged to decelerate marginally but remain robust, supported by higher public investment and improved corporate balance sheets, including in the banking sector (World Bank 2023m). Private consumption growth is likely to taper off, as the post-pandemic pent-up demand diminishes and persistent high food price inflation is likely to constrain spending, particularly among low-income households. Meanwhile, government consumption is expected to grow slowly, in line with the central government's efforts to lower the share of current spending.

In Bangladesh, growth is forecast to slow to 5.6 percent in FY2023/24 (July 2023 to June 2024). Inflation is likely to remain elevated, weighing on private consumption. As foreign exchange reserves are likely to stay low, import restrictions are expected to continue and impede private investment. In contrast, public investment is envisaged to remain resilient. Growth is expected to rise in FY2024/25 as inflationary pressure recedes.

In Pakistan, the economic outlook for FY2023/24 (July 2023 to June 2024) remains subdued, with growth projected at only 1.7 percent. Monetary policy is expected to remain tight to contain inflation, while fiscal policy is also set to be contractionary, reflecting pressures from high debt-service payments. Weak confidence stemming from political turmoil will contribute to the slow growth in private demand. As inflationary pressure eases, growth is expected to pick up to 2.4 percent in FY2024/25.

Maldives' economy is projected to expand by 5.2 percent in 2024 and 5.5 percent in 2025. A continued recovery in tourism from major economies, including China, is expected to contribute to robust growth. Investment related to the tourism sector, particularly the expansion of Velana International Airport, will also support growth.

In Bhutan, growth is expected to slow to 4 percent in FY2023/24 (July 2023 to June 2024), partly reflecting reductions in public investment and capital expenditure. Despite this, the economy will still benefit from a strong performance in tourism-related services. In FY2024/25, growth is projected to pick up to 4.6 percent, reflecting a recovery in industrial and services activities and the commissioning of a new hydro plant.

In Nepal, growth is projected to pick up to 3.9 percent in FY2023/24 (mid-July 2023 to mid-July 2024) and 5 percent in FY2024/25. Expansion of industrial and services activities will be supported

## FIGURE 2.5.2 **SAR: Outlook**

*Growth in the region is projected to dip slightly to 5.6 percent in 2024, before firming to 5.9 percent in 2025. In 2024, fiscal deficits are projected to narrow marginally. Long-term growth forecasts remain strong, and potential growth in the region is projected to remain broadly stable. Robust growth is expected to contribute to a further decline in the number of people living in poverty.*

**A. GDP growth**

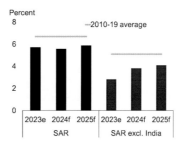

**B. Fiscal balances**

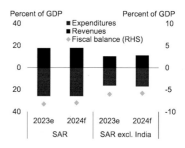

**C. Long-term GDP growth forecasts**

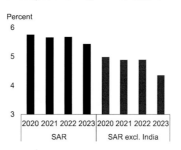

**D. Number of poor people**

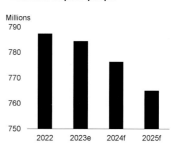

*Sources:* Consensus Economics; International Monetary Fund; World Bank.
*Note:* e = estimate; f = forecast; SAR = South Asia.
A.C. Aggregates are calculated as weighted averages using GDP weights at average 2010-19 prices and market exchange rates.
B. Aggregates are calculated as weighted averages using nominal GDP in U.S. dollars as weights.
C. Long-term GDP growth forecasts are defined as 10-year-ahead GDP growth forecasts in the long-term consensus forecasts in October of each year by Consensus Economics. The horizontal axis refers to the year of forecast surveys. Sample includes four countries (Bangladesh, India, Pakistan, and Sri Lanka).
D. The number of poor people is defined by using the lower middle-income poverty threshold of 3.65 international dollars per day in 2017 purchasing power parity. Sample includes five countries (Bangladesh, Bhutan, India, Pakistan, and Sri Lanka).

by monetary policy easing and the lagged effects of the removal of import restrictions. In Sri Lanka, the economic outlook remains uncertain, amid debt restructuring negotiations with private creditors and the implementation of structural reforms to improve growth potential.

Fiscal policies in the region are expected to be a modest drag on growth, with deficits set to narrow marginally in 2024 (figure 2.5.2.B). In India, government revenues are expected to gain from solid corporate profits, and current expenditures are likely to decrease with the conclusion of pandemic-related measures. Interest payments are projected to be large in countries with elevated debt levels, including India, Pakistan, and Sri Lanka.

Over the long run, growth prospects in the region are expected to remain strong, despite some moderation (figure 2.5.2.C). Potential growth in the region is expected to be broadly stable, partly supported by demographic dividends (Kose and Ohnsorge 2023). However, the region will see a shift in the distribution of workers toward older cohorts, underscoring a need to raise labor supply. As gender inequality is widespread in regional labor markets, there is ample opportunity to advance female labor force participation, which could, in turn, enhance the potential for economic growth.

Per capita income growth is projected to fall to 4.5 percent in 2024, from a 2010-19 average of 5.4 percent a year. Excluding India, regional per capita income growth is expected to be a modest 2.3 percent a year. Despite the slowdown, the decline in poverty in the region is expected to continue (figure 2.5.2.D).

## Risks

Risks to the baseline forecast remain tilted to the downside, with the most pressing concerns revolving around higher energy and food prices caused by an escalation of the conflict in the Middle East and adverse spillovers stemming from larger-than-expected increases in policy rates in advanced economies. Other downside risks in the region include large financing needs, extreme weather events, further weakness in China, and heightened uncertainty around elections in some countries. However, the implementation of growth-friendly policies following these elections could improve growth prospects.

An escalation of the conflict in the Middle East, as well as elevated geopolitical risks because of Russia's invasion of Ukraine, could have signifi-cant implications for commodity markets. A surge in oil prices caused by the intensification of the conflict would likely raise the cost of food and other commodities due to higher production and

transportation expenses (World Bank 2023g). SAR is vulnerable to higher prices of food and energy, as a surge in global prices would lead to a deterioration in external positions and destabilize the economy by dampening investment and overall economic activity. Food accounts for a significant share of household consumption baskets in the region (World Bank 2023n).

As poorer households spend more on food, rising food prices would disproportionately affect the poor and the vulnerable, resulting in an increase in poverty and inequality. The risk is particularly high in countries with limited fiscal buffers to mitigate adverse effects, including Nepal and Pakistan, and in countries under major security threats, including Afghanistan. In addition, an increase in food insecurity could be exacerbated by the escalation of the ongoing conflict in the Middle East (figure 2.5.3.A).

There remains uncertainty about the trajectory of global interest rates. Larger-than-anticipated increases in policy rates, particularly in advanced economies, driven by limited progress in reducing inflation, could cause further tightening of global financial conditions. Adverse spillovers from tighter financial conditions could undermine financial stability and economic activity in SAR, especially through increased borrowing costs, currency depreciations, and declines in foreign reserves. The effects could be compounded by elevated debt levels, as the financial sector is highly exposed to sovereign debt in SAR via the sovereign-bank nexus (World Bank 2023o). In addition, region-wide inflation expectations are increased among financial market participants (figure 2.5.3.B). If inflation expectations remain persistently high and are unanchored, additional domestic monetary policy tightening would be required, weighing on activity.

External and fiscal financing needs are elevated in several SAR economies, including Maldives, Pakistan, and Sri Lanka, increasing vulnerabilities to financial market disruptions (figure 2.5.3.C). In these economies, market sentiment can suddenly shift in response to financial sector stress or weakening fiscal positions. Vulnerability to such shifts is particularly high in countries with limited international reserves or fiscal buffers, or weak governance in the financial sector.

Extreme weather events also pose a major risk. In SAR, an increase in extreme weather events would contribute to an increase in poverty through multiple channels, including the deterioration of health conditions and a rise in food prices (Jafino et al. 2020). In 2023, the death toll from natural disasters remained high in SAR, mainly because of the devastating earthquake in Afghanistan and floods in India (figure 2.5.3.D). The growing frequency and severity of extreme weather events also pose risks to food production in the region.

Because SAR is relatively less open to trade, spillovers from weaker-than-projected growth in China would be smaller than in other EMDE regions. However, in countries where China is a major trading partner or key source of foreign investment, a sharper-than-expected slowdown in China could undermine growth. Additionally, in Bangladesh, slower-than-anticipated growth in its export destinations, particularly in the European Union, could pose a risk to growth prospects.

In a number of SAR economies (Bangladesh, Bhutan, India, Maldives, and Pakistan), parliamentary or national assembly elections are scheduled or planned in 2024. The heightened uncertainty around these elections could dampen activity in the private sector, including foreign investment. If combined with political or social unrest and elevated violence, this could further disrupt and weaken economic growth. In addition, particularly in countries with the weak fiscal positions, an increase in spending prior to these elections could exacerbate macro-fiscal vulnerabilities. However, the implementation of policies to reduce uncertainty and strengthen growth potential after elections could lead to an improvement in prospects.

## FIGURE 2.5.3 **SAR: Risks**

*An escalation of the conflict in the Middle East could increase food prices, worsening poverty and exacerbating food insecurity in the region. Further monetary policy tightening would be needed, if inflation expectations are unanchored, which could weigh on economic activity. Some regional economies face large financing needs and are more vulnerable to shifts in investor sentiment due to limited external or fiscal buffers. Natural disasters could continue to cause large human and economic losses.*

**A. Prevalence of hunger**

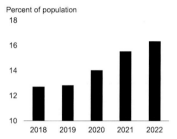

**B. Inflation expectations for 2024**

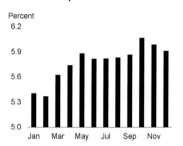

**C. External and fiscal financing needs, 2024**

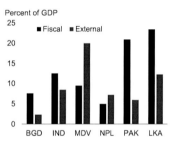

**D. Death toll from natural disasters**

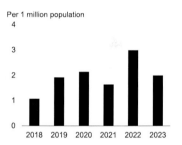

*Sources*: Consensus Economics; EM-DAT (database); Food and Agriculture Organization; International Monetary Fund; Kose et al. (2022); World Bank.
*Note*: BGD = Bangladesh; IND = India; LKA = Sri Lanka; MDV = Maldives; NPL = Nepal; PAK = Pakistan; SAR = South Asia.
A. Share of undernourishment, weighted by population. Sample includes six countries (Afghanistan, Bangladesh, India, Nepal, Pakistan, and Sri Lanka).
B. One-year-ahead inflation expectations, based on consensus forecast surveys in respective months of 2023. Aggregate is calculated using nominal GDP in U.S. dollars as weights. Sample includes four countries (Bangladesh, India, Pakistan, and Sri Lanka). Last observation is December 2023.
C. External financing needs are defined as the sum of amortization of long-term external debt, stock of short-term external debt in the previous year, and current account deficits. Fiscal financing needs are defined as a sum of short-term central government debt and fiscal deficits.
D. Total number of deaths caused by natural disasters in SAR, divided by population in millions.

## TABLE 2.5.1 South Asia forecast summary

(Real GDP growth at market prices in percent, unless indicated otherwise)

Percentage point differences from
June 2023 projections

| | 2021 | 2022 | 2023e | 2024f | 2025f | 2023e | 2024f | 2025f |
|---|---|---|---|---|---|---|---|---|
| **EMDE South Asia, GDP**[1,2] | **8.3** | **5.9** | **5.7** | **5.6** | **5.9** | **-0.2** | **0.5** | **-0.5** |
| GDP per capita (U.S. dollars) | 7.2 | 5.0 | 4.7 | 4.5 | 4.8 | -0.2 | 0.5 | -0.5 |
| EMDE South Asia excluding India, GDP | 6.1 | 3.3 | 2.8 | 3.8 | 4.1 | -0.1 | -0.5 | -0.6 |
| (Average including countries that report expenditure components in national accounts)[3] | | | | | | | | |
| EMDE South Asia, GDP[3] | 8.2 | 5.9 | 5.7 | 5.6 | 5.9 | -0.2 | 0.5 | -0.5 |
| PPP GDP | 8.2 | 5.9 | 5.7 | 5.6 | 5.9 | -0.2 | 0.5 | -0.5 |
| Private consumption | 10.6 | 6.8 | 4.3 | 4.9 | 6.0 | -0.6 | -1.1 | 1.1 |
| Public consumption | 7.5 | 2.1 | 2.2 | 5.5 | 5.4 | -0.3 | 1.4 | 2.5 |
| Fixed investment | 15.6 | 8.3 | 7.5 | 7.9 | 7.2 | 0.3 | 1.1 | 0.3 |
| Exports, GNFS[4] | 21.5 | 15.8 | 3.5 | 6.2 | 6.7 | -2.3 | -2.8 | 0.4 |
| Imports, GNFS[4] | 21.5 | 14.1 | 2.7 | 5.5 | 7.7 | -3.2 | -2.6 | 3.8 |
| Net exports, contribution to growth | -1.6 | -0.8 | 0.0 | -0.3 | -0.8 | 0.5 | 0.2 | -1.0 |
| **Memo items: GDP**[2] | | | | | | | | |
| | 2021/22 | 2022/23 | 2023/24e | 2024/25f | 2025/26f | 2023/24e | 2024/25f | 2025/26f |
| India | 9.1 | 7.2 | 6.3 | 6.4 | 6.5 | 0.0 | 0.0 | 0.0 |
| | 2020/21 | 2021/22 | 2022/23e | 2023/24f | 2024/25f | 2022/23e | 2023/24f | 2024/25f |
| Bangladesh | 6.9 | 7.1 | 6.0 | 5.6 | 5.8 | 0.8 | -0.6 | -0.6 |
| Pakistan (factor cost) | 5.8 | 6.2 | -0.2 | 1.7 | 2.4 | -0.6 | -0.3 | -0.6 |

*Source:* World Bank.
*Note:* e = estimate; f = forecast; EMDE = emerging market and developing economy; PPP = purchasing power parity. World Bank forecasts are frequently updated based on new information and changing (global) circumstances. Consequently, projections presented here may differ from those contained in other Bank documents, even if basic assessments of countries' prospects do not differ at any given moment in time.
1. GDP and expenditure components are measured in average 2010-19 prices and market exchange rates. Excludes Afghanistan because of the high degree of uncertainty.
2. National account data refer to fiscal years, while aggregates are presented in calendar year terms. The fiscal year runs from July 1 through June 30 in Bangladesh, Bhutan, and Pakistan; from July 16 through July 15 in Nepal; and April 1 through March 31 in India.
3. Subregion aggregate excludes Afghanistan, Bhutan, and Maldives, for which data limitations prevent the forecasting of GDP components.
4. GNFS refers to goods and non-factor services.

## TABLE 2.5.2 South Asia country forecasts

(Real GDP growth at market prices in percent, unless indicated otherwise)

Percentage point differences from
June 2023 projections

| | 2021 | 2022 | 2023e | 2024f | 2025f | 2023e | 2024f | 2025f |
|---|---|---|---|---|---|---|---|---|
| **Calendar year basis**[1] | | | | | | | | |
| Afghanistan[2] | -20.7 | .. | .. | .. | .. | .. | .. | .. |
| Maldives | 37.7 | 13.9 | 6.5 | 5.2 | 5.5 | -0.1 | -0.1 | -0.4 |
| Sri Lanka | 3.5 | -7.8 | -3.8 | 1.7 | 2.4 | 0.5 | 0.5 | 0.4 |
| **Fiscal year basis**[1] | 2020/21 | 2021/22 | 2022/23e | 2023/24f | 2024/25f | 2022/23e | 2023/24f | 2024/25f |
| Bangladesh | 6.9 | 7.1 | 6.0 | 5.6 | 5.8 | 0.8 | -0.6 | -0.6 |
| Bhutan | -3.3 | 4.8 | 4.6 | 4.0 | 4.6 | 0.1 | 0.9 | 0.3 |
| Nepal | 4.8 | 5.6 | 1.9 | 3.9 | 5.0 | -2.2 | -1.0 | -0.5 |
| Pakistan (factor cost) | 5.8 | 6.2 | -0.2 | 1.7 | 2.4 | -0.6 | -0.3 | -0.6 |
| | 2021/22 | 2022/23 | 2023/24e | 2024/25f | 2025/26f | 2023/24e | 2024/25f | 2025/26f |
| India | 9.1 | 7.2 | 6.3 | 6.4 | 6.5 | 0.0 | 0.0 | 0.0 |

*Source:* World Bank.
*Note:* e = estimate; f = forecast. World Bank forecasts are frequently updated based on new information and changing (global) circumstances. Consequently, projections presented here may differ from those contained in other Bank documents, even if basic assessments of countries' prospects do not significantly differ at any given moment in time.
1. Historical data are reported on a market price basis. National account data refer to fiscal years with the exception of Afghanistan, Maldives, and Sri Lanka, which report in calendar years. The fiscal year runs from July 1 through June 30 in Bangladesh, Bhutan, and Pakistan; from July 16 through July 15 in Nepal; and April 1 through March 31 in India.
2. Data for Afghanistan (beyond 2021) are excluded because of a high degree of uncertainty.

# SUB-SAHARAN AFRICA

*Growth in Sub-Saharan Africa (SSA) is projected to rebound to 3.8 percent in 2024 and 4.1 percent in 2025 as country-specific factors that have temporarily weighed on growth, including reduced fiscal support and metal-exporting economies' adjusting to lower prices, gradually ease. Nevertheless, elevated costs of living continue to limit consumption growth, and political instability has increased in parts of the region. High debt burdens and interest rates have narrowed fiscal space and heightened financing needs. Despite the projected pickup in growth, increases in per capita incomes will remain inadequate to enable the region's economies make significant progress in reducing extreme poverty. Risks to the baseline growth forecast remain tilted to the downside. They include a further rise in global or regional instability, such as the possible escalation of the conflict in the Middle East, which could drive up global energy and food prices; a sharper-than-expected global economic slowdown; increased frequency and intensity of adverse weather events; and increased defaults if attempts to reduce elevated public debt burdens were to fail. Materialization of these risks would also exacerbate poverty and limit the ability of many countries to cope with climate change.*

## Recent developments

Growth in SSA decelerated to an estimated 2.9 percent in 2023, which is 0.3 percentage point lower than projected in June. Various country-specific challenges, including higher input prices for businesses in Nigeria and an energy crisis in South Africa, contributed to a slowdown in the region's economic activity during 2023 (figure 2.6.1.A). Growth in the region's three largest economies—Nigeria, South Africa, and Angola—slowed to an average of 1.8 percent in 2023. In the region's other countries, growth softened to 3.9 percent, partly reflecting a sharp decline in metal exporters' growth alongside lower global metals prices (chapter 1). Moreover, growth in several countries was hampered by intense and protracted conflicts, most notably that in Sudan, and recent flareups of violence in Chad and Niger, contributing to an increase in violent events in the region (figure 2.6.1.B). Moreover, post-pandemic recoveries were slowed by weakening external demand and domestic policy tightening to address persistent inflation.

In *Nigeria*, the region's largest economy, growth softened to an estimated 2.9 percent in 2023. While services growth weakened markedly in 2023, partly driven by a disruptive currency demonetization policy in the first quarter of 2023, annual oil production increased after a notable decline in previous years (figure 2.6.1.C).

In *South Africa*, growth weakened further in 2023, to an estimated 0.7 percent, reflecting the effects structural constraints, especially the energy crisis and transport bottlenecks, and weaker demand in a context of weak job creation, high prices and monetary policy tightening. Power outages hit record highs in 2023, holding back manufacturing and mining production.

Growth in *Angola* weakened to an estimated 0.5 percent in 2023, with maturing oil fields contributing to markedly lower oil production, leading to revenue shortfalls and triggering public expenditure cuts.

Elsewhere in the region, activity in resource-rich countries weakened. Growth in Botswana softened owing to declines in global demand and prices for diamonds, while growth in Namibia, a mineral and metal resource-rich country, slowed owing to

---

*Note:* This section was prepared by Dominik Peschel.

## FIGURE 2.6.1 SSA: Recent developments

*Economic activity in SSA slowed in the second half of 2023, while the number of violent events picked up. Oil production declined in 2023 in Angola but increased in Nigeria after several years of decline. Inflation in the region declined in 2023 but remained at high levels.*

**A. Purchasing managers' index**

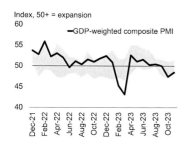

**B. Incidence of violent events**

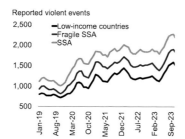

**C. Oil production**

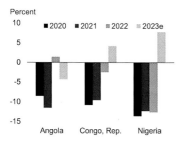

**D. Consumer price inflation in SSA**

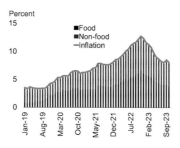

*Sources*: ACLED (database); Haver Analytics; International Energy Agency; International Monetary Fund; World Bank.
*Note*: EMDEs = emerging markets and developing economies; SSA = Sub-Saharan Africa.
A. GDP-weighted average. Sample comprises Ghana, Kenya, Mozambique, Nigeria, South Africa, Uganda, and Zambia. Shaded area indicates the interquartile range. Last observation is November 2023.
B. Three-month moving averages. Violent events include battles, explosions, riots, and violence against civilians. Last observation is November 2023.
C. Year-on-year increase. Year to November 2023 relative to corresponding period of 2022.
D. Change in prices from 12 months earlier. Unweighted averages for the sample of 20 SSA EMDEs. Non-food includes housing, utilities, fuel, transport, and other goods and services. Last observation is October 2023.

the loss of momentum in mining output growth and tighter monetary policy weighing on domestic demand. In Niger, also a metal exporter, growth slowed sharply following a coup in late July, which was followed by international economic and financial sanctions against the junta. More broadly, lower metal prices weighed on growth in many metal-exporting economies (Botswana, Democratic Republic of Congo, Liberia, Sierra Leone, Zambia).

Amid persistently large current account and fiscal deficits, and the associated need for fiscal consolidation, growth in non-resource-rich countries generally weakened in 2023, even

though most of these countries are agricultural commodity exporters benefiting from declining fertilizer prices. Despite a pickup in its agricultural sector, Ethiopia—SSA's largest agricultural commodity producer and its most populous low-income country—saw its growth slow to 5.8 percent in 2023, as a result of increased fiscal and external pressures. In contrast, growth in Tanzania and Uganda edged up in 2023, supported by higher government spending.

Headline consumer price inflation in SSA moderated in 2023 following sharp rises in global food and energy prices in 2022, yet it remained elevated (figure 2.6.1.D). The cost of living continues to be high, which has worsened the economic hardship of the poor and increased food insecurity across the region. In West Africa, a significant portion of the population—often even the majority in countries like Burkina Faso, Chad, Guinea, Mali, Niger, and Sierra Leone—has insufficient food (World Bank 2023p).

## Outlook

Growth in SSA is expected to accelerate to 3.8 percent in 2024 and firm further to 4.1 percent in 2025 as inflationary pressures fade and financial conditions ease (table 2.6.1). The projections for regional growth in 2024 and 2025 are little changed from June forecasts, but these aggregates mask a mix of upgrades and downgrades at the country level. While growth in the largest economies in SSA is expected to lag the rest of the region, non-resource-rich economies are forecasted to maintain a growth rate above the regional average. Excluding the three largest SSA economies, growth in the region is expected to accelerate from 3.9 percent in 2023 to 5 percent in 2024, and further 5.3 percent in 2025 (figure 2.6.2.A). Non-resource-rich countries are expected to continue benefiting from the moderation in fertilizer prices. Although metal exporters are expected to recover from their growth slump in 2023, downgrades are still concentrated among these economies, with continued weak growth in demand from China expected to be a drag on activity (figure 2.6.2.B).

More broadly, limited fiscal space, resulting from high debt levels and increased borrowing costs, along with tight monetary policies, are expected to weigh on investment growth across the region. Although waning inflationary pressures should allow for a gradual easing of interest rates, thereby bolstering private consumption and investment during the forecast period, the weaknesses in the region's three largest economies will limit the pickup in SSA's growth.

Growth in *Nigeria* is projected at 3.3 percent this year and 3.7 percent in 2025—up 0.3 and 0.6 percentage point, respectively, since June—as macro-fiscal reforms gradually bear fruits. The baseline forecast implies that per capita income will reach its pre-pandemic level only in 2025. Growth is expected to be driven mainly by agriculture, construction, services, and trade. Inflation should gradually ease as the effects of last year's exchange rate reforms and removal of fuel subsidies fade. These structural reforms are expected to boost fiscal revenue over the forecast period.

Growth in *South Africa* is projected to firm to a still-subdued 1.3 percent in 2024 and then edge up to 1.5 percent in 2025. While energy sector reforms are expected to improve energy availability in the medium term, increasingly prevalent infrastructure bottlenecks, exacerbated by the slow pace of structural reforms, are likely to continue to limit the country's growth potential. Domestically, fiscal pressures from underperforming revenue and the rising costs of social transfers and subsidies of state-owned enterprises, as well as rising public sector wages and debt-service payments, may require curbs on other government spending to reduce the fiscal deficit. In addition, constrained rail and port capacity are expected to weigh on export performance.

Growth in *Angola* is projected to pick up to 2.8 percent this year, half a percentage point lower than anticipated in the June *Global Economic Prospects* report, as investment grows more slowly than expected. Non-oil economic activity will be the main driver of growth, while the oil and gas industry is expected to grow by a mere 1 percent a year on account of field depletion and lack of investment. Projected growth is broadly in line with Angola's population growth, implying that

## FIGURE 2.6.2 SSA: Outlook

*Growth in SSA is expected to pick up in 2024-25, approaching its average rate of the past two decades. Growth in the largest economies in SSA is expected to lag that in the rest of the region, while it is forecast to remain above the regional average in non-resource-rich countries. Forecast downgrades are concentrated in metal-exporting countries amid weak demand from China. Per capita incomes in SSA in 2025 are expected to be barely above those of 2019, and they will be notably lower in the largest economies. The current account balances in many industrial-commodity-exporting countries are expected to deteriorate further in 2024-25.*

**A. Growth in SSA**

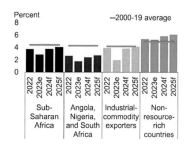

**B. Growth forecast revisions since June 2023**

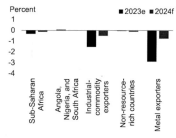

**C. Income per capita**

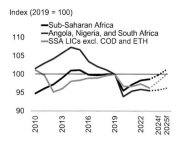

**D. Current account balance**

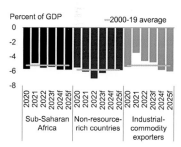

*Sources:* International Monetary Fund; World Bank.
*Note:* e = estimates; f = forecasts. COD = Democratic Republic of Congo; ETH = Ethiopia; LICs = low-income countries; SSA = Sub-Saharan Africa.
A. Aggregate growth rates calculated using constant GDP weights at average 2010-19 prices and market exchange rates.
B. Revisions relative to forecast published in the June 2023 edition of the *Global Economic Prospects* report.
C. Panel reflects the evolution of real per capita GDP, rebased to 2019 = 100.
D. Simple averages of country groupings. Sample includes 45 SSA countries.
A.B.D. Industrial-commodity exporters excludes Angola, Nigeria, and South Africa. Non-resource-rich countries represent agricultural commodity-exporting and commodity-importing countries.

average per capita incomes will be broadly unchanged at the end of 2025 from current levels, which are nearly 13 percent lower than before the pandemic. Inflationary pressures are expected to ease in 2024, declining toward the central bank's target of 7 percent.

Growth in SSA's resource-rich countries is expected to pick up in 2024 and 2025. Industrial commodity exporters in the region, excluding the three largest economies, are forecast to grow by

3.8 percent in 2024 and 4.1 percent in 2025, up from 2.0 percent in 2023. This uptick is due to the diminishing impact of the sharp fall in commodity prices from their 2022 peak. Growth in the non-mining sectors, especially services, is expected to pick up as inflation gradually declines (Botswana, Cameroon, Democratic Republic of Congo).

Growth in non-resource-rich countries is projected to strengthen to 5.4 percent in 2024 and 5.7 percent in 2025. Increasing investment is expected to drive growth in Kenya and Uganda, partly owing to improved business confidence. Uganda will also benefit from infrastructure investment ahead of new oil production in 2025, and investment in Kenya should be boosted by increased credit to the private sector as the government reduces domestic borrowing. In Tanzania, reforms to improve the business climate are expected to lift growth.

Per capita income in SSA, on average, is projected to grow by a meager 1.2 percent this year and 1.5 percent in 2025 (figure 2.6.2.C). However, per capita income is expected to fall in both years in Chad, Equatorial Guinea, and Sudan, with particularly sharp declines in Sudan. Additionally, it is anticipated to stagnate in 2025 after shrinking in 2024 in Angola and the Central African Republic. By 2025, per capita gross domestic product (GDP) in about 30 percent of the region's economies, with a total population of more than 250 million, will not have fully recovered to their pre-pandemic levels. This implies that these economies will have lost several years in advancing per capita income.

External financing needs across the region have increased since the onset of the pandemic, partly reflecting higher import bills and debt-service costs. Consequently, current account deficits remain elevated in many economies. Higher deficits for industrial-commodity-exporting countries outweigh improvements for non-resource-rich economies (figure 2.6.2.D). The gross financing needs of the median SSA country in the Low-Income Country Debt Sustainability Framework have more than quadrupled since 2012, rising from 2.4 percent to 11 percent of GDP in 2022 (World Bank 2023q).

Meanwhile access to external finance has become more challenging with the tightening of global financial conditions, especially for countries with reduced donor support or shrinking foreign exchange reserves. The need to boost fiscal revenues, and, where adequate, implement fiscal consolidation has become even more pressing throughout SSA, especially in highly indebted countries facing risks of debt distress.

## Risks

Risks to the baseline growth forecast are tilted to the downside. They include a rise in political instability and violence, such as the intensification of the conflict in the Middle East, disruptions to global or local trade and production, increased frequency and intensity of adverse weather events, a sharper-than-expected global economic slowdown, and higher risk of government defaults, especially if debt restructuring attempts by highly indebted countries prove unsuccessful.

An escalation of the conflict in the Middle East could acerbate the situation in SSA in terms of food insecurity (figure 2.6.3.A; World Bank 2023g). A conflict-induced sustained oil price spike would not only raise food prices by increasing production and transportation costs but could also disrupt supply chains, leading to less affordable food and an uptick in malnutrition rates in the region.

Although global food and energy prices have retreated from their peaks in 2022, disruptions to global or local trade and production could reignite consumer price inflation, especially food price inflation, throughout the region. Such disruptions, especially in mining and agriculture, could be triggered by extreme weather events linked partly to climate change. The region is highly vulnerable to such events. For instance, the current El Niño weather pattern could bring above-average rainfall and flooding to East Africa, and drought to Southern Africa (figure 2.6.3.B; WMO/WHO 2023). Subsistence agriculture is the main source of livelihood and employment for many poor and vulnerable people in SSA. An increase in the frequency and severity of droughts, floods, and tropical cyclones would aggravate poverty across

SSA, while increasing food insecurity in many countries. Over the period 1991-2021, SSA has been the most affected region in terms of lost value added in agriculture due to extreme events affecting crops and livestock (FAO 2023). In the long term, climate change-induced rises in average temperatures could adversely affect crop yields across the region, reducing food supplies as well as exports.

Global growth could weaken more than expected, perhaps owing to tighter financing conditions or further deterioration in China's growth (chapter 1). In such a scenario, the prices of many of SSA's export commodities, especially metals and minerals, could weaken. Countries that rely heavily on China as an export destination for these commodities would be hit especially hard by slower-than-projected Chinese growth.

Public-debt-service costs have risen sharply in many SSA economies since the pandemic (figure 2.6.3.C). This has increased the need for debt reduction, particularly in highly indebted countries. If global or domestic inflation turns out to be higher than expected, interest rates could remain elevated for a longer duration than assumed in the baseline scenario, leading to tighter financial conditions globally and in SSA. This could limit access to financial markets and increase risks of financial distress and government debt defaults (figure 2.6.3.D).

Many SSA economies suffer from fragility stemming from persistent poverty, as well as festering violence and conflict, including the Democratic Republic of Congo, Ethiopia, Somalia, South Sudan, and Sudan. Peacemaking efforts in the Democratic Republic of Congo and Ethiopia have borne fruit, but recent coups d'état—in Niger and Gabon in 2023; Burkina Faso in 2022; and Chad, Guinea, Mali, and Sudan in 2021—have resulted in an escalation of political instability in much of the region. Further increases in violent conflicts could push growth below the baseline and result in extended humanitarian crises in many of SSA's most economically vulnerable countries. These nations are already frequently facing high levels of debt (or even debt distress), heavy dependence on food and fuel imports, and elevated inflation.

**FIGURE 2.6.3 SSA: Risks**

*Food insecurity in the region remains elevated and could worsen if the conflict in the Middle East intensifies. The share of the population affected by adverse weather events has increased in recent years. Interest payments on public debt are expected to rise as a result of the increase in global interest rates, while the number of countries in debt distress or facing high risk of debt distress will likely remain elevated.*

**A. Food insecurity in SSA**

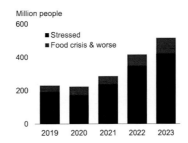

**B. Share of population affected by adverse weather events**

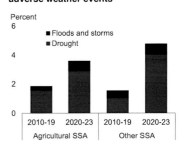

**C. Public debt and interest payments in SSA**

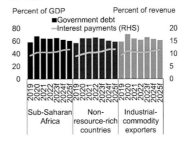

**D. Risk of debt distress in SSA**

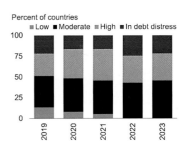

*Sources*: EM-DAT (database); FSIN and GNAFC (2023); International Monetary Fund (IMF); World Bank.
*Note*: SSA = Sub-Saharan Africa.
A. Number of people facing food security stress or food security crisis and worse. Sample includes up to 41 countries in Sub-Saharan Africa. United Nations World Food Programme estimates for 2023.
B. Bars indicate percent of population affected. "Other SSA" refers to non-agriculture exporting countries. Last observation is December 5, 2023.
C. Simple averages of country groupings. Sample includes 45 SSA countries. Industrial-commodity exporters excludes Angola, Nigeria, and South Africa. Non-resource-rich countries represent agricultural commodity-exporting and commodity-importing countries.
D. Panel shows the share of SSA countries eligible to access the IMF's concessional lending facilities by level of debt distress. The sample size varies between 36 and 37 countries. Eritrea is excluded because of data restrictions.

## TABLE 2.6.1 Sub-Saharan Africa forecast summary

(Real GDP growth at market prices in percent, unless indicated otherwise)

Percentage point differences from
June 2023 projections

| | 2021 | 2022 | 2023e | 2024f | 2025f | 2023e | 2024f | 2025f |
|---|---|---|---|---|---|---|---|---|
| **EMDE SSA, GDP** [1] | **4.4** | **3.7** | **2.9** | **3.8** | **4.1** | **-0.3** | **-0.1** | **0.1** |
| GDP per capita (U.S. dollars) | 1.8 | 1.2 | 0.3 | 1.2 | 1.5 | -0.3 | -0.1 | 0.0 |
| (Average including countries that report expenditure components in national accounts) [2] | | | | | | | | |
| EMDE SSA, GDP [2,3] | 4.7 | 3.9 | 2.8 | 3.9 | 4.2 | -0.5 | -0.3 | -0.1 |
| PPP GDP | 4.6 | 3.9 | 2.7 | 4.0 | 4.3 | -0.7 | -0.3 | -0.1 |
| Private consumption | 4.8 | 3.6 | 2.3 | 3.7 | 3.8 | -0.9 | 0.1 | 0.1 |
| Public consumption | 2.7 | 2.8 | 1.6 | 2.0 | 2.2 | 0.6 | -1.3 | -0.7 |
| Fixed investment | 8.0 | 6.7 | 5.6 | 6.2 | 6.3 | -1.0 | -0.1 | -0.8 |
| Exports, GNFS [4] | 6.8 | 8.0 | 4.2 | 4.5 | 5.2 | -2.1 | -1.9 | -0.8 |
| Imports, GNFS [4] | 10.9 | 10.5 | 4.9 | 4.7 | 4.8 | -1.6 | -1.4 | -1.4 |
| Net exports, contribution to growth | -1.2 | -0.9 | -0.3 | -0.2 | 0.0 | 0.2 | 0.1 | 0.5 |
| **Memo items: GDP** | | | | | | | | |
| Eastern and Southern Africa | 4.7 | 3.7 | 2.5 | 3.6 | 3.8 | -0.6 | -0.3 | -0.2 |
| Western and Central Africa | 4.0 | 3.8 | 3.3 | 4.0 | 4.3 | 0.0 | 0.1 | 0.3 |
| SSA excluding Nigeria, South Africa, and Angola | 4.9 | 4.8 | 3.9 | 5.0 | 5.3 | -0.7 | -0.3 | -0.1 |
| Oil exporters [5] | 3.2 | 3.2 | 2.6 | 3.1 | 3.6 | 0.0 | 0.1 | 0.3 |
| CFA countries [6] | 4.3 | 4.7 | 4.2 | 5.3 | 5.3 | -0.3 | -0.2 | 0.2 |
| CEMAC [7] | 1.7 | 3.0 | 2.7 | 2.6 | 2.8 | 0.0 | -0.2 | -0.2 |
| WAEMU [8] | 6.0 | 5.7 | 5.0 | 6.9 | 6.6 | -0.5 | -0.1 | 0.4 |
| SSA3 | 3.9 | 2.7 | 1.8 | 2.4 | 2.8 | 0.1 | 0.0 | 0.3 |
| Nigeria | 3.6 | 3.3 | 2.9 | 3.3 | 3.7 | 0.1 | 0.3 | 0.6 |
| South Africa | 4.7 | 1.9 | 0.7 | 1.3 | 1.5 | 0.4 | -0.2 | -0.1 |
| Angola | 1.2 | 3.0 | 0.5 | 2.8 | 3.1 | -2.1 | -0.5 | 0.0 |

*Source*: World Bank.

*Note*: e = estimate; f = forecast; PPP = purchasing power parity; EMDE = emerging market and developing economy. World Bank forecasts are frequently updated based on new information and changing (global) circumstances. Consequently, projections presented here may differ from those contained in other Bank documents, even if basic assessments of countries' prospects do not differ at any given moment in time.

1. GDP and expenditure components are measured in average 2010-19 prices and market exchange rates.

2. Subregion aggregate excludes the Central African Republic, Eritrea, Guinea, Nigeria, São Tomé and Príncipe, Somalia, and South Sudan, for which data limitations prevent the forecasting of GDP components.

3. Subregion growth rates may differ from the most recent edition of Africa's Pulse (https://www.worldbank.org/africas-pulse) because of data revisions.

4. Exports and imports of goods and nonfactor services (GNFS).

5. Includes Angola, Cameroon, Chad, the Republic of Congo, Equatorial Guinea, Gabon, Ghana, Nigeria, and South Sudan.

6. The Financial Community of Africa (CFA) franc zone consists of 14 countries in Sub-Saharan Africa, each affiliated with one of two monetary unions.

7. The Central African Economic and Monetary Union (CEMAC) comprises Cameroon, the Central African Republic, Chad, the Republic of Congo, Equatorial Guinea, and Gabon.

8. The West African Economic and Monetary Union (WAEMU) comprises Benin, Burkina Faso, Côte d'Ivoire, Guinea-Bissau, Mali, Niger, Senegal, and Togo.

## TABLE 2.6.2 Sub-Saharan Africa country forecasts[1]

(Real GDP growth at market prices in percent, unless indicated otherwise)

Percentage point differences from June 2023 projections

| | 2021 | 2022 | 2023e | 2024f | 2025f | 2023e | 2024f | 2025f |
|---|---|---|---|---|---|---|---|---|
| Angola | 1.2 | 3.0 | 0.5 | 2.8 | 3.1 | -2.1 | -0.5 | 0.0 |
| Benin | 7.2 | 6.3 | 5.8 | 6.0 | 6.0 | -0.2 | 0.1 | -0.1 |
| Botswana | 11.8 | 5.8 | 3.8 | 4.1 | 4.3 | -0.2 | 0.1 | 0.3 |
| Burkina Faso | 6.9 | 1.5 | 4.3 | 4.8 | 5.1 | 0.0 | 0.0 | 0.0 |
| Burundi | 3.1 | 1.8 | 2.9 | 4.2 | 4.5 | -0.1 | 0.2 | 0.3 |
| Central African Republic | 1.0 | 0.5 | 1.3 | 1.6 | 3.1 | -1.7 | -2.2 | -0.7 |
| Cabo Verde | 5.6 | 17.1 | 4.5 | 4.7 | 4.7 | -0.3 | -0.7 | -0.6 |
| Cameroon | 3.6 | 3.8 | 4.0 | 4.2 | 4.5 | 0.1 | 0.0 | 0.0 |
| Chad | -1.2 | 2.2 | 3.0 | 2.8 | 2.7 | -0.2 | -0.6 | -0.4 |
| Comoros | 2.1 | 2.6 | 3.0 | 3.5 | 4.0 | 0.2 | 0.6 | 0.4 |
| Congo, Dem. Rep. | 6.2 | 8.9 | 6.8 | 6.5 | 6.2 | -0.9 | -1.1 | -1.3 |
| Congo, Rep. | 1.0 | 1.5 | 3.2 | 4.1 | 3.0 | -0.3 | -0.2 | 0.2 |
| Côte d'Ivoire | 7.0 | 6.7 | 6.3 | 6.5 | 6.5 | 0.1 | 0.0 | 0.0 |
| Equatorial Guinea | -0.9 | 3.1 | -2.5 | -6.1 | -3.9 | 1.2 | -0.1 | -0.8 |
| Eritrea | 2.9 | 2.5 | 2.6 | 3.2 | 3.3 | -0.1 | 0.3 | 0.5 |
| Eswatini | 10.7 | 0.5 | 3.6 | 2.9 | 2.8 | 0.6 | 0.0 | 0.1 |
| Ethiopia[2] | 6.3 | 6.4 | 5.8 | 6.4 | 7.0 | -0.2 | -0.2 | 0.0 |
| Gabon | 1.5 | 3.0 | 2.7 | 3.0 | 2.8 | -0.4 | 0.0 | -0.2 |
| Gambia, The | 4.3 | 4.3 | 4.8 | 5.3 | 5.5 | -0.2 | -0.2 | -0.3 |
| Ghana | 5.1 | 3.1 | 2.3 | 2.8 | 4.4 | 0.7 | -0.1 | -0.4 |
| Guinea | 4.3 | 4.7 | 5.1 | 5.8 | 6.2 | -0.5 | 0.0 | 0.6 |
| Guinea-Bissau | 6.4 | 3.5 | 2.8 | 5.6 | 4.5 | -1.7 | 1.1 | 0.0 |
| Kenya | 7.6 | 4.8 | 5.0 | 5.2 | 5.3 | 0.0 | 0.0 | 0.0 |
| Lesotho | 1.6 | 1.8 | 2.2 | 2.5 | 2.1 | -0.4 | -0.6 | -1.2 |
| Liberia | 5.0 | 4.8 | 4.5 | 5.4 | 6.2 | 0.2 | -0.1 | 0.6 |
| Madagascar | 5.7 | 3.8 | 4.0 | 4.8 | 4.7 | -0.2 | 0.0 | -0.4 |
| Malawi | 2.8 | 0.9 | 1.6 | 2.8 | 3.3 | 0.2 | 0.4 | 0.3 |
| Mali | 3.1 | 3.7 | 4.0 | 4.0 | 5.0 | 0.0 | 0.0 | 0.0 |
| Mauritania | 0.7 | 6.4 | 4.8 | 5.1 | 5.5 | 0.3 | -0.5 | -1.3 |
| Mauritius | 3.4 | 8.8 | 5.0 | 4.6 | 3.6 | 0.3 | 0.5 | 0.0 |
| Mozambique | 2.3 | 4.2 | 6.0 | 5.0 | 5.0 | 1.0 | -3.3 | -0.3 |
| Namibia | 3.5 | 4.6 | 2.8 | 2.9 | 3.1 | 0.4 | 1.2 | 1.0 |
| Niger | 1.4 | 11.5 | 2.3 | 12.8 | 7.4 | -4.6 | 0.3 | -1.7 |
| Nigeria | 3.6 | 3.3 | 2.9 | 3.3 | 3.7 | 0.1 | 0.3 | 0.6 |
| Rwanda | 10.9 | 8.2 | 6.9 | 7.5 | 7.8 | 0.7 | 0.0 | 0.3 |
| São Tomé and Príncipe | 1.9 | 0.1 | 0.5 | 2.5 | 3.3 | -1.6 | -0.9 | -0.4 |
| Senegal | 6.5 | 4.2 | 4.1 | 8.8 | 9.3 | -0.6 | -1.1 | 4.1 |
| Seychelles | 5.4 | 9.0 | 4.3 | 4.1 | 3.9 | 0.5 | 1.1 | 0.8 |
| Sierra Leone | 4.1 | 3.5 | 3.1 | 3.7 | 4.3 | -0.3 | 0.0 | -0.1 |
| South Africa | 4.7 | 1.9 | 0.7 | 1.3 | 1.5 | 0.4 | -0.2 | -0.1 |
| Sudan | -1.9 | -1.0 | -12.0 | -0.6 | 0.2 | -12.4 | -2.1 | -1.8 |
| South Sudan[2] | -5.1 | -2.3 | -0.4 | 2.3 | 2.4 | 0.0 | 0.0 | 0.0 |
| Tanzania | 4.3 | 4.6 | 5.1 | 5.5 | 6.1 | 0.0 | -0.1 | -0.1 |
| Togo | 6.0 | 5.8 | 5.2 | 5.2 | 5.8 | 0.3 | -0.1 | 0.3 |
| Uganda[2] | 3.4 | 4.7 | 5.3 | 6.0 | 6.6 | -0.4 | -0.2 | -0.1 |
| Zambia | 4.6 | 4.7 | 2.7 | 4.6 | 4.8 | -1.5 | -0.1 | 0.0 |
| Zimbabwe | 8.5 | 6.5 | 4.5 | 3.5 | 3.5 | 1.6 | 0.1 | 0.1 |

*Source*: World Bank.

*Note*: e = estimate; f = forecast. World Bank forecasts are frequently updated based on new information and changing (global) circumstances. Consequently, projections presented here may differ from those contained in other Bank documents, even if basic assessments of countries' prospects do not significantly differ at any given moment in time.

1. Data are based on GDP measured in average 2010-19 prices and market exchange rates.
2. Fiscal year-based numbers.

# References

ACLED (Armed Conflict Location & Event Data Project) database. Accessed on December 18, 2023. https://acleddata.com/data-export-tool

Arroyo Marioli, F., A. Fatás, and G. Vasishtha. 2023. "Fiscal Policy Volatility and Growth in Emerging Markets and Developing Economies." Policy Research Working Paper 10409, World Bank, Washington, DC.

Arteta, C., S. Kamin, and F. U. Ruch. 2022. "How Do Rising U.S. Interest Rates Affect Emerging and Developing Economies? It Depends." Policy Research Working Paper 10258, World Bank, Washington, DC.

Cai, W., G. Wang, A. Santoso, M. J. McPhaden, L. Wu, F. Jin, A. Timmermann, et al. 2015. "Increased Frequency of Extreme La Niña Events under Greenhouse Warming." *Nature Climate Change* 5 (2): 132-37.

Davies, S., T. Pettersson, and M. Öberg. 2023. "Organized Violence 1989-2022, and the Return of Conflict between States." *Journal of Peace Research* 60 (4): 691-708.

Dieppe, A., S. Kilic Celic, and C. Okou. 2020. "Implications of Major Adverse Events on Productivity." Policy Research Working Paper 9411, World Bank, Washington, DC.

EM-DAT (The International Disaster Database) database. Centre for Research on the Epidemiology of Disasters (CRED), UCLouvain, Brussels. Accessed December 18, 2023. https://www.emdat.be

FAO (Food and Agriculture Organization of the United Nations). 2023. *The Impact of Disasters on Agriculture and Food Security 2023—Avoiding and Reducing Losses through Investment in Resilience*. Rome: Food and Agriculture Organization of the United Nations.

Feenstra, R. C., R. Inklaar, and M. P. Timmer. 2015. "The Next Generation of the Penn World Table." *American Economic Review* 105 (10): 3150-82.

Gatti, R., D. Lederman, N. Elmallakh, J. Torres, J. Silva, R. Lotfi, and I. Suvanov. 2023. *Balancing Act: Jobs and Wages in the Middle East and North Africa When Crises Hit*. Middle East and North Africa Economic Update. October. Washington, DC: World Bank.

Gatti, R., D. Lederman, A. M. Islam, C. A. Wood, R. Y. Fan, R. Lotfi, M. E. Mousa, and H. Nguyen. 2022. *Reality Check: Forecasting Growth in the Middle East and North Africa in Times of Uncertainty*. Middle East and North Africa Economic Update. April. Washington, DC: World Bank.

Grekou, C., V. Mignon, and L. Ragot. 2023. "Russie: Sanctions Occidentales et échappatoires Orientales." La Lettre du CEPII N°439, Centre d'Etudes Prospectives et d'Informations Internationales, Paris.

Jafino, B. A., B. Walsh, J. Rozenberg, and S. Hallegatte. 2020. "Revised Estimates of the Impact of Climate Change on Extreme Poverty by 2030." Policy Research Working Paper 9417, World Bank, Washington, DC.

Kose, M. A., S. Kurlat, F. Ohnsorge, and N. Sugawara. 2022. "A Cross-Country Database of Fiscal Space." *Journal of International Money and Finance* 128 (November): 102682.

Kose, M. A., and F. Ohnsorge, eds. 2023. *Falling Long-Term Growth Prospects: Trends, Expectations, and Policies*. Washington, DC: World Bank.

Maloney, W., D. Riera-Crichton, E. I. Ianchovichina, G. Vuletin, G. Beylis, and G. Vuletin. 2023. *The Promise of Integration: Opportunities in a Changing Global Economy*. April. Washington, DC: World Bank.

OECD (Organisation for Economic Co-operation and Development). 2018. "Climate-Resilient Infrastructure." OECD Environment Policy Paper 14, Organisation for Economic Co-operation and Development, Paris.

Pfeiffer, P., J. Varga, and J. in 't Veld. 2023. "Unleashing Potential: Model-Based Reform Benchmarking for EU Member States." Luxembourg, European Commission.

Pigato, M. A., ed. 2019. *Fiscal Policies for Development and Climate Action*. Washington, DC: World Bank.

Schady, N., A. Holla, S. Sabarwal, J. Silva, and A. Y. Chand. 2023. *Collapse and Recovery: How the COVID-19 Pandemic Eroded Human Capital and What to Do about It*. Washington, DC: World Bank.

Wang, B., X. Luo, Y. Yang, W. Sun, M. A. Cane, W. Cai, S. Yeh, and J. Liu. 2019. "Historical Change of El Niño Properties Sheds Light on Future Changes of Extreme El Niño." *Proceedings of the National Academy of Sciences* 116 (45): 22512-17.

WHO (World Health Organization) and WMO (World Meteorological Organization). 2023. "Health and the El Niño-Southern Oscillation (ENSO)." Brief, WHO-WMO Climate and Health Office, Geneva.

World Bank. Forthcoming. "Bulgaria Public Finance Review." World Bank, Washington, DC.

World Bank. 2022a. *Catching Up: Inclusive Recovery & Growth for Lagging States.* Malaysia Economic Monitor. June. Washington, DC: World Bank.

World Bank. 2022b. *China Country Climate and Development Report.* Washington, DC: World Bank.

World Bank. 2023a. *Services for Development.* East Asia and Pacific Economic Update. October. Washington, DC: World Bank.

World Bank. 2023b. *Sustaining Growth through the Recovery and Beyond.* China Economic Update. June. Washington, DC: World Bank.

World Bank. 2023c. "Leveraging Diaspora Finances for Private Capital Mobilization." Migration and Development Brief 39, World Bank, Washington, DC.

World Bank. 2023d. *Sluggish Growth, Rising Risks.* Europe and Central Asia Update. October. Washington, DC: World Bank.

World Bank. 2023e. *Toward Sustainable Growth.* Western Balkans Regular Economic Report 24. October. Washington, DC: World Bank.

World Bank. 2023f. *Women, Business and the Law 2023.* September. Washington, DC: World Bank.

World Bank. 2023g. *Commodity Markets Outlook: Under the Shadow of Geopolitical Risks.* October. Washington, DC: World Bank.

World Bank. 2023h. *The Business of the State.* November. Washington, DC: World Bank.

World Bank. 2023i. *Toward a Framework for the Sustainable Heating Transition in Europe and Central Asia.* September. Washington, DC: World Bank.

World Bank. 2023j. "Bangladesh Development Update: New Frontiers in Poverty Reduction." October. World Bank, Washington, DC.

World Bank. 2023k. "Nepal Development Update: Restoring Export Competitiveness." October. World Bank, Washington, DC.

World Bank. 2023l. "Afghanistan Development Update: Uncertainty after Fleeting Stability." October. World Bank, Washington, DC.

World Bank. 2023m. "India Development Update." October. World Bank, Washington, DC.

World Bank. 2023n. *South Asia Development Update: Toward Faster, Cleaner Growth.* October. Washington, DC: World Bank.

World Bank. 2023o. *Expanding Opportunities: Toward Inclusive Growth.* South Asia Economic Focus. April. Washington, DC: World Bank.

World Bank 2023p. "Food Security Update." October. Global Market Outlook, World Bank, Washington, DC.

World Bank. 2023q. *Africa's Pulse: Delivering Growth to People through Better Jobs.* October. Washington, DC: World Bank.

World Bank and DRC (Development Research Center of the State Council, the People's Republic of China). 2022. *Four Decades of Poverty Reduction in China: Drivers, Insights for the World, and the Way Ahead.* Washington, DC: World Bank.

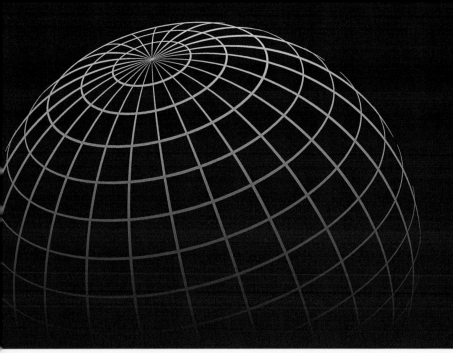

# CHAPTER 3

# THE MAGIC OF INVESTMENT ACCELERATIONS

*Investment powers economic growth, helps drive down poverty, and will be indispensable for tackling climate change and achieving other key development goals in emerging market and developing economies (EMDEs). Without further policy action, investment growth in these economies is likely to remain tepid for the remainder of this decade. But it can be boosted. This chapter offers the first comprehensive analysis of investment accelerations—periods in which there is a sustained increase in investment growth to a relatively rapid rate—in EMDEs. During these episodes over the past seven decades, investment growth typically jumped to more than 10 percent per year, which is more than three times the growth rate in other (non-acceleration) years. Countries that had investment accelerations often reaped an economic windfall: output growth increased by about 2 percentage points and productivity growth increased by 1.3 percentage points per year. Other benefits also materialized in the majority of such episodes: inflation fell, fiscal and external balances improved, and the national poverty rate declined. Most accelerations followed, or were accompanied by, policy shifts intended to improve macroeconomic stability, structural reforms, or both. These policy actions were particularly conducive to sparking investment accelerations when combined with well-functioning institutions. A benign external environment also played a crucial role in catalyzing investment accelerations in many cases.*

# Introduction

Over the past two decades, capital accumulation is estimated to have accounted for more than half of potential output growth in emerging market and developing economies (EMDEs), highlighting the critical role of investment in driving economic growth (figure 3.1).[1] Yet, investment growth in these economies is going through a prolonged, broad-based slowdown since the global financial crisis that began in 2008. Investment growth in EMDEs (excluding China) averaged about 6 percent per year in the 2000s, before slowing to an annual average of 3 percent in the 2010s (World Bank 2023a). During the 2020 global recession triggered by the COVID-19 pandemic, investment contracted much more deeply than it did during the 2009 global recession. Despite a cyclical rebound in 2021, investment growth in EMDEs will likely be subdued over the medium term.

Prolonged weak investment growth dampens potential output growth and makes it more difficult to achieve climate-related and other development goals. It also exacerbates the challenges associated with sizeable unmet investment needs in many EMDEs: substantial investment is required to fill infrastructure gaps, enable adaptation to climate change, facilitate the energy transition away from fossil fuels, accelerate poverty reduction, and advance shared prosperity (G20-IEG 2023; Rozenberg and Fay 2019; Stamm and Vorisek 2023; UNEP 2023).[2]

Although there is extensive discussion about the urgent need to raise investment growth, there is insufficient research on past investment accelerations—defined as periods in which there is a sustained increase in investment growth to a relatively rapid rate. A fuller understanding of these accelerations could provide useful lessons for achieving long-term growth and development goals in EMDEs.

This chapter examines the drivers of investment accelerations and associated economic outcomes by addressing the following questions:

---

*Note*: This chapter was prepared by Kersten Stamm and Shu Yu. It is based on and extends Stamm, Yu, and de Haan (2024).

[1] This estimate is derived by applying the standard growth accounting framework to decompose output growth into estimated contributions of the growth in factor inputs and the growth of total factor productivity. See Kose and Ohnsorge (2023).

[2] To reach the climate targets of the Paris Agreement alone, there is a global need of more than US$4 trillion in annual investment through 2030 (IRENA 2023). EMDEs are projected to require annual investment equivalent to 1 to 8 percent of GDP through 2030 to reduce greenhouse gas emissions by 70 percent by 2050 and meet other development goals (World Bank 2022a). The costs of adaptation are estimated to be in a plausible range of US$215 billion-US$387 billion per year through 2030 (UNEP 2023). Even if these needs are fulfilled, there would be significant investment gaps for delivering the nationally determined contributions of the Paris Climate Agreement (IEA and IFC 2023; McCollum et al. 2018). These gaps imply that large amounts of private funding must be mobilized to complement the limited public sources (G20 and IEG 2023; Zattler 2023).

## FIGURE 3.1 Evolution of investment growth

*Capital accumulation is a key driver of potential output growth. Since the global financial crisis, most EMDEs have experienced prolonged, broad-based investment growth slowdowns that have exacerbated their unmet investment gaps. They especially need a resilient and low-carbon pathway of growth.*

**A. Contributions to average annual potential output growth**

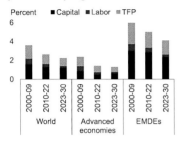

**B. Average annual investment growth, by country group**

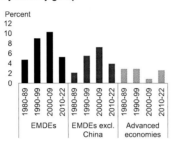

**C. Average annual investment growth, by income level**

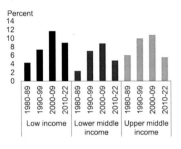

**D. Investment growth forecasts**

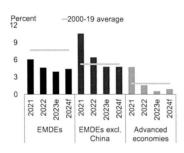

**E. Investment needs for a resilient and low-carbon pathway, 2022-30**

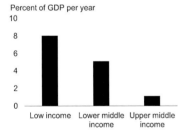

**F. The climate adaptation finance gap in developing countries**

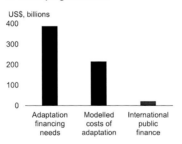

*Sources:* Haver Analytics; Feenstra, Inklaar, and Timmer (2015); Kose and Ohnsorge (2023); United Nations Environment Programme (2023); WDI (database); World Bank (2022a); World Bank.

*Note:* e = estimate; f = forecast. "Investment" refers to gross fixed capital formation. EMDEs = emerging market and developing economies.

A. Advanced economy and EMDE averages are calculated using GDP weights at average 2010-19 prices and market exchange rates. Sample includes 30 advanced economies and 53 EMDEs. See Kose and Ohnsorge (2023) for estimation details.

B.C. Investment growth averages are calculated using GDP weights at average 2010-19 prices and market exchange rates. Sample includes up to 35 advanced economies and 69 EMDEs.

D. Investment growth is calculated with countries' real annual investment in constant U.S. dollars as weights. Sample includes 35 advanced economies and 68 EMDEs.

E. Bars show estimates of the annual investment needs to build resilience to climate change and put countries on track to reduce emissions by 70 percent by 2050. Depending on data availability, estimates include investment needs related to transport, energy, water, urban adaptations, industry, and landscape.

F. Comparison of adaptation financing needs, modelled costs and actual international public adaptation finance flows (red) in developing countries. Values for needs and flows are for this decade through 2030, while international public finance flows are for 2021. Domestic and private finance flows are excluded.

- What are the main features of investment accelerations?

- What are the key macroeconomic and development outcomes associated with investment accelerations?

- What policy interventions are most likely to spark investment accelerations?

## Contributions

The chapter makes the following contributions to the literature:

**Exclusive focus on investment accelerations.** This is the first study that examines periods characterized by a sustained increase in investment growth to a relatively rapid rate.[3] The earlier literature often examined the drivers of investment growth in the context of standard cross-country growth regressions. The event-study approach employed here demonstrates a stronger link between investment accelerations on the one hand and initial conditions and policy interventions on the other.[4]

**Detailed analysis of investment accelerations.** The chapter presents a comprehensive analysis of the evolution of investment, output, and other key macroeconomic and financial variables during investment accelerations. It examines 104 economies—35 advanced economies and 69 EMDEs—from 1950 to 2022. This analysis documents the macroeconomic correlates of investment accelerations, such as capital accumulation, total factor productivity (TFP) growth, and employment growth, which contribute to output growth. It also studies how

---

[3] Macroeconomic studies of cross-country investment include Anand and Tulin (2014); Caselli, Pagano, and Schivardi (2003); and Qureshi, Diaz-Sanchez, and Varoudakis (2015). Kose et al. (2017) and World Bank (2019, 2023a) also examine investment trends and correlates in a large sample of EMDEs.

[4] The chapter builds upon studies identifying accelerations in real GDP per capita. Hausmann, Pritchett, and Rodrik (2005) and Jong-A-Pin and de Haan (2011) identify output accelerations and show that these are related to trade, investment, and positive regime changes. Jones and Olken (2008) document that most countries experience output accelerations and slowdowns. Berg, Ostry, and Zettelmeyer (2012) find that adverse external shocks and macroeconomic volatility reduce the duration of output accelerations while strong institutions are positively correlated with longer-lasting accelerations.

some key macroeconomic and financial indicators—such as fiscal balances, trade, exchange rates, and credit—evolve around these episodes. Finally, this study analyzes the association between investment accelerations and key development outcomes, such as changes in poverty and inequality.

**In-depth study of policies.** The chapter draws both on empirical models and country case studies (box 3.1) to analyze the linkages between policies and investment accelerations. The empirical models assess the roles played by various initial conditions and policy interventions in triggering an investment acceleration. They also consider the interplay between policies and institutional environments in accelerating investment. The case studies zoom in on the experiences of selected countries to present more detailed accounts of the roles of policies, initial conditions, and the external environment in specific investment accelerations.

## Main findings

The chapter's principal findings are:

**Investment accelerations have happened in many EMDEs, but they have become less common.** The chapter identifies 192 investment accelerations in 93 economies (34 advanced economies and 59 EMDEs) over 1950-2022. On average, the probability that an EMDE experienced an investment acceleration in any decade was 40 percent. Along with the protracted slowdown in investment growth since the global financial crisis, the number of investment accelerations in EMDEs has declined over time. In parallel, the external environment has become less supportive and domestic reform drives of the early 2000s lost momentum (Kose and Ohnsorge 2019; Stamm and Vorisek 2023).

**Faster investment growth has often been driven by both the public and private sectors.** The median annual growth of investment was 10.4 percent in EMDEs during investment accelerations, slightly more than three times the growth rate of 3.2 percent in other years. Often, both public and private investment growth have picked up during these episodes. Although the extent of

the increase in public and private investment growth around investment accelerations differs across EMDE regions, the differences were relatively small.

**Investment accelerations often coincided with periods of transformative growth.** During investment accelerations, output growth in EMDEs reached 5.9 percent per year, which is 1.9 percentage points higher than in other years. This rapid growth rate translates into an expansion of almost two-fifths in GDP over six years, almost one-and-a-half times the median expansion during a comparable period outside accelerations. Investment accelerations are associated with higher output growth as they help boost capital accumulation, increase employment growth and strengthen growth of TFP—that is, the portion of growth that is not due to increased inputs of labor and capital and is generally considered a measure of efficiency. Specifically, an investment acceleration in EMDEs, on average, was associated with an increase of almost 1.3 percentage points in annual TFP growth, from slightly above zero in other years. Also, there was much higher growth of employment and output in the manufacturing and services sectors because investment accelerations support faster shifts of resources from less productive sectors, mainly agriculture, to more productive sectors.

**Accelerations have coincided with better macroeconomic and development outcomes.** Investment accelerations have also frequently been accompanied by improved fiscal balances, faster credit expansion, and larger net capital inflows. In addition, they have tended to coincide with better development outcomes, including faster poverty reduction, lower inequality, and improved access to infrastructure, such as the internet.

**Policies have helped to ignite investment accelerations.** Both the chapter's empirical analysis and its country case studies arrive at three key observations about the role of policies in investment accelerations:

- Policy interventions that improve macroeconomic stability—such as fiscal consolidations (actions to reduce deficits) and inflation targeting—and structural reforms, including measures that ease cross-border trade and financial flows, have been instrumental in sparking investment accelerations.

- Although individual policy interventions have played a role, country-specific comprehensive packages of policies fostering macroeconomic stability and addressing structural issues have tended to be more potent in driving investment accelerations. When a country's primary fiscal balance and openness to trade and financial flows have substantially improved, the probability of igniting an investment acceleration has increased by 9 percentage points. Country cases, such as the Republic of Korea in the late 1990s and Türkiye in the early 2000s, illustrate the potential efficacy of comprehensive policy packages.

- Having high quality institutions (such as a well-functioning and impartial legal system) is critical for the success of policy interventions in starting investment accelerations. The likelihood of investment accelerations and the ultimate impact of policy reforms have been greater in countries with better institutions.

# Database and identification methodology

## Database

Investment is defined as real gross fixed capital formation, including both private and public investment (World Bank 2023a). Data on investment are taken from Penn World Table 10.01 (PWT), extended to 2022 using data from Haver Analytics, and databases from the World Bank's World Development Indicators and Global Economic Prospects (see annex 3.2 for details on data). This chapter focuses on growth in investment per capita because it presents a clear parallel with growth in GDP per capita, which is the most basic measure of growth in living standards and, as such, central to the analysis of long-term economic growth (Libman, Montecino, and Razmi 2019). Investment and output data are converted into per capita terms using population data from PWT and the United Nations World

Population Prospects database. The dataset covers up to 35 advanced economies and 69 EMDEs for 1950-2022. The IMF Investment and Capital Stock dataset, which covers the period 1960-2019, is used to separate public from private investment (for information on other data used in the chapter, see annex 3.2).

## Identification methodology

A simple event study approach is employed to identify investment accelerations. The approach follows earlier studies on accelerations of output and capital stock, but it is adjusted to ensure that the identified episodes are characterized by *sustained increases in per capita investment growth to a relatively rapid rate.*[5] The methodology imposes the following rules, based on the data and the literature:

- *Sustained.* Each episode must be sustained for at least six years. The duration of episodes is selected to exclude purely cyclical rebounds in investment growth (Barro and Sara-i-Martin 1992; Christiano and Fitzgerald 2003).

- *Rapid.* The average annual growth rate of investment in the acceleration (of at least six years) must be at least 4 percent. Only one-third of the countries in the sample had a median annual per capita investment growth rate exceeding 4 percent between 1950 and 2022. Because of the volatile nature of investment growth, a 4 percent threshold was selected because it is sufficiently high, and surpassing an average growth rate of 4 percent is unlikely to be driven by one year of very high growth.

- *Higher growth rate.* To ensure that the episode is an acceleration, the average per capita growth rate of investment must be at least 2 percentage points higher than the average of

---

[5] Hausmann, Pritchett, and Rodrik (2005), Jong-A-Pin and de Haan (2011), and Libman, Montecino, and Razmi (2019) employ similar methods to identify output and capital stock accelerations (see annex 3.1). Alternative rules (involving the duration of episodes and other thresholds used in the baseline event study) do not change the headline results (see annex 3.3 for an extensive list of sensitivity exercises).

the previous six years. In addition, to ensure that the episode is not merely a cyclical recovery, the capital stock at the end of the period must exceed its pre-episode peak.

An acceleration is considered to end when per capita investment growth turns negative, or when the inclusion of the current year reduces the average annual per capita investment growth rate since the start of the acceleration to below 4 percent. Investment accelerations can end for a variety of reasons: diminishing returns to capital stock that naturally reduce the average investment growth rate, domestic shocks driven by the accumulation of macroeconomic and financial imbalances, or external shocks such as a regional or global financial crisis. In general, accelerations have rarely been followed by crises or major recessions: four-fifths of those in the sample were not followed by a currency, debt, or banking crisis in the four years after the acceleration.

The rest of the chapter focuses on growth rates of investment, output, and other macroeconomic variables in the three stages around an investment acceleration—namely *before, during,* and *after,* with *during* capturing the full duration of acceleration years. To report comparable statistics across these three stages, the analysis focuses mainly on the medians of changes in variables in each stage.

# Features of investment accelerations

## Number of accelerations

The method identifies 192 investment accelerations in 93 economies (34 advanced economies and 59 EMDEs) over the period 1950-2022 (see annex 3.1). For a typical country, the probability of an investment acceleration in any given decade was 44 percent, slightly higher than the probability in an EMDE (40 percent). Among the countries that experienced at least one investment acceleration, fewer than one-third of them had three or more investment accelerations. In countries with multiple accelerations, the average time between two episodes was about 10 years, with a few exceptions.

Eleven of the 104 countries in the sample experienced no acceleration. These countries had periods of rapid investment growth, but no true accelerations. In some countries, investment was so volatile that no significant increase in investment growth lasted as long as six years (Guatemala, and Iceland). In other countries, periods of rapid investment growth followed declines in the capital stock, were relatively short-lived, and were insufficient to raise the capital stock to its preacceleration peaks (Côte d'Ivoire, Ghana, Niger, South Africa).

## Distribution of accelerations over time and across countries

Globally, 42 percent of countries had an investment acceleration in the 2000s. In the following decade only about a quarter of the world's economies had one. This decline was fully accounted for by EMDEs, as the share of advanced economies with accelerations was virtually unchanged (figure 3.2). The wave of investment accelerations in these economies during the early 2000s was partially supported by benign global conditions, strong cross-border trade and financial flows, and structural reforms that improved many countries' policy frameworks (Kose and Ohnsorge 2019). Since the global financial crisis, the combination of an increasingly difficult external environment and a loss of domestic reform momentum has weighed on investment growth in EMDEs (Stamm and Vorisek 2023).

An EMDE, on average, experienced about 1.7 investment accelerations between 1950 and 2022, compared with about 2.2 such episodes in the average advanced economy. A typical low-income country (LIC) experienced fewer investment accelerations than a high-income country, but its number was similar to those in a typical EMDE. Across EMDE regions, the highest number of investment accelerations per country (nearly 2.4) occurred in East Asia and Pacific, which registered much higher investment growth than other regions over the past seven decades. Reflecting the high volatility of their investment, commodity exporters, economies facing fragile and conflict-affected situations (FCS), and small states experienced fewer investment accelerations than other country groups.

## FIGURE 3.2 Frequency of investment accelerations

*For EMDEs, the share of investment accelerations peaked in the 2000s and fell by about half in the 2010s. More investment accelerations per country have been observed in East Asia and the Pacific, on average, than in other EMDE regions. Investment accelerations have occurred less frequently in commodity exporters, fragile and conflict-affected situations, and small states—groups of countries where output growth performance is relatively volatile.*

**A. Share of countries with investment accelerations, by decade**

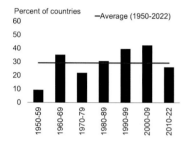

**B. Share of countries with investment accelerations, by decade and country group**

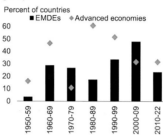

**C. Number of investment accelerations, by country group**

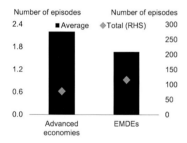

**D. Number of investment accelerations, by income level**

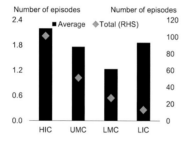

**E. Number of investment accelerations, by EMDE region**

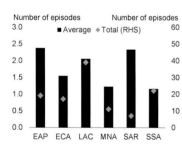

**F. Number of investment accelerations, by EMDE country group**

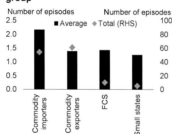

*Sources:* Feenstra, Inklaar, and Timmer (2015); Haver Analytics; WDI (database); World Bank.
*Note:* EAP = East Asia and Pacific; ECA = Europe and Central Asia; EMDEs = emerging market and developing economies; FCS = fragile and conflict-affected situations; HIC = high-income countries; LAC = Latin America and the Caribbean; LIC = low-income countries; LMC = low-middle income countries; UMC = upper-middle income countries; MNA = Middle East and North Africa; SAR = South Asia; SSA = Sub-Saharan Africa. Sample includes 192 investment accelerations in 93 economies, including 34 advanced economies and 59 EMDEs.
A.B. Bars and diamonds show the share of countries starting an investment acceleration during the corresponding decade. The red line in A shows the long-run average share of countries starting an investment acceleration over the past seven decades. The number of accelerations in the 1950s is constrained to episodes starting in 1956 or later by the filter criteria.
C.-F. Bars show the average number of investment accelerations per country over the period 1950-2022, while diamonds show the total number of episodes between 1950 and 2022.
E.F. The sample contains EMDEs alone.

## Amplitude and duration of accelerations

In EMDEs, the median annual growth rate of investment was 10.4 percent in a typical investment acceleration during 1950-2022, just over three times the median growth rate in other years of 3.2 percent (figure 3.3). The rate of investment growth typically exceeded 5 percent in the first year of an acceleration episode and peaked at 13 percent in the following year. In one-fourth of the episodes, annual investment growth reached a peak of at least 21 percent. EMDEs typically experienced a greater increase in investment growth than advanced economies. Reflecting the higher volatility of investment, EMDEs also typically experienced a larger decline in investment growth in the six years following the end of an acceleration than did advanced economies. The basic pattern of investment growth over the three stages of acceleration episodes shows only minor differences across EMDEs in different regions and country groups. Most accelerations lasted six to seven years, with a median duration of seven years. One-fifth of accelerations lasted longer than 10 years.

During a typical investment acceleration, median private and public investment growth both improved significantly from the preceding six years—by about 7 percentage points per year globally—and by somewhat more in EMDEs than in advanced economies (figure 3.4). Of the 192 accelerations, just over half saw higher private than public investment growth. The subsequent decline in growth was slightly more pronounced in private than public investment—by about 1 to 2 percentage points a year—perhaps because of the supportive role that fiscal policy tends to play in periods of weaker private investment growth. The decline in private investment after accelerations was also more pronounced in EMDEs than in advanced economies. The behavior of public and private investment growth around investment accelerations did not differ much across EMDE regions. Across the six regions, LAC and SSA had the lowest share of accelerations with higher private than public investment growth, with 37 percent in LAC and almost 32 percent in SSA.

# Correlates of investment accelerations

Investment accelerations are associated with faster output growth because they help boost capital accumulation and the growth of productivity and employment, and also because they tend to be accompanied by significant shifts of resources from less productive to more productive uses. Investment accelerations tend to coincide with improvements in some key macroeconomic and financial variables. In addition, they are associated with stronger progress toward some of the key development goals, such as reduction in poverty and inequality and increased access to infrastructure.

## Output growth and its underlying channels

**Output growth.** Output growth has tended to surge during investment accelerations (figure 3.5). In EMDEs, output growth reached 5.9 percent per year during investment accelerations over the period 1950-2022—1.9 percentage points more than in other years. This rapid growth rate translates into an expansion of almost 40 percent in GDP over a six-year period, more than one-and-a-half times the expansion in a comparable six-year period outside acceleration years. In LICs, output growth was higher during accelerations than before and after them, but not to a statistically significant extent. This is partly due to the highly volatile nature of output growth in these economies and the small sample of LICs. Similarly, FCS display very volatile growth in periods before accelerations, with higher growth during and after accelerations. For small states, GDP growth rose particularly rapidly during accelerations, from 2.5 percent before a typical investment acceleration to more than 7.4 percent during one. After accelerations, output growth fell back to 4.7 percent. For small states, these changes in output growth are statistically significant.

Investment accelerations are associated with higher output growth through their impact on capital accumulation and the growth of both TFP and employment.

## FIGURE 3.3 Investment growth during accelerations

*During an investment acceleration, the annual investment growth rate has typically reached 9 percent, significantly higher than the pace of the preceding and following years, by 7 and 8 percentage points, respectively.*

**A. Investment growth accelerations, world**

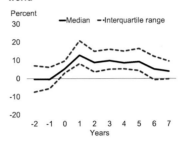

**B. Investment growth around investment accelerations, world**

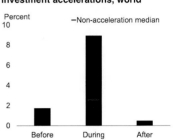

**C. Investment growth around investment accelerations, by country group**

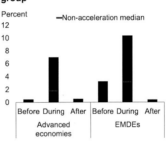

**D. Duration of investment accelerations**

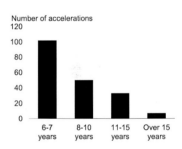

**E. Investment growth around accelerations, by EMDE region**

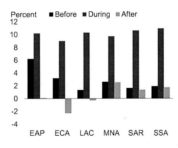

**F. Investment growth around accelerations, by EMDE country group**

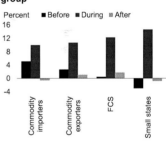

*Sources:* Feenstra, Inklaar, and Timmer (2015); Haver Analytics; WDI (database); World Bank.
*Note:* EAP = East Asia and Pacific; ECA = Europe and Central Asia; EMDEs = emerging market and developing economies; FCS = fragile and conflict-affected situations; LAC = Latin America and the Caribbean; LICs = low-income country; MNA = Middle East and North Africa; SAR = South Asia; SSA = Sub-Saharan Africa. The sample includes 192 investment acceleration episodes in 93 economies, including 34 advanced economies and 59 EMDEs.
A. *t* = 0 refers to the start year of an investment acceleration episode. The blue line shows the median, red dashed lines show the 25th and 75th percentile of investment growth in each year around an investment acceleration.
B.C.E.F. Bars show median annual investment growth during the six years before, the entire duration of, and the six years after an investment acceleration. At the 10 percent level, differences between before, during, and after periods are statistically significant unless otherwise specified.
B.C. Red tick mark indicates the median investment growth rate during non-acceleration years in the sample.
D. Bars show the number of investment accelerations that fall into each duration category.
F. For small states, the difference between before and during is not statistically significant.

## FIGURE 3.4 Public versus private investment during investment accelerations

*Both public and private investment growth have increased during investment accelerations. While the rise and subsequent decline in growth has been similar in magnitude in regard to both private and public investment in EMDEs, the rise and decline in private investment has been more notable than that in public investment in advanced economies. The behavior of public and private investment growth before and during investment accelerations has not differed notably across EMDE regions, except that public investment has accounted for a larger share of accelerations in Latin America and the Caribbean and Sub-Saharan Africa.*

**A. Public investment growth around investment accelerations, world**

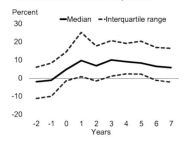

**B. Private investment growth around investment accelerations, world**

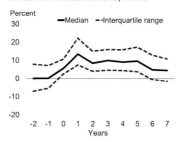

**C. Public investment growth around investment accelerations**

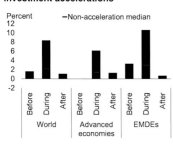

**D. Private investment growth around investment accelerations**

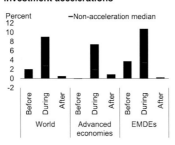

**E. Share of investment accelerations driven by private investment**

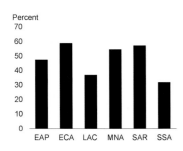

**F. Private investment growth around investment accelerations, by EMDE region**

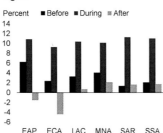

*Sources:* Feenstra, Inklaar, and Timmer (2015); Haver Analytics; IMF, Investment and Capital Stock dataset; WDI (database); World Bank.

*Note:* EAP = East Asia and Pacific; ECA = Europe and Central Asia; EMDEs = emerging market and developing economies; LAC = Latin America and the Caribbean; MNA = Middle East and North Africa; SAR = South Asia; SSA = Sub-Saharan Africa. Sample includes 192 investment acceleration episodes in 93 economies, including 34 advanced economies and 59 EMDEs.

A.B. *t* = 0 refers to the start year of an investment acceleration episode. The blue line shows the median and the red dashed lines show the 25th and 75th percentile of investment growth (public in A, private in B) in each year around an investment acceleration.

C.D.F. Bars show median annual investment growth during the six years before, the entire duration of, and the six years after an investment acceleration. At the 10 percent level, differences between before, during, and after periods are statistically significant unless otherwise specified.

C.D. Red tick mark indicates the median public investment growth rate (in C) and private investment growth rate (in D) during non-acceleration years in the sample.

E. Bars show the share of accelerations in each EMDE region during which median private investment growth exceeded public investment growth.

- *Capital accumulation.* Investment accelerations are associated with stronger output growth directly through their links with faster capital accumulation (Kose and Ohnsorge 2023; Loayza and Pennings 2022). Capital accumulation alone accounted for 45 percent of output growth during investment accelerations globally in 1950-2022 (figure 3.6). The share of output growth explained by capital accumulation is markedly higher in EMDEs—almost half—than in advanced economies, where it accounts for one-third during these episodes. This contribution remains sizable after accelerations, contributing to 77 percent of growth in EMDEs, compared with 48 percent in the years before an acceleration. Globally, the annual growth rate of the capital stock increased by almost 50 percent from its preceding level during a typical investment acceleration, reaching 5.2 percent, and kept growing at a faster rate after an acceleration compared with before. For EMDEs, the pickup in capital stock growth during investment accelerations was significantly larger, and from lower initial levels, than for advanced economies. Growing at 6.2 percent a year, the capital stock in EMDEs expanded by nearly 44 percent over the first six years of an investment acceleration, almost 45 percent more than the expansion over a similar period outside an acceleration.

- *Productivity growth.* Heightened output growth during an investment acceleration is also often accompanied by increased TFP growth (figure 3.7). During 1950-2022, TFP typically grew by 1.7 percent a year in EMDEs during accelerations, significantly faster than in other years. While TFP growth tended to return close to its preceding rate after accelerations in advanced economies, it dropped below its preacceleration pace in EMDEs. Along with TFP growth, labor productivity growth, one of the main drivers of per capita income growth, also significantly increases during these episodes.

- *Employment growth.* Investment accelerations were often accompanied by significant increases in employment growth (figure 3.7).

Globally, the employment rate expanded significantly by 0.3 percentage point a year during accelerations, compared with slight contractions in the six years before and after accelerations. Though still significant, the pickup in employment growth during investment accelerations in EMDEs was smaller than in advanced economies, while EMDEs avoided a decrease in the employment rate after accelerations and advanced economies did not.

**Sectoral shifts.** Investment accelerations are also associated with higher productivity growth through intersectoral resource shifts (Dieppe 2021; Hoyos, Libman, and Razmi 2021). During a typical investment acceleration, the composition of employment has moved significantly away from the agriculture sector toward manufacturing and services, and output growth in manufacturing and services has registered significant increases (figure 3.7). The pace of sectoral shifts has tended to gain momentum during accelerations as the growth rates of employment in the manufacturing and services sectors tend to be significantly higher than in other years. The reallocation of workers from less productive sectors to more productive sectors is a substantial source of productivity growth—particularly in recent decades in EMDEs, such as China. It is estimated, for instance, that such reallocations accounted for two-thirds of productivity growth in LICs in the decades leading up to the global financial crisis (Dieppe 2021).

## Other macroeconomic and financial correlates

**Consumption.** During investment accelerations, both public and private consumption growth improved significantly, by about 1 and 1.6 percentage point a year globally, respectively (figure 3.8). In EMDEs, the increase in the growth of public consumption (including all government current expenditures) during accelerations was comparable to that in private consumption, whereas in advanced economies, public consumption increased much less. Both public and private consumption growth tended to fall back to preacceleration rates.

**FIGURE 3.5 Growth of output during investment accelerations**

*Output growth has risen notably during investment accelerations. In EMDEs, annual output growth has typically reached 5.9 percent during an investment acceleration—about 2 percentage points higher than that in other years. Cumulatively, GDP has typically expanded by two-fifths during an investment acceleration. The increase in output growth during these episodes has varied across EMDE regions.*

**A. Output growth during investment accelerations, world**
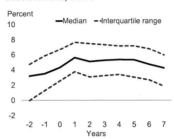

**B. Output growth around investment accelerations**
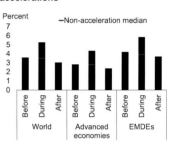

**C. Cumulative change in output around investment accelerations, world**
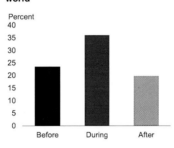

**D. Cumulative change in output around investment accelerations, by country group**
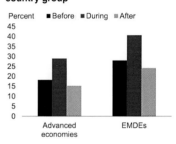

**E. Output growth around investment accelerations, by EMDE country group**
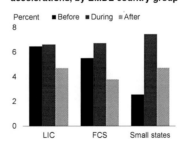

**F. Output growth around investment accelerations, by EMDE region**
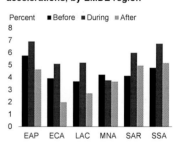

Sources: Feenstra, Inklaar, and Timmer (2015); WDI (database); World Bank.
Note: EAP = East Asia and Pacific; ECA = Europe and Central Asia; EMDEs = emerging market and developing economies; FCS = fragile and conflict-affected situations; LAC = Latin America and the Caribbean; LIC = low-income country; MNA = Middle East and North Africa; SAR = South Asia; SSA = Sub-Saharan Africa; TFP = total factor productivity. Sample includes 192 investment acceleration episodes in 93 economies, including 34 advanced economies and 59 EMDEs.
A. t = 0 refers to the start of an investment growth acceleration. The blue line shows the median and the red dashed lines show the 25th and 75th percentile of output growth in each year around an investment acceleration.
B.E.F. Bars show median annual GDP growth during the six years before, the entire duration of, and the six years after an investment acceleration. The red tick mark in B indicates the median GDP growth rate during non-acceleration years in the sample. At the 10 percent level, differences between before, during, and after periods are statistically significant unless otherwise specified.
C.D. Cumulative change is calculated for a six-year period based on annual median growth rates by group and period.
E. For LICs, the difference in values before and during is not statistically significant.
F. For MNA, the difference in values before and during is not statistically significant.

## FIGURE 3.6 Contributions to GDP growth during investment accelerations

*Capital accumulation made a major contribution to output growth in 1950-2022, especially in EMDEs. During an investment acceleration in EMDEs, annual growth of capital almost doubled from its preceding rate. Both total factor productivity (TFP) growth and employment growth contributed more to output growth during investment accelerations than during other periods. The moderation in TFP growth after investment accelerations was sharper in EMDEs than in advanced economies.*

**A. Decomposition of GDP growth during accelerations, world**

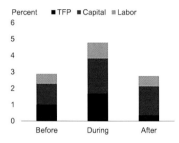

**B. Decomposition of GDP growth during accelerations, by country group**

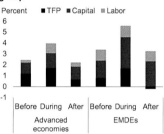

**C. Capital stock growth around investment accelerations**

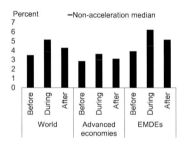

**D. Capital stock growth around investment accelerations, by EMDE region**

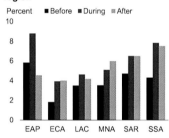

**E. Capital stock growth around investment accelerations, by income level**

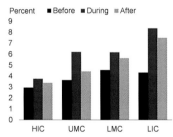

**F. Capital stock growth around investment accelerations, by EMDE country group**

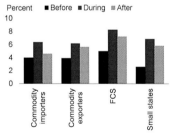

*Sources:* Feenstra, Inklaar, and Timmer (2015); Haver Analytics; WDI (database); World Bank.
*Note:* EAP = East Asia and Pacific; ECA = Europe and Central Asia; EMDEs = emerging market and developing economies; FCS = fragile and conflict-affected situations; HIC = high-income country; LAC = Latin America and the Caribbean; LIC = low-income country; LMC = lower-middle-income country; MNA = Middle East and North Africa; SAR = South Asia; SSA = Sub-Saharan Africa; TFP = total factor productivity; UMC = upper-middle-income country. Sample includes 192 investment acceleration episodes in 93 economies, including 34 advanced economies and 59 EMDEs.
A.B. Bars show the median contribution of TFP growth, capital accumulation, and labor to output growth. Capital accumulation and labor are weighted by the labor share.
C.-F. Bars show median annual capital stock growth during the six years before, the entire duration of, and the six years after an investment acceleration. The red tick marks in C indicate the median capital stock growth rate during non-acceleration years in the sample. At the 10 percent level, differences between before, during, and after periods are statistically significant unless otherwise specified.
D. For all regions except EAP and LAC, the difference in capital stock growth between during and after the acceleration is not statistically significant.
E. For LMC, the difference in capital stock growth between during and after the acceleration is not statistically significant.
F. For small states, the difference in capital stock growth between during and after the acceleration is not statistically significant.

**Fiscal positions.** Fiscal balances have tended to improve during investment accelerations (figure 3.8). Globally the primary balance (which excludes net interest on government debt) shifted from a small deficit in the preceding six years to a small surplus during accelerations. In EMDEs, it remained unchanged, while the overall fiscal deficit narrowed by about 1 percentage point of GDP. During accelerations, the ratio of government debt to GDP fell by 9 percentage points both in EMDEs and globally, largely reflecting, in EMDEs, both faster GDP growth and improvements in primary balances. However, as output growth moderated after investment accelerations, improvements in fiscal and primary balances have tended to erode.

**International trade.** Trade growth has tended to increase significantly during investment accelerations, partly reflecting shifts of resources to the tradeable manufacturing sector and increased growth in imports of capital goods (figure 3.8; Irwin 2021; Lee 1995). Both import and export growth increased markedly during accelerations, with import growth roughly tripling the rate prior to accelerations. The surges in import and export growth were slightly larger in EMDEs than in advanced economies; the larger increase in import growth in EMDEs may partly reflect EMDEs' greater reliance on imports for capital goods (Bustein, Cravino, and Vogel 2013). As a result of the growth of imports relative to exports, current account deficits tended to widen somewhat in EMDEs and globally during and after accelerations.

**Capital inflows.** Capital inflows increased notably during investment accelerations (figure 3.8). In EMDEs, capital inflows rose by about 2 percentage points of GDP during accelerations, relative to their preceding levels, partly on account of increases in FDI inflows relative to GDP. Increases in capital inflows seem to have supported some investment accelerations in EMDEs—such as those in Türkiye in the 2000s and Poland in the 1990s (box 3.1). Increases in capital inflows were often sustained after the acceleration.

**Credit and saving.** Both domestic credit and gross domestic saving grew significantly faster during investment accelerations. In EMDEs, credit growth increased by about 4.5 percentage points a year during accelerations, while the real interest rate fell by more than half. Growth of saving increased by 3 percentage points a year. The increases in both credit growth and saving growth were larger in EMDEs than in advanced economies. While saving growth tended to moderate after investment accelerations in EMDEs, credit growth tended to remain elevated. Accelerations that were supported by credit growth lasted longer and saw significantly higher output growth than accelerations that were not accompanied by credit growth.

**Inflation and real effective exchange rates.** Falling inflation rates have often preceded or accompanied investment accelerations (for example, Korea in the late 1990s; see box 3.1). Globally, annual inflation fell during 1950-2022, from about 7 percent before to about 4 percent during accelerations, while in EMDEs, it dropped from 8 percent to 6 percent. The low inflation rates were typically sustained after investment accelerations (especially after the 1980s).

Real effective exchange rates have not changed materially during investment accelerations, but rose slightly (statistically significantly) afterward, with domestic currencies thus appreciating in real effective terms. There is evidence that, at least in EMDEs, a competitive exchange rate can facilitate capital accumulation both through households' saving and investment behaviors and by expanding the tradeable sector, which supports investment growth.[6] Some countries, such as Germany, Japan, and Korea, have at times relied largely on exports to achieve faster growth. These countries eventually had to allow their currencies to appreciate after the period of rapid growth (Rodrik 2010).

---

[6] Rodrik (2008) argues that currency undervaluation helps the rapid development of the tradeable sector, which is more reliant on investment in EMDEs. Bleaney and Greenaway (2001) suggest that there are two reasons why currency overvaluation can hurt investment in Sub-Saharan Africa: first, overvaluation reduces the returns to investment in the tradables sector, and second, the accompanying current account deficit may cause a tightening of import licensing procedures, which further reduces the returns to investment. There are also drawbacks, such as increases in income inequality and lack of product diversification, associated with currency undervaluation (Bergin 2022; Ribeiro, McCombie, and Lima 2020).

**FIGURE 3.7 Total factor productivity growth, employment growth, and sectoral shifts around investment accelerations**

*Investment accelerations have often been accompanied by improvements in productivity growth, stronger employment growth, and greater reallocation across sectors.*

A. TFP growth around investment accelerations

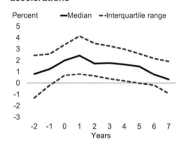

B. TFP growth around investment accelerations, by country group

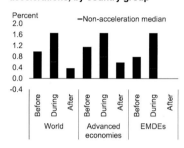

C. Change in labor productivity growth around investment accelerations

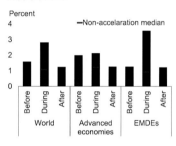

D. Change in employment rate around investment accelerations, by country group

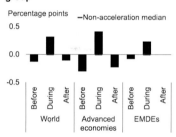

E. Output growth, by sector, around investment accelerations

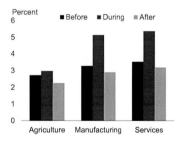

F. Employment growth, by sector, around investment accelerations

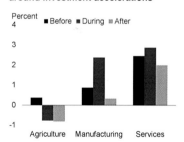

*Sources:* Dieppe (2021); Feenstra, Inklaar, and Timmer (2015); Haver Analytics; WDI (database); WEO (database); World Bank.
*Note:* EMDEs = emerging market and developing economies; TFP = total factor productivity. Sample includes up to 192 investment acceleration episodes in 93 economies, including 34 advanced economies and 59 EMDEs.
A. $t = 0$ refers to the start year of an investment acceleration episode. The blue line shows the median, red dashed lines show the interquartile range of TFP growth in each year around an acceleration.
B.-F. At the 10 percent level, differences between before, during, and after periods are statistically significant unless otherwise specified.
B.-D. Bars show median annual growth (median annual change in the employment rate in D) during the six years before, the entire duration of, and the six years after an investment acceleration. Red tick mark indicates the median annual growth (annual change in the employment rate in D) during non-acceleration years.
C. Difference between before and during for advanced economies is not statistically significant.
E.F. Bars show median annual sector output (in E; employment in F) growth during the six years before, the entire duration of, and the six years after an investment acceleration. In E, the difference in output growth between the before and during periods for the agriculture sector are not statistically significant. In F, the difference in growth rates in the agriculture sector during and after the acceleration are not statistically significant, as well as the difference in the growth rate of employment in the services sector before and during the acceleration.

## FIGURE 3.8 Macroeconomic indicators around investment accelerations

*Investment accelerations in EMDEs have been accompanied by improvements in key macroeconomic variables: both private and public consumption growth have picked up; fiscal deficits and government debt, relative to GDP, have declined; the growth of credit has increased; and inflation has declined. While the growth of both imports and exports has picked up during such accelerations, the rise in imports growth has been relatively larger in EMDEs, partly reflecting their greater reliance on imports for capital goods.*

**A. Public and private consumption growth**

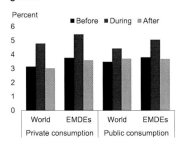

**B. Fiscal indicators**

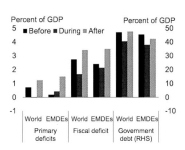

**C. International trade**

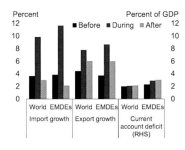

**D. Capital inflows**

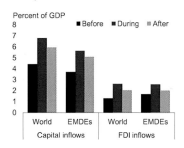

**E. Domestic credit growth and real interest rates**

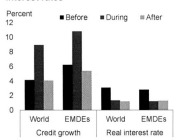

**F. Inflation and exchange rates**

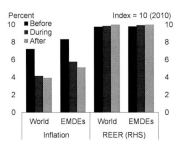

*Sources:* Bank for International Settlements; Feenstra, Inklaar, and Timmer (2015); Ha, Kose, and Ohnsorge (2021); Haver Analytics; IMF, International Financial Statistics; WDI (database); WEO (database); World Bank.

*Note:* EMDEs = emerging market and developing economies. FDI = foreign direct investment; REER = real effective exchange rate. Sample includes up to 192 investment acceleration episodes in 93 economies, including 34 advanced economies and 59 EMDEs.

A.-F. Bars show the median values for the six years before, the entire duration of, and six years following investment accelerations. At the 10 percent level, differences between before, during, and after periods are statistically significant unless otherwise specified.

B. For EMDEs, differences between before and during in primary and fiscal deficits are not statistically significant.

C. For World and EMDE current accounts, differences between before and during, and during and after are not statistically significant.

D. For EMDE capital inflows, differences between during and after are not statistically significant.

E. For World and EMDE real interest rates, differences between during and after are not statistically significant.

F. For World inflation, differences between during and after are not statistically significant. For World and EMDE REERs, differences between before and during are not statistically significant.

## Development outcomes

**Poverty and inequality.** During investment accelerations, more progress has often been made in reducing both poverty and inequality (figure 3.9). The share of the population in extreme poverty barely changed in the six years before a typical investment acceleration in 1950-2022, but declined significantly, by 0.2 percentage point per year, during the acceleration. Similarly, the Gini coefficient, which measures income inequality, fell significantly during the typical investment acceleration after rising slightly in the years preceding it. Measured at national poverty lines, the fall in poverty was even more pronounced with a 0.5 percentage point improvement in the national poverty headcount ratio per year.

**Income convergence.** These gains in poverty and equality are underpinned by the rapid increase in per capita output growth during investment accelerations, which led to faster income convergence toward advanced-economy income levels. Specifically, the median per capita output growth in EMDEs was 0.6 percentage point higher than in advanced economies (4.3 percent compared with 3.7 percent). In contrast, EMDEs registered weaker per capita output growth than advanced economies in other years (1.8 percent versus 2.1 percent per year).

**Access to infrastructure.** Access to infrastructure improved during investment accelerations. For example, the share of the population with access to basic sanitation increased by 0.4 percentage point globally during investment accelerations, while the incidence of stunting among children aged 5 or younger fell by 0.6 percentage point. Since the 1990s, access to the internet has also tended to rise significantly during investment accelerations: 2.4 percent of the population per year gained access to the internet during a typical acceleration, two times the increase during the prior period.

# Drivers of investment accelerations

A rich body of empirical research has shown that investment growth in a country is affected by both global (or regional) conditions and the country's initial conditions, economic policies and institutional settings.[7] However, this literature has not considered the roles of these factors in sparking investment accelerations. This section presents the results of a series of empirical exercises and compares these with insights from the country case studies (box 3.1) on how these factors help trigger investment accelerations.

## Initial conditions

Initial conditions have influenced the onset of investment accelerations (figure 3.10). For example, economies with higher institutional quality have been more likely to experience an investment acceleration: specifically, moving from the bottom quartile to the top quartile in institutional quality increases the probability of starting an investment acceleration by 5.6 percentage points. Similarly, a more undervalued currency is associated with a significantly higher likelihood of an investment acceleration, whereas overvalued currencies have often been a sign of macroeconomic and financial imbalances. In EMDEs, a competitive exchange rate can facilitate capital accumulation either by boosting higher-income households' propensity to save and invest or by supporting the tradables sector (Gluzmann, Levy-Yeyati, and Sturzenegger 2012, 2013; Guzman, Ocampo, and Stiglitz 2018). In both cases, maintaining a competitive currency may help initiate and sustain investment accelerations.

Benign global economic conditions, proxied by strong global output growth, also substantially increase the likelihood of an acceleration. In the sample period of this study, raising global GDP growth from the bottom to the top quartile—from 2.1 percent to 3.5 percent—increased the

---

[7] Kose et al. (2017) show how the slowdown in investment growth in EMDEs following the global financial crisis was driven by spillovers from slowing growth in advanced economies, heavier debt burdens, and falling commodity prices. Libman, Montecino, and Razmi (2019) show how capital stock accumulation is positively correlated with higher human capital endowments, exchange rate undervaluation, low capital-output ratios, and net capital outflows. Manzano and Saboin (2022) find that higher institutional quality is correlated with capital stock accelerations. Stamm and Vorisek (2023) document the contribution of the COVID-19 pandemic to the slowdown in investment growth and show how the weak investment recovery coincides with subdued growth in output, trade, productivity, and credit, and high debt levels.

## FIGURE 3.9 Development outcomes during investment accelerations

*Investment accelerations have typically been accompanied by faster poverty reduction, larger improvements in income equality and human development indicators, and greater enhancements in access to infrastructure than at other times.*

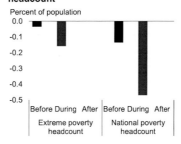

A. Change in extreme poverty headcount

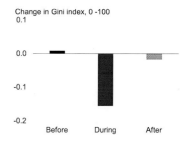

B. Change in Gini coefficient

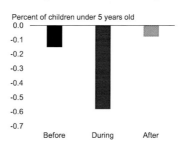

C. Change in incidence of stunting

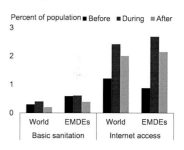

D. Change in access to infrastructure

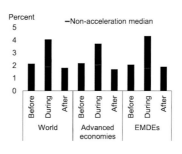

E. Output growth per capita around investment accelerations

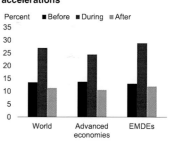

F. Cumulative change in output per capita around investment accelerations

*Sources:* Feenstra, Inklaar, and Timmer (2015); SDG data dashboard; WDI (database); World Bank.

*Note:* EMDEs = emerging market and developing economies.

A.-D. Bars are medians of the annual changes in the corresponding indicators during the six years before, entire duration of, and six years after investment accelerations. Sample includes up to 192 investment acceleration episodes in 93 economies, including 34 advanced economies and 59 EMDEs. At the 10 percent level, differences between before, during, and after periods are statistically significant unless otherwise specified.

A. The difference in national poverty change between before and during is not significant for World, but is statistically significant for EMDEs.

B. The Gini coefficient is a measure of income inequality. The smaller the coefficient, the more income is equally distributed.

D. Data availability limited to 1998 and later. Differences for basic sanitation indicator not statistically significant.

E. Bars show median per capita growth of output in the six years before, entire duration of, and six years following an acceleration. Red tick marks indicate non-acceleration-year medians.

F. Cumulative change is based on the median growth rates shown in E and calculated for a six-year period.

## FIGURE 3.10 Initial conditions and the start of investment accelerations

*Economies with better institutional quality and a more competitive exchange rate are more likely to experience an investment acceleration. Additionally, benign global economic conditions have also tended to increase the likelihood of accelerations. Conversely, the probability of initiating an investment acceleration tends to be lower with higher levels of per capita GDP.*

**A. Probability an acceleration will start, by institutional quality**

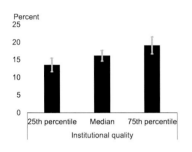

**B. Probability an acceleration will start, by exchange rate undervaluation**

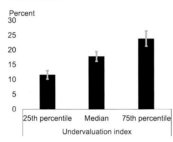

**C. Probability an acceleration will start, by global GDP growth**

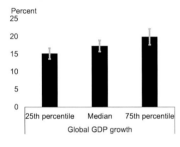

**D. Probability an acceleration will start, by per capita GDP**

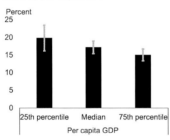

*Sources*: Feenstra, Inklaar, and Timmer (2015); Haver Analytics; PRS Group; WDI (database); World Bank.
*Note*: Figure is based on the regression results of table A3.2.1, column (6). See annex 3.2 for a description of the data and sources.
A. The bars show the predicted probability of an investment acceleration at different levels of the lagged International Country Risk Guide Law and Order index. Yellow whiskers refer to the 90 percent confidence interval. The percentile thresholds of the index are 3, 4, and 5.
B. The bars show the predicted probability of an investment acceleration at different levels of the lagged exchange rate undervaluation index. Yellow whiskers refer to the 90 percent confidence interval. The percentile thresholds of the log index are -0.32, -0.01, and 0.25.
C. The bars show the predicted probability of an investment acceleration at different levels of lagged global GDP growth. Yellow whiskers refer to the 90 percent confidence interval. The percentile thresholds are 2.1 percent, 2.8 percent, and 3.5 percent.
D. The bars show the predicted probability of an investment acceleration at different levels of lagged per capita GDP levels (in logs). Yellow whiskers refer to the 90 percent confidence interval. The percentile thresholds are 8.3, 9.2, and 10.1.

probability of starting an investment acceleration for an average economy by 4.7 percentage points. Several of the country case studies (box 3.1) illustrate how commitment to comprehensive reforms enables countries to seize on supportive external factors, such as high commodity prices or international assistance. The probability of an investment acceleration also increased significantly in countries with lower per capita income. For instance, the likelihood of an acceleration was about one-fourth higher in countries in the bottom quartile of income per capita compared with those in the top quartile.

## Macroeconomic policies and structural reforms

Investment accelerations have often been preceded or accompanied by policy measures to improve macroeconomic stability or reduce restrictions on cross-border trade or financial flows. An improved primary fiscal balance or reduced capital flow restrictions tended to precede or accompany about a third of investment accelerations during 1956-2017. Trade restrictions were relaxed by policy measures prior to 70 percent of accelerations in this period. The adoption or tightening of an inflation target was followed or accompanied by 10 percent of accelerations (figure 3.11).[8]

A combination of more stringent fiscal policies, the adoption of an inflation target, and structural reforms to promote trade and financial openness can raise the likelihood of an investment acceleration by more than might be deduced from the effects of each of these individual policy improvements in isolation. Using the sample of accelerations, it is estimated that if the primary balance and trade and financial openness indices were all improved by one standard deviation, there would be a marked increase of 9 percentage points in the probability of starting an investment acceleration. If these reforms were also accompanied by the adoption of an inflation-targeting regime, the probability would be raised by an additional 33 percentage points.[9] These results underline the case for a comprehensive package of stabilization and reform policies to spark an investment acceleration.

---

[8] Inflation targeting has become a policy tool in recent decades, with New Zealand being the first economy adopting it in 1990 in the sample. It is typically implemented as a one-time policy measure.

[9] Specifically, a one-standard-deviation increase in all of the following three policy measures (excluding the adoption of inflation-targeting) results in 9 percentage point increase in the probability of starting an acceleration: a one-standard-deviation increase involves a 35 percent increase in the capital openness index (ranges from 0 to 1 with a higher value indicating more capital openness), an 8 percent increase in the trade openness index (ranges from 0 to 1 with a higher value indicating more trade openness), and a 2.3 percentage point increase in the primary balance. For details, see annex 3.2.

The country cases also highlight the role of policies aimed at stabilizing the macroeconomy and implementing structural reforms, particularly when these are part of a comprehensive package, in initiating accelerations (box 3.1). In general, the country cases show that investment accelerations were preceded by at least one of the two types of policy intervention: those aimed at improving macroeconomic stability (such as Türkiye in the early 2000s) and those intended to address structural shortcomings (such as ending public-sector monopolies in India in the 1990s). Often, comprehensive packages containing both types of policy intervention (such as in Korea in the late 1990s and Morocco in the 1990s and 2000s) accompanied or preceded strong growth accelerations. Demonstrated commitment to such reforms allowed countries to seize favorable external conditions and turn them into investment accelerations.

## Institutional quality

The effect of economic policies on the likelihood of accelerations depends on institutional quality. There was a greater likelihood that improved fiscal policies and trade reforms were associated with investment accelerations in countries with better institutions than in those with weaker institutions. Specifically, in countries with institutional quality in the top quartile of the sample, improvements in the primary fiscal balance or reductions in trade restrictions significantly increased the likelihood of starting an acceleration, whereas such policies had no statistically significant impact in countries where the quality of institutions was in the bottom quartile of the sample (figure 3.11).

## Robustness

A broad array of robustness exercises was conducted, including employing different thresholds to identify investment accelerations; adding additional control variables to check whether the results were driven by global economic conditions or financial cycles; and using aggregate investment growth, rather than per capita investment growth (see annexes 3.3 and 3.4). These changes did not alter the headline results.

**FIGURE 3.11 Policy improvements and the start of investment accelerations**

*Improvements in the primary fiscal balance, the adoption or reduction of inflation targets, and structural reforms that increase openness to international trade or financial flows have been conducive to investment accelerations. The scale of the effects of improvements in the fiscal balance and trade liberalization have depended on the institutional environment.*

**A. Share of investment accelerations preceded by fiscal or monetary policy improvements**

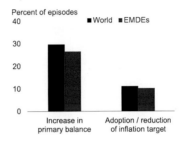

**B. Share of investment accelerations preceded by structural policy improvements**

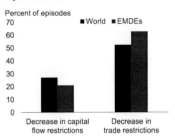

**C. Average marginal effect of an improvement in fiscal or monetary policy**

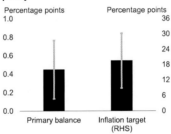

**D. Average marginal effect of an improvement in international trade or capital flow restrictions**

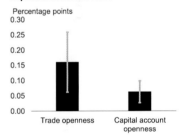

**E. Average marginal effect of an improvement in primary balance, by institutional quality**

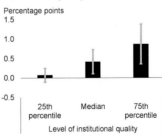

**F. Average marginal effect of a reduction in trade restrictions, by institutional quality**

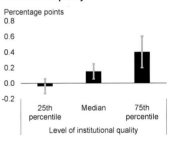

*Sources:* Alesina et al. (2020); Chinn and Ito (2008); IMF, International Financial Statistics; PRS Group; WDI (database); WEO (database); World Bank.

*Note:* EMDEs = emerging market and developing economies. See annex 3.2 for a description of the data and sources.

A.B. Bars show the share of investment accelerations that were preceded by or coincided with an improvement in the policy variables of at least 2 percent (trade restrictions index or capital account openness index) or 2 percentage points of GDP (primary balance) or an adoption or tightening of an inflation target all within the preceding five years. For the trade restrictions index, primary balance to GDP ratio, and capital account openness index, an improvement is an increase in the variable. Data on inflation targeting are available from 1990.

C.D. Panels are based on regression results shown in table A3.2.2. Bars show the average marginal effect of improvements in economic policies. Yellow whiskers refer to the 90 percent confidence interval.

E.F. Panels are based on regression results shown in table A3.2.2. Bars show the average marginal effect of improvements in economic policies at different quartiles of the institutional quality index (based on International Country Risk Guide's Law and Order index). Yellow whiskers refer to the 90 percent confidence interval. The quartile thresholds for institutional quality are 3, 4, and 5.

**FIGURE 3.12 Enabling factors for investment accelerations**

*Policy and institutional conditions that have helped trigger investment accelerations have been more prevalent in advanced economies than in EMDEs. Over the past few decades, EMDEs have made some progress in removing trade restrictions, but less progress in enhancing institutional quality and reducing fiscal imbalances. The number of restrictive trade policy measures in EMDEs has increased significantly over the past eight years.*

**A. Institutional quality**

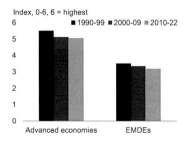

**B. Fiscal policy**

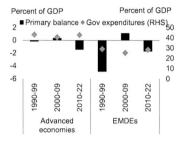

**C. FDI inflows, by decade**

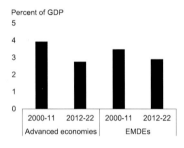

**D. EMDE trade growth**

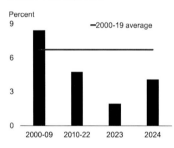

**E. Trade restrictions**

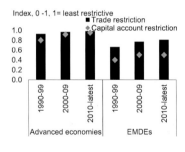

**F. Trade policy interventions**

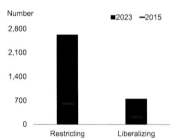

*Sources*: Alesina et al. (2020); Chinn and Ito (2008); Global Trade Alerts; IMF, International Financial Statistics; PRS Group; WDI (database); WEO (database); World Bank.
*Note*: See annex 3.2 for a description of the data and sources. EMDEs = emerging market and developing economies; FDI = foreign direct investment.
Bars show simple averages by country classification.
A. Institutional quality is proxied with the International Country Risk Guide Law and Order index, which ranges from 0 (lowest) to 6 (highest).
C. Average FDI-to-GDP ratio of a median country. Balanced sample of 35 advanced economies, 135 EMDEs and 4 unclassified economies.
D. Trade refers to volume of goods and nonfactor services and is defined as an average of exports and imports. Aggregate is calculated using trade weights at average 2010-19 prices and market exchange rates. Data for 2023 are estimates, and data for 2024 are forecasts.
E. Latest available data for trade restrictions are from 2014, and those for capital account restrictions are from 2019.
F. Panel shows the number of implemented trade policy interventions since November 2008. Restricting (Liberalizing) measures are interventions that discriminate against (benefit) foreign commercial interests. Adjusted data as of November 26, 2023.

# Policies to start investment accelerations

To promote investment accelerations, EMDEs need to implement a comprehensive package of policies, tailored to their specific circumstances. This package typically includes fiscal and monetary interventions, structural policies, and efforts to improve institutional quality (figure 3.12).

## Fiscal and monetary policies

Both the empirical analysis and country cases highlight the important role that fiscal policy can play in sparking investment accelerations. Expenditure and revenue measures, and fiscal rules, can help improve fiscal positions.

**Revenue measures** that can improve fiscal balances include reforming tax administrations, enlarging tax bases, and increasing tax rates. In many EMDEs, particularly those in South Asia and Sub-Saharan Africa, revenue-to-GDP ratios are much lower than in advanced economies (World Bank 2015, 2016b). Eliminating tax exemptions and strengthening the administration of tax collection could improve fiscal positions by increasing revenues. Tax policies can also be used to improve incentives, particularly for investment in the private sector (Djankov et al. 2010). For example, the elimination of fossil fuel subsidies, together with the introduction of carbon taxes, can incentivize investment into energy-efficient technologies (World Bank 2023b).

**Expenditure measures** that can improve fiscal balances include eliminating distortive agriculture and fossil fuel subsidies, which currently account for sizable shares of government expenditure in many EMDEs. EMDEs can also enhance the efficiency and predictability of their expenditures. By eliminating wasteful spending and prioritizing public investment in assets such as productive infrastructure and human capital, through education and healthcare spending, they can improve fiscal positions and contribute to both investment accelerations and improved output growth. Efficient public investment in infrastructure can also crowd in private investment by stimulating economic development (Ansar et al. 2016; World Bank 2023b).

**Fiscal rules**, over the past three decades, have reduced the volatility of fiscal policy in EMDEs and allowed governments to respond to adverse events countercyclically by conserving fiscal space (IMF 2022; Marioli, Fatas, and Vasishtha 2023). Fiscal rules that ensure that current expenditures are fully financed by revenues over the cycle can provide appropriate protection for public investment. By implementing fiscal rules and utilizing stabilization funds, commodity-exporting EMDEs can improve budget positions while reducing the procyclicality of fiscal policies (World Bank 2022e).

If excessive, government borrowing to fund deficits can put pressure on credit markets, tighten financial conditions, and crowd out private investment (Huang, Pagano, and Panizza 2020; World Bank 2023c). Conversely, improving fiscal positions can, under certain circumstances, boost (crowd in) private investment (Essl et al. 2019). This is particularly true for EMDEs that are in or near debt distress, as measures to improve their fiscal positions, when feasible, can yield benefits. In many EMDEs, fiscal policy in the near term needs to be calibrated to regain the ability to take appropriate expansionary measures when needed—creating so-called "fiscal space," which was eroded during the pandemic.

**Monetary policy** reforms, such as the establishment or reinforcement of central bank independence or the adoption of an inflation-targeting regime, may also be important to securing a stable macroeconomic environment that supports investment growth. Low and stable inflation in the medium term is a key requirement of macroeconomic stability and healthy investment growth.

## Structural policies

A broad range of structural policies can promote investment accelerations.

**Trade policy.** Reducing restrictions on cross-border trade can play an important role in sparking investment accelerations. Such measures have significantly increased the likelihood of starting an investment acceleration and have often preceded accelerations, such as in India, Morocco,

and Türkiye (box 3.1). In recent decades, tariffs have been lowered substantially in many EMDEs, but costly and widespread non-tariff barriers remain.

Easing these de facto restrictions, which include unwieldy customs procedures, poor trade-related infrastructure, and uncompetitive domestic logistics sectors, can significantly improve trade flows and support investment growth (Kose and Ohnsorge 2023, Breton, Farrantino, and Maliszewska 2022; World Bank 2021a). A comprehensive reform package could lower trade costs by more than one-half among the EMDEs that perform worst in shipping and logistics—which account for the bulk of trade costs. Digital technology can facilitate many of these reforms, for example, by enabling the electronic processing of documents ahead of time, linking logistics services at borders, and helping lower barriers to entry for small and medium-sized enterprises.

The nontariff costs involved in border crossings can be reduced by lessening wait times created by lengthy administrative procedures and unclear or extensive documentation requirements. The WTO Agreement on Trade Facilitation, for example, provides a framework to simplify border procedures. Harmonizing inspection requirements and labeling standards between countries can also lower firms' costs and smooth border crossings (World Bank 2021a). Regarding logistics, improving physical infrastructure, like ports, airports, and roads, can reduce travel time and variability.

Membership in trade agreements—for example, the African Continental Free Trade Area agreement—can help solidify trade facilitation reforms and lower tariffs. Further, trade treaties can boost economies of scale and lower costs by standardizing regulatory requirements across multiple jurisdictions. Trade agreements also promote regional and global value chain participation by codifying intellectual property rights, and competition and investment protocols. This can significantly benefit small countries and countries that are geographically isolated from trade hubs (Echandi, Maliszewska, and Steenbergen 2022; Moïsé and Le Bris 2013; World Bank 2020b).

**Financial sector policies.** Improvements in access to external finance have tended to raise the probability of starting an investment acceleration. Actions to enhance access to external finance include the loosening of regulations on capital flows (Alesina et al. 2020). Since restrictions on outflows tend also to discourage inflows, the easing of restrictions on both capital inflows and outflows will generally need to be considered (Chinn and Ito 2008; Lee 1997). Nevertheless, the easing of capital flow restrictions may need to be accompanied by measures to mitigate risks arising from instability in capital inflows and outflows, which could destabilize the domestic economy. Such measures include safeguards to prevent capital inflow surges from generating boom-and-bust cycles, as was experienced by Malaysia in the 1990s (box 3.1). A well-regulated domestic financial sector is essential. Also important are measures to reduce country risk, including sound macroeconomic policies (Fratzscher 2012; Koepke 2019).

Policies that help develop domestic capital markets can also support investment accelerations. Capital market development can improve access to credit and financing in local currency, especially long-term financing. Policies to promote capital market development include improving contract enforcement to reduce collateral requirements, mitigating country-specific risks or market failures through partial credit guarantees to intermediaries, and developing digital infrastructure to allow small firms and financial institutions to participate in financial markets at low cost (United Nations 2022; World Bank 2022d).

The establishment of local currency equity and debt markets can help attract institutional investors to EMDEs with less-developed financial intermediation infrastructure. For instance, pension funds and private equity firms, which tend to have higher risk tolerance, may provide financing in situations where traditional banks are unwilling to do so (United Nations 2022). Multilateral development banks play a critical role in supporting these markets by providing liquidity through innovative products, including catastrophe bonds, blue and green bonds, provisioning of loans in local currencies in the most illiquid markets and offering guarantees

against political and other noncommercial risks (World Bank 2015a, 2022d).

In many EMDEs, it is critical to improve the digital and technological infrastructure. This enhancement is essential to lower the costs of access to finance and running a business, and to enable rural residents to access broadband networks. Facilitating investment in digital infrastructure requires aligning regulations with international standards, encouraging competition among providers to lower prices and improve services, and educating the workforce in relevant skills (OECD and IDB 2016). Increasing access to the internet has been shown to boost foreign direct investment, increase the incomes of rural households, and lower poverty rates (Bahia et al. 2020; Mensah and Traore 2022).

Institutional quality

In EMDEs with better institutions, particularly those emphasizing the improvement in law and order and property rights protection, the likelihood of initiating an investment acceleration is higher. Additionally, in such environments, policies have been more effective in leading to investment accelerations. The potential for institutional improvements in EMDEs is indicated by the fact that the quality of institutions is much lower than in advanced economies (figure 3.12).

Policymakers can improve institutions by, for example, defining property rights more clearly and protecting them more effectively, increasing the independence of the judiciary and strengthening the rule of law, and improving the enforcement of contracts. In many EMDEs, reforms are also needed to improve and unify regulatory and institutional structures, which are often fragmented, to help ease excessive constraints on private investors and businesses, and to ensure the effective enforcement of necessary regulations.

To enhance the quality of public infrastructure investment, countries can establish public investment management systems, robust project appraisal systems, and effective procurement and monitoring frameworks to mitigate the problems of asymmetric information and moral hazard (Gardner and Henry 2021; Kim, Fallov, and

Groom 2020). Public-private partnerships are commonly utilized for delivering public investment and services, while limiting fiscal risks, provided that a robust framework of contract preparation, procurement and management is in place (Dappe et al. 2023; Dappe, Melecky, and Turkgulu 2022; Engel, Fischer, and Galetovic 2020). These reforms tend to be especially important in LICs, where regulatory frameworks are often inadequate (World Bank 2020a). Countries with better governance of public investment projects tend to register larger improvements in macroeconomic and fiscal outcomes (Schwartz et al. 2020).

## Interventions at the micro level

In addition to macro-level policy interventions, micro-interventions also play a pivotal role in supporting investment, especially in the private sector. For instance, training and mentorship programs targeted at entrepreneurs can enhance their capabilities in scaling up their businesses, adopting new technologies, and conducting long-term profitable investment (Donald et al. 2022; Karlan, Knight, and Udry 2012; McKenzie and Woodruff. 2014). Providing financial education to the general public can improve financial literacy, which is positively correlated with planning for savings and wealth accumulation (Hastings, Madrian, and Skimmyhorn 2013; Kaiser and Menkhoff 2017).

## Designing a policy package

Policies to accelerate investment need to take account of country-specific conditions, be formulated in a well-designed package, and be carefully sequenced. The empirical analysis and country case studies demonstrate the importance of combining policies that enhance macroeconomic stability with policies that address structural barriers facing private-sector development and institutional weaknesses. Country experiences, such as those in Korea in the late 1990s and Türkiye in the early 2000s, support the view that a comprehensive package of policies can be potent in triggering an investment acceleration.

**FIGURE 3.13 Policy packages and potential growth**

*In the past several decades, comprehensive policy packages that have improved macroeconomic stability and promoted cross-border trade and financial flows have significantly increased the likelihood of initiating an investment acceleration. Based partly on this evidence, a scenario in which EMDEs that experienced an acceleration between 2000 and 2022 start another in 2023 and all EMDEs replicate their best reform efforts in a decade, suggests that the slowdown in potential growth projected in the baseline for 2022-30 would not occur.*

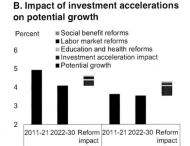

*Sources:* Kose and Ohnsorge (2023); World Bank.
*Note:* EMDE = emerging market and developing economies.
A. Blue bars show the potential output growth rates based on production function approach. GDP-weighted averages for a sample of 53 EMDEs.
B. The scenario assumes that in 40 EMDEs (excluding China) that experienced an investment acceleration between 2000 and 2022, investment growth will increase to 10.4 percent per year from 2023-28 before returning to 0.4 percent per year in 2029-30. The 40 EMDEs were chosen because they have the highest expected average investment growth for 2021-25 and are included in the Kose and Ohnsorge (2023) sample. The increase in investment growth to 10.4 percent and subsequent fall to 0.4 percent matches the median investment growth during and after investment accelerations in EMDEs between 1950-2022.

When designing a policy package, the sequencing of measures should be carefully planned. For example, fiscal measures may need to take precedence in countries with significant fiscal challenges. The implementation of institutional policies, including measures to improve the business climate and regulatory structures, may need to be advanced particularly in countries that have difficulty mobilizing private investment. Policies to strengthen the regulation of the financial system and reform exchange rate arrangements may need to be implemented before the liberalization of capital flows. Such careful sequencing helps countries gird against potential disruptions that could otherwise imperil reform efforts, and lays the groundwork to take advantage of any favorable turn in the external environment.

In the absence of additional policy reforms, potential output growth in EMDEs is projected to decline from an annual average of 4.9 percent in

2011-21 to 4.0 percent a year in 2022-30 (figure 3.13; Kose and Ohnsorge 2023). Nevertheless, if the EMDEs that registered an investment acceleration since 2000 were able to spark another such episode between 2022 and 2030, their annual potential output growth would be 0.3 percentage point higher than projected in the baseline.[10] Furthermore, in a scenario where all EMDEs replicated their best 10-year performance in labor force participation reforms, as well as health and education improvements, potential growth for 2022-30 could increase by 0.5 percentage points per year higher, reaching 4.6 percent. This increase would almost eliminate the decline projected in the baseline (figure 3.13).

## Conclusion

Raising investment growth is a critical objective for EMDEs. They have significant investment needs to enable them to deliver sustainable and inclusive output growth, cope with climate change, and make progress toward broader development goals. Nevertheless, EMDEs face many obstacles in seeking to accelerate investment: the near-term investment growth outlook is weak, long-term growth prospects have deteriorated, fiscal resources are limited, and external borrowing costs are elevated.

This chapter has presented the first study of investment accelerations using a large sample of countries over an extended period. Investment accelerations are often associated with much improved macroeconomic and development outcomes. The median annual growth rate of investment jumped to 10.4 percent during these episodes, three times the median in other years. Investment accelerations also coincided with substantial increases in output growth coming alongside faster capital accumulation and growth of TFP and employment, relative to non-acceleration years. In addition, poverty and inequality declined during these episodes.

These results collectively suggest a strong association between investment accelerations and improved macroeconomic and development

outcomes. However, it is important to highlight that they do not imply a one-way causal link. Indeed, there can be self-reinforcing dynamics between investment accelerations and other beneficial developments during these episodes. That said, the regular coincidence of investment accelerations and transformative phases of macroeconomic and developmental progress underscores the critical importance of periods of rapid and sustained investment growth.

National policies have played an important role in sparking investment accelerations. For example, both fiscal consolidation measures and structural reforms to liberalize international trade and financial flows have facilitated investment accelerations. However, while individual policy measures can help ignite accelerations, comprehensive packages of measures have tended to be more effective. In addition, an enabling institutional environment has tended to significantly amplify the impact of policies on investment growth and increase the likelihood of accelerations. A country that is bolstering its institutions, fostering macroeconomic stability, and demonstrating commitment to structural reforms is particularly well placed to turn supportive external conditions into a transformative investment acceleration.

To boost private capital mobilization, multilateral development banks (MDBs) can offer various financial instruments and support (G20-IEG 2023). These include providing credit enhancement and disaster risk management instruments, enhancing liquidity in local-currency debt and equity markets in EMDEs with less-developed financial markets, and promoting innovative investment products such as blue and green bonds. In situations where market failures prevent investors from insuring risks, MDBs can also offer loan guarantees. Additionally, MDBs can provide technical assistance by advising governments on creating the regulatory and institutional framework for well-functioning markets. This assistance extends to supporting the formulation of prudent fiscal policies, and providing guidance on achieving the energy transition and facilitating adaptation to climate change.

---

[10] Forty-one out of 67 EMDEs in the sample used for this exercise have experienced an investment acceleration since 2000.

## BOX 3.1 Sparking investment accelerations: Lessons from country case studies

*Investment accelerations often have been preceded by at least one of two types of policy intervention: measures to improve macroeconomic stability and reforms to address structural problems. While each type of policy measure has helped trigger investment accelerations, comprehensive packages of policies that combine both types appear to have sparked faster investment and output growth than might have been expected from the individual effects of each type of measure. A benign external environment has also played a crucial role in catalyzing investment accelerations in most cases.*

### Introduction

The empirical analysis in this chapter documents the common features of investment accelerations—periods in which there are sustained increases in investment growth to a relatively rapid rate—and the policies that have been associated with them. It also highlights some substantial differences across investment accelerations. This box presents a brief account of notable investment accelerations in select countries. Specially, it aims to answer the following questions:

- What types of policy changes have triggered investment accelerations?

- How have the macroeconomic implications of investment accelerations differed depending on the underlying policy drivers?

The box focuses on 13 investment accelerations in 10 countries (tables B3.1.1, B3.1.2, and B3.1.3): Chile (1986-93), Colombia (2001-07), India (1994-99), Malaysia (1988-97), Morocco (1996-2009), Poland (1992-2000 and 2003-08), Republic of Korea (1985-96 and 1999-2007), Türkiye (2003-08), Uganda (1993-2012), and Uruguay (1991-98 and 2004-14).[a]

### East Asia and Pacific

#### Malaysia (1988-97)

**Economic performance.** Malaysia experienced an investment acceleration from 1988 to 1997. Annual

investment growth averaged 17.9 percent during this period, exceeding the level in other years by 20.9 percentage points (figure B3.1.1). Private investment growth increased more than public investment growth. Both credit growth and capital inflows played major roles in triggering this episode. During the acceleration in investment, output growth averaged 9.2 percent, enabling Malaysia to attain upper-middle-income-country status in 1992.

**Policy drivers.** The 1988 acceleration was triggered by policy changes that reduced restrictions on capital flowing in and out of the country (so-called capital account liberalization), which translated into a sharp increase in capital inflows and improved access to domestic credit, as well as structural reforms in the Fifth Malaysia Plan. Net capital inflows increased from -2 percent of GDP (that is, a net outflow) in 1988 to 16 percent at the peak in 1993, and the financial sector undertook an expanding array of activities that increased credit flow especially through bank lending (Ghani and Suri 1999). With improved access to credit and foreign capital, exports of manufactured goods rose (Naguib and Smucker 2009). A currency devaluation and tax reform improved the business climate while public revenue shortfalls were prevented through the elimination of tax loopholes (Somogyi 1991). However, the episode was not accompanied by policy changes to control financial excesses associated with the rapid opening of the capital account, a major factor in the financial crisis of 1997.

#### Republic of Korea (1985-96 and 1999-2007)

**Economic performance.** The Republic of Korea experienced two investment accelerations since the 1980s—one in 1985-96 and the other in 1999-2007. Investment growth surged during both accelerations, reaching 9.2 percent a year (figure B3.1.1). Output growth picked up by 4 percentage points per year during the accelerations, relative to other years. While capital accumulation had played a large role in Korea's growth miracle since the 1960s, the two episodes were

---

Note: This box was prepared by Marie Albert, Jongrim Ha, Reina Kawai, Philip Kenworthy, Jeetendra Khadan, Dohan Kim, Emiliano Luttini, Joseph Mawejje, Valerie Mercer-Blackman, Kersten Stamm, Guillermo Verduzco, Collette Wheeler, and Shu Yu.

[a] The 13 investment accelerations covered here are not all of the accelerations these 10 countries have experienced since 1980. The accelerations were chosen because they are representative of the fiscal, monetary, or structural reform efforts that often precede accelerations. The other accelerations in these countries were: Chile (2002-08), India (1985-90; 2004-12), Malaysia (2006-18), Poland (1983-88; 2017-22), the Republic of Korea (2013-18), and Türkiye (2010-17). Tables B3.1.1, B3.1.2 and B3.1.3 present an overview of the accelerations and accompanying policies for each country.

## BOX 3.1 Sparking investment accelerations: Lessons from country case studies (*continued*)

### FIGURE B3.1.1 Investment accelerations in the Republic of Korea and Malaysia

*Malaysia experienced an investment acceleration from 1988 to 1997. In that episode, private investment growth increased more than public investment growth. Both credit growth and capital inflows played major roles in triggering this episode. The Republic of Korea experienced two investment accelerations—in 1985-96 and in 1999-2007. While capital accumulation played a large role in Korea's growth miracle, the two episodes were also associated with faster growth of employment and productivity.*

**A. Output and investment growth in Malaysia**

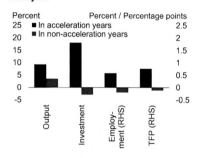

**B. Macroeconomic conditions in Malaysia**

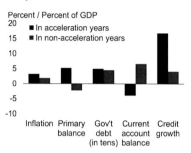

**C. Net capital inflows and public and private investment growth in Malaysia**

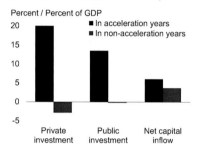

**D. Output and investment growth in the Republic of Korea**

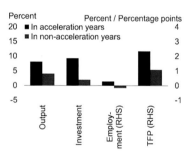

**E. Macroeconomic conditions in the Republic of Korea**

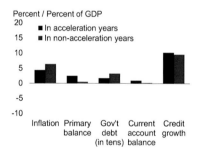

**F. Net capital inflows and public and private investment growth in the Republic of Korea**

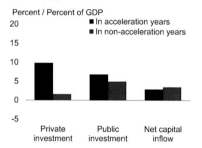

*Sources*: Bank for International Settlements; Feenstra, Inklaar, and Timmer (2015); Ha, Kose, and Ohnsorge (2021); Haver Analytics; IMF, International Financial Statistics; IMF, Investment and Capital Stock dataset; WDI (database); WEO (database); World Bank.
*Note*: The sample period is 1980-2022. Acceleration years cover the full duration of the episode. Non-acceleration years exclude acceleration years that were not included in this box; CPI = consumer price index; TFP = total factor productivity.
A.D. Bars are simple averages of growth in output, investment, and TFP, as well as the percentage point change in the employment rate.
B.E. Bars are simple average of the change in CPI in percent, primary balance as a percent of GDP, government debt as a percent of GDP, current account balance as a percent of GDP, and real credit growth in percent.
C.F. Bars are simple averages of growth in private investment and public investment in percent, and the net capital-inflow-to-GDP ratio in percent of GDP.

also associated with much faster growth of employment and productivity, and improvements in human capital (Rodrik 1995; Kim and Lau 1994).

Furthermore, enhanced price stability, strengthened fiscal positions, and improved current account balances accompanied both accelerations: on average across the two accelerations, inflation fell to 4.3 percent; government debt declined by 15 percentage points of GDP; the primary balance was in surplus by 2.4 percent of GDP and the current account balance was in a slight surplus of 0.9 percent of GDP. A notable 8.3

percentage point increase in annual private investment growth underpinned both acceleration episodes. Korea attained high-income-country status in 1995, fell back in 1998 because of the 1997 Asian financial crisis, and then regained high-income status in 2001.

**Policy drivers.** The 1985 acceleration was preceded by a comprehensive set of macroeconomic stabilization policies. First, to curb inflation that was partly driven by the government-led growth strategy in the late 1970s, fiscal policy was tightened based on a balanced budget principle. This ended the subordination of

**BOX 3.1 Sparking investment accelerations: Lessons from country case studies (*continued*)**

monetary policy to government financing (Koh 2007; Cho and Kang 2013). Second, the number of price controls was reduced, and the Monopoly Regulation and Fair-Trade Act was established to ensure market competition (Nam 1988). Third, restrictions on imports were loosened which helped relieve pressure on inflation by promoting domestic competition (Dornbusch and Park 1987; Koh 2010).

Against a backdrop of broader measures to bolster macroeconomic stability, the acceleration that began in 1999 benefited from structural reforms to address financial and corporate sector problems that contributed to the 1997 crisis. These included comprehensive steps to liberalize capital markets and foreign investment (Lee 2013; Vashakmadze et al. 2023). Extensive restructuring of corporates and financial institutions also strengthened financial soundness, governance, and profitability. Notably, reforms geared toward Chaebol groups (family-controlled large conglomerates) required their affiliated firms to exit nonviable businesses, which improved loan availability for smaller firms (Krueger and Yoo 2002). In addition, a floating exchange rate system was adopted in late 1997, and an inflation-targeting regime with enhanced central bank independence was established in 1998.

Europe and Central Asia

**Poland (1992-2000 and 2003-08)**

**Economic performance.** Poland experienced two investment accelerations, during 1992-2000 and 2003-08 (figure B3.1.2). During these accelerations there were sharp increases in both investment growth (which averaged 10.4 percent per year) and output growth (which averaged 5 percent per year). In contrast, in non-acceleration years since 1980, investment fell 3 percent per year and output declined 0.7 percent per year. Both private and public investment growth rose sharply in these episodes, with the 2003 episode driven by a more pronounced increase in public investment. The two accelerations were also accompanied by an improvement in the fiscal position and an uptick in net capital inflows. Inflation declined notably during the 1992 acceleration.

**Policy drivers.** The 1992 acceleration in Poland was preceded by reforms to stabilize the economy and structural policy shifts that helped transition from a

centrally planned economy toward a market-oriented one. Prior to the 1992 acceleration, the collapse of the Soviet Union caused output and investment to plummet and inflation to skyrocket in Poland. To curb inflation, a stabilization program was employed to tighten monetary policy, restrict credit flow, and enhance central bank independence. The exchange rate system transitioned from a fixed regime in 1990 to a crawling peg in 1991, and then progressively to a fully floating regime in 2000.

Fiscal sustainability improved because of a comprehensive set of interventions: cuts in subsidies and spending by public enterprises; the introduction of personal, corporate, value added, and excise taxes; the implementation of a more targeted system of social transfers; and sizable debt reliefs granted by the Paris Club (Berg and Blanchard 1994; World Bank 2022c). Poland also undertook structural policy changes—liberalizing international trade to become a key exporter to Western Europe, encouraging capital inflows (especially FDI), privatizing state-owned enterprises, recapitalizing the financial system, and lowering entry barriers for new firms (Georgiev, Nagy-Mohacsi, and Plekhanov 2017). Private sector development was also supported by capital market deepening, reinforced by the creation of regulatory bodies, the Stock Exchange, and an increasing role of foreign banks (de Haas and van Lelyveld 2006).

The 2003 acceleration was triggered by reforms tied to Poland's EU accession process which granted the country access to the single European market and additional EU structural funds (IMF 2003; IMF 2008; World Bank 2022b). To become an EU member, Poland maintained prudent fiscal policy and transitioned to an inflation-targeting regime in 1998. Lower corporate income taxes and research and development tax allowances were introduced to promote investment (Murgasova 2005).

Attaining full EU membership accelerated Poland's structural changes and integration with the global economy. The EU accession process led to improvements in institutional quality as Poland aligned policies and regulations to European standards, privatized the telecommunications and energy sectors, strengthened banking regulation, and improved access to public infrastructure (Bruszt and Campos 2016). Labor market policies became more flexible. Capital

**BOX 3.1 Sparking investment accelerations: Lessons from country case studies (*continued*)**

**FIGURE B3.1.2 Investment accelerations in Poland and Türkiye**

*Poland had two investment accelerations—in 1992-2000 and 2003-08. Both private and public investment growth rose sharply in these episodes, with the 2003 episode driven by a more pronounced increase in public investment. The two episodes were also accompanied by improved fiscal positions and higher net capital inflows. Türkiye's investment acceleration occurred during 2003-08. Both private and public investment growth surged to similar degrees, while credit growth and net capital inflows more than tripled.*

A. Output and investment growth in Poland

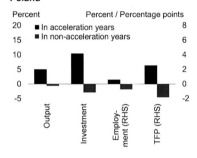

B. Macroeconomic conditions in Poland

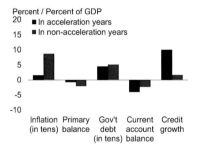

C. Net capital inflows and public and private investment growth in Poland

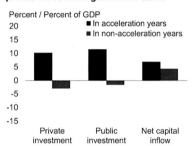

D. Output and investment growth in Türkiye

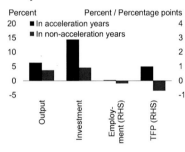

E. Macroeconomic conditions in Türkiye

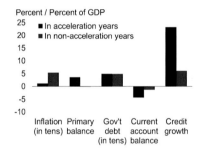

F. Net capital inflows and public and private investment growth in Türkiye

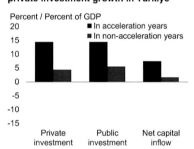

*Sources*: Bank for International Settlements; Feenstra, Inklaar, and Timmer (2015); Ha, Kose, and Ohnsorge (2021); Haver Analytics; IMF, International Financial Statistics; IMF, Investment and Capital Stock dataset; WDI (database); WEO (database); World Bank.
*Note*: The sample period is 1980-2022. Acceleration years cover the full duration of the episode. Non-acceleration years exclude acceleration years that were not included in this box; CPI = consumer price index; TFP = total factor productivity.
A.D. Bars are simple averages of growth in output, investment, and TFP, as well as the percentage point change in the employment rate.
B.E. Bars are simple average of the change in CPI in percent, primary balance as a percent of GDP, government debt as a percent of GDP, current account balance as a percent of GDP, and real credit growth in percent.
C.F. Bars are simple averages of growth in private investment and public investment in percent, and the net capital-inflow-to-GDP ratio in percent of GDP.

inflows surged as Poland integrated further into the supply chains of Western Europe (Georgiev, Nagy-Mohacsi, and Plekhanov 2017).

**Türkiye (2003-08)**

**Economic performance.** Türkiye experienced an investment acceleration during 2003-08. Average investment growth rose to 14.3 percent per year during the acceleration, compared with 4.6 percent in other years (figure B3.1.2). Output growth reached more than 6 percent per year during this episode, up from 3.7 percent per year in other years. During this period, the primary balance improved, and inflation was brought

under control—falling from 65 percent in the six years before the acceleration to about 11 percent during the acceleration. Both private and public investment growth surged to similar degrees, while credit growth and net capital inflows more than tripled. Rapid output growth allowed Türkiye to attain upper-middle-income status in 2004.

**Policy drivers.** Policy reforms implemented in the early 2000s, accompanied by a benign external environment, laid the foundation for the 2003 acceleration. Prior to the acceleration, a series of macroeconomic stabilization policies were implemented in response to the 2000-01

**BOX 3.1 Sparking investment accelerations: Lessons from country case studies (*continued*)**

economic crisis. Fiscal discipline was established with a primary surplus target of 6.5 percent of GNP, and the central bank became an independent institution (IMF 2007). The result was a virtuous cycle of disinflation, lower interest rates, and higher economic growth (Macovei 2009). These macroeconomic policies were complemented by structural reforms in several areas, including enterprise restructuring and privatization, improvements to the business climate, trade liberalization, labor market liberalization, and comprehensive reform of the banking sector. As a result, both access to credit and foreign direct investment inflows improved (World Bank 2008).

## Latin America and the Caribbean

### Uruguay (1991-98 and 2004-14)

**Economic performance.** Uruguay experienced two investment accelerations: 1991-98 and 2004-14. Average annual investment growth reached 10.3 percent, exceeding the level in non-acceleration years by 14.7 percentage points (figure B3.1.3). Output growth rose to 5 percent per year during the acceleration episodes (from near zero in non-acceleration years) as both employment and productivity growth surged. In both episodes, private investment grew much faster than public investment. Each acceleration was accompanied by improved macroeconomic conditions, including lower government debt, subdued inflation, larger primary surpluses, and higher credit growth compared with non-acceleration years. Uruguay attained high-income-country status in 2012.

**Policy drivers.** Following a period of stagnation between 1983 and 1990, policies to stabilize the economy and promote trade laid the foundation for the 1991 acceleration (Marandino and Oddone 2019). Fiscal policy measures included reducing external debt by 5 percentage points of GDP and restructuring short-term debt through the 1991 Brady Plan, as well as broader fiscal consolidation (Rial and Vicente 2003). Following high inflation in the 1980s, these fiscal adjustments fed into a price stabilization plan which also included a preannounced crawling exchange rate peg (Peluffo 2013). The country's first Central Bank Act was approved in 1995 to strengthen monetary policy and establish limits on central bank financing of the public sector. The 1991 acceleration was also

associated with further trade liberalization, marked by the signing of the Treaty of Asunción that formed the Southern Common Market.

The 2004 acceleration coincided with a series of macroeconomic and structural policy reforms. After a major banking crisis in 2002 and several external shocks between 1999 and 2001, the government adopted a range of measures to improve macroeconomic stability and debt sustainability (de la Plaza and Sirtaine 2005; Marandino and Oddone 2019). Fiscal consolidation and better debt management were combined with monetary policy measures including greater exchange rate flexibility, adoption of an inflation target, and enhanced central bank independence. Banking regulations were introduced in 2008 to mitigate risks associated with currency mismatches between banking sector assets and liabilities (Marandino and Oddone 2019).

This acceleration episode was also supported by structural reforms that improved the investment climate. These included strengthening the national investment office and improving physical infrastructure and the business environment (IMF 2008, 2010). The 2004 acceleration was accompanied by elevated agricultural commodity prices, favorable global financial conditions, and stronger regional trade linkages. Late in the 2000s investment acceleration, Uruguay regained an investment grade sovereign rating (Che 2021).

### Colombia (2001-07)

**Economic performance.** Colombia experienced an investment acceleration between 2001 and 2007. Annual investment growth reached 12.7 percent during the acceleration, exceeding the level of non-acceleration years by 10.3 percentage points (figure B3.1.3). Output growth averaged 4.5 percent during the investment acceleration compared with 3.3 percent outside of that period. During the acceleration, private investment grew over six times faster than during non-acceleration years, at 13.8 percent, while public investment growth increased from 4.2 percent to 6.1 percent. Inflation declined to single digits in the year before the acceleration for the first time in more than two decades. The overall fiscal deficit was less than 1 percent of GDP by 2004, while the primary balance reached a surplus. Government debt fell from 48 percent of GDP at its peak in 2002 to 33 percent of GDP in 2007.

**BOX 3.1 Sparking investment accelerations: Lessons from country case studies (*continued*)**

**FIGURE B3.1.3 Investment accelerations in Colombia and Uruguay**

*Uruguay experienced two investment accelerations: in 1991-98 and 2004-14. Private investment grew much faster than public investment during the two episodes. Both accelerations were accompanied by more favorable macroeconomic conditions, including lower government debt, subdued inflation, larger primary surpluses, and higher credit growth. Colombia experienced an investment acceleration between 2001 and 2007. During the acceleration, private investment grew more than six times faster than during non-acceleration years, while public investment growth increased from 4.2 to 6.1 percent. Both employment and TFP grew strongly.*

**A. Output and investment growth in Uruguay**

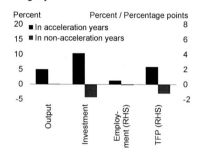

**B. Macroeconomic conditions in Uruguay**

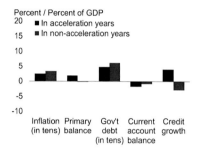

**C. Net capital inflows and public and private investment growth in Uruguay**

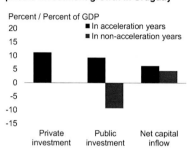

**D. Output and investment growth in Colombia**

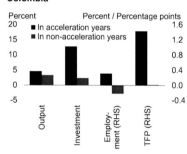

**E. Macroeconomic conditions in Colombia**

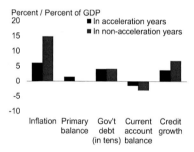

**F. Net capital inflows and public and private investment growth in Colombia**

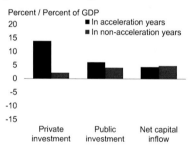

*Sources*: Bank for International Settlements; Feenstra, Inklaar, and Timmer (2015); Ha, Kose, and Ohnsorge (2021); Haver Analytics; IMF, International Financial Statistics; IMF, Investment and Capital Stock dataset; WDI (database); WEO (database); World Bank.
*Note*: The sample period is 1980-2022. Acceleration years cover the full duration of the episode. Non-acceleration years exclude acceleration years that were not included in this box; CPI = consumer price index; TFP = total factor productivity.
A.D. Bars are simple averages of growth in output, investment, and TFP, as well as the percentage point change in the employment rate.
B.E. Bars are simple average of the change in CPI in percent, primary balance as a percent of GDP, government debt as a percent of GDP, current account balance as a percent of GDP, and real credit growth in percent.
C.F. Bars are simple averages of growth in private investment and public investment in percent, and the net capital-inflow-to-GDP ratio in percent of GDP.

**Policy drivers.** The 2001 acceleration came after a difficult decade and was preceded by a series of reforms that significantly improved macroeconomic stability. First, a floating exchange rate regime was introduced in 1999 that helped reduce the impact of shocks on international reserve buffers. Second, in 2000, inflation targeting was adopted, accompanied by several legal measures to improve central bank independence and transparency (IMF 2006a). Third, on the fiscal front, government finances were improved by the introduction of tax reforms in the early 2000s, spending

restraint, a pension reform, and a series of reforms to public spending management (Clavijo 2009; IMF 2006b). Rising oil prices increased fiscal revenues during this period. Colombia's external position was also boosted by strong export growth in industrial goods. Domestic financial markets were deepened via the privatization and liquidation of public banks and improved supervision (IMF 2005, 2006b). Significant improvements in administrative procedures also supported the business environment.

**BOX 3.1 Sparking investment accelerations: Lessons from country case studies (*continued*)**

## Chile (1986-93)

**Economic performance.** Chile experienced an investment acceleration between 1986 and 1993 which resulted in annual average investment growth of 12.3 percent—8.4 percentage points higher than in other years (figure B3.1.4). Output growth doubled during this episode, exceeding 7.6 percent per year, supported by both productivity and employment growth. Broad improvements in macroeconomic indicators accompanied this acceleration. These included the primary balance moving from deficit to surplus, a significant decline in inflation (from almost 20 percent in the first year of the acceleration to 12.7 percent in 1993), and a substantial improvement in the current account from -6 percent of GDP in 1986 to -0.25 percent of GDP at its peak in 1991. Trade openness (the sum of exports plus imports relative to GDP) increased from about 50 percent of GDP to 63 percent of GDP at its peak in 1989, and proportion of exports from sectors other than mining increased by about 5 percentage points. Chile became an upper-middle-income country in 1993.

**Policy drivers.** Several policy interventions preceded or coincided with the acceleration. After the 1982 debt crisis during which output contracted by 15 percent, macroeconomic stability was an essential enabler (De Gregorio 2005; Corbo, Hernández, and Parro 2005). After the debt crisis, Chile took steps to reduce government borrowing, resulting in several consecutive years of fiscal surplus. The public debt-to-GDP ratio declined to roughly 50 percent by 1993, from 120 percent in 1986. The adoption of an inflation targeting regime in 1991 also helped to bring inflation under control.

Structural reforms—including trade liberalization, pension system reform, and banking sector reforms—were essential to sparking the investment acceleration (Corbo, Hernández, and Parro 2005, Gallego and Loayza 2002). The 1981 pension reform from a pay-as-you-go system toward a capitalization scheme helped deepen domestic financial markets by creating an additional source of credit for the private sector (Edwards 1998). Reforms that bolstered the ability of banks to provide credit and set up bankruptcy proceedings with well-defined property rights were critical factors in improving resource allocation (Bergoing et al. 2002).

## Middle East and North Africa

### Morocco (1996-2009)

**Economic performance.** Morocco underwent a significant economic transformation during the investment acceleration between 1996 and 2009 (figure B3.1.4). Annual investment growth rose from 2.3 percent in non-acceleration years to 7.5 percent during acceleration years, with annual output growth improving from 3.2 percent to 5 percent (despite a brief recession in 1997 during which investment growth did not contract). The period coincided with improvements in the fiscal position, external balance, and productivity growth, as well as higher credit growth. Both inflation and government debt (as a share of GDP) declined during the period.

**Policy drivers.** The acceleration followed and was accompanied by a range of fiscal and monetary reforms to foster macroeconomic stability (Harrigan and El-Siad 2010; IMF 2001, 2004). Fiscal revenue capacity was strengthened, including through the privatization of the telecommunications sector, tax reforms in the 1980s, and the strategic allocation of privatization revenues in 2001 (IMF 2001, 2004). During this period, improved fiscal capacity, exemplified by a large reduction in the external debt-to-reserves ratio, lessened marginal borrowing costs, allowing the government to finance much-needed social development initiatives.

Trade integration was strengthened by the Association Accord with the EU in 1996 and a free trade agreement with the United States in 2004. Morocco's trade openness surged by 31 percentage points of GDP during the acceleration. Financial reforms and price liberalization created a more conducive business and trade environment (Moreira 2019). Strategic policies supporting vital and internationally competitive sectors such as agriculture and renewable energy helped improve production (Paus 2012; Agénor and Aynaoui 2015). Other significant reforms included improvements in governance and competitiveness, measures to streamline public investment processes, and incentives to increase tourism revenues. This broad suite of growth-friendly reforms helped increase the net-capital-inflows-to-GDP ratio to 2 percent of GDP during the acceleration, from -2 percent prior to the episode (World Bank 2001; Achy 2011).

**BOX 3.1 Sparking investment accelerations: Lessons from country case studies (*continued*)**

**FIGURE B3.1.4 Investment accelerations in Chile and Morocco**

*Chile experienced an investment acceleration between 1986 and 1993. Output growth doubled during this episode, exceeding 7.6 percent per year, supported by both productivity and employment growth. Morocco underwent a significant economic transformation during an investment acceleration between 1996 and 2009. This period coincided with improvements in the fiscal position, the external balance, and productivity growth, as well as higher credit growth. Both inflation and government debt (as a share of GDP) declined.*

**A. Output and investment growth in Chile**

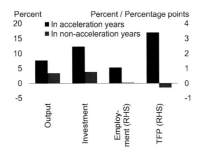

**B. Macroeconomic conditions in Chile**

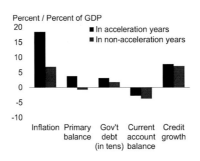

**C. Net capital inflows and public and private investment growth in Chile**

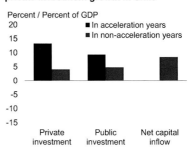

**D. Output and investment growth in Morocco**

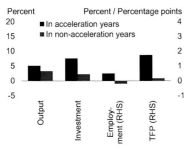

**E. Macroeconomic conditions in Morocco**

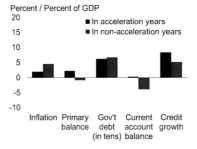

**F. Net capital inflows and public and private investment growth in Morocco**

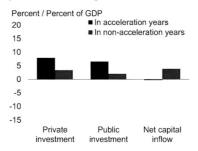

*Sources*: Bank for International Settlements; Feenstra, Inklaar, and Timmer (2015); Ha, Kose, and Ohnsorge (2021); Haver Analytics; IMF, International Financial Statistics; IMF, Investment and Capital Stock dataset; WDI (database); WEO (database); World Bank.
*Note*: The sample period is 1980-2022. Acceleration years cover the full duration of the episode. Non-acceleration years exclude acceleration years that were not included in this box; CPI = consumer price index; TFP = total factor productivity.
A.D. Bars are simple averages of growth in output, investment, and TFP, as well as the percentage point change in the employment rate.
B.E. Bars are simple average of the change in CPI in percent, primary balance as a percent of GDP, government debt as a percent of GDP, current account balance as a percent of GDP, and real credit growth in percent.
C.F. Bars are simple averages of growth in private investment and public investment in percent, and the net capital-inflow-to-GDP ratio in percent of GDP.

## South Asia

### India (1994-99)

**Economic performance.** India experienced an investment acceleration from 1994 to 1999 (figure B3.1.5). During this acceleration, driven mostly by the private sector, average annual investment growth reached 10 percent per year, about 5.9 percentage points higher than in other years. The government debt -to-GDP ratio was about 6 percentage points lower during this episode than in non-acceleration years, while the primary fiscal deficit and current account

deficit widened slightly. Net capital inflows to GDP improved slightly during the acceleration compared with those in the years before the acceleration while credit growth rose to over 7 percent compared with 4.8 percent in non-acceleration years. At the same time, TFP growth almost doubled during the acceleration, from 1.9 percent in nonacceleration years to 3.8 percent.

**Policy drivers.** The 1994 investment acceleration had its roots in reforms that started in 1991, addressing four major economic distortions (Ahluwalia 2002). First,

**BOX 3.1 Sparking investment accelerations: Lessons from country case studies (*continued*)**

### FIGURE B3.1.5 Investment accelerations in India and Uganda

*India had an investment acceleration from 1994 to 1999. During this episode, driven mostly by the private sector, average annual investment growth reached 10 percent per year, while the government-debt-to-GDP ratio declined materially. Uganda's investment acceleration lasted from 1993 to 2012. The episode was accompanied by a significant reduction in inflation and an improved primary fiscal balance, as well as a notable increase in credit growth. Private investment also grew.*

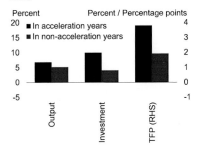

A. Output and investment growth in India

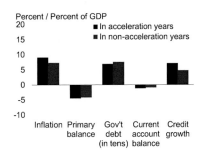

B. Macroeconomic conditions in India

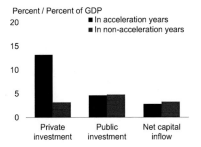

C. Net capital inflows and public and private investment growth in India

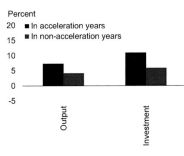

D. Output and investment growth in Uganda

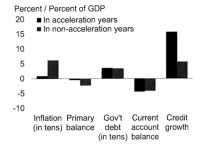

E. Macroeconomic conditions in Uganda

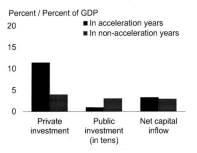

F. Net capital inflows and public and private investment growth in Uganda

*Sources*: Bank for International Settlements; Feenstra, Inklaar, and Timmer (2015); Ha, Kose, and Ohnsorge (2021); Haver Analytics; IMF, International Financial Statistics; IMF, Investment and Capital Stock dataset; WDI (database); WEO (database); World Bank.
*Note*: The sample period is 1980-2022. Acceleration years cover the full duration of the episode. Non-acceleration years exclude acceleration years that were not included in this box; CPI = consumer price index; TFP = total factor productivity.
A.D. Bars are simple averages of growth in output, investment, and TFP, as well as the percentage point change in the employment rate.
B.E. Bars are simple average of the change in CPI in percent, primary balance as a percent of GDP, government debt as a percent of GDP, current account balance as a percent of GDP, and real credit growth in percent.
C.F. Bars are simple averages of growth in private investment and public investment in percent, and the net capital-inflow-to-GDP ratio in percent of GDP.

tariff and non-tariff barriers on imports were lifted, making it easier to import capital goods. Second, capital account restrictions were loosened to allow greater capital inflows. Third, state control of the banking and insurance sectors was reduced to facilitate greater competition and efficiency, leading to increased domestically supplied credit to the private sector.

Finally, most of the public sector monopolies were ended. Sectors reserved to public firms shrank from 18 important industries (including iron and steel, electricity, and telecommunications) to three (atomic energy, rail transport, and national defense-related

aircraft and warships). A further reform was the transition to a market-determined exchange rate in 1993. These reforms promoted international investment and trade, and strengthened the private sector generally (Ahmad et al. 2018; Gupta et al. 2018).

## Sub-Saharan Africa

### Uganda (1993-2012)

**Economic performance.** Uganda, a low-income country, had a long period of investment acceleration between 1993 and 2012 (figure B3.1.5). Annual average investment growth, estimated at 10.9 percent

**BOX 3.1 Sparking investment accelerations: Lessons from country case studies (*continued*)**

during the acceleration period, was 5 percentage points higher than during non-acceleration years. Output growth was similarly elevated during the acceleration, but to a lesser extent—averaging 7.4 percent in acceleration years, compared with 4.2 percent otherwise. The episode was accompanied by a significant drop in inflation, an improved primary balance, a sizable reduction in the debt-service-to-exports ratio, and a notable increase in credit growth. Both private and public investment grew robustly during the acceleration. The proportion of the population in poverty fell from 68 percent in 1993 to 35 percent in 2013 (World Bank 2016).

**Policy drivers.** The 1993 acceleration was supported by a wide range of policies (World Bank 2007). Prior to the acceleration, Uganda committed to fiscal measures encompassing public enterprise and civil service reforms which helped stabilize the macroeconomy (Kuteesa et al. 2010; Mawejje and Odhiambo 2021). Public enterprise reforms, especially the privatization of key government-owned enterprises and the introduction of private sector participation in public utilities, sought to reduce the role of the government (Reinikka and Collier 2001; World Bank 2004). In addition, a comprehensive debt strategy formulated in 1991 strengthened debt management (Kitabire 2010). Monetary policy reforms focused on attaining a flexible exchange rate and price stability (Henstridge and Kasekende 2001).

A variety of structural reforms were implemented in the early 1990s to improve efficiency in the banking sector, liberalize the capital account, reduce trade barriers, and eliminate tax, legal, and other regulatory burdens on firms (Kuteesa et al. 2010; World Bank 2004). Debt relief initiatives and development assistance programs championed by the international community also played a significant role in supporting the acceleration. For example, Uganda was the first country to qualify for the Heavily Indebted Poor Countries debt relief initiative in 1998 and benefited from the Multilateral Debt Relief Initiative in 2006 (Andrews et al. 1999; Kitabire 2010). Uganda's participation in these initiatives reduced the debt-service-to-exports ratio by more than half, creating fiscal space that allowed more fiscal resources to be channeled into investment (Muwanga-Zake and Ndhaye 2001; Kitabire 2010).

Conclusion

These country studies show how initial conditions, together with comprehensive efforts to improve fiscal, monetary, and structural policies, can spark investment accelerations (tables B3.1.1, B3.1.2, and B3.1.3). The policy packages documented above allowed the 10 countries to seize favorable external conditions and turn them into accelerations. The case studies also demonstrate how such accelerations can be the source of sizable economic and development achievements.

The comprehensive policy packages overlapped considerably, even if the subsequent accelerations differed in some important dimensions (such as the split between private and public investment growth, or levels of credit growth). First, at about the start of each acceleration, improvements in the credibility and independence of monetary policy helped achieve lower and more stable inflation (for example, the Republic of Korea in 1998). Second, all accelerations were preceded by fiscal consolidation, either through stricter expenditure controls, the elimination of subsidies, tax reforms, or privatization of state-owned enterprises (for example, Colombia, India, or Uganda). Third, all accelerations were accompanied structural reforms. These encompassed trade and capital account liberalization efforts, the strengthening and deepening of financial markets and their regulation, and improvements to business climates, including policies to promote greater competition (for example, India, Poland in 1992, and Türkiye).

Investment accelerations were crucial for economic and human development. Output growth was substantially higher during these 13 accelerations than in non-acceleration years. Further, for many countries, productivity and employment growth was only positive, on average, during accelerations. Several countries either became high-income countries during the acceleration (for example, the Republic of Korea in 2001, Poland in 2009, or Uruguay in 2012), or saw sizable gains in the fight against extreme poverty (Colombia, India, Morocco, Uganda).

In some cases, the international community played a critical role in addressing long-standing debt problems, such that investment accelerations could take hold. For example, well-calibrated debt relief preceded or accompanied accelerations in Uganda and Uruguay.

**BOX 3.1 Sparking investment accelerations: Lessons from country case studies (*continued*)**

### TABLE B3.1.1 Investment and output growth during and outside investment accelerations

| Country | Acceleration episode | Investment growth | | Private investment growth | | Public investment growth | | Output growth | |
|---|---|---|---|---|---|---|---|---|---|
| | | During | Outside | During | Outside | During | Outside | During | Outside |
| Chile | 1986-93 | 12.3 (13.2) | 3.9 (5.1) | 13.2 (16.0) | 4.0 (5.9) | 9.2 (20.6) | 4.8 (3.1) | 7.6 (7.1) | 3.4 (3.4) |
| Colombia | 2001-07 | 12.7 (11.8) | 2.3 (3.1) | 13.8 (13.4) | 2.1 (2.8) | 6.1 (5.7) | 4.2 (2.9) | 4.5 (4.7) | 3.3 (3.4) |
| India | 1994-99 | 10.0 (9.0) | 4.1 (4.6) | 13.2 (11.9) | 3.2 (3.4) | 4.6 (5.9) | 4.8 (2.5) | 6.8 (7.1) | 5.2 (6.1) |
| Korea, Rep. | 1985-96 | 12.2 (11.2) | 1.9 (1.2) | 12.9 (12.1) | 1.5 (-0.1) | 9.4 (8.2) | 4.9 (4.5) | 9.3 (9.4) | 4.0 (3.3) |
| Korea, Rep. | 1999-2007 | 5.2 (5.1) | 1.9 (1.2) | 5.7 (5.3) | 1.5 (-0.1) | 3.3 (2.4) | 4.9 (4.5) | 6.3 (5.3) | 4.0 (3.3) |
| Morocco | 1996-2009 | 7.5 (7.2) | 2.2 (2.0) | 7.8 (7.8) | 3.3 (2.8) | 6.5 (4.0) | 2.0 (-0.3) | 5.0 (5.4) | 3.2 (4.0) |
| Malaysia | 1988-97 | 17.9 (16.3) | -3.0 (-1.2) | 19.9 (20.1) | -2.9 (-2.3) | 13.4 (11.7) | -0.2 (-10.3) | 9.2 (9.2) | 3.4 (5.4) |
| Poland | 1992-2000 | 10.4 (8.5) | -3.0 (-2.1) | 10.7 (10.2) | -3.0 (-3.7) | 8.5 (6.4) | -1.7 (0.3) | 5.0 (4.7) | -0.7 (1.3) |
| Poland | 2003-08 | 10.4 (8.9) | -3.0 (-2.1) | 9.3 (7.2) | -3.0 (-3.7) | 15.8 (17.4) | -1.7 (0.3) | 4.9 (4.6) | -0.7 (1.3) |
| Türkiye | 2003-08 | 14.3 (17.1) | 4.6 (2.8) | 14.3 (17.1) | 4.3 (2.3) | 14.3 (17.1) | 5.5 (4.7) | 6.2 (6.4) | 3.7 (4.9) |
| Uganda | 1993-2012 | 10.9 (10.3) | 5.9 (2.1) | 11.4 (10.6) | 4.0 (2.5) | 9.6 (11.0) | 31.0 (12.2) | 7.4 (7.1) | 4.2 (4.7) |
| Uruguay | 1991-98 | 10.9 (9.3) | -4.4 (-4.6) | 12.0 (7.0) | -0.1 (-4.7) | 9.5 (7.9) | -9.3 (-6.6) | 4.5 (4.7) | 0.0 (0.8) |
| Uruguay | 2004-14 | 9.9 (10.7) | -4.4 (-4.6) | 10.5 (13.4) | -0.1 (-4.7) | 8.9 (9.8) | -9.3 (-6.6) | 5.4 (5.0) | 0.0 (0.8) |

*Source*: World Bank.
*Note*: All numbers are average growth rates in percent with median growth rates in parentheses for the respective acceleration years, or all non-acceleration years in a country since 1980. During refers to statistics for the acceleration years between 1980-2022. Outside refers statistics for all non-acceleration years over the same period. For details about the acceleration episodes, see box 3.1.

### TABLE B3.1.2 Economic indicators during and outside investment accelerations

| Country | Acceleration episode | Real credit growth | | TFP growth | | Change in employment rate | | Net capital inflows (percent of GDP) | | Cumulative real GDP per capita growth (percent) |
|---|---|---|---|---|---|---|---|---|---|---|
| | | During | Outside | During | Outside | During | Outside | During | Outside | During |
| Chile | 1986-93 | 7.7 (7.4) | 7.1 (8.5) | 3.4 (3.2) | -0.3 (-0.2) | 1.1 (1.2) | 0.1 (0.2) | 0.1 (1.7) | 8.4 (9.9) | 52 |
| Colombia | 2001-07 | 3.7 (2.3) | 6.9 (6.1) | 1.4 (1.1) | 0.0 (0.2) | 0.3 (0.4) | -0.2 (-0.1) | 4.4 (5.0) | 4.9 (4.8) | 23 |
| India | 1994-99 | 7.1 (5.6) | 4.8 (5.4) | 3.8 (4.4) | 1.9 (2.0) | | | 2.8 (2.8) | 3.3 (2.6) | 27 |
| Korea, Rep. | 1985-96 | 14.0 (13.7) | 9.5 (7.6) | 2.3 (2.2) | 1.1 (0.8) | 0.1 (0.1) | -0.2 (0.1) | 2.3 (3.0) | 3.5 (3.6) | 140 |
| Korea, Rep. | 1999-2007 | 4.9 (4.6) | 9.5 (7.6) | 2.4 (1.9) | 1.1 (0.8) | 0.4 (0.3) | -0.2 (0.1) | 3.5 (3.5) | 3.5 (3.6) | 49 |
| Morocco | 1996-2009 | 8.3 (7.5) | 5.1 (3.5) | 1.7 (1.5) | 0.2 (1.1) | 0.5 (0.5) | -0.2 (0.0) | -0.3 (-0.2) | 3.9 (3.7) | 50 |
| Malaysia | 1988-97 | 16.7 (17.6) | 4.1 (3.6) | 0.8 (0.6) | -0.1 (1.6) | 0.6 (0.6) | -0.2 (-0.1) | 6.0 (5.6) | 3.7 (3.5) | 74 |
| Poland | 1992-2000 | 8.2 (11.2) | 1.6 (6.9) | 3.1 (3.1) | -1.9 (-0.0) | -0.5 (-1.8) | -0.8 (-0.5) | 5.4 (5.7) | 4.3 (4.7) | 50 |
| Poland | 2003-08 | 12.4 (14.2) | 1.6 (6.9) | 1.7 (2.0) | -1.9 (-0.0) | 2.1 (1.9) | -0.8 (-0.5) | 8.3 (7.5) | 4.3 (4.7) | 29 |
| Türkiye | 2003-08 | 23.2 (21.7) | 6.0 (6.3) | 1.0 (1.5) | -0.7 (0.7) | 0.0 (0.1) | -0.2 (-0.0) | 7.4 (7.5) | 1.7 (1.6) | 27 |
| Uganda | 1993-2012 | 15.7 (11.7) | 5.7 (5.0) | | | | | 3.3 (4.2) | 3.0 (3.0) | 114 |
| Uruguay | 1991-98 | 5.4 (7.3) | -2.9 (-0.4) | 2.0 (2.1) | -1.2 (-0.7) | -0.2 (-0.2) | -0.1 (-0.4) | 3.4 (3.4) | 4.5 (5.6) | 30 |
| Uruguay | 2004-14 | 2.8 (8.6) | -2.9 (-0.4) | 2.6 (2.3) | -1.2 (-0.7) | 1.0 (0.8) | -0.1 (-0.4) | 8.3 (7.8) | 4.5 (5.6) | 65 |

*Source*: World Bank.
*Note*: All numbers except last column are average growth rates in percent with median growth rates in parentheses for the respective acceleration years, or all non-acceleration years in a country since 1980. During refers to statistics for the acceleration years between 1980-2022. Outside refers statistics for all non-acceleration years over the same period. Empty cells reflect missing data. For details about the acceleration episodes, see box 3.1. GDP = gross domestic product; TFP = total factor productivity.

**BOX 3.1 Sparking investment accelerations: Lessons from country case studies (*continued*)**

**TABLE B3.1.3 Policy changes and reforms during investment accelerations**

| Country | Acceleration episode | Fiscal policy | Monetary policy | Structural policy | External environment |
|---|---|---|---|---|---|
| Chile | 1986-93 | Fiscal consolidation | Central bank independence (1989) Adoption of inflation target (1990) | Trade liberalization Financial sector deepening Banking reforms | Rising copper prices in the late 1980s |
| Colombia | 2001-07 | Fiscal consolidation Structural tax reforms SOE and public investment management reforms | Increased exchange rate flexibility Adoption of inflation target (1999) Enhanced central bank independence | Enhanced trade linkages Financial sector deepening | Rising oil prices<br><br>Strong global growth and supportive global financial conditions |
| India | 1994-99 | Fiscal consolidation Structural tax reforms | Increased exchange rate flexibility | Ended most public sector monopolies Capital account and trade liberalization Reduced state control of banking and insurance | Solid global growth |
| Malaysia | 1988-97 | Structural tax reforms (revenue collection focus) | Currency devaluation | Financial sector deepening (better access to credit) | |
| Morocco | 1996-2009 | Fiscal consolidation<br><br>Structural tax reforms | Reforms to balance fixed exchange rate | Trade liberalization (trade agreements with the EU and U.S.) Reduction in price controls and subsidies Financial sector deepening (better access to credit) | Strong global growth and supportive global financial conditions |
| Poland | 1992-2000 | Reduction of inefficient subsidies SOE management reforms Structural tax and entitlement reforms | Increased exchange rate flexibility Monetary tightening (curbing excess credit growth) Adoption of inflation targeting (1998) | Privatization of state-owned enterprises Trade liberalization (joined GATT and signed multiple trade agreements) Capital account liberalization Banking reforms and recapitalization Competition reforms | Paris Club debt forgiveness |
| Poland | 2003-08 | Targeted tax reductions to promote investment | Increased exchange rate flexibility | Financial sector deepening Alignment of many policies and regulations to the EU | Accession to the EU in 2004 Strong global growth and supportive global financial conditions |
| Korea, Rep. | 1985-96 | Fiscal consolidation and rules (balanced budget principle) Institutional fiscal improvements (establishing a budget council) | End central bank financing of government | Trade liberalization (reduced import restrictions) Reduction in price controls Competition reforms (Monopoly Regulation and Fair Trade Act) | |
| Korea, Rep. | 1999-2007 | Fiscal consolidation (especially lower spending growth) | Enhanced central bank independence Increased exchange rate flexibility Adoption of inflation targeting (1998) | Liberalization of capital markets (reduced FDI restrictions) Corporate governance reforms Restructuring of financial corporations | Strong global growth and supportive global financial conditions |

**BOX 3.1 Sparking investment accelerations: Lessons from country case studies (*continued*)**

**TABLE B3.1.3 Policy changes and reforms during investment accelerations (*continued*)**

| Country | Acceleration episode | Fiscal policy | Monetary policy | Structural policy | External environment |
|---------|---------------------|---------------|-----------------|-------------------|----------------------|
| Türkiye | 2003-08 | Fiscal consolidation and rules (primary surplus target) | Central bank independence (2001) | Privatizations and corporate restructuring<br>Business climate improvements<br>Trade liberalization<br>Labor market liberalization<br>Banking reform | Strong global growth and supportive global financial conditions |
| Uganda | 1993-2012 | Privatizations and SOE reforms<br>Institutional fiscal improvements (establishing Uganda Tax authority) | Increased exchange rate flexibility | Banking reform<br>Trade liberalization<br>Business climate improvements | HIPC and Multilateral Debt Relief<br>Development assistance |
| Uruguay | 1991-98 | Fiscal consolidation | Increased exchange rate flexibility<br>Limit central bank financing of government | Trade liberalization (MERCOSUR regional trade agreement) | Reduced external debt through Brady plan |
| Uruguay | 2004-14 | Institutional fiscal improvements (improved public balance sheet management) | Increased exchange rate flexibility<br>Enhanced central bank independence<br>Adoption of inflation targeting (2005) | Banking reform<br>Business climate improvements | Elevated agricultural commodity prices<br>Improving regional trade integration<br>Supportive global financial conditions |

*Source*: World Bank.
*Note*: EU = European Union. For details about the acceleration episodes, see box 3.1.

# ANNEX 3.1 Identification of investment accelerations

**Definition.** Investment accelerations are defined as episodes of rapid acceleration in investment per capita that are sustained for at least six years. Using per capita growth in investment takes into account the significance of population growth, which has averaged more than 2 percent in the typical EMDE between 1950 and 2022. Per capita growth rates also have a better link with GDP per capita growth, which is the focus of long-term growth analyses (Libman, Montecino, and Razmi 2019).

As suggested by Barro and Sala-i-Martin (1992) and Christiano and Fitzgerald (2003), economic indicators taken more than five calendar years apart are less influenced by business cycle fluctuations. According to Hausmann, Pritchett, and Rodrik (2005), output growth accelerations require heightened output growth to last at least eight years. Given the volatile nature of investment growth, the approach preferred here uses a time frame of a minimum of six years. In addition, the requirement that capital stock per capita at the end of an acceleration must exceed its pre-episode peak is added to ensure that the episodes identified are indeed accelerations and not merely periods of recoveries. The sensitivity analysis shows that shorter (or longer) periods of acceleration do not affect the main results of this chapter (see annexes 3.3 and 3.4 for details). Based on the length of six years and the sample's end year of 2022, the latest year an acceleration can start is in 2017. The distribution of episodes by country groups is shown in table A3.1.1, and the list of episodes in EMDEs detailed in table A3.1.2.

The chapter aims to identify the same type of large-scale investment acceleration with transformative development implications. To avoid pooling different types of accelerations, the same set of criteria detailed below is applied to per capita growth in investment in all economies in the sample:

- The average growth rate of investment over six years must be at least 4 percent a year.

- The average growth rate of investment over six years must be at least 2 percentage points higher than in the previous six years.

- The level of the capital stock per capita at the end of the acceleration must exceed its pre-episode peak.

The first two criteria are designed to identify rapid acceleration in investment per capita growth. The first criterion requires that growth is rapid, setting a threshold of at least 4 percent per capita growth per year. This rate corresponds to the long-run median growth rate of investment for the top one-third of countries in the sample.[11] The second criterion confirms that investment accelerates. It does so by requiring a minimum increase of 2 percentage points, which is the median difference in growth between two neighboring six-year periods for the top one-third of countries in the sample. Finally, the requirement that capital stock per capita at the end of an acceleration must exceed its pre-episode peak ensures that the episodes identified are indeed accelerations and not merely periods of recoveries. Three additional criteria are added to identify more reasonable episodes and starting years (see below).

**Comparison with other identification approaches.** The identification approach adopted here aligns with the existing studies on output and capital stock growth accelerations, but differs in two key dimensions: the duration of heightened growth required and the main criteria for identifying accelerations. First, all existing studies on accelerations typically adopt an eight-year framework without adapting to the volatile nature of investment growth (for instance, Libman, Montecino and Razmi, 2019; Manzano and Saboin 2022). Second, the values for various criteria detailed above are taken from sample statistics, while other approaches used ad-hoc values (for instance, Hausmann, Pritchett and Rodrik 2005; Jong-A-Pin and de Haan 2011). In addition, Libman, Montecino and Razmi (2019) study capital stock growth accelerations. Their approach differs slightly from the one used here in

---

[11] In the sensitivity analyses, alternative thresholds are used, which do not change the main results (see annex 3.3).

how they identify the correct starting years (that is, using a break test to smoothed capital stock growth series) and the focus on capital stock per capita growth. The use of capital stock growth makes their set of accelerations less linked with output performance.

**Additional requirements.** A few additional requirements are added to avoid overidentifying investment accelerations and to identify more reasonable episodes and starting years. These requirements are specifically added to tailor the filtering approach to the volatile nature of investment growth. Firstly, to exclude episodes driven by short-term surges in investment, the approach mandates that investment growth must be positive in at least five out of the six years of an acceleration period. Second, the investment per capita growth rate at the beginning of the six-year period should not be negative. Third, per capita investment has to accelerate and be higher in the second year of an episode than in the first year. Finally, if more than one year qualifies as the start of the investment acceleration episode, the first year that meets the criteria is identified as the start (Jong-A-Pin and De Haan 2008). The unconditional probability of experiencing an investment acceleration in a decade is calculated by dividing the number of identified investment accelerations by the total number of country-years in the sample (later converted to decades) during which an acceleration could occur.

**TABLE A3.1.1 Investment accelerations: Distribution over country groups**

| Grouping | Number of economies | Number of investment accelerations | EMDE groups | Number of economies | Number of investment growth accelerations |
|---|---|---|---|---|---|
| AEs | 35 | 77 | CIM | 25 | 54 |
| EAP | 8 | 19 | CEX | 44 | 61 |
| ECA | 11 | 17 | LICs | 7 | 13 |
| LAC | 19 | 39 | FCS | 7 | 10 |
| MNA | 9 | 11 | Small states | 4 | 5 |
| SAR | 3 | 7 | | | |
| SSA | 19 | 22 | | | |

*Source*: World Bank.
*Note*: Number of economies refers to economies for which data are available. All non-advanced economies have been classified in regions and EMDE groups as used by the World Bank in fiscal year 2024. AEs = advanced economies; CIM = commodity-importing EMDEs; CEX = commodity-exporting EMDEs; EAP = East Asia and Pacific; ECA = Eastern Europe and Central Asia; EMDEs = emerging market and developing economies; FCS = fragile and conflict-affected situations; LAC = Latin America and the Caribbean; LICs = low-income countries; MNA = Middle East and North Africa; SAR = South Asia; SSA = Sub-Saharan Africa.

## TABLE A3.1.2 List of investment accelerations in EMDEs

| Economy | Starting year(s) of investment accelerations | Economy | Starting year(s) of investment accelerations |
|---|---|---|---|
| Albania | 1999 | Malaysia | 1967, 1978, 1988, 2006 |
| Algeria | 1973, 1999 | Mali | 1971, 1984, 1992, 2002, 2014 |
| Argentina | 1967 | Mauritius | 1972, 1983 |
| Armenia | 1997 | Mexico | 1991, 2003 |
| Bahrain | 2012 | Mongolia | 1976, 2005 |
| Belarus | 1999 | Morocco | 1996 |
| Belize | 1986 | Mozambique | 2007 |
| Benin | 1966 | Namibia | 2005 |
| Bolivia | 2005 | Nepal | 2014 |
| Botswana | 1996 | Nicaragua | 1961, 2010 |
| Brazil | 1968, 2005 | Nigeria | 1969 |
| Bulgaria | 1994 | North Macedonia | 2006 |
| Burkina Faso | 1968, 2002, 2017 | Oman | 2002 |
| Cambodia | 2011 | Panama | 1965, 1990, 2005 |
| Chile | 1977, 1986, 2002 | Paraguay | 1971, 2005, 2016 |
| China | 1977, 1991 | Peru | 1961, 1969, 1992, 2002 |
| Colombia | 2001 | Philippines | 1973, 2012 |
| Costa Rica | 1973, 1983, 2004 | Poland | 1983, 1992, 2003, 2017 |
| Dominican Republic | 1970, 2005, 2014 | Romania | 1969, 1999, 2014 |
| Ecuador | 2007 | Rwanda | 1970, 2002 |
| El Salvador | 1970, 1984, 1991, 2017 | Saudi Arabia | 2003 |
| Equatorial Guinea | 1994 | Sri Lanka | 1974, 1990, 2002 |
| Honduras | 2003 | Tanzania | 2002 |
| Hungary | 1993, 2013 | Thailand | 1958, 1976, 1987, 2001 |
| India | 1985, 1994, 2004 | Togo | 1974 |
| Indonesia | 1987, 2003 | Türkiye | 1969, 2003, 2010 |
| Iran, Islamic Rep. | 1963, 1999 | Uganda | 1993 |
| Jamaica | 1966 | Uruguay | 1974, 1991, 2004 |
| Kenya | 2007 | Viet Nam | 2002, 2013 |
| Kuwait | 1990, 2001, 2012 | | |

*Source*: World Bank.
EMDEs = emerging market and developing economies.

# ANNEX 3.2 Methodological annex

## Data

Data for investment, GDP, capital stock, and population for the period 1950-2019 are sourced from the Penn World Table (PWT) 10.01 because this database covers many more countries than alternative databases. To update the investment data provided by PWT, investment growth data for 2020-22 is sourced from Haver Analytics, World Bank Development Indicators (WDI), and *Global Economic Prospects* (GEP). To compute per capita series of GDP and investment after 2019, population data are taken from the United Nations population prospects database. The final sample of economies includes 35 advanced economies and 69 EMDEs (table A3.1.1). These economies represent about 97 percent of global GDP since the mid-2000s (World Bank 2023a).

Data on the explanatory variables are taken from a variety of sources. Institutional quality is proxied by the "law and order" subcomponent of the PRS Group's *International Country Risk Guide* (ICRG). The undervaluation index is constructed following Rodrik (2008) using data from PWT. Global GDP growth is computed using GDP weights at average 2010-19 prices and market exchange rates. Primary balance as a share of GDP is taken from the IMF's *World Economic Outlook*. Inflation data are taken from Ha, Kose, and Ohnsorge (2021). Trade restrictions and inflation targeting indices are taken from the IMF structural reform database (Alesina et al. 2020) and IMF AREAER database. The capital account restrictions index is taken from (Chinn and Ito 2008). Additional covariates for the robustness checks include natural resource rent as a share of GDP from WDI; global recession years defined by Kose, Sugawara, and Terrones (2020); and global financial cycle factor, retrieved from Miranda-Agrippino and Rey (2020).

## Methodology

The correlates and probability of an investment acceleration starting in a given year are estimated using logit regressions. The following model is estimated:

$$Pr\ (Y_{i,t} = 1 \,|\, X_{i,t}) = \phi\ (\beta X_{i,t}),$$

where *Pr* denotes the probability that a sustained investment acceleration takes place in country *i* in year *t* ($Y_{i,t}$), conditioned on a set of variables ($X_{i,t}$), and $\phi$ denotes the cumulative distribution function. Because there is some uncertainty around the precise starting date of an acceleration, the approach of Hausmann, Pritchett, and Rodrik (2005) and Libman, Montecino, and Razmi (2019) is followed: the dependent variable takes the value 1 in the year immediately before and the year immediately after the beginning of the episode, and 0 otherwise. Also, the years an episode cannot take place (that is, year two until the end of an episode, as well as the first and last five years of the sample) are excluded. Because of data limitations, the regressions cover the period 1985-2017. Furthermore, to prevent a small number of countries from having a large influence on the results, estimates are unweighted.

The analysis focuses on the effect of institutional quality (*IQ*) and economic policy reforms (EPR) on the likelihood that an investment acceleration occurs. In the model, the level of institutional quality, the economic policy reform indicator, and their interaction are included.

The model is:

$$Pr\ (Y_{i,t} = 1 \,|\, X_{i,t}) = \phi(\beta_0 + \beta_1\,IQ_{i,t-1} + \beta_2\,EPR_{i,t} + \beta_3\,[IQ_{i,t-1} * EPR_{i,t}] + \beta_4\,CV_{i,t-1} + \mu_{i,t}),$$

where *CV* represents the control variables capturing the country's development status and domestic and external controls, such as the global GDP growth rate. Institutional quality is measured by the law and order subindex from ICRG. Economic policy reforms are calculated as the annual change in the trade restriction index and the Chin-Ito capital openness index (measured in percent), percentage points of GDP for the primary balance, or a dummy variable indicating whether a country has adopted an inflation target or tightened an inflation target since the preceding year.

## Empirical results

Table A3.2.1 shows the results for the impact of institutional quality and control variables on the probability of an investment acceleration starting in the following year. Column (1) shows the main institutional quality variable, and controls for country-specific conditions that capture the development status (GDP per capita), level of capital (capital-to-output ratio), and the undervaluation index following Rodrik (2008). Columns (2) through (6) add additional control variables for global economic conditions (global GDP growth), economic stability (inflation rate), and the level of fiscal and external policies of this chapter. Based on these results and the limits that the level of fiscal and external policy place on the sample size, column (2) is the preferred baseline specification for the analysis of policy impacts on the probability of an investment acceleration.

Table A3.2.2 presents the impact of policy changes on the probability of an investment acceleration using the set of controls in column (2) of table A3.2.1. To simplify the interpretation of the results, the institutional quality variable and the policy change variables are demeaned. The results mirror those in table A3.2.1, showing that higher institutional quality, as well as the four policy changes presented in table A3.2.2, increase the likelihood of an investment acceleration. Furthermore, the impact of a policy is dependent on the level of institutional quality. For two policy changes, the interaction term between the lagged institutional quality variable and the policy change are significant. Column (5) includes all four policy reforms concurrently but does not include an interaction term with institutional quality.

**TABLE A3.2.1 Institutional quality and initial conditions as drivers of the likelihood of investment accelerations**

| Dependent variable | (1) | (2) | (3) | (4) | (5) | (6) |
|---|---|---|---|---|---|---|
| | Investment per capita growth acceleration | | | | | |
| Lagged institutional quality (IQ) | 0.207*** | 0.204*** | 0.207*** | 0.219*** | 0.276*** | 0.222*** |
| | (3.49) | (3.45) | (3.48) | (2.96) | (4.50) | (2.91) |
| Lagged GDP per capita | -0.016 | -0.006 | -0.022 | -0.192** | -0.089 | -0.206** |
| | (-0.25) | (-0.09) | (-0.35) | (-2.33) | (-1.18) | (-1.97) |
| Lagged capital-to-output ratio | -0.521*** | -0.525*** | -0.504*** | -0.748*** | -0.376*** | -0.638*** |
| | (-3.84) | (-3.87) | (-3.71) | (-4.43) | (-2.58) | (-3.46) |
| Lagged under valuation index | 0.752*** | 0.766*** | 0.750*** | 1.432*** | 1.073*** | 1.634*** |
| | (4.74) | (4.82) | (4.75) | (7.23) | (5.89) | (8.17) |
| Lagged global GDP growth | | 0.109** | | | | 0.260*** |
| | | (2.14) | | | | (4.09) |
| Lagged inflation rate | | | -0.000 | | | -0.012* |
| | | | (-0.09) | | | (-1.85) |
| Lagged government expenditure to GDP | | | | 0.037*** | | 0.038*** |
| | | | | (4.31) | | (3.71) |
| Lagged net capital inflows to GDP | | | | | -0.009*** | -0.010*** |
| | | | | | (-3.50) | (-2.78) |
| Constant | -1.610*** | -1.965*** | -1.571*** | -0.877 | -1.296** | -1.384* |
| | (-3.47) | (-3.95) | (-3.39) | (-1.57) | (-2.11) | (-1.71) |
| Number of observations | 2,200 | 2,200 | 2,189 | 1,767 | 1,936 | 1,590 |
| Pseudo R² | 0.027 | 0.029 | 0.026 | 0.056 | 0.043 | 0.079 |
| Number of episodes | 117 | 117 | 117 | 93 | 107 | 88 |
| Number of economies | 96 | 96 | 96 | 96 | 95 | 95 |

*Source*: World Bank.
*Note*: This table shows the estimated coefficients for the change in log-odds. Robust standard errors in parentheses. ***, **, and * indicate significance at the 1, 5, and 10 percent levels, respectively. Investment per capita growth accelerations are identified as described in annex 3.1.

## TABLE A3.2.2 Institutional quality and policies as drivers of the likelihood of investment accelerations

| Dependent variable | (1) | (2) | (3) | (4) | (5) |
|---|---|---|---|---|---|
| | Investment per capita growth acceleration | | | | |
| Lagged institutional quality (IQ) | 0.227*** | 0.224*** | 0.249*** | 0.289*** | 0.472*** |
| | (3.60) | (3.66) | (3.27) | (3.71) | (5.06) |
| Lagged GDP per capita | -0.016 | -0.018 | -0.016 | 0.095 | -0.021 |
| | (-0.23) | (-0.28) | (-0.22) | (1.00) | (-0.17) |
| Lagged capital-to-output ratio | -0.556*** | -0.533*** | -0.593*** | -0.420** | -0.311 |
| | (-3.61) | (-3.86) | (-3.47) | (-2.18) | (-1.24) |
| Lagged under valuation index | 0.963*** | 0.764*** | 1.259*** | 1.392*** | 2.078*** |
| | (5.81) | (4.74) | (6.25) | (5.18) | (6.96) |
| Lagged global GDP growth | 0.162*** | 0.116** | 0.152*** | 0.062 | 0.125* |
| | (2.99) | (2.28) | (2.59) | (1.13) | (1.90) |
| Change in capital account openness | 0.005*** | | | | 0.004** |
| | (2.98) | | | | (2.01) |
| Interaction of lagged IQ and change in capital account openness (percent) | 0.001 | | | | |
| | (0.88) | | | | |
| Adoption or lowering of inflation target (dummy) | | 1.133*** | | | 1.463*** |
| | | (3.75) | | | (4.13) |
| Interaction of lagged IQ and adoption or lowering of inflation target (dummy) | | -0.058 | | | |
| | | (-0.31) | | | |
| Change in primary balance (percent of GDP) | | | 0.032** | | 0.124*** |
| | | | (2.20) | | (2.72) |
| Interaction of lagged IQ and change in primary balance (percent of GDP) | | | 0.027*** | | |
| | | | (3.58) | | |
| Change in trade restriction index (percent) | | | | 0.010** | 0.018*** |
| | | | | (2.41) | (2.96) |
| Interaction of lagged IQ and change in trade restriction index (percent) | | | | 0.014*** | |
| | | | | (2.88) | |
| Constant | -1.125* | -1.094* | -1.136* | -1.907** | -1.242 |
| | (-1.83) | (-1.85) | (-1.71) | (-2.28) | (-1.22) |
| Number of observations | 1,951 | 2,200 | 1,683 | 1,393 | 1,006 |
| Pseudo $R^2$ | 0.037 | 0.036 | 0.051 | 0.051 | 0.108 |
| Number of episodes | 106 | 117 | 87 | 83 | 60 |
| Number of economies | 94 | 96 | 95 | 74 | 71 |

*Source*: World Bank.
*Note*: This table shows the estimated coefficients for the change in log-odds. Robust standard errors in parentheses. ***, **, and * indicate significance at the 1, 5, and 10 percent levels, respectively. Investment per capita growth accelerations are identified as described in annex 3.1.

# ANNEX 3.3 Investment accelerations using different filtering algorithms

Table A3.3.1 displays the robustness of the identification approach when alternative parameter values of the minimum average investment growth rate and minimum length of investment acceleration are applied. Overall, setting lower thresholds for growth rates during accelerations or using shorter acceleration durations result in a larger number of identified episodes. Despite variations in the number of episodes identified under different parameter combinations, including those based on aggregate rather than per-capita investment growth, the findings show sustained and heightened investment and output growth, which supports the use of the baseline approach.

**TABLE A3.3.1 Investment accelerations using different filtering algorithms**

| (1)<br>Filtering method | (2)<br>Number of episodes | (3)<br>Investment per capita growth Before | (4)<br>Investment per capita growth During | (5)<br>t-test (p value) | (6)<br>Output per capita growth Before | (7)<br>Output per capita growth During | (8)<br>t-test (p value) | (9)<br>Countries without accelerations |
|---|---|---|---|---|---|---|---|---|
| **Benchmark** | 192 | 1.56 | 9.87 | 0.00 | 1.74 | 4.50 | 0.00 | 11 |
| 6 years, 4% not per capita | 226 | 3.34 | 10.73 | 0.00 | 1.97 | 4.13 | 0.00 | 11 |
| 5 years, 4% | 243 | 1.72 | 10.00 | 0.00 | 1.88 | 4.41 | 0.00 | 8 |
| 7 years, 4% | 142 | 0.20 | 9.96 | 0.00 | 1.64 | 4.60 | 0.00 | 23 |
| 6 years, 3% | 210 | 1.46 | 9.28 | 0.00 | 1.74 | 4.26 | 0.00 | 10 |
| 6 years, 5% | 165 | 1.77 | 10.74 | 0.00 | 1.81 | 4.78 | 0.00 | 16 |

*Source*: World Bank.
*Note*: This table displays the number of investment acceleration episodes identified using different thresholds for the algorithm as well as investment growth measured in aggregate rather than per capita terms. In column (1) years refers to the minimum duration of the acceleration, and the percent growth rate refers to the minimum average growth rate of (per capita) investment growth. The baseline as described in annex 3.1 uses a minimum 4 percent average growth and minimum duration of 6 years as parameters. Column (2) shows the number of identified accelerations. Columns (3) and (4) show the mean investment per capita growth rate during the six years before and during an acceleration. For the algorithm that does not use per capita investment growth in the second row, columns (3) and (4) show mean investment growth not in per capita terms. Column (5) shows the p-value from a two-sided test comparing investment growth rates before and during an acceleration. Columns (6), (7), and (8) show the per capita output growth rates before and during an investment acceleration along with the p-value of the two-sided test assessing if the means are equal. Column (9) shows the number of countries without identified investment accelerations for the given combination of parameters.

# ANNEX 3.4 Robustness exercises

The empirical results presented in annex 3.2 are robust to the use of alternative sets of episodes identified using different algorithm thresholds and duration parameters as well as controlling for additional variables. Table A3.4.1 reruns the main regression shown in table A3.2.2 using investment accelerations identified when alternative minimum duration length is required while holding the minimum required growth rate of 4 percent constant. Table A3.4.2 shows that the results are also robust to alternative minimum average investment

growth thresholds. In table A3.4.3, the following additional control variables are included in the baseline regression: lagged per capita investment growth, the global recession year dummies defined in Kose, Sugawara, and Terrones (2020), the global financial cycle factor provided by Miranda-Agrippino and Rey (2020), and natural resource rents as a share of GDP (taken from the World Development Indicators). Table A3.4.4 repeats the baseline regression using investment accelerations identified using the baseline parameters applied to aggregate investment growth (that is, not in per capita terms). Across all robustness tests, the baseline results presented in table A3.2.2 do not change in a meaningful way.

## TABLE A3.4.1 Investment accelerations using different duration parameters

| Policy variable | (1)<br>Change in<br>capital account openness | (2)<br>Adoption or reduction of<br>inflation target | (3)<br>Change in<br>primary balance | (4)<br>Change in trade<br>restrictiveness index |
|---|---|---|---|---|
| Model 1: minimum duration 5 years, average growth rate 4 percent | | | | |
| Lagged institutional quality (IQ) | 0.359*** | 0.360*** | 0.440*** | 0.435*** |
| | (6.01) | (6.21) | (5.82) | (5.59) |
| Policy | 0.003** | 0.769*** | 0.033** | 0.009** |
| | (1.98) | (2.64) | (2.25) | (2.21) |
| Interaction of policy with lagged IQ | 0.000 | 0.011 | 0.029*** | 0.013** |
| | (0.21) | (0.06) | (3.78) | (2.54) |
| Number of observations | 2,023 | 2,276 | 1,764 | 1,402 |
| Number of episodes | 122 | 138 | 98 | 92 |
| Model 2: minimum duration 7 years, average growth rate 4 percent | | | | |
| Lagged IQ | 0.325*** | 0.332*** | 0.508*** | 0.486*** |
| | (4.30) | (4.53) | (5.72) | (5.78) |
| Policy | 0.003** | 0.765** | 0.029* | 0.009* |
| | (2.05) | (2.27) | (1.67) | (1.66) |
| Interaction of policy with lagged IQ | 0.002** | 0.025 | 0.030*** | 0.023*** |
| | (2.00) | (0.10) | (3.45) | (3.86) |
| Number of observations | 1,956 | 2,198 | 1,661 | 1,447 |
| Number of episodes | 79 | 89 | 62 | 67 |

*Source:* World Bank.
*Note:* This table shows the estimated coefficients for the change in log-odds. Robust standard errors in parentheses. ***, **, and * indicate significance at the 1, 5, and 10 percent levels, respectively. The institutional quality variable and policy change variables have been demeaned for easier interpretation of the interaction term. All regressions use the baseline control variables in column (2) of table A3.2.1. The two models presented here use the baseline parameter of 4 percent minimum investment per-capita growth but a duration of five years (model 1), seven years (model 2) compared with six years in the baseline. See annex A3.3 on alternative algorithm specifications.

## TABLE A3.4.2 Investment accelerations using different duration and growth parameters

| Policy variable | (1) Change in capital account openness | (2) Adoption or reduction of inflation target | (3) Change in primary balance | (4) Change in trade restrictiveness index |
|---|---|---|---|---|
| Model 1: minimum duration 6 years, average growth rate 3 percent | | | | |
| Lagged institutional quality (IQ) | 0.271*** | 0.268*** | 0.288*** | 0.343*** |
| | (4.40) | (4.44) | (3.98) | (4.51) |
| Policy | 0.004*** | 1.277*** | 0.029** | 0.009** |
| | (2.62) | (4.32) | (2.10) | (2.10) |
| Interaction of policy with lagged IQ | 0.001 | -0.004 | 0.025*** | 0.013*** |
| | (0.58) | (-0.02) | (3.47) | (2.65) |
| Number of observations | 1,887 | 2,130 | 1,623 | 1,334 |
| Number of episodes | 115 | 126 | 97 | 91 |
| Model 2: minimum duration 6 years, average growth rate 5 percent | | | | |
| Lagged IQ | 0.182*** | 0.177*** | 0.266*** | 0.235*** |
| | (2.63) | (2.62) | (3.13) | (2.95) |
| Policy | 0.005*** | 1.206*** | 0.038** | 0.006 |
| | (3.03) | (3.92) | (2.25) | (1.36) |
| Interaction of policy with lagged IQ | 0.001 | 0.044 | 0.032*** | 0.009** |
| | (0.99) | (0.24) | (3.80) | (2.46) |
| Number of observations | 2,083 | 2,332 | 1,791 | 1,493 |
| Number of episodes | 85 | 96 | 69 | 68 |

*Source*: World Bank.

*Note*: This table shows the estimated coefficients for the change in log-odds. Robust standard errors in parentheses. ***, **, and * indicate significance at the 1, 5, and 10 percent levels, respectively. The institutional quality variable and policy change variables have been demeaned for easier interpretation of the interaction term. All regressions use the baseline control variables in column (2) of table A3.2.1. The two models presented here use varying minimum average growth and a minimum duration of six years to identify investment accelerations, around the baseline parameters of 4 percent and 6 years. Model 1 requires a minimum duration of 6 years and a minimum growth rate of 3 percent. Model 2 requires a minimum duration of 6 years but growth rate of 5 percent. See annex 3.3 for alternative algorithm specifications.

## TABLE A3.4.3 **Baseline regressions with additional controls**

| Policy variable | (1) Change in capital account openness | (2) Adoption or reduction of inflation target | (3) Change in primary balance | (4) Change in trade restrictiveness index |
|---|---|---|---|---|
| *Model 1: Add lagged investment growth to the baseline model* | | | | |
| Lagged institutional quality (IQ) | 0.235*** | 0.232*** | 0.253*** | 0.293*** |
| | (3.71) | (3.76) | (3.31) | (3.75) |
| Policy | 0.005*** | 1.115*** | 0.030** | 0.009** |
| | (2.97) | (3.74) | (2.03) | (2.21) |
| Interaction of policy with lagged IQ | 0.001 | -0.069 | 0.026*** | 0.013*** |
| | (0.94) | (-0.37) | (3.51) | (2.84) |
| Lagged investment growth | -0.013*** | -0.012*** | -0.014*** | -0.015*** |
| | (-2.94) | (-3.01) | (-2.85) | (-2.65) |
| Number of observations | 1,951 | 2,200 | 1,683 | 1,393 |
| Number of episodes | 106 | 117 | 87 | 83 |
| *Model 2: Add global recession dummy to the baseline model* | | | | |
| Lagged IQ | 0.223*** | 0.222*** | 0.245*** | 0.287*** |
| | (3.55) | (3.63) | (3.23) | (3.69) |
| Policy | 0.005*** | 1.124*** | 0.030** | 0.010** |
| | (2.95) | (3.73) | (1.97) | (2.42) |
| Interaction of policy with lagged IQ | 0.001 | -0.055 | 0.026*** | 0.014*** |
| | (0.89) | (-0.29) | (3.53) | (2.87) |
| Dummy for global recessions | -0.284 | -0.192 | -0.268 | -0.170 |
| | (-0.84) | (-0.65) | (-0.70) | (-0.51) |
| Number of observations | 1,951 | 2,200 | 1,683 | 1,393 |
| Number of episodes | 106 | 117 | 83 | 83 |
| *Model 3: Add global financial cycle factor to the baseline model* | | | | |
| Lagged IQ | 0.238*** | 0.230*** | 0.247*** | 0.296*** |
| | (3.76) | (3.71) | (3.27) | (3.80) |
| Policy | 0.005*** | 1.144*** | 0.033** | 0.009** |
| | (2.94) | (3.78) | (2.27) | (2.16) |
| Interaction of policy with lagged IQ | 0.001 | -0.069 | 0.027*** | 0.013*** |
| | (0.85) | (-0.37) | (3.62) | (2.83) |
| Global financial cycle factor | -0.154* | -0.080 | -0.075 | -0.192* |
| | (-1.74) | (-0.94) | (-0.69) | (-1.82) |
| Number of observations | 1,951 | 2,200 | 1,683 | 1,393 |
| Number of episodes | 106 | 117 | 87 | 83 |
| *Model 4: Add natural resource rents to the baseline model* | | | | |
| Lagged IQ | 0.236*** | 0.233*** | 0.254*** | 0.315*** |
| | (3.73) | (3.74) | (3.38) | (4.00) |
| Policy | 0.005*** | 1.105*** | 0.038** | 0.010** |
| | (2.85) | (3.63) | (2.23) | (2.49) |
| Interaction of policy with lagged IQ | 0.001 | -0.061 | 0.030*** | 0.014*** |
| | (0.84) | (-0.33) | (3.42) | (2.87) |
| Natural resource rents (share of GDP) | -0.017* | -0.010 | -0.024** | -0.036 |
| | (-1.93) | (-1.24) | (-2.42) | (-1.59) |
| Number of observations | 1,942 | 2,174 | 1,677 | 1,384 |
| Number of episodes | 105 | 116 | 87 | 82 |

*Source*: World Bank.
*Note*: This table shows the estimated coefficients for the change in log-odds. Robust standard errors in parentheses. ***, **, and * indicate significance at the 1, 5, and 10 percent levels, respectively. The institutional quality variable and policy change variables have been demeaned for easier interpretation of the interaction term. All regressions use the baseline control variables in column (2) of table A3.2.1. The four models presented here use additional control variables in the baseline regression. Model 1 controls for lagged per capita investment growth, Model 2 controls for global recession years, Model 3 controls for global financial cycles, and Model 4 controls for natural resource rents as a share of GDP. See annex 3.2 for variable sources and definitions.

**TABLE A3.4.4 Baseline regressions based on investment growth (not in per capita terms)**

| Policy variable | (1) Change in capital account openness | (2) Adoption or reduction of inflation target | (3) Change in primary balance | (4) Change in trade restrictiveness index |
|---|---|---|---|---|
| Lagged institutional quality (IQ) | 0.192*** | 0.201*** | 0.215*** | 0.271*** |
| | (3.16) | (3.45) | (3.00) | (3.64) |
| Policy | 0.004*** | 1.102*** | 0.030** | 0.010** |
| | (2.65) | (3.80) | (2.48) | (2.23) |
| Interaction of policy with lagged IQ | 0.001 | -0.074 | 0.013* | 0.015*** |
| | (1.03) | (-0.40) | (1.82) | (2.82) |
| Number of observations | 1,861 | 2,093 | 1,613 | 1,344 |
| Number of episodes | 101 | 112 | 84 | 80 |

*Source:* World Bank.
*Note:* This table shows the estimated coefficients for the change in log-odds. Robust standard errors in parentheses. ***, **, and * indicate significance at the 1, 5, and 10 percent levels, respectively. The institutional quality variable and policy change variables have been demeaned for easier interpretation of the interaction term. All regressions use the baseline control variables in column (2) of table A3.2.1. The dependent variable is a dummy for the start years of investment accelerations identified using the baseline parameters applied to investment growth not in per capita terms. See annex 3.3 for algorithm parameters.

# References

Achy, L. 2011. "The ADCR 2011: Poverty in the Arab World Successes and Limits of Morocco's Experience." Arab Development Challenges Report Background Paper 2011/9, United Nations Development Programme, New York.

Ahluwalia, M. 2002. "Economic Reforms in India Since 1991: Has Gradualism Worked." *Journal of Economic Perspectives* 16 (3): 67-88.

Ahmad, J., F. Blum, P. Gupta, and D. Jain. 2018. "India's Growth Story." Policy Research Working Paper 8599, World Bank, Washington, DC.

Alesina, A., D. Furceri, J. Ostry, C. Papageorgiou, and D. Quinn. 2020. "Structural Reforms and Elections: Evidence from a World-Wide New Dataset." NBER Working Paper 26720, National Bureau of Economic Research, Cambridge, MA.

Anand, R., and V. Tulin. 2014. "Disentangling India's Investment Slowdown." IMF Working Paper 14/47, International Monetary Fund, Washington, DC.

Andrews, D., A. R. Boote, S. S. Rizavi, and S. Singh. 1999. "Debt Relief for Low-Income Countries: The Enhanced HIPC Initiative." Pamphlet 51, International Monetary Fund, Washington, DC.

Ansar, A., B. Flyvbjerg, A. Budzier, and D. Lunn. 2016. "Does Infrastructure Investment Lead to Economic Growth or Economic Fragility? Evidence from China." *Oxford Review of Economic Policy* 32 (3): 360-90.

Bahia, K., P. Castells, G. Cruz, T. Masaki, X. Pedros, T. Pfutze, C. Rodriguez-Castelan, and H. Winkler. 2020. "The Welfare Effects of Mobile Broadband. Evidence from Nigeria." Policy Research Working Paper 9230, World Bank, Washington, DC.

Barro, R., and X. Sara-i-Martin. 1992. "Convergence." *Journal of Political Economy* 100 (2): 223-51.

Berg, A., and O. J. Blanchard. 1994. "Stabilization and Transition: Poland, 1990-91." In *The Transition in Eastern Europe*, 1 (Country Studies), 51-92. Chicago: University of Chicago Press.

Berg, A., Ostry, J., and J. Zettelmeyer. 2012. "What Makes Growth Sustained?" *Journal of Development Economics* 98 (2): 149-66.

Bergin, P. 2022. "Currency Undervaluation and Comparative Advantage." *European Economic Review* 150 (C): 104316.

Bergoeing, R., P. Kehoe, T. Kehoe, and R. Soto. 2002. "A Decade Lost and Found: Mexico and Chile in the 1980s." *Review of Economic Dynamics* 5 (1): 166-205.

Bleaney, M., and D. Greenaway. 2001. "The Impact of Terms of Trade and Real Exchange Rate Volatility on Investment and Growth in Sub-Saharan Africa." *Journal of Development Economics* 65 (2): 491-500.

Breton, P., M. J. Ferrantino, and M. Maliszewska. 2022. *Reshaping Global Value Chains in Light of COVID19.* Washington, DC: World Bank.

Bruszt, L., and N. Campos. 2016. "Deep Economic Integration and State Capacity: The Case of the Eastern Enlargement of the European Union." ADP Working Paper, Asian Development Bank, Manila, Philippines.

Caselli, F., P. Pagano, and F. Schivardi. 2003. "Uncertainty and the Slowdown in Capital Accumulation in Europe." *Applied Economics* 35 (1): 79-89.

Che, N. 2021. "Dissecting Economic Growth in Uruguay." IMF Working Paper 21/002, International Monetary Fund, Washington, DC.

Chinn, M., and H. Ito. 2008. "A New Measure of Financial Openness." *Journal of Comparative Policy Analysis* 10 (3): 309-22.

Cho, D., and Y. Kang. 2013. *2012 Modularization of Korea's Development Experience: Korea's Stabilization Policies in the 1980s.* KDI School of Public Policy and Management. Seoul, Korea: Ministry of Strategy and Finance.

Christiano L., and T. Fitzgerald. 2003. "The Band Pass Filter." *International Economic Review* 44 (2): 435-65.

Clavijo, S. 2009. "Social Security Reforms in Colombia: Striking Demographic and Fiscal Balances." IMF Working Paper 09/058, International Monetary Fund, Washington DC.

Corbo V., L. Hernández, and F. Parro. 2005. "Institutions, Economic Policies and Growth: Lessons from the Chilean Experience." Working Paper 317, Central Bank of Chile, Santiago, Chile.

Dappe, M. H., V. Foster, A. Musacchio, T. Ter-Minassian, and B. Turkgulu. 2023. *Off the Books: Understanding and Mitigating the Fiscal Risks of Infrastructure. Sustainable Infrastructure Series.* Washington, DC: World Bank.

Dappe, M. H., M. Melecky, and B. Turkgulu. 2022. "Fiscal Risks from Early Termination of Public-Private Partnerships in Infrastructure." Policy Research Working Paper 9972, World Bank, Washington, DC.

De Gregorio, J. 2005. "Crecimiento Económico en Chile: Evidencia, Fuentes y Perspectivas." *Estudios Públicos* 98.

De Haan, J., K. Stamm, and S. Yu. Forthcoming. "Drivers of Investment Accelerations." Mimeo, World Bank, Washington, DC.

De Haas, R., and I. Van Lelyveld. 2006. "Foreign Banks and Credit Stability in Central and Eastern Europe: A Panel Data Analysis." *Journal of Banking & Finance* 30 (7): 1927-52.

De la Plaza, L., and S. Sirtaine. 2005. "An Analysis of the 2002 Uruguayan Banking Crisis." Policy Research Working Paper 3780, World Bank, Washington, DC.

Dieppe, A., ed. 2021. *Global Productivity: Trends, Drivers, and Policies.* Washington, DC: World Bank.

Djankov, S., T. Ganser, C. McLiesh, R. Ramalho, and A. Shleifer. 2010. "The Effect of Corporate Taxes on Investment and Entrepreneurship." *American Economic Journal: Macroeconomics* 2 (3): 31-64.

Donald, A., M. Goldstein, L. Rouanet, and L. Rouanet. "2022. Two Heads Are Better Than One: Agricultural Production and Investment in Côte d'Ivoire." Policy Research Working Papers 10047, World Bank, Washington, DC.

Dornbusch, R., and Y. Park. 1987. "Korean Growth Policy." *Brookings Papers on Economic Activity* 2 (1987): 389-454.

Echandi, R., M. Maliszewska, and V. Steenberge. 2022. *Making the Most of the African Continental Free Trade Area.* Washington, DC: World Bank.

Edwards, S., 1998, "The Chilean Pension Reform: A Pioneering Program." In *Privatizing Social Security,* edited by M. Feldstein, 33-62. Chicago: University of Chicago Press.

Engel, E., R. Fischer, and A. Galetovic. 2020. "When and How to Use Public-Private Partnerships in Infrastructure: Lessons from the International Experience." NBER Working Paper 26766, National Bureau of Economic Research, Cambridge, MA.

Essl, S., S. K. Celik, P. Kirby, and A. Proite. 2019. "Debt in Low-Income Countries." Policy Research Working Paper 8794, World Bank, Washington, DC.

Feenstra, R. C., R. Inklaar and M. P. Timmer. 2015. "The Next Generation of the Penn World Table." *American Economic Review* 105 (10): 3150-82.

Fratzscher, M. 2012. "Capital Flows, Push Versus Pull Factors and the Global Financial Crises." *Journal of International Economics* 88 (2): 341-56.

G20-IEG. 2023. *The Triple Agenda: A Roadmap for Better, Bolder, and Bigger MDBs.* Report of the Independent Expert Group.

Gallego F., and N. Loayza. 2002. "La Época Dorada del Crecimiento en Chile: Un Problema Financiero." *Revista de Economía Chilena* 5 (1): 37-63.

Gardner, C., and P. B. Henry. Forthcoming. "The Global Infrastructure Gap: Potential, Perils, and a Framework for Distinction." *Journal of Economic Literature.*

Georgiev, Y., P. Nagy-Mohacsi, and A. Plekhanov. 2017. "Structural Reform and Productivity Growth in

Emerging Europe and Central Asia." ADB Economics Working Paper 532, Asian Development Bank, Manila, Philippines.

Ghani, E., and V. Suri. 1999. "Productivity Growth, Capital Accumulation, and the Banking Sector." Policy Research Working Paper 2252, World Bank, Washington, DC.

Gluzmann, P. A., F. Sturzenegger, and E. Levy-Yeyati. 2012. "Exchange Rate Undervaluation and Economic Growth: Díaz Alejandro (1965) Revisited." *Economics Letters* 117 (3): 666-72.

Gluzmann, P. A., F. Sturzenegger, and E. Levy-Yeyati. 2013. "Fear of Appreciation." *Journal of Development Economics* 101 (March): 233-47.

Gupta, P., F. Blum, D. Jain, S. John, S. Seth, and A. Singhi. 2018. *India Development Update: India's Growth Story.* Washington, DC: World Bank.

Guzman, M., J. Ocampo, and J. Stiglitz. 2018. "Real Exchange Rate Policies for Economic Development." *World Development* 110 (October): 51-62.

Ha, J., M. A. Kose, and F. Ohnsorge. 2021. "One-Stop Source: A Global Database of Inflation." Policy Research Working Paper 9737, World Bank, Washington DC.

Harrigan, J. R., and H. El-Said. 2010. "The Economic Impact of IMF and World Bank Programs in the Middle East and North Africa: A Case Study of Jordan, Egypt, Morocco and Tunisia, 1983-2004." *Review of Middle East Economics and Finance* 6 (2): 1-25.

Hastings, J., B. Madrian, and W. Skimmyhorn. 2013. "Financial Literacy, Financial Education, and Economic Outcomes." *Annual Review of Economies* 5 (August): 347-73.

Hausmann, R., L. Pritchett, and D. Rodrik. 2005. "Growth Accelerations." *Journal of Economic Growth*, 10 (4): 303-29.

Henstridge, M., and L. Kasekende. 2001. "Exchange Reforms, Stabilization, and Fiscal Management." In *Uganda's Recovery: The Role of Farms, Firms and Government,* edited by R. Reinikka and P. Collier. Washington, DC: World Bank.

Hoyos, M., E. Libman, and A. Razmi. 2021. "The Structural Outcomes of Investment Surges." *Structural Change and Economic Dynamics* 58 (September): 245-55.

Huang, Y., M. Pagano, and U. Panizza. 2020. "Local Crowding-Out in China." *The Journal of Finance* 75 (6): 2855-98.

IEA (International Energy Agency) and IFC (International Finance Corporation). 2023. "Scaling Up Private Finance for Clean Energy in Emerging and Developing Economies." International Finance Corporation, Washington DC.

IMF (International Monetary Fund). 2001. "Morocco: Article IV." International Monetary Fund, Washington DC.

IMF (International Monetary Fund). 2003. "Republic of Poland: Staff Report for the 2003 Article IV Consultation." IMF Country Report 2003/187, International Monetary Fund, Washington, DC.

IMF (International Monetary Fund). 2004. "Morocco: Staff Report for the 2004 Article IV Consultation." IMF Country Report 2004/162, International Monetary Fund, Washington, DC.

IMF (International Monetary Fund). 2005. "Colombia: Staff Report for the 2005 Article IV Consultation." International Monetary Fund, Washington, DC.

IMF (International Monetary Fund) 2006a. "Colombia: Selected Issues." IMF Country Report 06/401, International Monetary Fund, Washington, DC.

IMF (International Monetary Fund). 2006b. "Colombia: Letter of Intent, Memorandum of Economic and Financial Policies, and Technical Memorandum of Understanding for Stand-By Arrangement." International Monetary Fund, Washington, DC.

IMF (International Monetary Fund). 2007. "Türkiye: Article IV." International Monetary Fund, Washington, DC.

IMF (International Monetary Fund). 2008. "Uruguay: 2008 Article IV Consultation-Staff Report; Staff Statement; Public Information Notice on the Executive Board Discussion; and Statement by the Executive Director for Uruguay." International Monetary Fund, Washington, DC.

IMF (International Monetary Fund). 2010. "Uruguay: 2010 Article IV Consultation-Staff Report; Public Information Notice; and Statement by the Executive Director for Uruguay." International Monetary Fund, Washington, DC.

IMF - WEO (International Monetary Fund) database. "World Economic Outlook: October 2023." Accessed on October 11, 2023. https://imf.org/en/Publications/WEO/weo-database/2023/October.

IRENA (International Renewable Energy Agency). 2023. *World Energy Transitions Outlook 2023: 1.5°C Pathway.* New York: International Renewable Energy Agency.

Irwin, D. 2021. "From Hermit Kingdom to Miracle on the Han: Policy Decisions That Transformed South Korea into an Export Powerhouse." Working Paper 21-14, Peterson Institute for International Economics, Washington, DC.

Jones, B. F., and B. A. Olken. 2008. "The Anatomy of Start-Stop Growth." *Review of Economic and Statistics* 90 (3): 582-87.

Jong-A-Pin, R., and J. de Haan. 2008. "Growth Accelerations and Regime Changes: A Correction." *Econ Journal Watch* 5 (1): 51-58.

Jong-A-Pin, R., and J. de Haan. 2011. "Political Regime Change, Economic Liberalization and Growth Accelerations." *Public Choice* 146 (1): 93-115.

Kaiser, T., and L. Menkhoff. 2017. "Does Financial Education Impact Financial Literacy and Financial Behavior, and If So, When?" *The World Bank Economic Review* 31 (3): 611-30.

Karlan, D., R. Knight, and C. Udry. 2012. "Hoping to Win, Expected to Lose: Theory and Lessons on Micro Enterprise Development." *World Bank Research Observer* 27 (2): 263-95.

Kim, J., and L. Lau. 1994. "The Sources of Economic Growth of the East Asian Newly Industrialized Countries." *Journal of the Japanese and International Economies* 8 (3): 235-71.

Kim, J.-H., J. A. Fallov, and S. Groom. 2020. *Public Investment Management Reference Guide.* Washington, DC:World Bank.

Kitabire, D. 2010. "Debt Management and Debt Relief." In *Uganda's Economic Reforms: Insider Accounts,* edited by F. Kuteesa, E. Tumusiime-Mutebile, A. Whitworth, and T. Williamson, 264-76. Oxford, U.K.: Oxford University Press.

Koepke, R. 2018. "What Drives Capital Flows to Emerging Markets? A Survey of the Empirical Literature." *Journal of Economic Surveys* 33 (April): 516-40.

Koh, Y. 2007. "Reforming the Fiscal Management System in Korea." In *Fiscal Policy and Management in East Asia, Volume 16,* edited by T. Ito and A. K. Roses, 289-335. Chicago: University of Chicago Press.

Koh, Y. 2010. "The Growth of Korean Economy and the Role of Government." In *The Korean Economy: Six*

*Decades of Growth and Development,* Edited by I. Sakong and Y. Koh, Chapter 2. Sejong-si, Korea: Korea Development Institute.

Kose, M. A., F. Ohnsorge, and L. Ye, and E. Islamaj. 2017, "Weakness in Investment Growth: Causes, Implications and Policy Responses." Policy Research Working Paper 7990, World Bank, Washington, DC.

Kose, A., N. Sugawara, and M. E. Terrones. 2020. "Global Recessions." Policy Research Working Paper 9172, World Bank, Washington, DC.

Kose, M. A., and F. Ohnsorge, eds. 2019. *A Decade After the Global Recession: Lessons and Challengers for Emerging and Developing Economics.* Washington DC: World Bank.

Kose, M. A., and F. Ohnsorge, eds. 2023. *Falling Long-Term Growth Prospects: Trends, Expectations, and Policies.* Washington, DC: World Bank.

Krueger, A., and J. Yoo. 2002."Chaebol Capitalism and the Currency-Financial Crisis in Korea." eds. S. Edwards and J. Frankel, Chapter 13 in *Preventing Currency Crises in Emerging Markets.* University of Chicago Press.

Kuteesa, F., E. Tumusiime-Mutebile, A. Whitworth, and T. Williamson. 2010. *Uganda's Economic Reforms: Insider Accounts.* Oxford, U.K.: Oxford University Press.

Lee, J. 1995. "Government Interventions and Productivity Growth in Korean Manufacturing Industries." NBER Working Paper 5060, National Bureau of Economic Research, Cambridge, MA.

Lee, J. 2013. "Foreign Capital in Economic Development: Korean Experiences and Policies." In *(2012) Modularization of Korea's Development Experience.* KDI School of Public Policy and Management. Seoul, Korea: Ministry of Strategy and Finance.

Lee, J.-Y. 1997. *Sterilizing Capital Inflows.* Washington, DC: International Monetary Fund.

Libman, E., J. A. Montecino, and A. Razmi. 2019. Sustained Investment Surges. *Oxford Economic Papers* 71 (4): 1071-95.

Loayza, N., and S. Pennings. 2022. *The Long-Term Growth Model: Fundamentals, Extensions, and Applications.* Washington, DC: World Bank.

Macovei, M. 2009. "Growth and Economic Crises in Türkiye: Leaving Behind a Turbulent Past?" European Commission Economic Papers 386, European Commission, Brussels.

Manzano, O., and J. L. Saboin. 2022. "Investment Booms and Institutions: Implications for the Andean Region." IDB Technical Note 2479. Inter-American Development Bank, Washington, DC.

Marandino, J., and G. Oddone. 2018. "The Monetary and Fiscal History of Uruguay: 1960-2017." Working Paper 2018-60, Becker Friedman Institute for Economics, University of Chicago.

Marioli, F., A. Fatas, and G. Vasishtha. 2023. "Fiscal Policy Volatility and Growth in Emerging Markets and Developing Economies." Policy Research Working Paper 10409, World Bank, Washington, DC.

Mawejje, J., and N. M. Odhiambo. 2021. "Uganda's Fiscal Policy Reforms: What Have We Learned?" *Public Budgeting & Finance* 41 (2): 89-107.

McCollum, D. L., W. Zhou, C. Bertram, H. S. De Boer, V. Bosetti, S. Busch, J. Després, et al. 2018. "Energy Investment Needs for Fulfilling the Paris Agreement and Achieving the Sustainable Development Goals." *Nat Energy* 3 (7): 589-99.

McKenzie, D., and C. Woodruff. 2014. "What Are We Learning from Business Training and Entrepreneurship Evaluations around the Developing World?" *The World Bank Research Observer* 29 (1): 48-82.

Mensah, J., and N. Traore. 2022. "Infrastructure Quality and FDI inflows. Evidence from the Arrival of High-Speed Internet in Africa." Policy Research Working Paper 9946, World Bank, Washington, DC.

Miranda-Agrippino, S., H. Rey. 2020. "U.S. Monetary Policy and the Global Financial Cycle". *The Review of Economic Studies* 87 (6): 2754-76.

Moïsé, E., and F. Le Bris. 2013. "Trade Costs-What Have We Learned? A Synthesis Report." OECD Trade Policy Papers 150, Organisation for Economic Co-operation and Development, Paris.

Moreira, E. P. 2019. "Morocco's Growth and Employment Prospects: Public Policies to Avoid the Middle-Income Trap." Policy Research Working Paper 8769, World Bank, Washington, DC.

Murgasova, Z. 2005. "Post-Transition Investment Behavior in Poland: A Sectoral Panel Analysis." IMF Working Paper 2005/184, International Monetary Fund, Washington, DC.

Muwanga-Zake, E. S. K., and S. Ndhaye. 2001. "The HIPC Debt Relief Initiative Uganda's Experience." Discussion Paper 2001/94, UNU/WIDER, Helsinki.

Naguib, R., and J. Smucker. 2009. "When Economic Growth Rhymes with Social Development: The Malaysia Experience." *Journal of Business Ethics* 89 (November): 99-113.

Nam, S. 1988. "2 Alternative Growth and Adjustment Strategies of Newly Industrializeing Countries in Southeast Asia." In *Beyond Adjustment: The Asian Experience,* edited by P. Streeten, Chapter 2. Washington DC: International Monetary Fund.

OECD (Organisation for Economic Co-operation and Development) and IDB (Inter-American Development Bank). 2016. "Broadband Policies for Latin America and the Caribbean: A Digital Economy Toolkit." Organisation for Economic Co-operation and Development, Paris.

Paus, E. 2012. "Confronting the Middle-Income Trap: insights from small latecomers." *Studies in Comparative International Development* 47 (April): 115-38.

Peluffo, A. 2013. "Assessing Labor Market Impacts of Trade Opening in Uruguay." *SpringerPlus* 2 (1): 1-19.

PRS Group (Political Risk Services) database. "The International Country Risk Guide (ICRG)." Accessed on November 10, 2023. https://prsgroup.com/explore-our-products/icrg

Qureshi, Z., J. L. Diaz-Sanchez, and A. Varoudakis. 2015. "The Post-Crisis Growth Slowdown in Emerging Economies and the Role of Structural Reforms." *Global Journal of Emerging Market Economies* 7 (2): 179-200.

Reinikka, R., and P. Collier. 2001. *Uganda's Recovery: The Role of Farms, Firms and Government.* Washington, DC: World Bank.

Rial, I., and L. Vicente. 2003. Sostenibilidad y Vulnerabilidad de la Deuda Pública Uruguaya: 1988-2015." *Revista de Economía, Segunda Época* 10 (2): 143-220.

Ribeiro, R., J. McCombie, and G. Lima. 2020. "Does Real Exchange Rate Undervaluation Really Promote Economic Growth?" *Structural Change and Economic Dynamics* 52 (C): 408-17.

Rodrik, D. 2008. "The Real Exchange Rate and Economic Growth." *Social and Economic Studies* 56 (2): 365-412.

Rozenberg, J. and M. Fay, eds. 2019. *Beyond the Gap: How Countries Can Afford the Infrastructure They Need While Protecting the Planet.* Washington, DC: World Bank.

Schwartz, G., M. Fouad, T. Hansen, and G. Verdier, eds. 2020. *Well Spent: How Strong Infrastructure Governance Can End Waste in Public Investment.* Washington, DC: International Monetary Fund.

Somogyi, J. 1991. "Malaysia's Successful Reform Experience." *Finance and Development* 28 (001). Washington, DC: International Monetary Fund.

Stamm, K., and D. Vorisek. 2023. "The Global Investment Slowdown: Challenges and Policies." In *Falling Long-Term Growth Prospects: Trends, Expectations, and Policies*, edited by M. A. Kose and F. Ohnsorge, 153-210. Washington, DC: World Bank.

UNEP (United Nations Environment Programme). 2023. *Adaptation Gap Report 2023*. New York: United Nations Environment Programme.

United Nations, Inter-agency Task Force on Financing for Development. 2022. *Financing for Sustainable Development Report 2022*. New York: United Nations.

Vashakmadze, T., J. Ha, D. Fukuzawa, J. Zhou, W. Choi, S. Chung, and J. Pyun. 2023. "Leveraging Global Integration and International Trade." In *Innovative Korea: Leveraging Innovation and Technology for Development,* edited by H. Soh, Y. Koh, and A. Aridi, Chapter 4. Washington, DC: World Bank.

World Bank. 2001. "Kingdom of Morocco: Poverty Update, Volume 1. Main Report." World Bank, Washington, DC.

World Bank. 2004. *World Development Report 2005: A Better Investment Climate for Everyone*. Washington, DC: World Bank.

World Bank. 2007. "Uganda, Moving Beyond Recovery: Investment and Behavior Change for Growth." Country Economic Memorandum, World Bank, Washington, DC.

World Bank. 2008. "Turkey Country Economic Memorandum." World Bank, Washington, DC.

World Bank. 2015. "From Billions to Trillions: Transforming Development Finance." Development Committee Paper, World Bank, Washington, DC.

World Bank. 2016. "Farms, Cities and Good Fortune: Assessing Poverty Reduction in Uganda from 2006 to 2016." Uganda Poverty Assessment Report, World Bank, Washington, DC.

World Bank. 2019. *Global Economic Prospects: Heightened Tensions, Subdued Investment*. June. Washington, DC: World Bank.

World Bank. 2020a. "Benchmarking Infrastructure Development 2020: Assessing Regulatory Quality to Prepare, Procure, and Manage PPPs and Traditional Public Investment in Infrastructure Projects." World Bank, Washington, DC.

World Bank. 2020b. The African Continental Free Trade Area: Economic and Distributional Effects. Washington, DC: World Bank.

World Bank. 2021a. *Global Economic Prospects*. January. Washington, DC: World Bank.

World Bank. 2021b. *Global Economic Prospects*. June. Washington, DC: World Bank.

World Bank 2022a. "Climate and Development: An Agenda for Action—Emerging Insights from World Bank Group 2021-22 Country Climate and Development Reports." World Bank, Washington, DC.

World Bank. 2022b. "Poland Country Economic Memorandum: The Green Transformation in Poland – Opportunities and Challenges for Economic Growth." Country Economic Memorandum of Poland, World Bank, Washington, DC.

World Bank. 2022c. "Poland Public Finance Review." World Bank, Washington, DC.

World Bank. 2022d. "Update on World Bank Group Efforts to Facilitate Private Capital Investments." World Bank, Washington, DC.

World Bank. 2022e. *Global Economic Prospects*. January. Washington, DC: World Bank.

World Bank. 2023a. *Global Economic Prospects*. January. Washington, DC: World Bank.

World Bank. 2023b. *South Asia Development Update: Toward Faster, Cleaner Growth*. Washington, DC: World Bank.

World Bank. 2023c. *South Asia Development Update: Expanding Opportunities: Toward Inclusive Growth*. . Washington, DC: World Bank.

World Bank - WDI (World Development Indicators) database. ""World Development Indicators.." Accessed on Nov. 10, 2023. https://databank.worldbank.org/source/world-development-indicators.

Zattler, J. 2023. "The Annual Meetings: Time to Walk the Talk on Private Sector Mobilisation for Climate." *Center for Global Development Blog*, October 10, 2023. https://www.cgdev.org/blog/annual-meetings-time-walk-talk-private-sector-mobilisation-climate

# CHAPTER 4

# FISCAL POLICY IN
# COMMODITY EXPORTERS

## An Enduring Challenge

*Fiscal policy has been about 30 percent more procyclical and about 40 percent more volatile in commodity-exporting emerging market and developing economies (EMDEs) than in other EMDEs. Both procyclicality and volatility of fiscal policy—which share some underlying drivers—hurt economic growth because they amplify business cycles. Structural policies, including exchange rate flexibility and the easing of restrictions on international financial transactions, can help reduce both fiscal procyclicality and fiscal volatility. By adopting average advanced-economy policies regarding exchange rate regimes, restrictions on cross-border financial flows, and the use of fiscal rules, commodity-exporting EMDEs can increase their GDP per capita growth by about 1 percentage point every four to five years through the reduction in fiscal policy volatility. Such policies should be supported by sustainable, well-designed, and stability-oriented fiscal institutions that can help build buffers during commodity price booms to prepare for any subsequent slump in prices. A strong commitment to fiscal discipline is critical for these institutions to be effective in achieving their objectives.*

# Introduction

Commodity-exporting emerging market and developing economies (EMDEs) face significant fiscal challenges: Government debt in these countries has grown rapidly over the past decade—from about 33 percent of GDP in 2010 to about 58 percent in 2022, on average. Over the same period, their primary fiscal deficit (which does not include interest payments) averaged about three times that of commodity importers. Increased spending during the pandemic amplified the challenges confronting commodity-exporting EMDEs. The higher cost of servicing elevated debt levels, coupled with weaker growth prospects, is increasing the risk of debt distress among some of these economies (World Bank 2023). Along with the wide swings in commodity prices in recent years, these developments have brought to the fore the complex task of formulating fiscal policy in these economies (figure 4.1.A).

The main challenge faced by policy makers in commodity-exporting countries is coping with the swings in commodity prices; commodities are important sources of export and fiscal revenues for almost two-thirds of EMDEs, including three-fourths of low-income countries (LICs) (figures 4.1.B and 4.1.C; World Bank 2022). Shocks to commodity prices are often large and persistent. Commodity prices have undergone frequent cycles over the past five decades, with the average cycle lasting almost six years (figure 4.1.D). Price

slumps, on average, lasted somewhat longer (39 months) than booms (30 months), with prices falling and rising by 1 to 4 percent per month over the course of the average cycle, respectively (World Bank 2022).

Commodity dependence makes it harder for policy makers to formulate appropriate fiscal responses to commodity price fluctuations. The booms and busts in government revenues attributable to commodities tend to make fiscal policy both more procyclical and more volatile in commodity-exporting EMDEs, amplifying business cycles and harming growth.

- *Fiscal policy tends to be more procyclical*—that is, expansionary in good times and contractionary in bad times—in commodity-exporting EMDEs than in other EMDEs.[1] In commodity-exporting EMDEs, rising commodity prices can lead to procyclical increases in public spending and tax cuts. Conversely, declines in commodity prices can trigger procyclical tax increases and cuts in public expenditures as a result of reduced revenues from commodity production and exports. Moreover, because tax cuts and increases in public spending are generally easier to implement and more difficult to reverse, politically, than tax increases and reductions in public spending, government deficits and

*Note*: This chapter was prepared by Francisco Arroyo Marioli and Garima Vasishtha. It is based on background studies by Arroyo Marioli and Végh (2023) and Arroyo Marioli, Fatás, and Vasishtha (2023).

[1] See Kaminsky, Reinhart, and Végh (2004) and Talvi and Végh (2005) for early contributions to empirical research on the procyclicality of fiscal policy. More recent contributions include Carneiro and Garrido (2016), Frankel, Végh, and Vuletin (2013), and Richaud et al. (2019), as well as studies documenting evidence for select groups of commodity-exporting countries, including Bova, Medas, and Poghosyan (2016) and Céspedes and Velasco (2014).

## FIGURE 4.1 Commodities: Price volatility and importance for exports and revenues

*Commodity prices have fluctuated widely in recent years. Commodities are critical sources of export and fiscal revenues for almost two-thirds of EMDEs and three-quarters of LICs. Energy exporters are more reliant on their commodity exports than are agriculture- and metal-reliant EMDEs on theirs. Resource revenues are an important source of fiscal revenues for commodity exporters, particularly energy exporters. Commodity prices have undergone frequent cycles over the past five decades, with the average cycle lasting almost six years.*

**A. Commodity price movements since 2020**

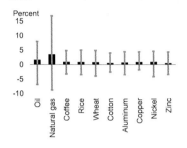

**B. Share of EMDE exports for key commodities**

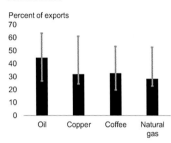

**C. Resource revenues as share of total fiscal revenues**

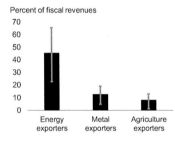

**D. Duration of commodity booms and slumps**

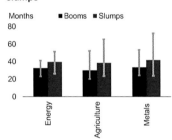

*Sources:* UNU-Wider; UN Comtrade (database); WITS (database); World Bank.

*Note:* EMDEs = emerging market and developing economies; LICs = low-income countries.

A. Bars show the average month-on-month change in commodity prices from January 2020 to November 2023. Whiskers show the interquartile ranges. The commodities used (from the World Bank's Pink Sheet database) are crude oil (average of West Texas Intermediate, Brent, and Dubai); natural gas index; coffee, Arabica; rice, Thai 5 percent; wheat, U.S. hard red winter; cotton, A Index; aluminum; copper; nickel; and zinc.

B. Panel displays the median export share of oil, copper, coffee, and natural gas for commodity-exporting EMDEs. The number of countries is 20 for oil, 6 for copper, 4 for coffee, and 5 for natural gas. Bars represent medians, while whiskers indicate interquartile ranges.

C. Unweighted average of resource revenues as a percentage of fiscal revenues for EMDE commodity exporters: 30 for energy, 14 for metals, and 10 for agricultural commodities. Whiskers show the interquartile range.

D. Duration measures the average length (in months) of a phase (boom or slump). Whiskers indicate minimum and maximum ranges.

ment services, and introduce a bias toward a deterioration in fiscal positions.

- *Fiscal policy tends to be more volatile* in commodity-exporting EMDEs than in other EMDEs. Swings in commodity prices often result in highly volatile commodity-related fiscal revenues in these countries, leading to more volatile business cycles, which historically move in tandem with commodity price cycles.[2] Over the past three decades, output volatility in commodity-exporting EMDEs was more than double that in commodity-importing ones. Revenues derived from the commodity sector are also prone to policies associated with rent-seeking behavior. In addition, fiscal policy volatility can act as a transmission mechanism for the "resource curse"—the term coined to describe how commodity abundance, if not managed properly, can damage overall growth.[3] Moreover, country-specific evidence suggests that large swings in commodity prices can be socially harmful, as shown in such indicators as poverty indices, highlighting the need for policies that mitigate the adverse effects of such price shocks (Álvarez, García-Marín, and Ilabaca 2021; Estrades and Terra 2012).

In the years ahead, the challenges associated with volatile and procyclical fiscal policies are likely to be compounded by sharp fluctuations in commodity prices as the impact of climate change on commodity markets becomes more pronounced.[4] The continuation of procyclical and volatile fiscal policies would be detrimental to growth and impede progress in achieving climate and other broader development goals. As the experience of

debt positions tend to ratchet up, deteriorating from cycle to cycle. This secular deterioration, in turn, will make it more difficult to implement countercyclical fiscal policy in bad times. In sum, the procyclical tendency of fiscal policy in commodity exporters can magnify the impact of commodity price movements on economic activity, lead to inefficient stops-and-starts in government investment and in the provision of government

[2] See IMF (2015a); Jacks, O'Rourke, and Williamson (2011); Richaud et al. (2019); and World Bank (2009, 2020, and 2022).

[3] On the detrimental effects of fiscal policy volatility on growth see, for example, Afonso and Furceri (2008); Fatás and Mihov (2003, 2007, and 2013); and Medina (2010). On the "resource curse," see Bleaney and Halland (2009) and Sachs and Warner (1995) for detailed discussions.

[4] Climate change has significant implications for commodity markets as it leads to severe alterations in weather patterns, affecting climate-sensitive industries such as agriculture and fishing. Droughts can reduce harvests, while floods can affect both harvests and transportation. Policies that address climate change can also generate gains for other commodities, such as metals that are used heavily in low-carbon technologies.

recent decades shows, governments have difficulties in establishing macroeconomic policy frameworks that are effective in helping maintain steady growth in the face of commodity price swings (IMF 2015b; UNCTAD 2021; World Bank 2022).

This chapter presents a comprehensive study of the role of fiscal policy in commodity-exporting EMDEs. Specifically, it addresses the following three questions:

- How different has fiscal policy been, in terms of its cyclicality and volatility, in commodity-exporting EMDEs relative to other EMDEs?

- How have fiscal procyclicality and volatility affected economic growth in commodity-exporting EMDEs?

- Which policy interventions can help improve the quality of fiscal policy by reducing procyclicality and volatility?

**Contributions to the literature.** This chapter makes several contributions to the literature, including:

- *Provides a thorough analysis of fiscal procyclicality and volatility.* This is the first study that examines the implications of fiscal policy procyclicality and volatility together. The empirical literature treats the concepts of fiscal cyclicality and volatility as distinct. While closely following the literature in terms of the methodology for analyzing the two concepts, this chapter goes beyond the literature in examining the linkages between cyclicality and volatility. It provides fresh comprehensive evidence on fiscal procyclicality and volatility for a larger sample of commodity exporters (agricultural, metals, and energy exporters) and commodity importers than previously examined. It also documents how fiscal policy challenges have manifested themselves in different EMDE regions; previous studies have covered either a geographically limited set of countries or mainly oil exporters.

- *Deepens the understanding of the implications of fiscal procyclicality and volatility for economic growth.* The chapter quantifies how procyclical fiscal policy responses have amplified business cycles in commodity-exporting EMDEs during periods of elevated commodity prices, taking a close look at the 2003-08 commodity price boom. It also quantifies the impact of higher output volatility on economic growth.

- *Presents a large menu of policies.* The chapter presents a comprehensive analysis of policies to reduce fiscal policy procyclicality and volatility. It uses several empirical approaches to examine the roles of cyclical and structural factors in improving the design of fiscal policy. In addition, the chapter illustrates the use of sovereign wealth funds (SWFs) and fiscal rules in coping with fiscal procyclicality and volatility by examining the experiences of a set of commodity-exporting countries. Insights from these cases complement the findings of the broader quantitative analysis and help identify best practices in the implementation of these fiscal frameworks and institutions.

**Main findings.** This chapter offers five main findings.

**Fiscal policy has tended to be both more procyclical and more volatile in EMDEs than in advanced economies, and more so in EMDE commodity exporters than commodity importers.** The average correlation between the cyclical components of real GDP and real government spending—the measure of fiscal cyclicality—is 0.40 for EMDEs and near zero for advanced economies. Within EMDEs, the correlation is 0.46 for commodity exporters and 0.36 for commodity importers. Fiscal policy volatility, measured by the volatility of real government expenditure, is about 40 percent higher in EMDE commodity exporters than in other EMDEs. Moreover, among EMDEs, the larger the commodity sector, the more volatile fiscal policy has tended to be. Both fiscal procyclicality and volatility have generally trended downward in EMDEs in recent decades. However, procyclicality has fallen less among commodity-exporting EMDEs than in other EMDEs. Fiscal volatility has declined by nearly half in EMDEs over the past three decades, but it remains much higher among commodity exporters than in other EMDEs.

**Fiscal procyclicality has amplified the business cycle in commodity-exporting EMDEs.** Because of its procyclical nature, fiscal policy in the average EMDE commodity exporter has increased the impact of commodity price shocks on output by more than one-fifth, relative to the counterfactual in which fiscal policy does not respond to the price shock (box 4.1). In contrast, fiscal policy in advanced-economy commodity exporters has, on average, offset the output effect of a commodity price shock by reacting countercyclically. When hit by a commodity price shock of the same magnitude, the change in output in the average commodity-exporting EMDE has tended to be more than three times larger than that in its average advanced-economy counterpart, because of the opposite responses of fiscal policy in the two country groups.

**Fiscal policy volatility has often amplified the business cycle and reduced growth.** Fiscal policy volatility has tended to be associated with more volatile business cycles and lower economic growth. Results from a counterfactual exercise show that if the average commodity-exporting EMDE were to adopt the policies of an average advanced economy in three areas—exchange rates, capital flow restrictions, and the use of fiscal rules—it could have added about 1 percentage point in per capita growth every four to five years by reducing fiscal policy volatility.

**Fiscal procyclicality and volatility are intertwined.** Procyclicality and volatility have been strongly interlinked in EMDEs, especially commodity exporters, and driven by similar factors. EMDEs with more procyclical fiscal policies have tended also to display more volatile fiscal policies. Procyclical fiscal policy amplifies the business cycle, which in turn exacerbates the volatility of output. That is, given a shock to output, a procyclical fiscal response further exacerbates the business cycle. Hence, the initial shock to output has larger overall economic impacts when there also is procyclicality, thereby amplifying volatility.

**Structural policies can help reduce fiscal procyclicality and volatility.** In particular, more stable governments, a stronger rule of law, greater capital account openness, fiscal rules to constrain government spending, and SWFs have all been associated with lower fiscal procyclicality. Fiscal rules and SWFs, essentially state-owned investment companies, have been most effective when surrounded by robust institutional frameworks. Stronger institutions and stricter constraints on fiscal policy have also been associated with less fiscal volatility. Specifically, the presence of fiscal rules, less constraints on international financial transactions, and flexible exchange rates are all associated with lower fiscal policy volatility. Medium-term expenditure frameworks can also help lower the procyclicality and volatility of fiscal policies by improving fiscal discipline.

## Fiscal policy procyclicality

### Conceptual definitions

Because the concept of fiscal policy cyclicality is important to guiding actual policy, it is critical to define policy cyclicality in terms of policy instruments (such as, government expenditure) rather than outcomes (such as, the fiscal balance). This chapter follows the literature and measures fiscal cyclicality as the correlation between annual percentage changes in real (primary) government expenditure and real GDP: a positive correlation indicates procyclicality while a negative correlation indicates countercyclicality.[5] These correlations are calculated for 182 countries using annual data for 1980-2020.

Economies are placed into two groups— "commodity exporters" and "commodity importers"—by applying the classification criteria used in World Bank (2022). An economy is classified as a commodity exporter if, on average in 2017-19, either its combined exports of all

---

[5] For details about this measure, see Frankel, Végh, and Vuletin (2013) and Kaminsky, Reinhart, and Végh (2004). The stylized facts reported in this section are based on the correlations between the cyclical components of real (primary) government expenditure and real GDP, using the Hodrick-Prescott filter to detrend the time series. The results are robust to the use of alternative filters, such as the Baxter-King filter. Results are also robust to the use of nonparametric filters, as documented by Carneiro and Garrido (2016) and Kaminsky, Reinhart, and Végh (2004).

commodities accounted for 30 percent or more of its total exports or its exports of any single commodity accounted for 20 percent or more of its total exports. Economies are excluded if they reached either threshold only because of re-exports (imports that were exported without being changed). Based on these criteria, 92 economies are classified as commodity exporters of which 87 are EMDEs and five are advanced economies. Commodity importers are economies not classified as commodity exporters (table A4.3.1). The panel is unbalanced because some countries do not have data for the whole sample period.

### Basic features of procyclicality

The analysis of correlations produces four stylized facts.

- In the period 1980-2020, fiscal policy in EMDEs has been procyclical while that in advanced economies has been acyclical (figure 4.2.A). The correlation between the cyclical components (derived using the Hodrick-Prescott filter) of real government expenditure and real GDP for EMDEs is 0.40, while that for advanced economies is slightly negative.

- Although fiscal policy in both commodity exporters and commodity importers has been procyclical among all EMDEs in the sample, commodity exporters are 30 percent more procyclical than commodity importers on average (figure 4.2.B). The correlation between the cyclical components of real government spending and real GDP for commodity exporters is 0.46 compared with 0.36 for commodity importers, with both coefficients as well as the difference between them being statistically significant. This procyclical behavior has been widespread across all EMDE regions (figure 4.2.C).

- The degree and nature of fiscal procyclicality have varied across country-income groups. Fiscal procyclicality in LICs and fragile and conflict-affected situations (FCSs) was higher than in lower- and upper-middle income countries, while in high-income countries fiscal policy was countercyclical (figure 4.2.D).

## FIGURE 4.2 Procyclicality of government expenditures

*Over the past four decades, fiscal policy in EMDEs has been strongly procyclical, while that in advanced economies has been acyclical, on average. Commodity-exporting EMDEs tend to display significantly higher procyclicality than other EMDEs. Procyclicality tends to be more pronounced in low-income countries than in lower- and upper-middle-income commodity exporters. On average, fiscal procyclicality has been declining in commodity exporters over the past decade and a half.*

**A. Fiscal procyclicality: EMDEs versus advanced economies**

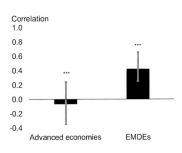

**B. Fiscal procyclicality: EMDE commodity exporters versus importers**

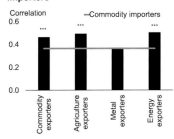

**C. Fiscal procyclicality in commodity exporters, by regions**

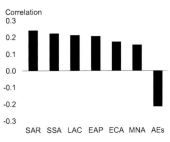

**D. Fiscal procyclicality in commodity exporters, by country-income groups**

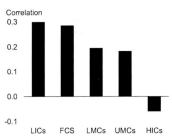

**E. Shifts in fiscal procyclicality, 1980-2020**

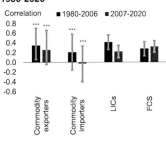

**F. Share of countries with procyclical fiscal policy**

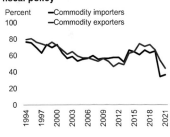

*Sources*: Arroyo Marioli and Végh (2023); International Monetary Fund; World Bank.
*Note*: AEs = advanced economies; EAP = East Asia and Pacific; ECA = Europe and Central Asia; EMDEs = emerging market and developing economies; FCS = fragile and conflict-affected situations; HIC = high-income country; LAC = Latin America and the Caribbean; LIC = low-income country; LMC = lower-middle-income country; MNA = Middle East and North Africa; SAR = South Asia; SSA = Sub-Saharan Africa; UMC = upper-middle-income country.
A.-E. Bars show average correlation between the (Hodrick-Prescott-filtered) cyclical components of real GDP and real government spending within groups. The sample period is 1980-2020.
A.B.E. Whiskers show the 25th and 75th percentiles. Black asterisks indicate a statistically significant difference in means.
A. Sample includes 36 advanced economies and 146 EMDEs. *** indicates that the difference between the average correlation for the two country groups is statistically significant at the 10 percent level or better.
B. Sample of EMDEs includes 87 commodity exporters (38 agricultural, 31 energy, and 21 metals) and 59 commodity importers. *** indicates that the difference between the average correlation for the particular country group and that for commodity importers is statistically significant at the 10 percent level or better.
C.D. Panels show the average of the procyclicality measure for the various country groups.
E. For 1980-2006, the sample includes 90 commodity exporters, 91 commodity importers, 22 LICs, and 31 FCS. For 2007-20, it includes 95 commodity exporters, 95 commodity importers, 21 LICs, and 31 FCS.
F. Share of countries with procyclical policies based on five-year rolling windows. Sample has 184 countries.

## FIGURE 4.3 Fiscal procyclicality and macroeconomic factors in commodity exporters

*Among commodity exporters, more capital account restrictions and the presence of fixed exchange rate regimes are associated with more procyclical policy, on average.*

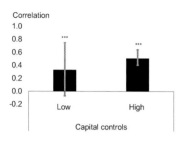

**A. Procyclicality in commodity-exporters, by degree of capital controls**

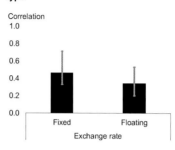

**B. Procyclicality in commodity-exporters, by exchange rate regime type**

*Sources*: Arroyo Marioli and Végh (2023); Chinn and Ito (2006); Ilzetzki, Reinhart, and Rogoff (2022); World Bank.

*Note*: Bars show average correlation between the cyclical components of real GDP and real government spending within groups. The cyclical components are derived using the Hodrick-Prescott filter. Vertical lines show 25th and 75th percentiles.

A. Based on Chinn-Ito index of financial openness. A country is classified as having high (low) capital account restrictions if its Chinn-Ito index score is below (above) the median. Sample has 36 countries with low capital controls and 54 countries with high capital controls. *** indicates that the difference between the means for the two country groups is statistically significant at the 10 percent level or better.

B. Sample has 63 countries with fixed exchange rates and 29 with floating rates, based on the classification in Ilzetzki, Reinhart, and Rogoff (2022). The difference between the means for the two country groups is not statistically significant.

- Fiscal procyclicality has declined over the past four decades. To examine the evolution of fiscal procyclicality, the sample is split into two subperiods: before and after 2006. This division reflects the observed increase in the willingness and ability of countries to pursue countercyclical fiscal policies following the 2007-09 global financial crisis (Alvarez and De Gregorio 2014; Végh and Vuletin 2014). Fiscal procyclicality in commodity exporters has been falling over the past decade-and-a-half. Nevertheless, procyclicality in commodity exporters still prevails and has fallen much less than in commodity-importing countries (which are, on average, acyclical since 2006) (figure 4.2.E). The fraction of countries running procyclical fiscal policies has declined over the past few decades. This decline was more pronounced for commodity importers (from 33 percent in the mid-1990s to 24 percent in 2021) compared with commodity exporters (from 40 percent in the mid-1990s to 36 percent in 2021) (figure 4.2.F).

## Determinants of fiscal procyclicality

To assess how fiscal cyclicality has varied with macroeconomic and institutional features of countries, this section first compares fiscal cyclicality across different groups of countries. It then presents a cross-country regression analysis to disentangle the roles of key factors in driving procyclicality.

The county groupings are based on certain macroeconomic characteristics, including the degree of capital account openness, the exchange rate regime, and the level of external debt. In addition to these macroeconomic characteristics, the degree of fiscal procyclicality can also depend on political economy considerations and institutional features. The choice of these variables is guided by the literature on fiscal procyclicality.

**Restrictions on international financial transactions.** Countries with more restrictions on the capital account tend to have more limited access to international financial markets, which makes the cost of borrowing more expensive. This may increase the procyclicality of fiscal policy by making the government's access to funds particularly limited during recessions, forcing government expenditures to shrink, thus amplifying the economic downturn and the cycle.[6] And the data indeed show that fiscal policy in commodity-exporting countries with more capital account restrictions has tended to be more procyclical than in those with fewer restrictions (figure 4.3.A).[7] On average, the correlation between cyclical components of real government spending and real GDP for countries with more capital controls is 0.51 compared with 0.33 for countries with fewer capital controls; the difference between the correlations is statistically significant.

**Exchange rate regime.** Flexible exchange rates are often associated with greater fiscal discipline

---

[6] For details of this argument, see Kose et al. (2010). This result is in line with insights from real business cycle models, where a steeper upward-sloping supply of funds (which makes borrowing from the rest of the world more costly) implies a more procyclical fiscal policy, as exemplified in Fernández et al. (2021).

[7] The results shown in figures 4.3 and 4.4 are broadly similar when an alternative threshold (the lower and upper one-third of observations) is used to classify countries into "low" and "high" groups for capital account openness, political risk, control of corruption, and law and order.

because of the immediacy of the repercussions of imprudent fiscal policies (Tornell and Velasco 2000). It is likely, then, that the degree of fiscal procyclicality is higher in countries with fixed exchange rate regimes. Indeed, the correlation between the cyclical components of government spending and GDP is higher (0.46) under fixed exchange rate regimes than under flexible exchange rates (0.36)—although the difference between the two is not statistically significant (figure 4.3.B).

**External debt.** Fiscal cyclicality is found not to have varied significantly with the level of external debt over the sample period. The correlation between cyclical components of real GDP and real government spending is essentially the same for countries with low and high external debt.[8]

**Political economy factors.** Extensive research has documented the role of political variables in driving fiscal procyclicality. Political pressures in good times tend to prompt policy makers to reduce primary surpluses, by reducing taxes or increasing spending. Given that more volatile primary surpluses offer more chances of fiscal appropriation, the more volatile output and therefore the tax base are, the more procyclical will fiscal policy tend to be (Talvi and Végh 2005).

The dispersion of political power—the so-called voracity effect, in which various fiscal claimants (including government ministries, provinces, and unions) attempt to appropriate resources in good times without considering the effects of their actions on other claimants—is another channel through which political economy factors can affect fiscal procyclicality (Tornell and Lane 1999). As the intensity of such fiscal competition increases in good times, the rise in government spending could

be greater than the windfall gains in revenues, resulting in procyclical fiscal expansion. The more claimants there are (that is, the more dispersed the power), the higher government spending may tend to be in good times.

**Quality of institutions.** The quality of institutions plays an important role in the ability of countries to conduct countercyclical fiscal policy.[9] Indeed, institutional factors, such as law and order, have been found to play a larger role than financial variables, such as financial openness and domestic credit to the private sector, in explaining differences in fiscal cyclicality between advanced and developing economies (Calderón and Schmidt-Hebbel 2008). Government stability and law and order are especially important factors in reducing fiscal procyclicality. They can help do so by shrinking government discretion and extending the horizon of policy decision-making.

To analyze the linkages between fiscal cyclicality and institutional quality, five country-specific indicators of institutional quality from the PRS Group database are used: political risk, quality of bureaucracy, control of corruption, government stability, and law and order (table A4.3.2). The association between procyclicality and the presence of fiscal rules is also examined here because these rules are a significant part of the fiscal institutions in many commodity-exporting countries (box 4.2).

The results indicate that higher political risk is associated with more procyclical fiscal policies. The correlation between the cyclical component of real GDP and real government spending in countries that rank higher on political risk is 0.49, compared with a correlation of 0.28 for countries that rank lower on political risk; the difference between the average correlations for the two country groups is statistically significant (figure 4.4.A). Part of the explanation may be that governments in countries with higher political risk may be more focused on short-term outcomes to stay in power.

---

[8] The degree of fiscal procyclicality can also potentially vary with the stance of the business cycle. In some countries, the lack of access to international credit markets during recessions introduces an asymmetry in their fiscal policy reaction in bad times versus good times. This could also be because the size of fiscal multipliers has been found to depend on the stance of the business cycle, with multipliers in bad times being larger than those in good times (Auerbach and Gorodnichenko 2012, 2013). This notion, however, is not supported by a comparison of procyclicality in expansions and recessions over the sample period under consideration. The difference in the measure of fiscal procyclicality in expansions (0.29) and recessions (0.23) is not statistically significant.

[9] See, for example, Calderón, Duncan, and Schmidt-Hebbel (2016); Carneiro and Garrido (2016); Céspedes and Velasco (2014); Frankel, Végh, and Vuletin (2013); and Jalles et al. (2023).

## FIGURE 4.4 Fiscal procyclicality, fiscal rules, and institutional factors

*The degree of fiscal procyclicality tends to be higher, on average, among commodity exporters with higher political risk. Countries with better-quality bureaucracies and more corruption control display less procyclical behavior. Government stability and better rule of law are also associated with lower procyclicality. The presence of fiscal rules has a dampening effect on procyclicality for the entire sample, but less so among commodity-exporting countries.*

### A. Procyclicality and political risk
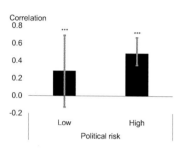

### B. Procyclicality and quality of bureaucracy
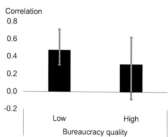

### C. Procyclicality and corruption control
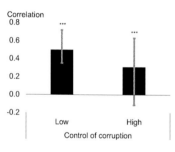

### D. Procyclicality and government stability
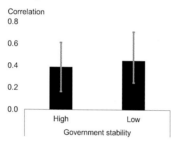

### E. Procyclicality and law and order
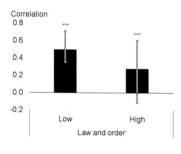

### F. Procyclicality and fiscal rules
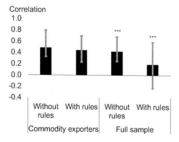

*Sources*: Arroyo Marioli and Végh (2023); International Monetary Fund; PRS Group (database).
*Note*: Bars show average correlation between the (Hodrick Prescott-filtered) cyclical components of real GDP and real government spending within groups. Vertical lines show 25th and 75th percentiles.
A. Countries with high (low) political risk are defined as those with political risk above (below) the sample median. Sample has 49 countries with high political risk and 24 countries with low political risk. *** indicates that the difference between the means for the two country groups is statistically significant at the 10 percent level or better.
B. Sample has 48 countries with low bureaucracy quality and 25 with high bureaucracy quality. The difference between the means for the two country groups is not statistically significant.
C. Sample has 45 countries with low control of corruption and 28 with high control of corruption. *** indicates that the difference between the means for the two country groups is statistically significant at the 10 percent level or better.
D. Sample has 32 countries with high government stability and four with low government stability. The difference between the means for the two country groups is not statistically significant.
E. Sample has 24 countries with high scores (above sample median) for the law-and-order index and 49 countries with low (below sample median) scores. *** indicates that the difference between the means for the two country groups is statistically significant at the 10 percent level or better.
F. For commodity exporters, the sample includes 28 countries with fiscal rules and 20 countries without fiscal rules. The entire sample includes 58 countries with fiscal rules and 47 countries without fiscal rules. The difference between the means for the two country groups (with and without fiscal rules) is statistically significant (indicated by ***) for the entire sample but not for the sample of commodity exporters.

Likewise, commodity-exporting countries with lower-quality bureaucracy have often implemented more procyclical fiscal policies than those with higher-quality bureaucracies, although the difference between the two country groups is not statistically significant (figure 4.4.B). Better bureaucracy may be expected to allow for better, rules-based, policy management and to limit unproductive discretionary spending.

Commodity exporters with better control of corruption have demonstrated lower fiscal procyclicality than those with weaker corruption control, and the difference between the procyclicality measures for the two country groups is statistically significant (figure 4.4.C). Weaker control of corruption makes it easier to capture rents. Likewise, countries with more government stability have tended to demonstrate less fiscal procyclicality than those with less government stability—although the difference in cyclicality measures is not statistically significant (figure 4.4.D). A more stable government allows for the formulation of fiscal policy with a longer horizon, weakening the incentive for procyclical policy. Better law and order has been associated with less procyclical fiscal policy (figure 4.4.E). The difference between the procyclicality measures for countries ranked lower in the law-and-order index and countries ranked higher is statistically significant.

Many commodity exporters have enacted fiscal rules, often in conjunction with stabilization funds—which essentially put aside revenue in good times that can be tapped in bad times. Fiscal rules may signal the intent of the government to dampen, if not eliminate, fiscal procyclicality as well as to safeguard long-term fiscal sustainability. Over the past four decades, the presence of fiscal rules has been associated with lower procyclicality across the full sample of countries, although results are less clear for commodity exporters (figure 4.4.F). Increased use of fiscal rules has not shielded EMDEs or commodity exporters from fiscal procyclicality, as evidenced by the continued procyclicality of fiscal policies in these countries after they adopted such rules. Nevertheless, there is evidence that some features of a second generation of fiscal rules—such as the use of

## BOX 4.1 How does procyclical fiscal policy affect output growth?

*Fiscal responses to commodity price shocks have differed considerably between emerging market and developing economies (EMDEs) and advanced economies. Commodity-exporting EMDEs have tended to react in a procyclical manner, increasing government expenditures when prices of exported commodities rise. Advanced-economy commodity exporters, by contrast, have tended to react countercyclically, reducing spending when prices rise. Fiscal policy procyclicality in the average EMDE commodity exporter has increased the effects of a commodity price shock on the business cycle by more than one-fifth.*

### Introduction

Procyclical fiscal policy amplifies the effect on output of a shock to economic activity—that is, "when it rains, it pours," using the analogy of Kaminsky, Reinhart, and Végh (2004). Such shocks could originate from various sources—from the financial sector or from supply or demand shocks associated with external or domestic developments. Kaminsky, Reinhart, and Végh (2004) focused on net capital inflows, finding that such flows were associated with an increase in government expenditure in emerging market and developing economies (EMDEs), while net capital outflows were associated with a decline in government expenditure. A variety of other drivers could lead to procyclical fiscal behavior.

This box examines how increases in commodity prices have affected the behavior of fiscal policy and, in turn, output growth. The total impact of the changes in commodity prices on output can be decomposed into two components. First, the "rains" component: in response to an increase in commodity prices, production rises in the commodity sector and other related sectors, and the associated increases in income generate further increases in private spending and output. The increases in output and spending, in turn, boost fiscal revenue, reducing the primary fiscal deficit. The second component depends on the response of fiscal policy. If the reduction in the fiscal deficit is conserved, fiscal policy will play a countercyclical role, dampening the increase in demand and activity. But if the reduction in the fiscal deficit leads the government to increase spending or lower taxes, fiscal policy will increase the effect of the shock on output. There will then be a "pours" component, with procyclical fiscal policy amplifying the business cycle.

This box addresses the following questions:

- How does fiscal policy in commodity-exporting countries react to changes in prices of commodity exports?

- How does the impact of this fiscal reaction on output growth differ between commodity-exporting-EMDEs and advanced economies?

### Methodology

To estimate the effect of fiscal policy on output, the analysis proceeds in four steps. First, to quantify the effects of changes in commodity prices on output, panel regressions are used to obtain the response of real GDP to changes in country-specific commodity price indexes.[a] The results show that a 10 percent increase in commodity export prices increases output by 0.63-0.85 percent in EMDE commodity exporters and 0.18-0.26 percent in advanced-economy commodity exporters (table A4.1.3).[b]

Second, panel regressions are used to estimate a fiscal policy reaction function (that is, the response of government spending to changes in commodity prices). Results show that EMDEs increase government spending when commodity export prices rise, indicating a procyclical fiscal policy (table A4.1.4). Specifically, a 10 percent increase in commodity export prices leads to an increase in government spending of about 0.6 percent to 0.8 percent. In contrast, advanced economies respond countercyclically: a 10 percent increase in commodity export prices elicits a reduction in government spending of about 0.7 percent to 1.2 percent. Third, an average fiscal multiplier is estimated for

---

a. Two control variables are used: overall terms of trade (which include terms of trade for all traded goods and services, not just commodities, using data from the IMF) to control for trade effects, and the lagged dependent variable to capture underlying growth unrelated to commodity prices. The country-specific commodity export price index is an index that weights commodities prices by their relevance in a country's exports. This index is a better measure of a commodity price shock for a particular country than global commodity price indexes that might include goods not exported by the particular country.

b. In table A4.1.3, the coefficient for EMDEs (0.085) in column (1) is about 3.5 times as much as the coefficient for advanced economies (0.024) in column (4).

**BOX 4.1 How does procyclical fiscal policy affect output growth? (*continued*)**

**FIGURE B4.1.1 The amplification effect of procyclical fiscal policy on output**

*Fiscal policy in commodity-exporting EMDEs has tended to amplify the effects of commodity price shocks on output, while in advanced economies it has tended to dampen the effects. More than three-fourths of the difference in growth between major commodity-exporting EMDEs and advanced economies during the 2003–08 commodity price boom can be explained by the difference in the cyclicality of fiscal policy between the two groups of countries.*

A. "Pours" as a fraction of "rains" in commodity exporters

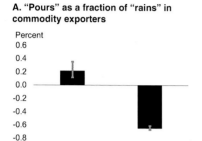

B. "Pours" versus "rains": 2003-08 commodity cycle

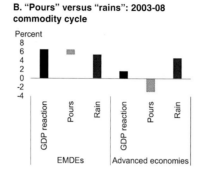

C. Cumulative fiscal response

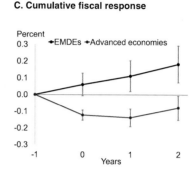

*Sources*: Arroyo Marioli and Végh (2023); International Monetary Fund; World Bank.
*Note*: EMDEs = emerging market and developing economies.
A.B. The sample has 4 advanced economies (Australia, Canada, New Zealand, and Norway) and 11 EMDEs (Argentina, Brazil, Chile, Colombia, Costa Rica, Ecuador, Honduras, Indonesia, Russian Federation, South Africa, and Ukraine).
A. Panel shows the change in GDP (in response to a commodity price shock) explained by the reaction of fiscal policy (the "pours" component) as a share of the direct effect of the commodity price shock on output (the "rain" component). The average of these shares for commodity-exporting EMDEs and advanced economies is shown by the blue bars. Whiskers shows the minimum and maximum range.
B. The orange bars represent the fraction of the change in GDP, in response to a commodity price shock, explained by the reaction of fiscal policy to the shock, averaged at the aggregate level. The red bars show the direct effect of a commodity price shock on GDP.
C. Panel shows the cumulative reaction of fiscal expenditure to a 1 percent increase in commodity exports prices in *t*=0, using panel regressions. The regression includes two leads and lags of commodity export prices.

commodity exporters using a panel structural vector autoregression (SVAR) model. [c]

Finally, the "amplification" effect (the "pours" component) of fiscal policy on output is obtained by combining the fiscal response in the second step with the fiscal multiplier obtained from the third step. The "pours" component represents changes in output growth that are due solely to changes in government expenditure in response to the initial shock. The "pours component" is then formally measured by:

*Pours = ΔCEP \* Fiscal reaction elasticity \* fiscal multiplier \* $\frac{g}{y}$*         (B4.1.1)

where *CEP* is the commodity export price, *fiscal reaction elasticity* is the estimated coefficient in the fiscal regression and $\frac{g}{y}$ is the ratio of government spending to GDP (computed as the average over the sample period for each country). Intuitively, changes in commodity export price (*CEP*) trigger a fiscal reaction (elasticity), which in turn affect GDP via the fiscal multiplier. The fiscal reaction is adjusted by the size of the government to measure the final impact in percentage points of GDP.[d]

---

c. The model is based on the Blanchard-Perotti (2002) identification method, employing quarterly data for GDP and government expenditure from the IMF's International Financial Statistics database for the period 1990-2019. In computing the "pours" component, the value of the multiplier after four quarters is used (given by 0.88).

---

d. The fiscal reaction elasticity is estimated using a panel of 15 commodity exporters (4 advanced economies and 11 EMDEs). The fiscal multiplier is estimated for the same panel following Blanchard and Perotti (2002). Government size is represented by the average government expenditure as a share of GDP for each country. The availability of quarterly data is critical for the Blanchard and Perotti (2002) identification method. This method assumes that output responds to government spending within the period, but that government spending does not respond to GDP. In other words, all contemporaneous correlation is attributed to fiscal policy affecting GDP. See Ilzetzki, Mendoza, and Végh (2013) for a detailed discussion.

### BOX 4.1 How does procyclical fiscal policy affect output growth? (*continued*)

#### Impact of procyclical fiscal policy on output

The results indicate that, if an increase in the price of the exported commodity boosts output by 1.0 percentage point (the "rains" effect), procyclical fiscal policy in commodity-exporting EMDEs increases GDP by another 0.21 percentage point (the "pours" effect), boosting the total change in GDP to 1.21 percent (figure B4.1.A). In contrast, fiscal policy in commodity-exporting advanced economies compensates for the cyclical effect by reacting in the opposite direction, reducing GDP by 0.65 percentage point. This leaves the net increase in GDP of 0.35 percentage point for advanced economies. These estimates suggest that, when faced with a commodity price shock of the same magnitude, the overall change in GDP can be more than three times bigger in EMDEs than in advanced economies solely because of the fiscal policy reaction.

The above approach is applied to the commodity price boom of 2003-08 to illustrate the role of fiscal policy. During this period, commodity export prices increased about 76 percent for the EMDEs and 66 percent for the advanced economies in the sample. The analysis estimates the direct effect of the commodity price shock on output (the "rain" component) by applying the 2003-08 cumulative price shock to the estimated parameters. The results indicate the effect on output to be 5.4 percent for EMDEs and 4.6 percent for advanced economies—that is, a difference of 0.8 percentage point (figure B4.1.1.B). The procyclical response of

fiscal policy in EMDEs ("pours" component) added another 1.1 percentage points to growth, bringing EMDE growth to 6.5 percent over this period.

In contrast, fiscal policy in advanced economies reacted in a countercyclical fashion, subtracting about 3 percentage points from growth, bringing advanced-economy growth to 1.6 percent. In other words, of the 4.9 percentage points difference between total EMDE and advanced-economy growth in the sample, 4.1 percentage points (or 84 percent) can be explained by the responses of fiscal policy—procyclical in EMDEs and countercyclical in advanced economies. Alternative estimates also indicate that fiscal expenditure in EMDEs reacts in a procyclical manner while that in advanced economies reacts in a countercyclical one (figure B4.1.1.C).

#### Conclusion

Fiscal procyclicality amplifies the effect of commodity price shocks on the business cycle in EMDEs. In the sample period examined, fiscal policy in the average EMDE commodity exporter is estimated to have increased the effect of a commodity price shock on output by more than one-fifth. The results indicate that in EMDE commodity exporters fiscal policy has tended to amplify the business cycle, whereas in advanced-economy commodity exporters fiscal policy has tended to dampen it.

---

cyclically adjusted targets and well-defined escape clauses, combined with strong legal and enforcement arrangements—have been associated with reduced procyclicality (Bova, Carcenac, and Guerguil 2014). The country cases examined in box 4.2 suggest that fiscal rules or SWFs are most effective in achieving their stated objectives when they are well-designed, closely linked to broader policy objectives, and supported by strong institutions and political commitment.

Armed with the insights from the correlates of fiscal procyclicality established above, the analysis uses cross-country regressions to identify the main drivers of fiscal procyclicality in commodity

exporters.[10] The dependent variable here is the correlation between the annual percentage changes of real government spending and real GDP. The explanatory variables are intended to capture the four explanations for the existence of procyclical fiscal policy described in the previous section: capital account openness (measured by an index of

---

[10] For an empirical analysis of the drivers of fiscal procyclicality in OECD countries, see Lane (2003). For an analysis of the role of financial and institutional variables, see Calderón and Schmidt-Hebbel (2008) and Calderón, Duncan, and Schmidt-Hebbel (2010). Ilzetzki (2011) provides a novel political economy explanation based on successive governments disagreeing on the desired distribution of public spending and examines different theories of procyclicality by running numerical simulations in calibrated models.

financial openness); political economy factors (measured by an index of political constraints, which reflects the extent to which policy changes are inhibited by institutional and political factors); macroeconomic stability (measured by the standard deviation of output); and institutional quality (measured by an index of control of corruption).

The coefficients of each of these four variables are statistically significant and three of the four have the expected sign (annex 4.1; table A4.1.1). More open capital accounts and better control of corruption are estimated to have helped reduce fiscal procyclicality while greater output volatility was associated with higher procyclicality. However, the coefficient of the political constraints index does not have the expected sign, suggesting either that the "voracity effect" did not hold or that the political constraints index fails to capture it. The variables are jointly significant when combined and explain about 18 percent of procyclical behavior across countries.[11]

Cross-country regressions are also used to analyze the role of institutional variables in driving fiscal cyclicality, as highlighted by the correlations reported in the previous section. The roles of SWFs and fiscal rules are also explored. SWFs can play an important role in reducing procyclicality by promoting the accumulation of government savings during commodity price booms, to be drawn down to some extent during price slumps (Asik 2017). The results show that greater government stability, better law and order, and the presence of SWFs and fiscal rules have all tended to reduce fiscal procyclicality (table A4.1.2). Overall, the analysis therefore provides empirical evidence that better institutions are associated with lower fiscal procyclicality. These results are also corroborated by the country case studies (box 4.2) which show that SWFs and fiscal rules are

most effective in meeting their goals when supported by strong institutions.

# Fiscal policy volatility

## Conceptual definitions

Country-specific measures of fiscal policy volatility are constructed based on the variance of exogenous changes in fiscal policy stance. These are simply derived from fiscal policy reaction functions, following the approach in Fatás and Mihov (2013) (annex 4.2 provides details). The analysis is based on four alternative measures of fiscal policy: primary expenditures (which exclude net interest payments), revenues, government consumption, and the primary budget balance (which excludes net interest). The first three variables are expressed in real (inflation-adjusted) terms and measured as log differences. The primary budget balance is expressed as the annual change of its ratio to GDP. Annual data are used for the 1990-2021 period for 184 countries, including 148 EMDEs and 36 advanced economies. The choice of the sample period is based on data availability. Of these 184 countries, 94 are commodity exporters and the remainder as commodity importers. Among commodity exporters, only five are advanced economies. Among commodity importers, 31 are advanced economies and 59 are EMDEs.

## Basic features of fiscal policy volatility

The following stylized facts emerge from a comparison of the measures of fiscal policy volatility between different country groups.

First, over the past three decades, *the volatilities of primary expenditures, government consumption, and revenues were all significantly higher in EMDEs than in advanced economies* (figure 4.5.A). The difference between the average volatility for these two groups of countries is statistically significant. Notably, the difference in the volatility of government consumption is larger than that of primary expenditures, highlighting the role of government consumption in fiscal policy volatility in EMDEs. The estimated volatility of the primary balance (as a percentage of GDP) is

---

[11] In line with Lane (2003), and to check the robustness of our results, GDP per capita, size of the public sector relative to GDP, and openness (the sum of exports and imports as a share of GDP) were added as controls, one at a time. While GDP per capita was significant at the 5 percent level, the two other control variables were not. In all three cases, the $F$-test for the joint significance of the three relevant explanatory variables was significantly different from zero at least at the 10 percent level.

relatively smaller and closer between the two country groups than with the other fiscal policy indicators.[12]

Second, EMDE *commodity exporters exhibited more volatility in fiscal policy than commodity importers* (figure 4.5.B). The difference in the average volatility for commodity exporters and commodity importers is statistically significant. Government revenues demonstrated greater volatility than the other indicators, although only by a slight margin.

Third, *fiscal policy volatility declined somewhat in EMDEs over the past three decades.* Volatility of government expenditure, consumption, revenue, and primary balance were all lower on average during 2007-20 than in 1980-2006 (figure 4.5.C). This reduction in fiscal policy volatility in EMDEs mirrors the increasing use of fiscal rules in these countries (Arroyo Marioli, Fatás, and Vasishtha 2023). In advanced economies, however, over the same period, revenue volatility declined while volatility of expenditures and primary balance increased (figure 4.5.D).

Fourth, *government expenditures, consumption, and revenue tend to be more volatile in LICs than in other EMDEs.* Over the past three decades, government expenditure, consumption and revenue were roughly twice as volatile in LICs as in other EMDEs (figure 4.5.E). The degree of fiscal volatility has also varied across emerging market regions. On average, expenditure volatility in LICs, particularly FCS economies, over the past three decades was higher than that in lower- and upper-middle income countries. Fiscal volatility was the highest among commodity exporters in Sub-Saharan Africa (SSA), the Middle East and North Africa (MNA), and East Asia and Pacific (EAP) than in other emerging market regions (figure 4.5.F).

---

[12] However, when comparing the volatility of the primary balance with the other fiscal variables, the average size of the government in EMDEs needs to be considered. For instance, a 1 percent increase in government spending will have a different impact on GDP in a country with a smaller government than in one with a larger government. Given that the average government size is about 30 percent, a 1 percent exogenous change in government expenditures only leads to a change in the primary balance of approximately 0.3 percent of GDP in the average EMDE.

## FIGURE 4.5 **Fiscal policy volatility**

*Over the past three decades, primary expenditure, government consumption, and revenues in EMDEs have been more volatile than those in advanced economies, on average. Within EMDEs, fiscal policy in commodity exporters has been more volatile than that in commodity importers and in LICs compared with non-LICs, on average. Fiscal policy volatility declined somewhat in EMDEs over the past three decades while the evolution of fiscal volatility in advanced economies has varied across different fiscal indicators. Expenditure volatility over the past three decades has been highest among commodity exporters in Sub-Saharan Africa, the Middle East and North Africa, and East Asia and Pacific.*

**A. Fiscal volatility: Advanced economies versus EMDEs**

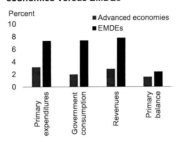

**B. Fiscal volatility: EMDE commodity exporters versus importers**

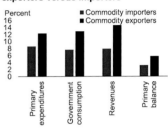

**C. Evolution of fiscal volatility in EMDEs**

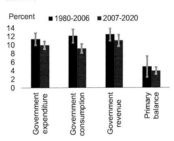

**D. Evolution of fiscal volatility in advanced economies**

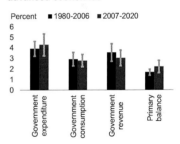

**E. Fiscal volatility: LICs versus non-LICs**

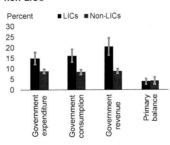

**F. Expenditure volatility in commodity exporters, by regions**

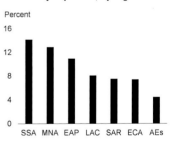

*Sources:* Arroyo Marioli, Fatás, and Vasishtha (2023); IMF WEO database; World Bank.
*Note:* AEs = advanced economies; EAP = East Asia and Pacific; ECA = Europe and Central Asia; EMDEs = emerging market and developing economies; LAC = Latin America and the Caribbean; LIC = low-income country; MNA = Middle East and North Africa; PPP = purchasing power parity; SAR = South Asia; SSA = Sub-Saharan Africa.
A.B. Panels show weighted averages (A) and simple averages (B), by country group, of the standard deviations of the residuals obtained from regressing four dependent variables—log differences of real primary expenditures, real government consumption, real revenues, and the change in primary balance (percent of GDP)—on real GDP growth. Weights used are the PPP GDP shares in the respective group's total GDP. Annual data for 36 advanced economies and 148 EMDEs over 1990-2021.
C.D.E. Panels show the weighted averages of the standard deviations of the residuals obtained from regressing four variables—log differences of real primary expenditures, real government consumption, real revenues, and the change in primary balance (percent of GDP)—on real GDP growth. Weights used are the PPP GDP shares in the respective group's total GDP. Annual data for 35 advanced economies and 142 EMDEs over 1980-2006, and 36 advanced economies and 144 EMDEs over 2007-20. Annual data for 22 LICs and 156 non-LICs.
F. Panel shows the average (unweighted) volatility in commodity exporters in each country group.

## Determinants of fiscal volatility

Cross-sectional regressions are used to investigate the role of country-specific factors—such as institutions, policy variables, the extent and nature of commodity dependence, and GDP per capita—in driving fiscal policy volatility. Like the analysis of procyclicality, the exercise focuses on the spending side of the budget. While each of the four fiscal policy indicators used above contains information about fiscal policy, the variation in primary expenditures provides a more accurate perspective on the volatility of fiscal policy. Since the automatic stabilizer component of expenditures tends to be small, changes in primary expenditures tend to be driven by discretionary measures and changes in nondiscretionary spending that are unrelated to the business cycle. It is these changes in primary expenditure net of cyclical components (such as unemployment benefits) that are captured in the volatility measure used in the analysis.

The findings indicate that commodity dependence can be a source of fiscal policy volatility by itself. Being both an EMDE and a commodity exporter explains up to 22 percent of the variation in fiscal policy volatility across countries (table A4.2.1).[13] That commodity exporters exhibit higher fiscal policy volatility even after their EMDE status is taken into account suggests that reliance on commodities in itself contributes to fiscal policy volatility.

EMDEs and commodity exporters are heterogenous groups of countries that display substantial variation in their level of development as well as degree of commodity dependence. To account for these differences across countries, two additional variables are introduced into the analysis. First, GDP per capita is included to represent the level of development in each country. Second, a variable measuring resource rents—specifically, income from natural resources as a percentage of GDP—is introduced to capture the degree of

commodity dependence. Resource rents are highly correlated with resource revenues as a share of GDP (Arroyo Marioli, Fatás, and Vasishtha 2023).

The results indicate that the lower GDP per capita in EMDEs does not by itself explain the differences in fiscal policy volatility across countries because the presence of larger commodity sectors contributes to greater volatility in fiscal policy. Overall, these findings suggest that both the level of development and the degree of commodity dependence contribute to explaining fiscal volatility.

Energy exporters display higher fiscal policy volatility than exporters of metals and agricultural commodities. Controlling for resource rents, however, the results indicate that commodity dependence is a more important determinant of fiscal volatility than the type of commodity exported (table A4.2.2).

A stable institutional environment and the use of sound fiscal rules can reduce fiscal policy volatility. The role of institutional factors in driving fiscal policy volatility is analyzed by including two additional variables often used in the literature: political constraints and control of corruption. These two variables are found to be significant and together help explain up to 40 percent of cross-country variation in fiscal policy volatility. Policy frameworks can also play an important role in driving fiscal policy volatility. The roles of three specific policy variables are examined: the capital account openness, exchange rate regime (floating versus fixed), and the presence of fiscal rules.

The presence of a more open capital account, more flexible exchange rates, and fiscal rules are all associated with lower fiscal policy volatility. Taken together, these explanatory variables can explain up to 71 percent of the cross-country variation in fiscal policy volatility. The estimates suggest that moving from a fixed exchange rate regime to a flexible one can lower expenditure volatility by 3 percentage points (table A4.2.1). Although a flexible exchange rate regime is not feasible or appropriate for all EMDEs, countries with those regimes may have more room for the exchange

---

[13] For brevity, table A4.2.1 only shows the regression results when primary expenditure is used as the dependent variable. The regression results with government consumption as the dependent variable are very similar.

rate adjustment needed to counteract the destabilizing effects of commodity prices on output. A more flexible exchange rate regime, in principle, facilitates a smoother cyclical adjustment to a terms-of-trade shock. For example, during the 2014-16 fall in commodity prices (mainly crude oil and natural gas), commodity-exporting countries such as Chile and Peru (two countries with flexible exchange rate regimes) were able to increase spending through countercyclical fiscal policy as they were equipped with sufficient fiscal space and the necessary medium-term fiscal frameworks to safeguard fiscal sustainability (Al-Sadiq, Bejar, and Otker 2021).[14] In contrast, countries with pegged regimes experienced a larger deterioration in their fiscal balance, on average, relative to those with flexible exchange rate regimes. Pegged exchange rates remain the dominant exchange rate regime among EMDEs (figure 4.6.A). While greater exchange rate flexibility can help build resilience to commodity price shocks, its macroeconomic implications need to be taken into account, particularly in cases where prices of a few key exports are globally determined, and exchange rate fluctuations may have adverse impacts on the balance sheets of public and private institutions.

The results also suggest that if the average degree of capital account openness in EMDEs were to be same as in the average advanced economy, expenditure volatility in EMDEs would be reduced by 1.7 percentage points. In principle, economies with greater access to international capital markets should be better able to smooth the impact of commodity price fluctuations on output volatility, although markets may respond in a procyclical manner for some countries (with capital flows increasing during commodity price booms and declining during slumps) (IMF 2012a). Capital account openness in commodity exporters has increased over the past few decades, but it remains lower than in commodity importers (figure 4.6.B). Measures to increase capital

## FIGURE 4.6 Exchange rate regimes and capital account openness

*Fixed exchange rates remain the dominant regime in EMDEs. Although capital account openness has increased in commodity exporters over the past few decades, it remains lower than that in commodity importers, and the gap between the two has widened.*

**A. Exchange rate regime flexibility in EMDEs**

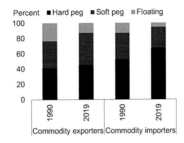

**B. Capital account openness**

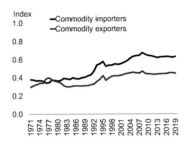

*Sources:* Chinn and Ito (2006); Ilzetzki, Reinhart, and Rogoff (2022); World Bank.
A. Panel shows the share of EMDEs with hard peg, soft peg, and floating exchange rate regimes, based on the classification in Ilzetzki, Reinhart, and Rogoff (2022).
B. Based on Chinn-Ito index of financial openness. The lines represent the average of the index in the represented year. Sample includes 98 commodity importers and 98 commodity exporters.

account openness always have to be considered with caution, in combination with consideration of the prudential and other measures that may be needed to avoid instability in the domestic financial system.

In addition, establishing a fiscal rule can reduce expenditure volatility in EMDEs by 0.7 percentage point (from 10.8 to 10.1 percent). The significance of these three variables—that is exchange rate regime, capital account openness, and fiscal rules—in driving fiscal policy volatility remains even after accounting for the level of development and the extent of commodity dependence. Although the presence of an SWF is also associated with lower fiscal volatility, the result is not statistically significant.[15]

## Implications of fiscal policy volatility for growth

Fiscal policy volatility reduces output growth by exacerbating macroeconomic volatility. Expenditure volatility is found to have significantly hurt

---

[14] Although a countercyclical fiscal policy response to a temporary commodity price shock is desirable under both fixed and flexible exchange rate regimes, these policies are more effective under a flexible exchange rate regime combined with inflation targeting when monetary policy complements fiscal policy by reducing inflation volatility (IMF 2012a).

[15] It is possible that the effect of establishing a sovereign wealth fund is captured by the other policy variables included in the analysis. For example, the decision to establish one may be correlated with volatility itself.

## FIGURE 4.7 **Fiscal policy volatility and procyclicality**

*The correlation between fiscal volatility and procyclicality among EMDEs and commodity exporters is mostly due to the procyclical behavior. While the correlation between fiscal procyclicality and volatility in advanced economies declined between 1980-2006 and 2007-20, it remained unchanged in EMDEs and commodity exporters. High- and upper-middle-income countries have had the highest correlations among country-income groups. Europe and Central Asia and Middle East and North Africa have had the highest correlations among EMDE regions.*

**A. Correlation between fiscal volatility and procyclicality**

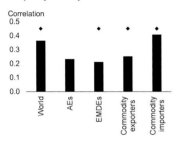

**B. Correlation between fiscal volatility and procyclicality over time**

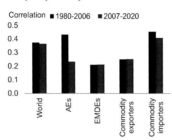

**C. Correlation between fiscal volatility and procyclicality, by country-income groups**

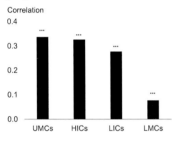

**D. Correlation between fiscal volatility and procyclicality, by regions**

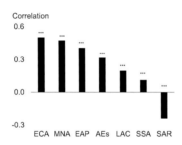

*Sources:* International Monetary Fund; World Bank.
*Note:* AEs = advanced economies; EAP = East Asia and Pacific; ECA = Europe and Central Asia; EMDEs = emerging market and developing economies; HIC = high-income country; LAC = Latin America and the Caribbean; LIC = low-income country; LMC = lower-middle-income country; MNA = Middle East and North Africa; SAR = South Asia; SSA = Sub-Saharan Africa; UMC = upper-middle-income country.
A.B.C.D. Bars represent the correlation between fiscal procyclicality and the measure of volatility that does not exclude the effect of the business cycle on fiscal policy changes.
A.C.D. Blue diamonds and asterisks represent statistical significance.

per capita output growth (annex 4.2 and table A4.2.3), which supports earlier research showing a negative association between macroeconomic volatility and economic growth (Kose, Prasad, and Terrones 2005; Ramey and Ramey 1995). The estimated impact of fiscal volatility on per capita growth is in line with other recent estimates (for example, Fatás and Mihov 2013).

Applying the above estimates in a counterfactual scenario, if the average commodity-exporting EMDE were to adopt the policies of an average advanced economy in three areas—capital account

openness, exchange rate flexibility, and use of fiscal rules—fiscal volatility would be reduced by roughly 3.1 percentage points—from 12.3 percent to 9.2 percent. That would result in an increase in the average per capita GDP growth rate for commodity-exporting EMDEs from about 1.4 to 1.7 percent per year. In other words, by adopting these policies the average commodity-exporting EMDE could have added about 1 percentage point in per capita growth every four to five years (figure 4.8.A). Over the 30-year sample period of the analysis, an overall 7.6 percentage points would have been added to average growth in GDP per capita in EMDEs.

## Links between procyclicality and volatility

Fiscal procyclicality and volatility are intimately related concepts and often driven by similar factors, as highlighted by the preceding analysis. Intuitively, a more procyclical fiscal policy would be expected to result in a more volatile fiscal policy to the extent that it amplifies the business cycle, thus exacerbating the effect of the initial source of volatility.[16] The measures of volatility and procyclicality are positively correlated, a finding in line with some previous studies (figure 4.7.A; IMF 2004). However, when EMDEs and advanced economies are considered separately, the correlation is significant only for EMDEs. The correlation is significant for both commodity exporters and commodity importers. This suggests that fiscal procyclicality is associated with more fiscal policy volatility only in EMDEs (which also tend to be procyclical). In advanced economies, because fiscal policy is countercyclical or acyclical on average, the volatility of fiscal policy is likely from other factors. The correlation between fiscal procyclicality and volatility has declined for advanced economies from the 1980-2006 period

---

[16] It is also possible that if fiscal policy is procyclical relative to the commodity cycle, it may end up being the main transmission channel from the commodity cycle itself. In countries where the commodity export sector is weakly linked with the rest of the economy, government expenditures could be the main link between the overall cycle and prices. However, in the analysis used here (which follows the empirical literature) fiscal volatility is defined as the volatility of changes in public expenditure that are not related to the business cycle (Fatás and Milhov 2013). Under this definition, the relation between the two is less obvious.

to the post-2007 period, while it has remained unchanged for EMDEs and commodity exporters (figure 4.7.B). High- and upper-middle-income countries present the highest correlation among country-income groups (figure 4.7.C). Finally, the Europe and Central Asia (ECA) and Middle East and North Africa (MNA) regions show higher correlation than other EMDE regions (figure 4.7.D).

# Fiscal institutions and frameworks

The results of the empirical analysis highlight the role of political pressures in driving fiscal policy procyclicality and volatility in commodity-exporting EMDEs. This section discusses how well-designed and credible institutional mechanisms—fiscal rules, sovereign wealth funds, and medium-term expenditure frameworks—can help foster fiscal discipline and counteract tendencies toward procyclicality. It also highlights the role of strong governance more generally in facilitating countercyclical fiscal policies in these economies.

## Fiscal rules

Fiscal rules can help reduce the volatility of fiscal policy and deliver better fiscal outcomes. Fiscal rules leave less space for discretionary spending, which tends to be procyclical and to exacerbate the business cycle (thereby adding more fiscal volatility). Fiscal rules can also provide a strong signal of prudence in fiscal policy (Debrun and Kumar 2008). Well-designed fiscal rules have been found to help lower fiscal deficits and reduce both fiscal procyclicality and volatility.[17]

Until the early 1990s only a handful of EMDEs had fiscal rules and virtually no LICs did. Since then, a growing number of EMDEs have adopted

---

[17] For empirical evidence on the importance of well-designed fiscal rules to deliver lower fiscal deficits, see Caselli and Reynaud (2020), Dahan and Strawczynski (2013), Debrun et al. (2008), and Fabrizio and Mody (2006). Badinger and Reuter (2017), Caselli and Reynaud (2020), Céspedes and Velasco (2014), and Martorano (2018) provide evidence on the association between fiscal rules and lower procyclicality while Badinger and Reuter (2017) show that fiscal rules also help lower fiscal policy volatility.

## FIGURE 4.8 Fiscal volatility, growth, and fiscal frameworks

*If the average commodity-exporting EMDE were to adopt the policies of an average advanced economy regarding exchange rates, capital account openness, and use of fiscal rules, it could have added about 1 percentage point in per capita growth every four to five years by reducing fiscal policy volatility. Since the early 1990s, fiscal rules have been adopted and sovereign wealth funds (SWFs) introduced by a growing number of EMDEs, particularly commodity exporters, to strengthen their fiscal frameworks. Fiscal rules are more prevalent in agriculture and energy exporters than in metal exporters. Among the major emerging market regions, the Middle East and North Africa ranks the highest in terms of total assets under management by SWFs—more than twice that in advanced-economy commodity exporters.*

**A. EMDE annual per capita growth**

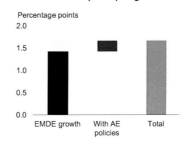

**B. Fiscal rules and SWFs**

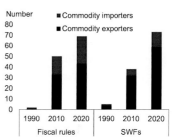

**C. Shares of fiscal rules, by type of commodity exporter**

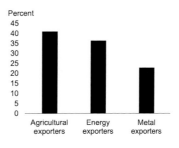

**D. Assets under management by SWFs in commodity exporters, by region, 2022**

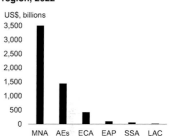

*Sources*: Davoodi et al. (2022); International Monetary Fund; Sovereign Wealth Fund Institute; World Bank.
*Note*: AEs = advanced economies; EAP = East Asia and Pacific; ECA = Europe and Central Asia; EMDEs = emerging market and developing economies; LAC = Latin America and the Caribbean; MNA = Middle East and North Africa; SSA = Sub-Saharan Africa; SWF = sovereign wealth fund.
A. The middle column in the panel illustrates how applying the average advanced-economy policies along three dimensions (exchange rate regimes, capital account openness, and fiscal rules) impacts GDP per capita growth in the average commodity-exporting EMDE. The last column shows the total commodity-exporting EMDE growth with these advanced-economy policies.
B. Number of EMDEs with fiscal rules and SWFs (sovereign wealth funds).
C. Panel shows the share of EMDEs with fiscal rules according to commodity exporter type, as of 2021.
D. Panel shows the amount of SWF assets under management in commodity-exporting countries, as of 2022.

such rules—including commodity exporters, such as Chile and Indonesia (Davoodi et al. 2022; box 4.2). By the end of 2020, 43 of 96 commodity-exporting EMDEs had at least one fiscal rule in place (figure 4.8.B). The adoption of fiscal rules has been most prevalent in energy and agricultural exporters followed by metal exporters (figure 4.8.C). The use of fiscal rules has been associated with more fiscal discipline.[18] However, only well-designed fiscal rules promote more fiscal discipline (Caselli and Reynaud 2020). Additionally, although while fiscal rules are associated with improved fiscal policy management, their success crucially depends on effective institutions and governance underpinned by the rule of law and strong accountability mechanisms (Ardanaz, Cavallo, and Izquierdo 2023; Bergman and Hutchison 2015).

The adoption of fiscal rules is associated with less procyclicality in fiscal policy. At the same time, fiscal rules can act as a constraint on the ability of incumbent politicians to generate political business cycles using fiscal and monetary expansions. Fiscal frameworks that do not have formal rules but focus on transparent and credible strategies backed by proper fiscal institutions could also provide a viable approach to support fiscal discipline (World Bank 2023b).

## Sovereign wealth funds

Over the past few decades, the number of SWFs established has increased rapidly, particularly by commodity-exporting countries. Many commodity exporters have established SWFs as a stabilization fund to channel windfall gains during commodity price booms to accumulate as savings that can be withdrawn during commodity price slumps to limit the impact on fiscal balances. Among the major emerging market regions, the MNA region ranks the highest in terms of total assets under management of SWFs—more than twice that in advanced-economy commodity exporters (figure 4.8.D).

In practice, the effectiveness of such stabilization funds in moderating fluctuations in government spending, and hence output, has varied across countries (Gill et al. 2014). Although poor fiscal

governance has hampered the successful implementation of sovereign stabilization funds in many EMDEs, the overall experience has been positive for smoothing the path of government spending (Sugawara 2014). There is evidence that SWFs can be effective in reducing fiscal procyclicality in some countries (Coutinho et al. 2022). In oil-exporting countries, stabilization funds have been associated with reduced macroeconomic variability and lower inflation (Shabsigh and Ilahi 2007).

An appropriate institutional framework and strong long-term political commitment, including transparent governance of the stabilization fund and prudent constraints on the discretion of fund managers, are critical for the effectiveness of these funds (Asik 2017; Bagattini 2011; Ossowski et al. 2008). Strong institutions help to shield these funds from political influences (Koh 2017; Mohaddes and Raissi 2017). In this context, sovereign wealth and stabilization funds work well to reduce government expenditure volatility in countries where fiscal rules are implemented (Sugawara 2014), but their effectiveness is hampered where there are inadequate controls and integration with the budget is limited (Le Borgne and Medas 2007). More broadly, cross-country evidence shows a strong causal link running from better institutions to less procyclical or more countercyclical fiscal policy in EMDEs (Frankel, Végh, and Vuletin 2013). These results are also corroborated by the country case studies presented in box 4.2, which suggest that the efficacy of SWFs is positively correlated with the presence of strong institutions.

## Medium-term expenditure frameworks

Medium-term expenditure frameworks (MTEFs) are intended to establish or enhance credibility in the budgetary process and to set out spending plans consistent with prevailing economic conditions and medium-term policy objectives (Raudla, Douglas, and MacCarthaigh 2022). Such frameworks can enhance clarity on the purposes of expenditures and help ensure a transparent budgetary process, where government agencies allocate public resources based on strategic priorities. MTEFs foster greater fiscal transparency and accountability by providing a

---

[18] See, for example, Apeti, Basdevant, and Salins (2023); Bergman, Hutchison, and Jensen (2016); and Tapsoba (2012). It is important to note that establishing causality from fiscal rules to fiscal discipline is not straightforward because of endogeneity issues (more disciplined and prudent governments are more likely to adopt fiscal rules) and reverse causality issues (many fiscal rules are adopted after a crisis).

clear basis for monitoring government performance against approved plans, making it easier to hold governments accountable for their fiscal policies.

The number of countries with MTEFs has increased notably over the past three decades. Initially adopted by a few advanced economies in the early 1980s to address public overspending, MTEFs became widely accepted as integral components of fiscal governance throughout the 1990s and 2000s. Among EMDEs, MTEFs were introduced to strengthen public finance management and to realign expenditures consistent with long-term development needs (World Bank 1998). The adoption of MTEFs accelerated in the aftermath of financial crises, with the objective of reconciling short-term pressures with longer-term priorities (Raudla, Douglas, and MacCarthaigh 2022).[19]

Evidence suggests that credible MTEFs can significantly improve fiscal discipline (Vlaicu et al. 2014; World Bank 2013). Robust implementation of these frameworks is closely related to linkages with broader economic and social policy objectives, to the reliability of the relevant data, and to the forecasting capability of the authorities (Allen et al. 2017). The success of these frameworks crucially depends on strong government ownership and support (Schiavo-Campo 2009). For example, South Africa, a commodity exporter, introduced an MTEF when government debt was high, the central government was underspending, and provincial governments were overspending. With widespread support at the top levels of government, the underspending and overspending were both reduced following the introduction of the MTEF (World Bank 2013).

MTEFs need clearly defined legal frameworks and strong supporting institutions to be effective. They can also complement other fiscal frameworks to achieve desired fiscal policy objectives. For example, combined with fiscal rules, MTEFs can improve fiscal balances and the quality of budget

forecasts. More advanced MTEFs can also be associated with lower spending volatility and higher spending efficiency. Nevertheless, MTEFs may fail to meet their objectives where institutions are weak and where key government functions are hindered by capacity constraints in critical technical and administrative areas. For instance, the improvements in fiscal discipline following the adoption of MTEFs tend to be transient in nature, especially in the case of frameworks lacking comprehensive metrics for monitoring and evaluating fiscal performance. In addition, lack of fiscal transparency can impair budget credibility and increase uncertainty about fiscal policy and outturns in EMDEs.[20]

## Institutional quality and governance

Resource abundance can be advantageous to a country if the government has a sound long-term plan for extracting the resources and a robust mechanism for using resource revenues to meet economic and social needs to achieve sustained economic growth. However, resource wealth can undermine institutions and longer-term growth by promoting rent-seeking, corruption, and the squandering of resources through unproductive spending, poor-quality investment, and the depletion of government savings. For mineral rich countries, there is also evidence that mineral wealth can provoke or fuel internal conflicts (Collier and Hoeffler 2004). In general, resource-rich countries with stronger economic and political institutions tend to have better macroeconomic and growth outcomes (Arezki and Bruckner 2010; Arezki, Hamilton, and Kazimov 2011; van der Ploeg 2011).

Higher quality political institutions help limit procyclicality of fiscal expenditures (Ossowski et al. 2008; Sugawara 2014). The observed decline in fiscal procyclicality in EMDEs over the past decade and a half has been mainly attributed to the improved quality of institutions, as measured by indicators on law and order, bureaucracy

---

[19] Vlaicu et al. (2014) estimated that the number of countries with MTEFs increased from 11 in 1990 to 132 at the end of 2008. The lack of data makes it difficult to estimate the current number of countries with MTEFs.

[20] On the role of institutions, see Filc and Scartascini (2010) and Schiavo-Campo (2009). On the role of fiscal rules, see Hansen (2020) and von Hagen (2010). For evidence on the impact of MTEFs on spending volatility and efficiency, see Vlaicu et al. (2014) and World Bank (2013). Elberry and Goeminne (2021) provide evidence on how lack of fiscal transparency affects fiscal outcomes.

quality, and corruption (Frankel, Végh, and Vuletin 2013). In LICs, the quality of budget institutions—measured through the quality of the various stages on the budget process and the number of checks and balances in place—tends to be positively associated with the ability of these countries to conduct countercyclical policies (Dabla-Norris et al. 2010).

The case studies of Norway, Chile, and Botswana show that the quality of their institutions—which is higher than that of their peers—helped limit the negative impact of commodity price volatility (box 4.2; Bova, Medas, and Poghosyan 2016). These country cases also demonstrate that fiscal rules or SWFs work best when they are well-designed, closely linked to broader policy objectives, and supported by strong institutions and political commitment. In the absence of strong institutions and political commitment, fiscal rules and SWFs tend not to be followed closely, which reduces their effectiveness.

## Conclusions

Many EMDEs are commodity-dependent—in terms of fiscal and export revenues as well as economic activity. The challenges posed by this commodity dependence have again been apparent in recent years because of gyrations in commodity prices, resulting partly from geopolitical tensions. These challenges are likely to be exacerbated in coming years as commodity prices become more volatile during the transition from fossil fuels to more climate-friendly sources of energy. If not adequately managed, the response of fiscal policy to this increased commodity price volatility is likely to impede growth.

This chapter has focused on two features of fiscal policy in commodity-exporting EMDEs, procyclicality and volatility. Fiscal policy tends to be both more procyclical and more volatile in EMDEs than in advanced economies, and more so in commodity exporters than in commodity importers. Fiscal procyclicality and volatility amplify the effect of commodity price shocks on the business cycle in EMDEs, with detrimental effects on economic growth.

The chapter offers insights for policy makers in commodity-exporting EMDEs about the appropriate design of fiscal policies and institutional frameworks. Both institutional and policy factors play important roles in explaining the cross-country variation in fiscal policy volatility. Greater government stability, a stronger rule of law, easier access to international financial markets, greater exchange rate flexibility, and the presence of fiscal rules and SWFs have all been associated with lower fiscal policy volatility and procyclicality.

The broader macroeconomic effects of commodity price fluctuations also depend on the policy mix, particularly the interaction of fiscal policy with the monetary and exchange rate policies (IMF 2012b; World Bank 2022). Additionally, the role that commodity revenues play in the budgets of commodity-exporting EMDEs and their impact on fiscal policy volatility suggests potential benefits from diversification of their economies, away from production of commodities.[21]

---

[21] For a detailed discussion, see Bleaney and Greenaway (2001); Ghosh and Ostry (1994); Gill et al. (2014); Hesse (2008); Joya (2015); and World Bank (2022).

**BOX 4.2 Do fiscal rules and sovereign wealth funds make a difference? Lessons from country case studies**

*Commodity price movements often induce more procyclical and volatile fiscal policy, which leads to boom-bust cycles and hinders growth in commodity-exporting emerging market and developing economies (EMDEs). In recent decades, many commodity exporters have adopted fiscal rules and established sovereign wealth funds (SWFs) to partly address these challenges. The adoption of these institutional arrangements, as well as their effectiveness in reducing fiscal procyclicality and fiscal volatility, has not been uniform across countries. Overall, fiscal rules and SWFs are found to have been most effective in addressing procyclicality and volatility when well-designed and supported by strong institutions. Chile and Norway, in particular, have managed their commodity exposure relatively successfully owing to their rigorous fiscal frameworks and strong institutions, offering lessons for other resource-dependent countries.*

## Introduction

Commodity dependence presents substantial challenges for many emerging market and developing economies (EMDEs). Commodity price volatility generally results in unpredictable swings in commodity-related export and fiscal revenues, particularly in countries where commodities account for a large share of fiscal revenue, which leads to volatile and procyclical public expenditure—that is, expenditure that reinforces rather than moderates a business cycle. To manage the impact of commodity price volatility on fiscal policy, commodity-exporting countries have adopted a variety of policy frameworks, such as fiscal rules and sovereign wealth funds (SWFs). Over the past two decades, several countries have also set up publicly funded independent fiscal institutions, such as "fiscal councils," to monitor fiscal policy. The independent fiscal monitoring institutions are supposed to act as watchdogs by highlighting fiscal risks. However, these policy frameworks and institutions are far from homogenous and often take different forms in different countries.

This box assesses the effectiveness of fiscal rules and SWFs in managing commodity price shocks in selected commodity-exporting countries. It addresses the following questions:

- How do fiscal rules and SWFs differ among commodity-exporting countries?

- How have fiscal rules and SWFs helped in reducing fiscal procyclicality and volatility?

## Sovereign wealth funds and fiscal rules

### Sovereign wealth funds

SWFs are special purpose investment funds or arrangements that are owned by the government and are designed to expand national wealth and stabilize business cycles. SWFs hold, manage, or administer assets to achieve financial objectives and employ a set of investment strategies. The objectives of SWFs depend on country-specific circumstances, which may evolve over time. SWFs include: [a]

- *Stabilization funds.* These funds are established to insulate the economy from commodity price volatility—for example, the Economic and Social Stabilization Fund in Chile. Revenue flows into the funds when government receipts are above a benchmark and money can be withdrawn from the fund when government revenue is below the benchmark level.

- *Savings funds.* The primary objective of a savings fund is to build wealth for future generations and ensure intergenerational equity in countries that rely on nonrenewable natural resources, such as oil. Examples include the Petroleum Fund in Timor-Leste and the Pula Fund in Botswana. These funds are characterized by fixed inflows of government revenue and discretionary outflows—reflecting a higher tolerance for short-term volatility and a focus on longer-term returns. Savings funds are established when a government can put aside funds for the future and be reasonably confident that the assets in the fund will not need to be liquidated in the short- and medium-run (Al-Hassan et al. 2018).

- *Financing funds.* A financing fund combines the characteristics of a stabilization fund and a savings fund, such as the SWF of Norway. It is fully integrated into the government budget process.

---

a. Other types of SWFs are reserve investment corporations and development wealth funds. These types of funds are not included in this analysis.

**BOX 4.2 Do fiscal rules and sovereign wealth funds make a difference? Lessons from country case studies (*continued*)**

### FIGURE B4.2.1 Fiscal rules, fiscal expenditures, and SWFs in commodity exporters

*Since the 1990s, the adoption of fiscal rules by commodity exporters has increased, with budget balance and debt rules being the most prevalent type of rules. Sovereign wealth funds in Australia and Norway have consistently accumulated resources in line with their long-term objectives.*

| A. Types of fiscal rules in commodity exporters | B. Australia | C. Norway |
|---|---|---|
| 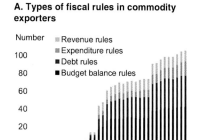 | 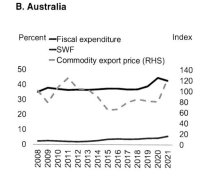 | 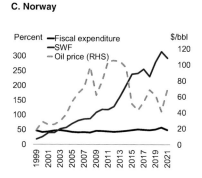 |

*Sources*: Davoodi et al. (2022); Future Fund (website); International Monetary Fund; Norges Bank; World Bank.
*Note*: bbl = billion barrels; SWF = sovereign wealth fund.
A. Panel shows types of fiscal rules for commodity-exporting countries. The sample consists of four advanced economies and 44 emerging market and developing economies.
B.C. Fiscal expenditure and assets under management of SWFs are expressed as percentages of GDP.

Typically, inflows to the fund come from the resource revenues of the government and the returns on the fund's investments. The outflows are transfers to cover any nonresource budget deficit. As a result, the fund receives positive net transfers if, and only if, the government runs a budget surplus when resource revenues are included. This is not necessarily the case for stabilization and savings funds (for example, that of New Zealand) because these funds are not linked to government budget deficits or surpluses (Al-Hassan et al. 2018). A key feature of the financing fund model is the fiscal policy guideline (or rule) which specifies the desired trajectory of the nonresource budget deficit that is to be financed by transfers from the fund.

### Fiscal rules

Since the 1990s, rules-based fiscal frameworks have become increasingly prevalent across the world. Although fiscal rules were designed to be rigid to constrain government actions and promote compliance, these rules have been evolving, especially in response to economic crises (Budina et al. 2013).

There are four main types of fiscal rules, based on the budgetary aggregate they aim to constrain (Davoodi et al. 2022):

- *Budget balance rules.* The objective of a budget balance rule is to constrain the size of the deficit and thereby control the evolution of the debt ratio (for example, Indonesia, Mexico, and Nigeria). Because such rules do not set numerical limits on budgetary aggregates, they are typically considered procedural rather than numerical fiscal rules. If followed properly, they can help prevent debt sustainability issues. However, in some cases, budget balance rules can also induce procyclicality by forcing expenditures to follow revenues, which are usually procyclical.

- *Revenue rules.* These rules set ceilings and floors on revenues and are aimed at boosting revenue collection and/or preventing an excessive tax burden. Most of these rules are not linked directly to the control of public debt because they do not constrain spending. Furthermore, setting ceilings/ floors on revenues can be challenging because

## BOX 4.2 Do fiscal rules and sovereign wealth funds make a difference? Lessons from country case studies (*continued*)

revenues often have a large cyclical component—fluctuating in line with the business cycle. Revenue rules alone could result in procyclical fiscal policy because floors generally do not account for automatic stabilizers (such as unemployment benefits) in a downturn and ceilings don't account for them in an upturn. Revenue rules can, however, directly target the size of the government.

- *Expenditure rules.* Expenditure rules set limits on total, primary, or current government expenditures to limit the procyclicality of fiscal policy (for example, Botswana, Chad, and Ecuador). Such limits are typically set either in absolute terms, or growth rates, and occasionally, as a percentage of GDP. The time horizon often ranges between three and five years. Expenditure rules can constrain spending during booms, when windfall revenue receipts are temporarily high and deficit limits are easy to comply with. Such rules, however, are not directly linked to the objective of debt sustainability because they do not constrain the revenue side. Moreover, expenditure rules do not allow much scope for discretionary fiscal stimulus during bad economic times.

- *Debt rules.* These rules focus on long-term sustainability by setting an explicit anchor or ceiling for public debt (often as a percentage of GDP). A debt rule is relatively easy to communicate and, by definition, most effectively ensures convergence to a debt target. However, debt rules do not provide clear short-term guidance for policy makers because it takes time for budgetary measures to affect debt levels.[b] Moreover, fiscal policy may become procyclical if the economy is hit by shocks and the debt target, defined as a percentage of GDP, is binding. Conversely, when debt is well below its ceiling, such a rule does not provide binding guidance (Budina et al. 2013).

As of 2021, budget balance and debt rules were the most prevalent type of rules in commodity-exporting countries. Budget balance rules accounted for about 41

percent of fiscal rules followed by debt rules which were about 33 percent of total fiscal rules (figure B4.2.1.A). Expenditure rules (15 percent) and revenue rules (11 percent) accounted for the rest.

### Country case studies

This box analyzes the use of SWFs and fiscal rules in seven diverse commodity-exporting countries: Argentina, Australia, Botswana, Chile, Indonesia, Norway, and Timor-Leste. The analysis aims to include a diverse set of commodity exporters both in terms of the types of commodity exports (agriculture, energy, and minerals) as well as the concentration of commodity exports (that is, single-commodity exporters as well as countries with a more diverse export portfolio). To draw useful insights for resource-rich countries considering adopting fiscal rules and SWFs to mitigate fiscal procyclicality and volatility, the box analyzes countries with well-functioning fiscal rules and SWFs, countries with mixed experiences, and countries without fiscal rules and SWFs. Finally, the sample includes both advanced economies and EMDEs in different geographical regions.

### *Australia, Chile, and Norway*

These countries have designed their SWFs to help manage the fiscal effects of fluctuations in commodity export prices and revenues. Australia and Norway have designed their funds for long-term purposes, while Chile has designed its fund for short-term purposes. These countries have also established fiscal rules and a strong institutional framework that allows them to reduce or avoid fiscal procyclicality (Arezki et al. 2012; Bauer 2014; Frankel 2011). The combination of good institutions, SWFs, and fiscal rules has enabled these countries to manage their commodity-based revenues and create sustainable frameworks. Australia combines well-developed fiscal frameworks with broad principles (for example, on debt sustainability) with more flexible numerical rules or guidelines. Chile and Norway also rely on more flexible guidelines and rules supported by strong institutions and transparency on fiscal plans, and are often regarded as countries with the most successful fiscal frameworks and institutions to manage natural resource wealth (Lam et al. 2023).

**Australia.** Australia's commodity exports comprise iron ore, coal, gold, liquified natural gas, and animal meat.

---

b. Debt levels can also be affected by developments outside the control of the government, such as changes in interest rates and the exchange rate, as well as "below-the-line" financing operations (such as financial sector support measures), which could result in large fiscal adjustments.

**BOX 4.2 Do fiscal rules and sovereign wealth funds make a difference? Lessons from country case studies (*continued*)**

FIGURE B4.2.2 **Fiscal expenditures and SWFs in Chile, Botswana, and Timor-Leste**

*Chile used its stabilization fund as needed during its 2019 social crisis and the pandemic. Botswana and Timor-Leste have demonstrated more procyclical fiscal policy, although fiscal rules have supported the accumulation of sizable financial assets. The quality of institutions seems to play an important role in influencing how these countries manage resource abundance.*

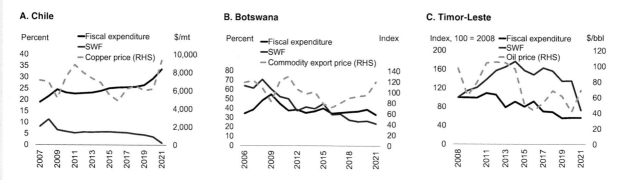

*Sources*: Bank of Botswana; Fondo de Estabilización Económica y Social (website); International Monetary Fund; Timor-Leste Petroleum Fund (website); World Bank.
*Note*: bbl = billion barrels; mt = metric ton; SWF = sovereign wealth fund.
A.B. Fiscal expenditure and assets under management of SWFs are expressed as percentages of GDP.
C. An index for fiscal expenditure and SWF assets under management was constructed starting in 2008.

The country's fiscal framework is based on the Charter of Budget Honesty Act 1998 (Commonwealth of Australia 2014), which provides for "constrained discretion," that advocates a principles-based approach rather than a numerically oriented, rules-based approach. It adds transparency and discipline to the budget formation and execution process (Bhattacharyya and Williamson 2011; Chohan 2017). The Charter defines the principles of sound fiscal management as comprising several components, including an expectation that fiscal policy contributes to adequate national saving and to moderating cyclical fluctuations in economic activity, as appropriate (Chohan 2017). The country's SWF, the Future Fund, was established in 2006 and accumulates revenue from budget surpluses for long-term purposes, such as pensions (figure B4.2.1.B).ᶜ The minister of finance may make certain discretionary transfers from time to time.

---

c. The Future Fund has also received contributions from the proceeds of the sale of the government's stake in Telstra in late 2006 and the approximately 2 billion shares in Telstra that remained after this sale process. Also, it received contributions from a combination of budget surpluses, proceeds from the sale of the government's holding of Telstra, and the transfer of remaining Telstra shares (Al-Hassan et al. 2018).

**Norway.** Commodity exports of Norway are concentrated in crude oil and petroleum gas. The country has a SWF comprising two separate investment funds.

• The Government Pension Fund-Global (GPFG), formerly the Petroleum Fund, was established in 1990 to collect revenue from oil-related income sources to support government saving and to promote an intergenerational transfer of resources (Velculescu 2008). In this way, the government's revenue from petroleum production does not enter the government budget directly. Norway's GFPG is the largest natural-resource-based SWF in the world with its latest annual holdings at more than US$1.2 trillion, equivalent to 256 percent of GDP at the end of 2022 (figure B4.2.1.C).

• The Government Pension Fund Norway (GPFN) saves surpluses of the national insurance scheme and held assets of US$32.7 billion, or 6 percent of 2022 GDP (Lam et al. 2023).

Political will to turn nonrenewable resources into wealth for future generations paved the road for Norway's fund. The GPFG is fully integrated with the

**BOX 4.2 Do fiscal rules and sovereign wealth funds make a difference? Lessons from country case studies (*continued*)**

state budget and builds on existing institutions to strengthen the budget process. It finances the non-oil budget without constraints from any inflow or outflow rules between the fund and the budget. Norway has consistently sustained budget surpluses over the past two decades (except for 2020), with net inflows to the GPFG accumulating over time. The central government in Norway has the so-called "bird-in-hand rule" or "spending rule" (established in 2001), which stipulates that the non-oil structural deficit, and thus withdrawals from the fund over time, should correspond to the estimated annual real return of the fund, which has been 3 percent since 2017.

Norway's spending rule implies that the non-oil budget, and hence the economy, are isolated from both the large variations in oil revenues that result from oil price fluctuations as well as the volatility in the value of the fund due to variations in stock prices. This, in turn, helps to dampen the cyclical swings in the economy. The linking of the structural, and not the actual, non-oil fiscal deficit to the expected real return on the assets of the wealth fund allows automatic stabilizers to work. Norway (unlike its Nordic peers) does not have a publicly funded independent body to monitor fiscal or other economic policy. Instead, it established a Model and Method Commission in 2011, which advises the Ministry of Finance.

**Chile.** Chile is the world's biggest copper exporter—the metal accounts for about half of the country's total exports. Chile's fiscal policy management has been anchored on the successful implementation of SWFs, fiscal rules, and the recent creation of a fiscal council. Chile's SWFs comprise two types of funds.

- The Economic and Social Stabilization Fund (ESSF) was established with the Fiscal Responsibility Law of 2006. The ESSF has been designed for short-term purposes, with the main objective of stabilizing fiscal spending and insulating the budget from economic downturns and volatile copper prices, thus reducing the need to issue debt. Provisions for contributions to and withdrawal from the ESSF are well established in the law and closely tied to the fiscal rules. The ESSF has followed its mandate successfully and helped Chile finance countercyclical fiscal policy when needed. During the pandemic, the

government utilized the stabilization fund to provide fiscal support.

- The Pension Reserve Fund (PRF) aims to accumulate resources on a longer-term horizon. The PRF was created to support the state guarantee of pension and disability benefits. The funds' governance and assets management strategy match international best practices (Lam et al. 2023).

Chile's fiscal rule, in place since 2001, limits the growth of budgeted central government spending to an estimate of structural revenue growth. The rule's operation is supported by two expert panels that estimate long-term copper prices and the output gap. According to the rule, the authorities can run a deficit larger than the target if: (1) in a recession, output falls short of its long-run trend, or (2) the price of copper is below its medium-term (10-year) equilibrium (Frankel 2011). The ESSF is closely linked to the structural budget balance rule and has followed international best practices to have a flexible inflow and outflow mechanism, a feature similar to the arrangement in Norway (Lam et al. 2023). In addition to the fiscal rule, in January 2018 Chile created the Autonomous Fiscal Council to replace the Advisory Fiscal Council established in 2013. The new fiscal council also continues to have legal independence, its own resources, and has a broader mandate.

The presence of credible fiscal rules; the strong governance structures that provide the space for their implementation; and the recent creation of competent, independent, and adequately resourced fiscal councils have enabled Chile to develop some of the best fiscal management institutions among commodity-exporting EMDEs (Izquierdo et al. 2008). For example, in the aftermath of the 2009 global recession, Chile was able to conduct a countercyclical fiscal policy and maintain a low risk of debt distress. Government expenditures grew from about 23 percent of GDP in 2012-14 to about 25 percent of GDP in 2015-17 (figure B4.2.2.A). This helped mitigate output volatility, with GDP growth declining by 2 percentage points between 2012-14 and 2015-17, compared with an average decline of 2.6 percent among other metal exporters (Richaud et al. 2019). Chile's fiscal sustainability was maintained on account of its fiscal rule, which allowed the country to save a substantial proportion of commodity revenues into its SWF during the commodity supercycle (World

**BOX 4.2 Do fiscal rules and sovereign wealth funds make a difference? Lessons from country case studies (*continued*)**

### FIGURE B4.2.3 Institutional quality and fiscal procyclicality

*Indonesia's use of fiscal rules has enabled it to follow a prudent fiscal balance path despite increases in its export prices. Argentina's fiscal balance has been deteriorating since the mid-2000s despite generally increasing export prices. Australia, Chile, and Norway have followed prudent fiscal paths, with a relatively low correlation between government spending and commodity export prices. Establishing sovereign wealth funds and fiscal rules supported by strong institutional frameworks have allowed these countries to reduce or avoid fiscal procyclicality.*

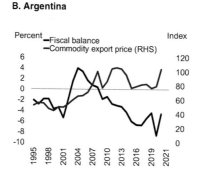

A. Indonesia

B. Argentina

C. Institutional quality and fiscal procyclicality

*Sources*: Arroyo Marioli and Végh (2023); International Monetary Fund; PRS Group (database); World Bank.
*Note*: EMDEs = emerging market and developing economies.
A.B. Fiscal balance as a percentage of GDP.
C. The institutional quality indexes give higher scores to countries with better metrics. "EMDEs" shows the simple average of 68 commodity-exporting countries across the three indicators from 1990-2019. The correlation is calculated between the GDP and the real government expenditure of a country after using the Hodrick-Prescott filter to remove the trend component of the time series.

Bank 2017). Part of these savings were drawn down to boost the economy in the wake of the global financial crisis. More recently, the SWF was crucial in financing a big fiscal stimulus package during the COVID-19 pandemic.

### *Botswana and Timor-Leste*

**Botswana.** Diamond mining is the dominant economic sector in Botswana. The government established a sovereign wealth fund—the Pula Fund—in 1994 to serve both as a savings fund and as a short-term stabilization fund. The main objective of the fund is to put aside part of the income from diamond exports to benefit future generations. Another objective is to provide a stabilization mechanism for the government budget and foreign reserves during an economic downturn or slump in mineral prices. For example, the Pula Fund helped stabilize revenue and output during the 2007-09 global financial crisis. During 2008-10, the fiscal deficit in Botswana averaged about 9.4 percent of GDP, as mining revenues declined, and expenditures surged because of an increase in infrastructure spending to offset the adverse effects of the global economic

downturn and to boost long-term productivity (figure B4.2.2.B). The government financed this deficit by drawing upon savings from the Pula Fund and issuing new debt (World Bank 2016).

To prevent excessive spending and bolster fiscal sustainability, the government has established a set of fiscal rules, which have been mostly set in terms of non-binding political commitments. Botswana has four main rules, which target public spending, the fiscal balance, and debt:

- An indicative expenditure rule, the Sustainable Budgeting Index (SBI), was established in 1994 to ensure that mineral revenue is directed toward investments and savings, rather than consumption (Apeti, Basdevant, and Salins 2023; Kojo 2010). The SBI computes the ratio of recurrent spending (excluding development spending) over non-diamond revenue, with the objective of keeping the ratio below 1. Adhering to this rule sets aside diamond revenue to finance the accumulation of financial assets and development spending.

**BOX 4.2 Do fiscal rules and sovereign wealth funds make a difference? Lessons from country case studies (*continued*)**

- There is an indicative target on the composition of spending, which specifies that development spending should be at least 30 percent of total spending.

- An indicative target of a nonnegative fiscal balance was established in 2003.

- Foreign and domestic debt are each prohibited from exceeding 20 percent of GDP.

Surplus fiscal savings are deposited into the Pula Fund, which invests in long-term instruments overseas, and dividends from these investments are paid to the Treasury.

However, Botswana's fiscal framework has limitations. The sustainable budgeting principle does not directly incorporate a sustainability concept, and the Pula Fund has been reducing its overall size with withdrawals that are far larger than its inflow (Basdevant 2008; Jefferis 2016). The Pula Fund is not governed by clearly defined withdrawal or deposit rules, with deposits determined by the size of the budget surplus and withdrawals determined by the size of deficits (Markowitz 2020). On balance, however, Botswana has run a fairly prudent fiscal policy, avoiding many pitfalls experienced by other commodity-dependent countries. The strength and stability of Botswana's institutions have been key in achieving this success (Kojo 2010; Richaud et al. 2019).

**Timor-Leste.** Offshore oil and gas reserves are the main sources of Timor-Leste's resource revenues. The Petroleum Fund (PF) was established in 2005 to collect oil revenues and is managed by the central bank. The PF primarily invests in offshore assets, such as U.S. Treasury bonds. The PF's only expenditures are transfers to the budget, payment of operational management fees, and refunds of overpaid taxes. The government has adopted two fiscal rules to guide the use of oil revenue although these rules are not binding.

- The Estimated Sustainable Income (ESI), established in 2005, is a mechanism for integrating the Petroleum Fund and the budget. The ESI is calculated as 3 percent of total wealth plus the present value of projected future oil receipts. That combined amount is what the government is

authorized to spend each year. The value of future oil receipts is determined using the U.S. Energy Information Administration's forecasts for West Texas Intermediate crude oil. Transfers exceeding the ESI are allowed only if the government provides a justification that is approved by Parliament. The requirement is designed to constrain the government's ability to spend government resources without considering long-term fiscal sustainability (Apeti, Basdevant, and Salins 2023).

- The second rule is a political commitment to maintain a ceiling on the cost of external debt at 3 percent per year. It requires the government to benchmark the costs of external borrowing against the average rate of investment returns of the PF.

Channeling all oil revenues into the PF and requiring that the ESI rule is consistent with the sustainable use of funds should, in principle, mitigate the impact of oil price cycles on fiscal expenditure. However, the escape clauses have hindered the effectiveness of Timor-Leste's fiscal frameworks. Until 2008, government spending of oil revenue was conservative and transfers to the budget to finance the non-oil budget deficit were lower than the ESI. As a result, the net assets of the Petroleum Fund grew rapidly from US$371 million in 2005 to US$4.2 billion in 2008, the equivalent of 647 percent of non-oil GDP.

However, beginning in 2009, the country started to withdraw funds from the PF in excess of the ESI to finance large infrastructure projects (IMF 2012b). This led to a significant slowdown in accumulation of assets, but the PF still reached a level of about US$19 billion in 2020. Since the global financial crisis, expenditures have followed oil prices closely (figure B4.2.2.C). Additionally, systematic excess withdrawals have been authorized in recent years, even prior to the pandemic. Given the low expected remaining lifetime of the country's oil fields, the PF is at serious risk of being depleted within the next decade (World Bank 2021).

In sum, escape clauses and weak institutions have diminished the effectiveness of fiscal rules in both Botswana and Timor-Leste, even when the rules were well-designed for long-run sustainability.

**BOX 4.2 Do fiscal rules and sovereign wealth funds make a difference? Lessons from country case studies (*continued*)**

*Argentina and Indonesia*

**Indonesia.** The main commodity exports of Indonesia are crude oil, gas, coal, palm oil, and rubber. Indonesia established a fiscal rule in 2003, which stipulates a fiscal deficit ceiling of 3 percent of GDP and a debt ceiling of 60 percent of GDP. At that time, the government's deficit was 1.7 percent of GDP, debt was at 57 percent of GDP, and the economy was well on its path to recovery after the Asian financial crisis. The aim of the fiscal rule was to solidify these gains and to promote future fiscal discipline by enacting these fiscal responsibility criteria into law (Blöndal, Hawkesworth, and Choi 2009). The rules have been respected and only temporarily lifted during the pandemic within legally pre-established norms.

Although Indonesia's fiscal rule has provided a solid nominal anchor and has safeguarded debt sustainability, fiscal spending has not been disconnected from the commodity price cycle (figure B4.2.3.A; Ismal 2011). For example, over 1993-2008, fiscal policy in Indonesia was not countercyclical (IMF 2009). The factors underlying limited fiscal responses to output fluctuations originated from structural weaknesses in public finance management and a lack of budget flexibility. This weakness included a high dependence on revenue from natural resources, narrow and volatile tax bases, low discretionary spending, and problems with budget execution.

Additionally, like many EMDEs, Indonesia relies on external financing which tends to be procyclical. Liquidity constraints, particularly during downturns, weaken the government's ability to run an expansionary fiscal policy to offset the effects of an economic slowdown. For example, during the 2007-09 global financial crisis, Indonesia's external borrowing spreads increased sharply, by nearly 1,200 basis points, much higher than its regional peers—Malaysia, the Philippines, and Thailand (IMF 2009). Another factor contributing to fiscal procyclicality is the high subsidy component of the budget, particularly energy subsidies, which leaves little room to respond to the economic cycle. However, the subsidies bill has been declining since 2015 owing to a series of reforms.

**Argentina.** The country's commodity export basket is based on agricultural goods. Unlike the other countries analyzed here, Argentina has neither a sovereign wealth fund nor a set of fiscal rules. Fiscal policy in Argentina has been highly procyclical, with expenditures growing closely in line with commodity export prices during the commodity price cycle of the 2000s (Kaminsky 2010; Tenreyro 2012). The lack of strong institutions and fiscal rules contributed to a deterioration in fiscal outcomes once the commodity price boom ended (figure B4.2.3.B). As a result, the country has faced persistent fiscal challenges in the past decade (IMF 2020).

## Conclusions

This box analyzes the experiences of selected commodity-exporting countries, all but one of which adopted fiscal rules and SWFs, in managing commodity price shocks. Insights from these case studies lead to the following conclusions.

First, *SWFs and fiscal rules differ among countries in objectives and design.* SWFs can have a long-term purpose (such as the accumulation of pension funds) or a short-term one (such as dampening the impact of temporary economic shocks). Some rules are designed to make an SWF sustainable, others to make them accessible when needed (Bauer 2014; Richaud et al. 2019). This aspect plays an important role in procyclicality because the criteria governing accessibility will determine the extent to which a government can access funds (and spend them). The sustainability conditions might also impose a limit on the amount that can be used even in times of need.

Second, *when supported by well-designed fiscal rules and institutions, SWFs can help reduce procyclicality.* International experience suggests that a strong political commitment to fiscal discipline, as well as strong institutions of good governance, are needed for SWFs to work well. Countries with good corruption control and law and order have been able to construct effective SWFs that reduce procyclicality by serving as a buffer against revenue volatility or as a source of financing during downturns (figures B4.2.3.C). In the cases of Norway (oil) and Chile (copper), commodity revenues are channeled directly into the SWFs, severing links from resource revenue to government spending. These funds are then available for specific purposes under certain conditions, avoiding or limiting fiscal

> **BOX 4.2 Do fiscal rules and sovereign wealth funds make a difference? Lessons from country case studies (*continued*)**
>
> procyclicality. In other cases, despite the presence of well-designed rules, the existence of escape clauses and weak institutions can render SWFs less useful (Perry 2007). These observations are in line with the findings of the analysis in this chapter, which shows that weak institutions limit the ability of governments to follow countercyclical fiscal policy despite having fiscal tools at their disposal.
>
> Finally, *commodity-exporters without SWFs or robust fiscal rules are more prone not only to procyclical fiscal behavior but* *also to debt sustainability issues.* In both Indonesia and Argentina, the two countries without an SWF in the sample, fiscal policies have been procyclical.[d] While Indonesia has benefited from a set of rules aimed at debt sustainability, the absence of rules in Argentina has allowed more discretionary spending policies that have contributed to successive crises.
>
> ---
>
> d. Indonesia established a SWF in 2021 that leverages state assets as well as public and private investment for infrastructure spending. It is not designed for fiscal stabilization.

# ANNEX 4.1 Determinants of fiscal procyclicality

Cross-country regressions for commodity exporters are used to identify the main drivers of fiscal procyclicality. The dependent variable is the correlation between the cyclical components of real government spending and real GDP. The explanatory variables capture each of the four explanations for the existence of procyclical fiscal policy: the financial openness index; the political constraints index; the standard deviation of GDP; and control of corruption. Each of these four variables is significant and three of the four coefficients have the expected sign (table A4.1.1). More financial openness and better control of corruption reduce procyclicality while greater output volatility increases procyclicality. However, the effect of the political constraints index is counterintuitive, suggesting that either the "voracity effect" does not hold or that the political constraint index is not an appropriate proxy for the detrimental effects of more fiscal claimants on available resources. When all these variables are included together, they are jointly significant.

**Robustness checks.** In line with Lane (2003), GDP per capita, size of the public sector relative to GDP, and openness (sum of exports and imports as a percentage of GDP) are used as controls in the regression one at a time. GDP per capita is significant at the 5 percent level but the two other control variables are not significant. In all three cases, the *F*-test for the joint significance of the four relevant explanatory variables is significantly different from zero at least at the 10 percent level.

The cross-country regressions are also used to analyze the role of institutional variables in driving fiscal procyclicality, as highlighted by the correlations reported in figure 4.4. The role of sovereign wealth funds (SWFs) and fiscal rules is also explored. To capture SWFs, a dummy variable is included that takes the value of 1 if a country has a SWF, and 0 otherwise. SWFs can play an important role in reducing procyclicality because these funds are designed to save during commodity price booms and dis-save during price slumps (Asik 2017). Results show that higher government stability, better law and order, and the presence of SWFs and fiscal rules all tend to reduce fiscal procyclicality (table A4.1.2). Overall, the analysis provides evidence that better institutions are associated with lower fiscal procyclicality.

Although fiscal rules may reduce procyclicality, the existence of fiscal procyclicality may prompt policy makers to adopt fiscal rules. To account for this potential endogeneity, instrumental variable estimation (two-stage least squares) is used with bureaucracy quality (from the PRS database) as an instrument.

## TABLE A4.1.1 Drivers of fiscal procyclicality

| | Dependent variable: Correlation between real government spending and real GDP | | | | |
|---|---|---|---|---|---|
| | (1) | (2) | (3) | (4) | (5) |
| Financial openness | -0.25** | | | | -0.19 |
| Corruption control | | -0.12*** | | | -0.07 |
| Political constraint index | | | -0.47** | | -0.08 |
| GDP volatility | | | | 1.58** | 1.26 |
| *F*-test | | | | | ** |
| Observations | 92 | 74 | 92 | 97 | 72 |
| *R*-squared | 0.05 | 0.13 | 0.05 | 0.06 | 0.18 |

*Source*: World Bank.
*Note*: Cross-sectional OLS regressions for commodity exporters. For regression (5), the *F*-test evaluates the joint significance of financial openness, corruption control, and GDP volatility. *, **, and *** denote significance at the 10, 5, and 1 percent level, respectively.

## TABLE A4.1.2 Institutional drivers of fiscal procyclicality

| | Dependent variable: Correlation between real government spending and real GDP | | | | | | |
|---|---|---|---|---|---|---|---|
| | (1) | (2) | (3) | (4) | (5) | (6) | (7) |
| Government stability | -0.09** | | | | | -0.01 | -0.07 |
| Law and order | | -0.13*** | | | | -0.12*** | -0.06 |
| Fiscal rules | | | -0.61*** | | -2.11*** | -0.31** | -1.26** |
| Sovereign wealth funds | | | | -0.53** | | -0.37** | -0.21 |
| *F*-test | | | | | | *** | *** |
| Observations | 137 | 137 | 106 | 194 | 83 | 83 | 83 |
| *R*-squared | 0.05 | 0.24 | 0.17 | 0.13 | n/r | 0.47 | 0.15 |

*Source*: World Bank.
*Note*: Cross-section regression for full sample. Regressions (1)-(4) and (6): OLS. Regressions (5) and (7): IV (two-stage least squares). n/r means not reported by STATA. For regressions (6) and (7), the *F*-test reported evaluates the joint significance of the three institutional variables. Regression (7), centered *R*-squared. Overidentification tests do not apply to regressions (5) and (7) since equations are perfectly identified. In regressions (5) and (7), the first-stage *F*-test of excluded instruments implies rejection of the null hypothesis of weak identification (p-value = 0.00) in both cases. *, **, and *** denote significance at the 10, 5, and 1 percent level, respectively.

## TABLE A4.1.3 Output growth and commodity prices

| | Dependent variable: GDP growth | | | | | |
|---|---|---|---|---|---|---|
| | (1) | (2) | (3) | (4) | (5) | (6) |
| | EMDEs | | | Full sample | | |
| Commodity export price index | 0.085*** | 0.063*** | 0.080*** | 0.024 | 0.018 | 0.026 |
| Terms of trade | | 0.029 | | | 0.026 | |
| GDP (*t* − 1) | | | 0.367*** | | | 0.366*** |
| Commodity export price index x EMDE | | | | 0.062** | 0.046* | 0.054** |
| *F*-test | | | | *** | *** | *** |
| Observations | 381 | 364 | 370 | 533 | 436 | 518 |
| Countries | 11 | 11 | 11 | 15 | 15 | 15 |

*Source*: World Bank.
*Note*: Panel least squares with country fixed effects. All variables are in log-differences. The estimates in columns (1)-(3) are based on the sample of emerging market and developing economies (EMDEs) only while those in columns (4)-(6) are based on the full sample that includes advanced-economy commodity exporters. *F*-test in columns (4)-(6) evaluates the joint significance of commodity export price index and the interaction of the index with the dummy variables for EMDEs. *, **, and *** indicate statistical significance at 10, 5, and 1 percent, respectively.

**TABLE A4.1.4 Government spending and commodity prices**

| | Dependent variable: Real government spending | | | | | |
|---|---|---|---|---|---|---|
| | (1) | (2) | (3) | (4) | (5) | (6) |
| | **EMDEs** | | | **Full sample** | | |
| Commodity export price index | 0.061* | 0.08* | 0.061* | -0.123*** | -0.072 | -0.121*** |
| Terms of trade | | -0.060 | | | -0.072 | |
| GDP ($t-1$) | | | 0.688*** | | | 0.625*** |
| Commodity export price index x EMDE | | | | 0.184*** | 0.158*** | 0.183*** |
| *F*-test | | | | *** | ** | *** |
| Observations | 276 | 269 | 276 | 415 | 341 | 413 |
| Countries | 11 | 11 | 11 | 15 | 15 | 15 |

*Source:* World Bank.
*Note:* Panel least squares with country fixed effects. All variables are in log-differences. The estimates in columns (1)-(3) are based on the sample of emerging market and developing economies (EMDEs) only while those in columns (4)-(6) are based on the full sample that includes advanced-economy commodity exporters. *F*-test in columns (4)-(6) evaluates the joint significance of commodity export price index and the interaction of the index with the dummy variables for EMDEs. *, **, and *** indicate statistical significance at 0.10, 0.05, and 0.01 percent, respectively. GDP = gross domestic product.

# ANNEX 4.2 Linkages between fiscal policy volatility and economic growth

## Estimating fiscal policy volatility

The framework used to estimate fiscal policy volatility is based on the approach in Fatás and Mihov (2013), which involves estimating a fiscal policy reaction function of the following form:

$$Fiscal\ Policy_t = \alpha + \beta\ Economic\ Activity_t + \gamma\ Controls_t + \epsilon_t \qquad (4.2.1)$$

where *"Fiscal Policy"* is a variable that captures the stance of fiscal policy. Four alternative measures of fiscal policy are used: primary expenditures, revenues, primary budget balance, and government consumption. Primary expenditures, revenues, and government consumption are all expressed in real terms and measured as log differences. The primary budget balance is expressed as the annual change of its ratio to GDP. *"Economic Activity"* denotes the cyclical stance of the economy and is represented by annual GDP growth. The alternatives—the output gap and the unemployment rate—are more difficult to construct or measure accurately for diverse economies.[22]

$\beta$ summarizes the cyclical behavior of fiscal policy and indicates whether fiscal policy is countercyclical or procyclical. It is composed of both automatic stabilizers and the discretionary response of governments to economic fluctuations.[23] The residual, $\epsilon$, captures changes in fiscal policy that are unrelated to the business cycle or any of the control variables. These decisions can be the result of political decisions (such as changes in tax rates or spending associated with the political cycle) or errors in policy (such as mismeasurement of the output gap). The uncertainty associated with the residual can be seen as generating excessive volatility in GDP and, possibly, reduced long-term growth. Following Fatás and Mihov (2013), the volatility of fiscal policy is measured as the standard deviation of the residual in the fiscal policy reaction function ($\sigma^{\epsilon}_i$).

## Implications of fiscal policy volatility for growth

The impact of fiscal policy volatility on per capita GDP growth is analyzed by estimating variants of a standard growth regression (Barro 1991). The benchmark specification is given by:

---

[22] HP-filtered GDP levels are also used as a measure of economic activity to check the robustness of the results. The results using this alternative measure are consistent with the baseline results.

[23] The specification has potential endogeneity issues since fiscal policy could affect economic activity contemporaneously. While the literature has acknowledged these issues, it has made use of OLS in many instances because of the lack of an obvious instrument (for example, Aghion, Hemous and Kharroubi 2014; Alesina, Campante and Tabellini 2008; and Lane 2003). Studies that have explored a set of instruments to test the robustness of the results presented in these earlier papers find similar results (for example, Fatás and Mihov 2013). Given this, and for the sake of simplicity, the analysis in this chapter makes use of OLS.

$$\overline{\Delta y_i} = \alpha' + \rho' \log(\sigma_i^\varepsilon) + \gamma' Z_i + u_i \qquad (4.2.2)$$

where $\overline{\Delta y_i}$ is the average per capita GDP growth for country $i$ ; $\sigma_i^\varepsilon$ is the measure of fiscal policy volatility—the key regressor; $Z_i$ is a vector of variables that have been found to have significant explanatory power for the cross-country variation in growth. Fiscal policy volatility is measured using primary expenditures. Equation (4.2.2) is estimated using both OLS as well as instrumental variables to address endogeneity concerns. Instruments used are political constraints and control of corruption from the PRS Group database, *International Country Risk Guide*.

The controls included in the regression are taken from the specification of Fatás and Mihov (2013), which are based on the growth regressions of Sala-i-Martin, Doppelhofer and Miller (2004).[24] The controls included are government size, initial GDP per capita, capital account openness, and the price of investment.

---

[24] For robustness, different specifications were estimated with a variety of controls, including the existence of a sovereign wealth fund. The results are not significant. Note that this variable is already included as an instrument for fiscal policy volatility.

**TABLE A4.2.1 Determinants of fiscal policy volatility: Cross-sectional regressions**

| | Dependent variable: Primary expenditure volatility | | | | | | |
|---|---|---|---|---|---|---|---|
| | (1) | (2) | (3) | (4) | (5) | (6) | (7) |
| EMDE | 4.930*** | 1.756** | | -2.381* | -0.398 | 0.536 | -1.255 |
| | (0.657) | (0.870) | | (1.266) | (1.276) | (1.151) | (0.970) |
| Commodity exporters | 3.295*** | -1.053 | | 0.661 | 3.356*** | 0.0398 | 1.082 |
| | (0.852) | (0.845) | | (0.747) | (1.134) | (0.849) | (0.753) |
| Resource rents | | 0.376*** | | 0.281*** | | 0.543*** | 0.402*** |
| | | (0.0814) | | (0.0688) | | (0.180) | (0.0678) |
| GDP per capita | | -1.240*** | | -0.548 | | 1.023 | 0.282 |
| | | (0.423) | | (0.464) | | (1.091) | (0.651) |
| SWF | | | | | | -0.324 | -0.349 |
| | | | | | | (0.832) | (0.703) |
| Political constraints | | | -11.27*** | -3.596 | | | 3.963 |
| | | | (2.502) | (3.224) | | | (4.676) |
| Control of corruption | | | -1.997*** | -1.836*** | | | -0.761* |
| | | | (0.421) | (0.570) | | | (0.388) |
| Fiscal policy rules | | | | | -0.947*** | -1.040** | -0.694** |
| | | | | | (0.348) | (0.411) | (0.308) |
| Capital account openness | | | | | -7.312*** | -4.256** | -4.202** |
| | | | | | (2.574) | (1.729) | (1.666) |
| Exchange rate regime | | | | | -4.722*** | -4.541*** | -3.206*** |
| | | | | | (1.093) | (1.294) | (0.857) |
| Constant | 3.930*** | 17.390*** | 17.92*** | 19.44*** | 14.04*** | 0.928 | 8.710 |
| | (0.460) | (4.495) | (1.305) | (5.025) | (2.836) | (10.191) | (5.579) |
| Observations | 178 | 177 | 133 | 132 | 93 | 93 | 77 |
| *R*-squared | 0.219 | 0.451 | 0.394 | 0.595 | 0.371 | 0.636 | 0.713 |

*Source*: World Bank.

*Note*: Robust standard errors in parentheses. "EMDE" is a dummy variable that takes the value 1 if a country is classified as an EMDE, and 0 otherwise. "Commodity exporters" is a dummy variable representing whether a country is a commodity exporter or not. "SWF" is a dummy equal to 1 if a country has a sovereign wealth fund and 0 otherwise. ***$p < 0.01$, **$p < 0.05$, *$p < 0.1$.

## TABLE A4.2.2 Determinants of fiscal policy volatility; by type of commodity

| | Dependent variable: Primary expenditure volatility | |
|---|---|---|
| | (1) | (2) |
| EMDE | 2.900*** | 1.794** |
| | (1.047) | (0.867) |
| Agriculture exporters | 0.712 | -0.592 |
| | (0.983) | (1.036) |
| Metal exporters | 2.236* | -0.136 |
| | (1.337) | (1.353) |
| Energy exporters | 6.185*** | -1.125 |
| | (1.625) | (1.252) |
| GDP per capita | -1.243** | -1.114** |
| | (0.523) | (0.453) |
| Resources rents | | 0.377*** |
| | | (0.089) |
| Constant | 17.081*** | 16.017*** |
| | (5.593) | (4.818) |
| Observations | 177 | 177 |
| R-squared | 0.292 | 0.450 |

*Source*: World Bank.
*Note*: Robust standard errors in parentheses. "Agriculture exporters," "metal exporters," and "energy exporters" are dummy variables that take the value 1 if a country is a net exporter of the respective commodity group, and 0 otherwise. ***$p < 0.01$, **$p < 0.05$, *$p < 0.1$.

## TABLE A4.2.3 Effects of fiscal policy volatility on GDP per capita growth

| | Dependent variable: GDP per capita growth | | | |
|---|---|---|---|---|
| | OLS | | IV | |
| | (1) | (2) | (3) | (4) |
| Fiscal policy volatility | -0.022 | -0.116*** | -0.110*** | 0.079* |
| | (0.060) | (0.022) | (0.036) | (0.042) |
| Government size | | 0.013 | 0.020 | 0.015 |
| | | (0.012) | (0.013) | (0.012) |
| Initial GDP per capita | | -0.659*** | -0.767*** | -0.774*** |
| | | (0.138) | (0.147) | (0.138) |
| Capital account openness | | 1.210*** | 1.230*** | 0.930*** |
| | | (0.302) | (0.314) | (0.342) |
| Investment price | | -1.481*** | -1.548*** | -1.546*** |
| | | (0.392) | (0.432) | (0.318) |
| Commodity exporter | | | | -0.734** |
| | | | | (0.318) |
| Constant | 1.986*** | 8.416*** | 9.202*** | 9.708*** |
| | (0.533) | (1.157) | (1.332) | (1.284) |
| Observations | 177 | 161 | 128 | 128 |
| R-squared | 0.006 | 0.356 | 0.403 | 0.433 |

*Source*: World Bank.
*Note*: Robust standard errors in parentheses. Fiscal policy volatility in all specifications is measured using primary expenditures. The estimates in columns (1) and (2) are based on ordinary least squares (OLS) regressions. Columns (3) and (4) is based on instrumental variables (IV) estimation, with the "political constraints" and "control of corruption" used as instruments. ***$p < 0.01$, **$p < 0.05$, *$p < 0.1$.

# ANNEX 4.3 Additional tables

**TABLE A4.3.1 List of economies for analysis of fiscal procyclicality and volatility**

| Commodity exporters | | | | | |
|---|---|---|---|---|---|
| **Agriculture** | | **Metals** | **Energy** | | |
| Argentina | New Zealand | Armenia | Algeria | Nigeria | |
| Belize | Nicaragua | Australia | Angola | Norway | |
| Benin | Paraguay | Botswana | Azerbaijan | Oman | |
| Brazil | Rwanda | Central African Republic | Bahrain | Qatar | |
| Burkina Faso | Senegal | Chile | Bolivia | Russian Federation | |
| Burundi | Seychelles | Congo, Dem. Rep. | Brunei Darussalam | Saudi Arabia | |
| Cabo Verde | Solomon Islands | Guinea | Cameroon | Timor-Leste | |
| Chad | Sudan | Kyrgyz Republic | Canada | Trinidad and Tobago | |
| Comoros | Tajikistan | Liberia | Chad | United Arab Emirates | |
| Costa Rica | Tanzania | Mauritania | Colombia | | |
| Côte d'Ivoire | Togo | Mongolia | Ecuador | | |
| Ethiopia | Uganda | Mozambique | Equatorial Guinea | | |
| Fiji | Ukraine | Namibia | Gabon | | |
| Guatemala | Uruguay | Niger | Ghana | | |
| Guinea-Bissau | Uzbekistan | Papua New Guinea | Guyana | | |
| Honduras | | Peru | Indonesia | | |
| Iceland | | Sierra Leone | Iran, Islamic Rep. | | |
| Kenya | | South Africa | Iraq | | |
| Lao PDR | | Sudan | Kazakhstan | | |
| Madagascar | | Suriname | Kuwait | | |
| Malawi | | Tajikistan | Libya | | |
| Mali | | Zambia | Myanmar | | |

| Commodity importers | | | | |
|---|---|---|---|---|
| Albania | Dominica | Italy | Moldova | Spain |
| Antigua and Barbuda | Dominican | Jamaica | Morocco | Sri Lanka |
| Austria | Egypt, Arab Rep. | Japan | Nepal | St. Kitts and Nevis |
| Bahamas, The | El Salvador | Jordan | Netherlands | St. Vincent and the Grenadines |
| Bangladesh | Eritrea | Kiribati | North Macedonia | Sweden |
| Barbados | Estonia | Korea, Rep. | Pakistan | Switzerland |
| Belarus | Eswatini | Latvia | Palau | Syrian Arab Republic |
| Belgium | Finland | Lebanon | Panama | Taiwan, China |
| Bhutan | France | Lesotho | Philippines | Thailand |
| Bosnia and Herzegovina | Georgia | Lithuania | Poland | Tonga |
| Bulgaria | Germany | Luxembourg | Portugal | Tunisia |
| Cambodia | Greece | Malaysia | Romania | Türkiye |
| China | Grenada | Maldives | Samoa | Tuvalu |
| Croatia | Hong Kong SAR, China | Malta | Serbia | United Kingdom |
| Cyprus | Hungary | Marshall Islands | Singapore | United States |
| Czechia | India | Mauritius | Slovak Republic | Vanuatu |
| Denmark | Ireland | Mexico | Slovenia | Viet Nam |
| Djibouti | Israel | Micronesia | | |

*Source*: World Bank.
*Note*: Commodity exports of economies can change over time implying the possibility of re-categorization.

## TABLE A4.3.2 Variables for analysis of fiscal procyclicality

| Variable | Description | Source |
|---|---|---|
| Government spending | Real government expenditure. | IMF, *World Economic Outlook* (WEO) |
| Political risk | Index based on 12 components with varying weights: government stability, socioeconomic conditions, investment profile, internal conflict, external conflict, corruption, military in politics, religious tensions, law and order, ethnic tensions, democratic accountability, and bureaucracy quality. | PRS Group (database) |
| Bureaucracy quality | Institutional strength and quality of the bureaucracy is a shock absorber that tends to minimize revisions of policy when governments change. In low-risk countries, the bureaucracy is somewhat autonomous from political pressure. Index measures the quality of bureaucracy from 0 to 6. | PRS Group (database) |
| Control of corruption | A measure of corruption within the political system that is a threat to foreign investment by distorting the economic and financial environment, reducing the efficiency of government and business by enabling people to assume positions of power through patronage rather than ability, and introducing inherent instability into the political process. Index ranges from 0 to 6. | PRS Group (database) |
| Government stability | A measure of both the government's ability to carry out its declared program(s) and to stay in office. The risk rating assigned is the sum of three subcomponents: government unity, legislative strength, and popular support. | PRS Group (database) |
| Law and order | "Law" assesses the strength and impartiality of the legal system, while the "order" element is an assessment of popular observance of the law. | PRS Group (database) |
| Capital account openness | The Chinn-Ito index (KAOPEN) measuring a country's degree of capital account openness; available from 1970-2019 for 182 countries. | Chinn and Ito (2006) |
| Exchange rate regime | A dummy indicator, where 1 is floating exchange rate regime and 0 is fixed. Classification codes 1-3 in the database have been classified as "0" and codes 4-6 as "1." | Ilzetzki, Reinhart, and Rogoff (2021) |
| Openness | Sum of exports and imports (percent of GDP). | World Integrated Trade Solution (World Bank) |
| Fiscal rules | Covers four types of rules: budget balance rules, debt rules, expenditure rules, and revenue rules, applying to the central or general government or the public sector. | Davoodi et al. (2022) |
| SWF (sovereign wealth fund) | Dummy variable: "0" if a country does not have a SWF and "1" if it has a SWF. | www.swfinstitute.org/fund-rankings/sovereign-wealth-fund |

*Source*: World Bank.

**TABLE A4.3.3 Variables for analysis of fiscal policy volatility**

| Variable | Description | Source |
|---|---|---|
| General government revenue | Consists of taxes, social contributions, grants receivable, and other revenue. | IMF, *World Economic Outlook* (WEO) |
| Primary balance | Primary net lending/borrowing is net lending (+)/borrowing (-) plus net interest payable/paid (interest expense minus interest revenue; percent of GDP) | WEO |
| Primary expenditure | Obtained by subtracting interest payments from general government total expenditures. Interest payments are calculated as the difference between overall fiscal balance and the primary balance (all in percent of GDP). | WEO and authors' calculations |
| Government consumption | General government final consumption expenditure includes all government current expenditures for purchases of goods and services (including compensation of employees) and most expenditures on national defense and security; excludes government military expenditures that are part of government capital formation. | World Development Indicators (World Bank) |
| Real GDP; real GDP per capita | | WEO |
| Political constraints | The Political Constraints Index (POLCON) measures the extent to which policy changes are constrained by institutional and political factors. | POLCON data set (Henisz 2000) |
| Control of corruption | An index measuring corruption within the political system; ranges from 0 to 6. | PRS Group (database) |
| Government size | General government total expenditure (percent of GDP). | WEO |
| Investment price | Price level of investment. | Penn World Table |
| Capital account openness | The Chinn-Ito index (KAOPEN) measuring a country's degree of capital account openness; available from 1970-2019 for 182 countries. | Chinn and Ito (2006) |
| Openness | Sum of exports and imports (percent of GDP). | World Integrated Trade Solution (World Bank) |
| Resources rents | Sum of oil rents, natural gas rents, coal rents (hard and soft), mineral rents, and forest rents. The estimates of natural resource rents are calculated as the difference between the price of a commodity and the average cost of producing it. | World Development Indicators (World Bank) |
| Fiscal rules | Covers four types of rules: budget balance rules, debt rules, expenditure rules, and revenue rules, applying to the central or general government or the public sector. | Davoodi et al. (2002) |
| SWF (sovereign wealth fund) | Dummy variable: 0 if a country does not have a SWF and 1 if it has a SWF. | www.swfinstitute.org/fund-rankings/sovereign-wealth-fund |

*Source*: World Bank.

# References

Afonso, A., and D. Furceri. 2008. "Government Size, Composition, Volatility and Economic Growth." Working Paper Series 849, European Central Bank, Frankfurt.

Aghion, P., D. Hemous, and E. Kharroubi. 2014. "Cyclical Fiscal Policy, Credit Constraints, and Industry Growth." *Journal of Monetary Economics* 62: 41-58.

Aizenman, J., and N. Marion. 1999. "Volatility and Investment: Interpreting Evidence from Developing Countries." *Economica* 66 (262): 157-79.

Al-Hassan, A., S. Brake, M.G. Papaioannou, and M. Skancke. 2018. "Commodity-based Sovereign Wealth Funds: Managing Financial Flows in the Context of the Sovereign Balance Sheet." IMF Working Paper 18/26, International Monetary Fund, Washington, DC.

Al-Sadiq, A., P. Bejar, and I. Otker. 2021. "Commodity Shocks and Exchange Rate Regimes: Implications for the Caribbean Commodity Exporters. IMF Working Paper 21/104, International Monetary Fund, Washington, DC.

Alesina, A., F. Campante, and G. Tabellini. 2008. "Why is Fiscal Policy Often Procyclical?" *Journal of the European Economic Association* 6 (5):1006-36.

Allen, R., T. Chaponda, L. Fisher, and R. Ray. 2017. "Medium-Term Budget Frameworks in Sub-Saharan African Countries." IMF Working Paper 17/203, International Monetary Fund, Washington, DC.

Alvarez, R., and J. De Gregorio. 2014. "Understanding Differences in Growth Performance in Latin America and Developing Countries between the Asian and the Global Financial Crises." *IMF Economic Review* 62 (4): 494-525.

Álvarez, R., Á. García-Marín, and S. Ilabaca. 2021. "Commodity Price Shocks and Poverty Reduction in Chile." *Resources Policy* 70 (March): 101177.

Apeti, A. E., O. Basdevant, and V. Salins. 2023. "Do Fiscal Rules Foster Fiscal Discipline in Resource-Rich Countries?" IMF Working Paper 23/088, International Monetary Fund, Washington, DC.

Ardanaz, M., E. A. Cavallo, and A. Izquierdo. 2023. Fiscal Rules: Challenges and Reform Opportunities for Emerging Markets. IDB Working Paper 1443, Inter-American Development Bank, Washington, DC.

Arezki, R., and M. Bruckner. 2010. "Commodity Windfalls, Polarization, and Net Foreign Assets: Panel Data Evidence on the Voracity Effect." IMF Working Paper 10/209, International Monetary Fund, Washington, DC.

Arezki, R., K. Hamilton, and K. Kazimov. 2011. "Resource Windfalls, Macroeconomic Stability and Economic Growth." IMF Working Paper 11/142, International Monetary Fund, Washington, DC.

Arezki, R., and K. Ismail. 2013. "Boom-bust Cycle, Asymmetrical Fiscal Response and the Dutch Disease." *Journal of Development Economics* 101(March): 256-67.

Arezki, R., C. A. Pattillo, M. G. Quintyn, and M. Zhu. 2012. "Commodity Price Volatility and Inclusive Growth in Low-Income Countries." Washington, DC: International Monetary Fund.

Arroyo Marioli, F., A. Fatás, and G. Vasishtha. 2023. "Fiscal Policy Volatility and Growth in Emerging Markets and Developing Economies." Policy Research Working Paper 10409, World Bank, Washington, DC.

Arroyo Marioli, F., and C. A. Végh. 2023. "Fiscal Procyclicality in Commodity Exporting Countries: How Much Does it Pour and Why?" NBER Working Paper 3143, National Bureau of Economic Research, Cambridge, MA.

Asik, A. 2017. "Effectiveness of Stabilization Funds in Managing Volatility in Oil-Rich Countries." Unpublished Manuscript, TOBB Economics and Technology University, Ankara, Türkiye.

Auerbach, A. J., and Y. Gorodnichenko. 2012. "Measuring the Output Responses to Fiscal Policy." *American Economic Journal: Economic Policy* 4 (2): 1-27.

Auerbach, A. J., and Y. Gorodnichenko. 2013. "Fiscal Multipliers in Recession and Expansion." In *Fiscal Policy after the Financial Crisis*, edited by A. Alesina and F. Giavazzi, 63-102. Chicago: University of Chicago Press.

Badinger, H., and W. H. Reuter. 2017. "The Case for Fiscal Rules." *Economic Modelling* 60 (January): 334-43.

Bagattini, G. 2011. "The Political Economy of Stabilization Funds: Measuring Their Success in Resource Dependent Countries." IDS Working Paper 356, Institute of Development Studies, University of Sussex, Brighton, U.K.

Barro, R. 1991. "Economic Growth in a Cross Section of Countries." *The Quarterly Journal of Economics* 106 (2): 407-43.

Basdevant, O. 2008. "Are Diamonds forever? Using the Permanent Income Hypothesis to Analyze Botswana's Reliance on Diamond Revenue." IMF Working Paper 08/80, International Monetary Fund, Washington, DC.

Bauer, A. 2014. "Fiscal Rules for Natural Resource Funds: How to Develop and Operationalize an Appropriate Rule." Policy Brief, Revenue Watch Institute, Vale Columbia Center on Sustainable International Investment, New York.

Bergman, U. M., and M. Hutchison. 2015. "Economic Stabilization in The Post-crisis World: Are Fiscal Rules The Answer?" *Journal of International Money and Finance* 52 (April): 82-101.

Bergman, U. M., M. Hutchison, and E. H. Jensen. 2016. "Promoting Sustainable Public Finances in the European Union: The Role of Fiscal Rules and Government Efficiency." *European Journal of Political Economy* 44 (September): 1-19.

Bhattacharyya, S., and J. G. Williamson. 2011. "Commodity Price Shocks and the Australian Economy since Federation." *Australian Economic History Review* 51(2): 150-77.

Blackburn, K., and A. Pelloni. 2004. "On the Relationship between Growth and Volatility." *Economics Letters* 83 (1): 123-27.

Blanchard, O., and R. Perotti. 2002. "An Empirical Characterization of the Dynamic Effects of Changes in Government Spending and Taxes on Output." *The Quarterly Journal of Economics* 117 (4): 1329-68.

Bleaney, M., and D. Greenaway. 2001. "The Impact of Terms of Trade and Real Exchange Volatility on Investment and Growth in Sub-Saharan Africa." *Journal of Development Economics* 65 (2): 491-500.

Bleaney, M., and H. Halland. 2009. "The Resource Curse and Fiscal Policy Volatility." Discussion Paper 09/09, Centre for Research in Economic Development and International Trade, University of Nottingham, Nottingham, U.K.

Blöndal, J., I. Hawkesworth, and H. Choi. 2009. "Budgeting in Indonesia." *OECD Journal on Budgeting* 9 (2).

Bova, E., N. Carcenac, and M. Guerguil. 2014. "Fiscal Rules and the Procyclicality of Fiscal Policy in the Developing World." IMF Working Paper 14/122, International Monetary Fund, Washington, DC.

Bova, M. E., M. P. A. Medas, and M. T. Poghosyan. 2016. "Macroeconomic Stability in Resource-Rich Countries: The Role of Fiscal Policy." IMF Working Paper 16/36, International Monetary Fund, Washington, DC.

Budina, N., T. Kinda, A. Schaechter, and A. Weber. 2013. "Numerical Fiscal Rules: International Trends." In *Public Financial Management and Its Emerging Architecture*, edited by M. Cangiano, T. Curristine, and M. Lazare. Washington, DC: International Monetary Fund.

Calderón, C., R. Duncan, and K. Schmidt-Hebbel. 2016. "Do Good Institutions Promote Countercyclical Macroeconomic Policies?" *Oxford Bulletin of Economics and Statistics* 78 (5): 650-70.

Calderón, C., and K. Schmidt-Hebbel. 2008. "Business Cycles and Fiscal Policies: The Role of Institutions and Financial Markets." Working Paper 481, Central Bank of Chile.

Carneiro, F., and L. Garrido. 2016. "Revisiting the Evidence on the Cyclicality of Fiscal Policy Across the World." MFM Discussion Paper 16, World Bank, Washington, DC.

Caselli, F., and J. Reynaud. 2020. "Do Fiscal Rules Cause Better Fiscal Balances? A New Instrumental Variable Strategy." *European Journal of Political Economy* 63 (June): 101873.

Céspedes, L. F., and A. Velasco. 2014. "Was this Time Different? Fiscal Policy in Commodity Republics." *Journal of Development Economics* 106 (January): 92-106.

Chinn, M. D., and H. Ito. 2006. "What Matters for Financial Development? Capital Controls, Institutions, and Interactions." *Journal of Development Economics* 81 (1): 163-192.

Chohan, U. W. 2017. "What Is a Charter of Budget Honesty? The Case of Australia." *Canadian Parliamentary Review* 40 (1): 11-15.

Collier, P., and A. Hoeffler. 2005. "Resource Rents, Governance, and Conflict." *Journal of Conflict Resolution* 49 (August): 625-33.

Commonwealth of Australia. 2014. "Charter of Budget Honesty Act 1998." Office of Parliamentary Counsel, Canberra.

Conteh, C. 2010. "The Challenges of Economic Development Policy Governance in Developing Countries: the Case of Botswana." *Canadian Journal of*

*Development Studies/Revue canadienne d'études du développement* 31(3-4): 401-16.

Coutinho, L., D. Georgiou, M. Heracleous, A. Michaelides, and S. Tsani. 2022. "Limiting Fiscal Procyclicality: Evidence from Resource-Dependent Countries." *Economic Modelling* 106 (January): 105700.

Dabla-Norris, E., R. Allen, L. Zanna, T. Prakash, E. Kvintradze, V. Lledo, I. Yackovlev, and S. Gollwitzer. 2010. "Budget Institutions and Fiscal Performance in Low-Income Countries." IMF Working Paper 10/80, International Monetary Fund, Washington, DC.

Dahan, M., and M. Strawczynski. 2013. "Fiscal Rules and the Composition of Government Expenditures in OECD Countries." *Journal of Policy Analysis and Management* 32 (3): 484-504.

Davoodi, H., P. Elger, A. Fotiou, D. Garcia-Macia, A. Lagerborg, R. Lam, and S. Pillai. 2022. "Fiscal Rules Dataset: 1985-2021." International Monetary Fund, Washington, DC.

Debrun, X., and M. Kumar. 2008. "Fiscal Rules, Fiscal Councils and All That: Commitment Devices, Signaling Tools or Smokescreens?" Workshop proceedings, Banca d'Italia, "Public Finance," Rome.

Debrun, X., L. Moulin, A. Turrini, J. Ayuso-i-Casals, and M. S. Kumar. 2008. "Tied to the Mast? National Fiscal Rules in the European Union." *Economic Policy* 23 (54): 298-362.

Elberry, N. A., and S. Goeminne. 2021. "Fiscal Transparency, Fiscal Forecasting and Budget Credibility in Developing Countries." *Journal of Forecasting* 40 (1): 144-61.

Estrades, C., and M. I. Terra. 2012. "Commodity Prices, Trade, and Poverty in Uruguay." *Food Policy* 37 (1): 58-66.

Fabrizio, S., and A. Mody. 2006. "Can Budget Institutions Counteract Political Indiscipline?" *Economic Policy* 21 (48): 689-739.

Fatás, A., and I. Mihov. 2001. "The Effects of Fiscal Policy on Consumption and Employment: Theory and Evidence." INSEAD Working Paper.

Fatás, A., and I. Mihov. 2003. "The Case for Restricting Fiscal Policy Discretion." *The Quarterly Journal of Economics* 118 (4): 1419-47.

Fatás, A., and I. Mihov. 2007. "Fiscal Discipline, Volatility and Growth." In *Fiscal Policy, Stabilization, and Growth: Prudence or Abstinence?*, edited by L. Serven, G. Perry, and R. Suescun. Washington, DC: World Bank.

Fatás, A., and I. Mihov. 2013. "Policy Volatility, Institutions, and Economic Growth." *The Review of Economics and Statistics* 95 (2): 362-76.

Fernández, A., D. Guzman, R. E. Lama, and C. A. Végh. 2021. "Procyclical Fiscal Policy and Asset Market Incompleteness." NBER Working Paper 29149, National Bureau of Economic Research, Cambridge, MA.

Filc, G., and C. Scartascini. 2010. "Is Latin America on the Right Track? An Analysis of Medium-Term Frameworks and the Budget Process." IDB Working Paper 160, Inter-American Development Bank, Washington, DC.

Fondo de Estabilización Económica y Social (website). Ministerio de Hacienda, Santiago, Chile. Accessed on August 31, 2023. https://www.hacienda.cl/areas-de-trabajo/finanzas-internacionales/fondos-soberanos/fondo-de-estabilizacion-economica-y-social

Frankel, J. A. 2011. "A Solution to Fiscal Procyclicality: The Structural Budget Institutions Pioneered by Chile." NBER Working Paper 16945, National Bureau of Economic Research, Cambridge, MA.

Frankel, J., C. A. Végh, and G. Vuletin. 2013. "On Graduation from Fiscal Procyclicality." *Journal of Development Economics* 100 (1): 32-47.

Future Fund (website). Australia's Sovereign Wealth Fund, Future Fund Management Agency, Melbourne, Australia. Accessed on August 31, 2023. https://www.futurefund.gov.au/

Ghosh, A. R., and J. D. Ostry. 1994. "Export Instability and the External Balance in Developing Countries." *IMF Staff Papers* 41 (2): 214-35.

Gill, I. S., I. Izvorski, W. van Eeghen, and D. De Rosa. 2014. *Diversified Development: Making the Most of Natural Resources in Eurasia*. Washington, DC: World Bank.

Hansen, D. 2020. "The Effectiveness of Fiscal Institutions: International Financial Flogging or Domestic Constraint?" *European Journal of Political Economy* 63 (June): 101879.

Hesse, H. 2008. "Export Diversification and Economic Growth." Commission on Growth and Development Working Paper 21, World Bank, Washington, DC.

Huidrom, R., Kose, M. A., and F. Ohnsorge. 2016. "Challenges of Fiscal Policy in Emerging and Developing Economies." World Bank Policy Research Working Paper 7725, World Bank, Washington, DC.

Ilzetzki, E. 2011. "Rent-seeking Distortions and Fiscal Procyclicality." *Journal of Development Economics* 96 (1): 30-46.

Ilzetzki, E., E. Mendoza, and C. A. Végh. 2013. "How Big (Small?) are Fiscal Multipliers?" *Journal of Monetary Economics* 60 (2): 239-54.

Ilzetzki, E., C. M. Reinhart, and K. Rogoff. 2022. "Rethinking Exchange Rate Regimes." In *Handbook of International Economics* 6, edited by G. Gopinath, E. Helpman, and K. Rogoff, 91-145. Amsterdam: Elsevier.

IMF (International Monetary Fund). 2004. *World Economic Outlook.* October. Washington, DC: International Monetary Fund.

IMF (International Monetary Fund). 2009. "Indonesia: Selected Issues." IMF Country Report 09/231, International Monetary Fund, Washington, DC.

IMF (International Monetary Fund). 2012a. *World Economic Outlook: Commodity Price Swings and Commodity Exporters.* International Monetary Fund, Washington, DC.

IMF (International Monetary Fund). 2012b. Macroeconomic Policy Frameworks for Resource-Rich Developing Countries. IMF Background Paper, International Monetary Fund, Washington, DC.

IMF (International Monetary Fund). 2015a. *World Economic Outlook: Uneven Growth: Short-and Long-Term Factors.* April. Washington, DC: International Monetary Fund.

IMF (International Monetary Fund). 2015b. *Fiscal Monitor: The Commodities Roller Coaster. A Fiscal Framework for Uncertain Times.* Chapter 1. October. Washington, DC: International Monetary Fund.

IMF (International Monetary Fund). 2020. "Argentina: Technical Assistance Report-Staff Technical Note on Public Debt Sustainability." IMF Country Report 20/83, International Monetary Fund, Washington, DC.

Ismal, R. 2011. "Assessing Economic Growth and Fiscal Policy in Indonesia." *East-West Journal of Economics and Business* 14 (1): 53-71.

Izquierdo, A., E. Talvi, L. Catão, E. Cavallo, and A. Powell. 2008. "All That Glitters May Not be Gold: Assessing Latin America's Recent Macroeconomic Performance." Research Department, Inter-American Development Bank, Washington, DC.

Jacks, D. S., K. H. O'Rourke, and J. G. Williamson. 2011. "Commodity Price Volatility and World Market Integration Since 1700." *The Review of Economics and Statistics* 93 (3): 800-13.

Jalles, J. T. 2018. "Fiscal Rules and Fiscal Counter-cyclicality." *Economics Letters* 170 (September): 159-62.

Jalles, J. T., Y. Kiendrebeogo, W. R. Lam, and R. Piazza. 2023. "Revisiting the Countercyclicality of Fiscal Policy." IMF Working Paper 23/89, International Monetary Fund, Washington, DC.

Jefferis, K. 2016. "Public finance and mineral revenues in Botswana." Technical Report. Waves Partnership Botswana Program.

Joya, O. 2015. "Growth and Volatility in Resource-Rich Countries: Does Diversification Help?" *Structural Change and Economic Dynamics* 35 (December): 38-55.

Kaminsky, G. L. 2010. "Terms of Trade Shocks and Fiscal Cycles." NBER Working Paper 15780, National Bureau of Economic Research, Cambridge, MA.

Kaminsky, G. L., C. M. Reinhart, and C. A. Végh. 2004. "When it Rains, It Pours: Procyclical Capital Flows and Macroeconomic Policies." *NBER Macroeconomics Annual* 19: 11-53.

Koh, W. C. 2017. "Fiscal Policy in Oil-Exporting Countries: The Roles of Oil Funds and Institutional Quality." *Review of Development Economics* 21 (3): 567-90.

Kojo, N. C. 2010. "Diamonds are Not Forever: Botswana Medium-Term Fiscal Sustainability." Policy Research Working Paper 5480, World Bank, Washington, DC.

Kose, M. A., F. Ohnsorge, K. Stamm, and N. Sugawara. 2023. "Government Debt Has Declined but Don't Celebrate Yet." *Brookings* (blog). February 21, 2023. https://brookings.edu/blog/future-development/2023/02/21/government-debt-has-declined-but-dont-celebrate-yet/

Kose, M. A., E. S. Prasad, and M. E. Terrones. 2005. "Growth and Volatility in an Era of Globalization." *IMF Staff Papers* 52 (Suppl 1): 31-63.

Kose, M. A., E. Prasad, K. Rogoff, and S. J. Wei. 2010. "Financial Globalization and Economic Policies." In *Handbook of Development Economics*, edited by D. Rodrik and M. Rosenzweig, 4283-359. Amsterdam: Elsevier.

Lam, R. W., Y. Cao, A. Lagerborg, and A. Scipioni. 2023. "Chile Technical Assistance Report—Fiscal Considerations in Managing Stabilization Funds." IMF Country Report 23/249, International Monetary Fund, Washington, DC.

Lane, P. R. 2003. "The Cyclical Behaviour of Fiscal Policy: Evidence from the OECD." *Journal of Public Economics* (87): 2661-75.

Le Borgne, E., and P. A. Medas. 2007. "Sovereign Wealth Funds in The Pacific Island Countries: Macro-Fiscal Linkages." IMF Working Paper 07/297, International Monetary Fund, Washington, DC.

Lensink, R., H. Bo, and E. Sterken. 1999. "Does Uncertainty Affect Economic Growth? An Empirical Analysis." *Review of World Economics* 135 (3): 379-96.

Lewin, M. 2011. "Botswana's Success: Good Governance, Good Policies, and Good Luck." In *Yes Africa Can*, edited by P. Chuhan-Pole and M. Angwafo, 81-90. Washington, DC: World Bank.

Manasse, P. 2006. "Procyclical Fiscal Policy: Shocks, Rules, and Institutions: A View from Mars." IMF Working Paper 06/027, International Monetary Fund, Washington, DC.

Markowitz, C. 2020. "Sovereign Wealth Funds in Africa: Taking Stock and Looking Forward." *Occasional Paper 304*, South African Institute of International Affairs, Johannesburg.

Martorano, B. 2018. "Cyclicality of Fiscal Policy in Latin America Over the Period 1990-2015." *Review of Development Economics* 22 (1): 67-90.

Medina, L. 2010. "The Dynamic Effects of Commodity Prices on Fiscal Performance in Latin America." IMF Working Paper 10/192, International Monetary Fund, Washington, DC.

Mohaddes, K., and M. Raissi. 2017. "Do Sovereign Wealth Funds Dampen the Negative Effects of Commodity Price Volatility?" *Journal of Commodity Markets* 8 (December): 18-27.

Ossowski, R., M. Villafuerte, P. A. Medas, and T. Thomas. 2008. "Managing the Oil Revenue Boom: The Role of Fiscal Institutions." IMF Occasional Paper 260, International Monetary Fund, Washington, DC.

Perry, G. E., ed. 2007. *Fiscal Policy, Stabilization, and Growth: Prudence or Abstinence?* Washington, DC: World Bank.

Ramey, G., and V. A. Ramey. 1995. "Cross-country Evidence on the Link Between Volatility and Growth." *American Economic Review* 85 (5): 1138-51.

Raudla, R., J. W. Douglas, and M. MacCarthaigh. 2022. "Medium-Term Expenditure Frameworks: Credible Instrument or Mirage?" *Public Budgeting & Finance* 42 (3): 71-92.

Richaud, C., A. G. M. Galego, F. Ayivodji, S. Matta, and S. Essl. 2019. "Fiscal Vulnerabilities in Commodity Exporting Countries and the Role of Fiscal Policy." MTI Discussion Paper 15, World Bank, Washington DC.

Sachs, J. D., and A. M. Warner. 1995. "Natural Resource Abundance and Economic Growth." NBER Working Paper 5398, National Bureau of Economic Research, Cambridge, MA.

Sala-i-Martin, X., G. Doppelhofer, and R. Miller. 2004. "Determinants of Long-Term Growth: A Bayesian Averaging of Classical Estimates (BACE) Approach." *American Economic Review* 94 (4): 813-35.

Schiavo-Campo, S. 2009. "Potemkin Villages: The Medium-Term Expenditure Framework in Developing Countries." *Public Budgeting & Finance* 29 (2): 1-26.

Shabsigh, G., and N. Ilahi. 2007. "Looking beyond the Fiscal: Do Oil Funds Bring Macroeconomic Stability?" IMF Working Paper 07/96, International Monetary Fund, Washington, DC.

Strong, C. O. Forthcoming. "Tying One's Hand: The Effect of Fiscal Rules on the Political Business Cycle in Africa." *Journal of African Economies.* https://doi.org/10.1093/jae/ejac014

Sugawara, N. 2014. "From Volatility to Stability in Expenditure: Stabilization Funds in Resource-Rich Countries." IMF Working Paper 14/43, International Monetary Fund, Washington, DC.

Talvi, E., and C. A. Végh. 2005. "Tax Base Variability and Procyclical Fiscal Policy in Developing Countries." *Journal of Development Economics* 78 (1): 156-90.

Tapsoba, R. 2012. "Do National Numerical Fiscal Rules Really Shape Fiscal Behaviours in Developing Countries? A Treatment Effect Evaluation." *Economic Modelling* 29 (4): 1356-69.

Temsumrit, N. 2022. "Democracy, Institutional Quality and Fiscal Policy Cycle: Evidence from Developing Countries." *Applied Economics* 54 (1): 75-98.

Tenreyro, S. 2012. The Argentine Crisis in Retrospect. *London School of Economics and Political Sciences.*

Timor-Leste Petroleum Fund (website). The Timor-Leste Institute for Development Monitoring and Analysis, Dili, Timor-Leste. Accessed on August 31, 2023. https://www.laohamutuk.org/Oil/PetFund/05PFIndex.htm

Tornell, A., and P. R. Lane. 1999. "The Voracity Effect." *American Economic Review* 89 (1): 22-46.

Tornell, A., and A. Velasco. 2000. "Fixed Versus Flexible Exchange Rates: Which Provides More Fiscal Discipline?" *Journal of Monetary Economics* 45: 399-436.

UNCTAD (United Nations Conference on Trade and Development). 2021. "Global Investment Trend Monitor 39." World Investment Forum Factsheet Edition. October. https://unctad.org/system/files/official-document/diaeiainf2021d2_en.pdf

Van der Ploeg, F. 2011. "Natural Resources: Curse or Blessing?" *Journal of Economic Literature* 49 (2): 366-420.

Végh, C. A., and G. Vuletin. 2014. "The Road to Redemption: Policy Response to Crises in Latin America." *IMF Economic Review* 62 (4): 526-68.

Velculescu, D. 2008. Norway's Oil Fund Shows the Way for Wealth Funds. *IMF Survey Magazine* 9: 600-03.

Vlaicu, R., M. Verhoeven, F. Grigoli, and Z. Mills. 2014. "Multiyear Budgets and Fiscal Performance: Panel Data Evidence." *Journal of Public Economics* 111 (March): 79-95.

Von Hagen, J. 2010. "Sticking to Fiscal Plans: The Role of Institutions." *Public Choice* 144: 487-503.

World Bank. 1998. "Public Expenditure Management Handbook." Washington, DC: World Bank.

World Bank. 2009. *Global Economic Prospects: Commodities at the Crossroads.* Washington, DC: World Bank.

World Bank. 2013. *Beyond the Annual Budget: Global Experience with Medium-Term Expenditure Frameworks.* Washington, DC: World Bank.

World Bank. 2016. *Public Finance and Mineral Revenues in Botswana Technical Report.* Washington, DC: World Bank. Available at https://econsult.co.bw/tempex/file/Mineral%20revenues%20and%20public%20finance_final_compressed.pdf

World Bank. 2017. "The Republic of Chile: Systematic Country Diagnostic." World Bank Publications. Washington, DC: World Bank.

World Bank. 2020. *Commodity Markets Outlook: Persistence of Commodity Shocks.* October. Washington, DC: World Bank.

World Bank. 2021. *Timor-Leste Public Expenditure Review: Changing Course Towards Better and More Sustainable Spending.* Washington, DC: World Bank

World Bank. 2022. *Global Economic Prospects.* January. Washington, DC: World Bank.

World Bank. 2023. *Global Economic Prospects.* June. Washington, DC: World Bank.

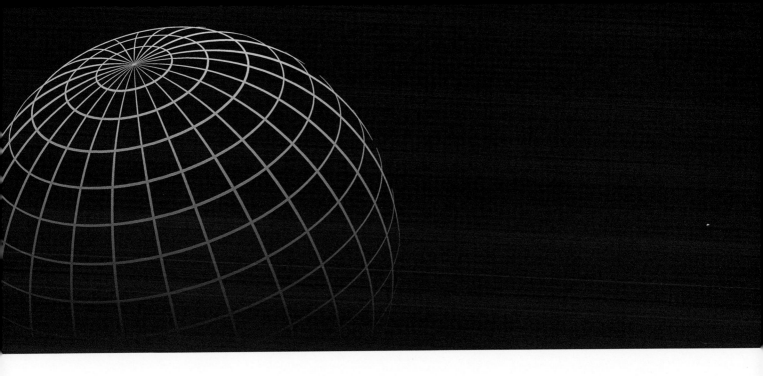

# STATISTICAL APPENDIX

# Real GDP growth

| | Annual estimates and forecasts [1] (Percent change) | | | | | Quarterly estimates [2] (Percent change, year-on-year) | | | | | |
|---|---|---|---|---|---|---|---|---|---|---|---|
| | 2021 | 2022 | 2023e | 2024f | 2025f | 22Q2 | 22Q3 | 22Q4 | 23Q1 | 23Q2 | 23Q3e |
| **World** | **6.2** | **3.0** | **2.6** | **2.4** | **2.7** | **3.0** | **3.0** | **1.8** | **2.4** | **2.9** | **..** |
| **Advanced economies** | **5.5** | **2.5** | **1.5** | **1.2** | **1.6** | **2.9** | **2.3** | **1.1** | **1.6** | **1.6** | **1.6** |
| United States | 5.8 | 1.9 | 2.5 | 1.6 | 1.7 | 1.9 | 1.7 | 0.7 | 1.7 | 2.4 | 2.9 |
| Euro area | 5.9 | 3.4 | 0.4 | 0.7 | 1.6 | 4.1 | 2.4 | 1.8 | 1.3 | 0.6 | 0.0 |
| Japan | 2.6 | 1.0 | 1.8 | 0.9 | 0.8 | 1.2 | 1.5 | 0.6 | 2.5 | 2.3 | 1.6 |
| **Emerging market and developing economies** | **7.0** | **3.7** | **4.0** | **3.9** | **4.0** | **3.1** | **4.0** | **2.8** | **3.7** | **4.8** | **..** |
| **East Asia and Pacific** | **7.5** | **3.4** | **5.1** | **4.5** | **4.4** | **1.3** | **4.5** | **3.2** | **4.6** | **6.0** | **4.8** |
| Cambodia | 3.0 | 5.2 | 5.4 | 5.8 | 6.1 | .. | .. | .. | .. | .. | .. |
| China | 8.4 | 3.0 | 5.2 | 4.5 | 4.3 | 0.4 | 3.9 | 2.9 | 4.5 | 6.3 | 4.9 |
| Fiji | -5.1 | 20.0 | 7.6 | 4.0 | 3.7 | .. | .. | .. | .. | .. | .. |
| Indonesia | 3.7 | 5.3 | 5.0 | 4.9 | 4.9 | 5.5 | 5.7 | 5.0 | 5.0 | 5.2 | 4.9 |
| Kiribati | 7.9 | 1.2 | 2.5 | 2.4 | 2.3 | .. | .. | .. | .. | .. | .. |
| Lao PDR | 2.5 | 2.7 | 3.7 | 4.1 | 4.3 | .. | .. | .. | .. | .. | .. |
| Malaysia | 3.3 | 8.7 | 3.9 | 4.3 | 4.2 | 8.8 | 14.1 | 7.1 | 5.6 | 2.9 | 3.3 |
| Marshall Islands [3] | 1.0 | -4.5 | 3.0 | 3.0 | 2.0 | .. | .. | .. | .. | .. | .. |
| Micronesia, Fed. Sts. [3] | -3.2 | -0.6 | 2.8 | 2.8 | 1.3 | .. | .. | .. | .. | .. | .. |
| Mongolia | 1.6 | 5.0 | 5.8 | 6.2 | 6.4 | 1.8 | 7.4 | 11.2 | 7.8 | 4.8 | 8.7 |
| Myanmar [3][4] | -12.0 | 4.0 | 1.0 | 2.0 | .. | .. | .. | .. | .. | .. | .. |
| Nauru [3] | 7.2 | 2.8 | 0.6 | 1.4 | 1.2 | .. | .. | .. | .. | .. | .. |
| Palau [3] | -13.4 | -2.0 | 0.8 | 12.4 | 11.9 | .. | .. | .. | .. | .. | .. |
| Papua New Guinea | -0.8 | 5.2 | 3.0 | 5.0 | 3.1 | .. | .. | .. | .. | .. | .. |
| Philippines | 5.7 | 7.6 | 5.6 | 5.8 | 5.8 | 7.5 | 7.7 | 7.1 | 6.4 | 4.3 | 5.9 |
| Samoa [3] | -7.1 | -5.3 | 8.0 | 4.5 | 3.6 | .. | .. | .. | .. | .. | .. |
| Solomon Islands | -0.6 | -4.1 | 1.8 | 2.7 | 3.1 | .. | .. | .. | .. | .. | .. |
| Thailand | 1.5 | 2.6 | 2.5 | 3.2 | 3.1 | 2.5 | 4.6 | 1.4 | 2.6 | 1.8 | 1.5 |
| Timor-Leste | 2.9 | 3.9 | 2.4 | 3.5 | 4.3 | .. | .. | .. | .. | .. | .. |
| Tonga [3] | -2.7 | -2.0 | 2.6 | 2.5 | 2.2 | .. | .. | .. | .. | .. | .. |
| Tuvalu | 1.8 | 0.7 | 3.9 | 3.5 | 2.4 | .. | .. | .. | .. | .. | .. |
| Vanuatu | 0.6 | 1.9 | 1.5 | 2.6 | 3.5 | .. | .. | .. | .. | .. | .. |
| Viet Nam | 2.6 | 8.0 | 4.7 | 5.5 | 6.0 | 7.8 | 13.7 | 5.9 | 3.3 | 4.1 | 5.3 |
| **Europe and Central Asia** | **7.1** | **1.2** | **2.7** | **2.4** | **2.7** | **0.6** | **-0.2** | **-0.2** | **0.4** | **3.7** | **..** |
| Albania | 8.9 | 4.8 | 3.6 | 3.2 | 3.2 | 3.2 | 4.9 | 4.4 | 2.8 | 3.2 | .. |
| Armenia | 5.8 | 12.6 | 7.1 | 4.7 | 4.5 | 13.1 | 14.8 | 12.7 | 12.1 | 9.1 | 7.4 |
| Azerbaijan | 5.6 | 4.6 | 1.5 | 2.4 | 2.5 | .. | .. | .. | .. | .. | .. |
| Belarus | 2.4 | -4.7 | 3.0 | 0.8 | 0.8 | -8.0 | -5.4 | -4.5 | -2.0 | 5.9 | .. |
| Bosnia and Herzegovina [5] | 7.4 | 3.9 | 2.2 | 2.8 | 3.4 | 5.6 | 2.9 | 2.5 | 1.7 | 1.2 | .. |
| Bulgaria | 7.7 | 3.9 | 1.7 | 2.4 | 3.3 | 4.2 | 3.3 | 3.6 | 2.2 | 1.9 | 1.5 |
| Croatia | 13.8 | 6.3 | 2.5 | 2.7 | 3.0 | 9.3 | 5.5 | 3.2 | 1.6 | 2.6 | 2.8 |
| Georgia | 10.5 | 10.4 | 6.5 | 4.8 | 4.5 | 7.1 | 10.3 | 10.0 | 8.0 | 7.8 | .. |
| Kazakhstan | 4.3 | 3.2 | 4.5 | 4.3 | 4.5 | 2.7 | 1.9 | 4.0 | 5.0 | 5.6 | .. |
| Kosovo | 10.7 | 5.2 | 3.2 | 3.9 | 4.0 | .. | .. | .. | .. | .. | .. |
| Kyrgyz Republic | 5.5 | 6.3 | 3.5 | 4.0 | 4.0 | .. | .. | .. | .. | .. | .. |
| Moldova | 13.9 | -5.0 | 1.8 | 4.2 | 4.1 | -0.9 | -10.3 | -10.6 | .. | .. | .. |
| Montenegro [2] | 13.0 | 6.4 | 4.8 | 3.2 | 3.1 | 13.0 | 3.6 | 3.6 | 6.2 | 6.9 | 6.6 |
| North Macedonia | 4.5 | 2.2 | 1.8 | 2.5 | 2.9 | 4.0 | 1.8 | 1.5 | 1.5 | 1.1 | 1.2 |
| Poland | 6.9 | 5.1 | 0.5 | 2.6 | 3.4 | 6.3 | 4.1 | 2.5 | -0.3 | -0.6 | 0.5 |
| Romania | 5.7 | 4.6 | 1.8 | 3.3 | 3.8 | 4.5 | 3.9 | 5.3 | 1.0 | .. | .. |
| Russian Federation | 5.6 | -2.1 | 2.6 | 1.3 | 0.9 | -4.5 | -3.5 | -2.7 | -1.8 | 4.9 | 5.5 |
| Serbia | 7.7 | 2.5 | 2.0 | 3.0 | 3.8 | 3.8 | 1.0 | 0.5 | 0.9 | 1.7 | .. |
| Tajikistan | 9.4 | 8.0 | 7.5 | 5.5 | 4.5 | .. | .. | .. | .. | .. | .. |
| Türkiye | 11.4 | 5.5 | 4.2 | 3.1 | 3.9 | 7.6 | 4.1 | 3.3 | 4.0 | 3.9 | 5.9 |
| Ukraine | 3.4 | -29.1 | 4.8 | 3.2 | 6.5 | -36.9 | -30.6 | -31.4 | -10.5 | 19.5 | 9.3 |
| Uzbekistan | 7.4 | 5.7 | 5.5 | 5.5 | 5.5 | .. | .. | .. | .. | .. | .. |

# Real GDP growth (*continued*)

| | Annual estimates and forecasts [1] (Percent change) | | | | | Quarterly estimates [2] (Percent change, year-on-year) | | | | | |
|---|---|---|---|---|---|---|---|---|---|---|---|
| | 2021 | 2022 | 2023e | 2024f | 2025f | 22Q2 | 22Q3 | 22Q4 | 23Q1 | 23Q2 | 23Q3e |
| **Latin America and the Caribbean** | **7.2** | **3.9** | **2.2** | **2.3** | **2.5** | **4.6** | **4.5** | **2.7** | **3.1** | **2.0** | **..** |
| Argentina | 10.7 | 5.0 | -2.5 | 2.7 | 3.2 | 6.8 | 5.7 | 1.5 | 1.4 | -5.0 | -0.8 |
| Bahamas, The | 17.0 | 14.4 | 4.3 | 1.8 | 1.6 | .. | .. | .. | .. | .. | .. |
| Barbados | -0.8 | 13.8 | 4.6 | 4.0 | 3.0 | .. | .. | .. | .. | .. | .. |
| Belize | 15.2 | 12.7 | 4.5 | 3.5 | 3.3 | 9.3 | 10.0 | 8.2 | 7.8 | 4.1 | 3.4 |
| Bolivia | 6.1 | 3.5 | 1.9 | 1.5 | 1.5 | 4.6 | 4.1 | 1.3 | 2.4 | 2.0 | .. |
| Brazil | 5.0 | 2.9 | 3.1 | 1.5 | 2.2 | 3.5 | 4.3 | 2.7 | 4.2 | 3.5 | 2.0 |
| Chile | 11.7 | 2.4 | -0.4 | 1.8 | 2.3 | 5.2 | 0.2 | -2.3 | -0.7 | -0.8 | 0.6 |
| Colombia | 11.0 | 7.3 | 1.2 | 1.8 | 3.0 | 12.3 | 7.4 | 2.1 | 3.0 | 0.4 | -0.3 |
| Costa Rica | 7.8 | 4.3 | 5.2 | 3.9 | 3.6 | 4.5 | 2.8 | 4.3 | 4.4 | 5.8 | 5.9 |
| Dominica | 6.9 | 5.9 | 4.9 | 4.6 | 4.0 | .. | .. | .. | .. | .. | .. |
| Dominican Republic | 12.3 | 4.9 | 2.5 | 5.1 | 5.0 | 5.2 | 5.0 | 3.3 | 1.4 | 0.9 | .. |
| Ecuador | 4.2 | 2.9 | 1.3 | 0.7 | 2.0 | 1.4 | 2.7 | 4.3 | 1.0 | 3.3 | .. |
| El Salvador | 11.2 | 2.6 | 2.8 | 2.3 | 2.3 | 2.5 | 2.2 | 1.2 | 0.8 | 3.1 | .. |
| Grenada | 4.7 | 6.4 | 3.9 | 3.8 | 3.5 | .. | .. | .. | .. | .. | .. |
| Guatemala | 8.0 | 4.1 | 3.4 | 3.5 | 3.5 | 4.5 | 3.8 | 3.5 | 3.7 | 3.8 | .. |
| Guyana | 20.1 | 63.4 | 29.0 | 38.2 | 15.2 | .. | .. | .. | .. | .. | .. |
| Haiti [3] | -1.8 | -1.7 | -2.5 | 1.3 | 2.2 | .. | .. | .. | .. | .. | .. |
| Honduras | 12.5 | 4.0 | 3.2 | 3.2 | 3.4 | 4.3 | 4.1 | 2.1 | 2.0 | 3.1 | .. |
| Jamaica [2] | 4.6 | 5.2 | 2.3 | 2.0 | 1.4 | 4.8 | 5.9 | 3.8 | 4.2 | 2.3 | .. |
| Mexico | 5.8 | 3.9 | 3.6 | 2.6 | 2.1 | 3.3 | 5.0 | 4.5 | 3.5 | 3.4 | 3.3 |
| Nicaragua | 10.3 | 3.8 | 3.1 | 3.2 | 3.5 | 4.5 | 3.4 | 2.5 | 3.5 | 3.9 | 6.2 |
| Panama | 15.8 | 10.8 | 4.9 | 4.6 | 5.3 | 9.6 | 10.0 | 10.4 | 9.3 | 8.2 | .. |
| Paraguay | 4.0 | 0.1 | 4.6 | 3.8 | 3.8 | -3.3 | 2.9 | 1.7 | 4.9 | 5.9 | .. |
| Peru | 13.4 | 2.7 | -0.4 | 2.5 | 2.3 | 3.4 | 2.0 | 1.7 | -0.4 | -0.5 | -1.0 |
| St. Lucia | 12.2 | 15.9 | 3.2 | 2.9 | 2.3 | .. | .. | .. | .. | .. | .. |
| St. Vincent and the Grenadines | 0.8 | 4.9 | 6.0 | 4.8 | 3.7 | .. | .. | .. | .. | .. | .. |
| Suriname | -2.4 | 2.4 | 2.0 | 2.6 | 3.0 | .. | .. | .. | .. | .. | .. |
| Uruguay | 5.3 | 4.9 | 1.2 | 3.2 | 2.6 | 8.7 | 3.4 | -0.1 | 1.6 | -2.5 | -0.2 |
| **Middle East and North Africa** | **3.8** | **5.8** | **1.9** | **3.5** | **3.5** | **6.3** | **6.0** | **4.7** | **3.9** | **2.8** | **..** |
| Algeria | 3.4 | 3.2 | 2.5 | 2.6 | 2.6 | 2.9 | 3.7 | 3.8 | 3.0 | .. | .. |
| Bahrain | 2.7 | 4.9 | 2.8 | 3.3 | 3.2 | 6.6 | 3.4 | 4.2 | 2.0 | 2.0 | .. |
| Djibouti | 4.5 | 3.1 | 4.7 | 5.1 | 5.7 | .. | .. | .. | .. | .. | .. |
| Egypt, Arab Rep. [3] | 3.3 | 6.6 | 3.8 | 3.5 | 3.9 | 3.2 | 4.4 | 3.9 | 3.9 | 2.9 | .. |
| Iran, Islamic Rep. [3] | 4.7 | 3.8 | 4.2 | 3.7 | 3.2 | 2.2 | 3.2 | 4.1 | 5.7 | 6.4 | .. |
| Iraq [2] | -2.1 | 7.0 | -2.9 | 4.2 | 2.9 | 10.4 | 6.0 | -1.3 | 2.6 | .. | .. |
| Jordan | 3.7 | 2.4 | 2.6 | 2.5 | 2.6 | 2.9 | 2.4 | 2.0 | 2.8 | 2.6 | .. |
| Kuwait | 1.3 | 7.9 | 0.8 | 2.6 | 2.7 | .. | .. | .. | .. | .. | .. |
| Lebanon [4] | -7.0 | -0.6 | 0.2 | .. | .. | .. | .. | .. | .. | .. | .. |
| Libya | 31.4 | -1.2 | 14.1 | 4.1 | 4.3 | .. | .. | .. | .. | .. | .. |
| Morocco | 8.0 | 1.3 | 2.8 | 3.1 | 3.3 | 2.2 | 1.7 | 0.7 | 3.5 | 2.3 | 2.4 |
| Oman | 3.1 | 4.3 | 1.4 | 2.7 | 2.9 | 4.1 | 6.8 | 7.4 | 4.0 | -0.2 | .. |
| Qatar | 1.5 | 4.9 | 2.8 | 2.5 | 3.1 | 4.0 | 4.4 | 6.2 | 2.2 | 1.0 | .. |
| Saudi Arabia | 3.9 | 8.7 | -0.5 | 4.1 | 4.2 | 11.2 | 8.6 | 5.3 | 3.8 | 1.2 | -4.4 |
| Syrian Arab Republic [4] | 1.3 | -3.5 | -5.5 | .. | .. | .. | .. | .. | .. | .. | .. |
| Tunisia | 4.4 | 2.4 | 1.2 | 3.0 | 3.0 | 2.8 | 3.4 | 1.8 | 1.8 | 0.6 | -0.2 |
| United Arab Emirates | 3.5 | 6.6 | 3.4 | 3.7 | 3.8 | 8.0 | 8.3 | 5.5 | 3.7 | 3.7 | .. |
| West Bank and Gaza | 7.0 | 3.9 | -3.7 | -6.0 | 5.4 | 3.4 | 4.6 | 2.2 | 3.1 | 2.9 | .. |
| Yemen, Rep. [4] | -1.0 | 1.5 | -0.5 | 2.0 | .. | .. | .. | .. | .. | .. | .. |

# Real GDP growth (*continued*)

| | Annual estimates and forecasts [1] (Percent change) | | | | | Quarterly estimates [2] (Percent change, year-on-year) | | | | | |
|---|---|---|---|---|---|---|---|---|---|---|---|
| | 2021 | 2022 | 2023e | 2024f | 2025f | 22Q2 | 22Q3 | 22Q4 | 23Q1 | 23Q2 | 23Q3e |
| **South Asia** | **8.3** | **5.9** | **5.7** | **5.6** | **5.9** | **11.9** | **5.1** | **3.7** | **4.9** | **6.4** | **..** |
| Afghanistan [4] | -20.7 | .. | .. | .. | .. | .. | .. | .. | .. | .. | .. |
| Bangladesh [3] | 6.9 | 7.1 | 6.0 | 5.6 | 5.8 | .. | .. | .. | .. | .. | .. |
| Bhutan [3] | -3.3 | 4.8 | 4.6 | 4.0 | 4.6 | .. | .. | .. | .. | .. | .. |
| India [3] | 9.1 | 7.2 | 6.3 | 6.4 | 6.5 | 13.1 | 6.2 | 4.5 | 6.1 | 7.8 | 7.6 |
| Maldives | 37.7 | 13.9 | 6.5 | 5.2 | 5.5 | 27.5 | 12.0 | 1.2 | 4.4 | 0.0 | .. |
| Nepal [2][3] | 4.8 | 5.6 | 1.9 | 3.9 | 5.0 | 9.0 | 1.7 | -1.1 | .. | .. | .. |
| Pakistan [2][3][5] | 5.8 | 6.2 | -0.2 | 1.7 | 2.4 | 7.2 | 1.0 | 1.8 | -0.6 | -2.7 | 2.1 |
| Sri Lanka | 3.5 | -7.8 | -3.8 | 1.7 | 2.4 | -7.4 | -11.5 | -12.4 | -11.5 | -3.1 | 1.6 |
| **Sub-Saharan Africa** | **4.4** | **3.7** | **2.9** | **3.8** | **4.1** | **2.8** | **3.7** | **2.9** | **2.1** | **2.7** | **..** |
| Angola | 1.2 | 3.0 | 0.5 | 2.8 | 3.1 | 3.6 | 3.9 | 2.6 | 0.3 | 0.0 | .. |
| Benin | 7.2 | 6.3 | 5.8 | 6.0 | 6.0 | .. | .. | .. | .. | .. | .. |
| Botswana | 11.8 | 5.8 | 3.8 | 4.1 | 4.3 | 5.2 | 5.3 | 5.9 | 5.4 | 3.4 | .. |
| Burkina Faso | 6.9 | 1.5 | 4.3 | 4.8 | 5.1 | .. | .. | .. | .. | .. | .. |
| Burundi | 3.1 | 1.8 | 2.9 | 4.2 | 4.5 | .. | .. | .. | .. | .. | .. |
| Cabo Verde | 5.6 | 17.1 | 4.5 | 4.7 | 4.7 | .. | .. | .. | .. | .. | .. |
| Cameroon | 3.6 | 3.8 | 4.0 | 4.2 | 4.5 | .. | .. | .. | .. | .. | .. |
| Central African Republic | 1.0 | 0.5 | 1.3 | 1.6 | 3.1 | .. | .. | .. | .. | .. | .. |
| Chad | -1.2 | 2.2 | 3.0 | 2.8 | 2.7 | .. | .. | .. | .. | .. | .. |
| Comoros | 2.1 | 2.6 | 3.0 | 3.5 | 4.0 | .. | .. | .. | .. | .. | .. |
| Congo, Dem. Rep. | 6.2 | 8.9 | 6.8 | 6.5 | 6.2 | .. | .. | .. | .. | .. | .. |
| Congo, Rep. | 1.0 | 1.5 | 3.2 | 4.1 | 3.0 | .. | .. | .. | .. | .. | .. |
| Côte d'Ivoire | 7.0 | 6.7 | 6.3 | 6.5 | 6.5 | .. | .. | .. | .. | .. | .. |
| Equatorial Guinea | -0.9 | 3.1 | -2.5 | -6.1 | -3.9 | .. | .. | .. | .. | .. | .. |
| Eritrea | 2.9 | 2.5 | 2.6 | 3.2 | 3.3 | .. | .. | .. | .. | .. | .. |
| Eswatini | 10.7 | 0.5 | 3.6 | 2.9 | 2.8 | .. | .. | .. | .. | .. | .. |
| Ethiopia [3] | 6.3 | 6.4 | 5.8 | 6.4 | 7.0 | .. | .. | .. | .. | .. | .. |
| Gabon | 1.5 | 3.0 | 2.7 | 3.0 | 2.8 | .. | .. | .. | .. | .. | .. |
| Gambia, The | 4.3 | 4.3 | 4.8 | 5.3 | 5.5 | .. | .. | .. | .. | .. | .. |
| Ghana | 5.1 | 3.1 | 2.3 | 2.8 | 4.4 | 3.5 | 2.7 | 3.7 | 3.3 | 3.2 | .. |
| Guinea | 4.3 | 4.7 | 5.1 | 5.8 | 6.2 | .. | .. | .. | .. | .. | .. |
| Guinea-Bissau | 6.4 | 3.5 | 2.8 | 5.6 | 4.5 | .. | .. | .. | .. | .. | .. |
| Kenya | 7.6 | 4.8 | 5.0 | 5.2 | 5.3 | 5.2 | 4.3 | 3.7 | 5.5 | 5.4 | .. |
| Lesotho | 1.6 | 1.8 | 2.2 | 2.5 | 2.1 | -1.4 | 4.2 | -3.1 | -2.2 | 1.4 | .. |
| Liberia | 5.0 | 4.8 | 4.5 | 5.4 | 6.2 | .. | .. | .. | .. | .. | .. |
| Madagascar | 5.7 | 3.8 | 4.0 | 4.8 | 4.7 | .. | .. | .. | .. | .. | .. |
| Malawi | 2.8 | 0.9 | 1.6 | 2.8 | 3.3 | .. | .. | .. | .. | .. | .. |
| Mali | 3.1 | 3.7 | 4.0 | 4.0 | 5.0 | .. | .. | .. | .. | .. | .. |
| Mauritania | 0.7 | 6.4 | 4.8 | 5.1 | 5.5 | .. | .. | .. | .. | .. | .. |
| Mauritius | 3.4 | 8.8 | 5.0 | 4.6 | 3.6 | .. | .. | .. | .. | .. | .. |
| Mozambique | 2.3 | 4.2 | 6.0 | 5.0 | 5.0 | 4.7 | 3.6 | 4.2 | 4.2 | 4.7 | 5.9 |
| Namibia | 3.5 | 4.6 | 2.8 | 2.9 | 3.1 | 5.9 | 5.4 | 4.9 | 8.3 | 5.5 | 7.2 |
| Niger | 1.4 | 11.5 | 2.3 | 12.8 | 7.4 | .. | .. | .. | .. | .. | .. |
| Nigeria | 3.6 | 3.3 | 2.9 | 3.3 | 3.7 | 3.4 | 2.4 | 3.6 | 2.4 | 2.6 | 3.1 |
| Rwanda | 10.9 | 8.2 | 6.9 | 7.5 | 7.8 | 7.5 | 10.0 | 7.3 | 9.2 | 6.3 | 7.5 |
| São Tomé and Príncipe | 1.9 | 0.1 | 0.5 | 2.5 | 3.3 | .. | .. | .. | .. | .. | .. |
| Senegal | 6.5 | 4.2 | 4.1 | 8.8 | 9.3 | .. | .. | .. | .. | .. | .. |
| Seychelles | 5.4 | 9.0 | 4.3 | 4.1 | 3.9 | 7.6 | 8.8 | 1.7 | 3.5 | -2.4 | .. |
| Sierra Leone | 4.1 | 3.5 | 3.1 | 3.7 | 4.3 | .. | .. | .. | .. | .. | .. |

# Real GDP growth (*continued*)

| | Annual estimates and forecasts[1] (Percent change) | | | | | Quarterly estimates[2] (Percent change, year-on-year) | | | | | |
|---|---|---|---|---|---|---|---|---|---|---|---|
| | 2021 | 2022 | 2023e | 2024f | 2025f | 22Q2 | 22Q3 | 22Q4 | 23Q1 | 23Q2 | 23Q3e |
| **Sub-Saharan Africa (*continued*)** | | | | | | | | | | | |
| South Africa | 4.7 | 1.9 | 0.7 | 1.3 | 1.5 | 0.2 | 4.1 | 0.8 | 0.2 | 1.5 | -0.7 |
| South Sudan [3] | -5.1 | -2.3 | -0.4 | 2.3 | 2.4 | .. | .. | .. | .. | .. | .. |
| Sudan | -1.9 | -1.0 | -12.0 | -0.6 | 0.2 | .. | .. | .. | .. | .. | .. |
| Tanzania | 4.3 | 4.6 | 5.1 | 5.5 | 6.1 | .. | .. | .. | .. | .. | .. |
| Togo | 6.0 | 5.8 | 5.2 | 5.2 | 5.8 | .. | .. | .. | .. | .. | .. |
| Uganda [3] | 3.4 | 4.7 | 5.3 | 6.0 | 6.6 | 5.9 | 9.0 | 4.5 | 1.8 | 5.4 | 5.3 |
| Zambia | 4.6 | 4.7 | 2.7 | 4.6 | 4.8 | 4.3 | 5.8 | 6.1 | 5.5 | 7.7 | .. |
| Zimbabwe | 8.5 | 6.5 | 4.5 | 3.5 | 3.5 | .. | .. | .. | .. | .. | .. |

*Sources:* Haver Analytics; World Bank.

*Note:* e = estimate; f = forecast. Since Croatia became a member of the euro area on January 1, 2023, it has been added to the euro area aggregate and removed from the EMDE and ECA aggregate in all tables to avoid double counting.

1. Aggregate growth rates calculated using GDP weights at average 2010-19 prices and market exchange rates.

2. Quarterly estimates are based on non-seasonally-adjusted real GDP, except for advanced economies, as well as Algeria, Ecuador, Morocco, and Tunisia. In some instances, quarterly growth paths may not align to annual growth estimates, owing to the timing of GDP releases. Quarterly data for Iraq, Jamaica, Nepal, and Pakistan are gross value added. Quarterly data for Montenegro are preliminary. Data for Timor-Leste represent non-oil GDP.

Regional averages are calculated based on data from the following economies.

East Asia and Pacific: China, Indonesia, Malaysia, Mongolia, the Philippines, Thailand, and Viet Nam.

Europe and Central Asia: Albania, Armenia, Belarus, Bosnia and Herzegovina, Bulgaria, Georgia, Hungary, Kazakhstan, Moldova, Montenegro, North Macedonia, Poland, Romania, the Russian Federation, Serbia, Türkiye, and Ukraine.

Latin America and the Caribbean: Argentina, Belize, Bolivia, Brazil, Chile, Colombia, Costa Rica, the Dominican Republic, Ecuador, El Salvador, Guatemala, Honduras, Jamaica, Mexico, Nicaragua, Panama, Paraguay, Peru, and Uruguay.

Middle East and North Africa: Bahrain, the Arab Republic of Egypt, the Islamic Republic of Iran, Jordan, Morocco, Oman, Qatar, Saudi Arabia, Tunisia, the United Arab Emirates, and West Bank and Gaza.

South Asia: India, Maldives, Pakistan, and Sri Lanka.

Sub-Saharan Africa: Angola, Botswana, Ghana, Kenya, Lesotho, Mozambique, Namibia, Nigeria, Rwanda, the Seychelles, South Africa, Uganda, and Zambia.

3. Annual GDP is on fiscal year basis, as per reporting practice in the country. For Bangladesh, Bhutan, Egypt, Nepal, and Pakistan, the column for 2022 refers to FY2021/22. For India and the Islamic Republic of Iran, the column for 2022 refers to FY2022/23.

4. Data for Afghanistan (beyond 2021), Lebanon (beyond 2023), Myanmar (beyond 2024), the Syrian Arab Republic (beyond 2023), and the Republic of Yemen (beyond 2024) are excluded because of a high degree of uncertainty.

5. Data for Bosnia and Herzegovina are from the production approach. Annual GDP for Pakistan are based on factor cost.

# Data and Forecast Conventions

The macroeconomic forecasts presented in this report are prepared by staff of the Prospects Group of the Equitable Growth, Finance and Institutions Vice-Presidency, in coordination with staff from the Macroeconomics, Trade, and Investment Global Practice and from regional and country offices, and with input from regional Chief Economist offices. They are the result of an iterative process that incorporates data, macroeconometric models, and judgment.

**Data.** Data used to prepare country forecasts come from a variety of sources. National Income Accounts (NIA), Balance of Payments (BOP), and fiscal data are from Haver Analytics; the World Development Indicators by the World Bank; the *World Economic Outlook*, *Balance of Payments Statistics*, and *International Financial Statistics* by the International Monetary Fund. Population data and forecasts are from the United Nations World Population Prospects. Country- and lending-group classifications are from the World Bank. The Prospects Group's internal databases include high-frequency indicators such as industrial production, consumer price indexes, emerging markets bond index (EMBI), exchange rates, exports, imports, policy rates, and stock market indexes, based on data from Bloomberg, Haver Analytics, IMF Balance of Payments Statistics, IMF *International Financial Statistics*, and J.P. Morgan.

**Aggregations.** Aggregate growth for the world and all subgroups of countries (such as regions and income groups) is calculated using GDP weights at average 2010-19 prices and market exchange rates of country-specific growth rates. Income groups are defined as in the World Bank's classification of country groups.

**Forecast process.** The process starts with initial assumptions about advanced-economy growth and commodity price forecasts. These are used as conditioning assumptions for the first set of growth forecasts for EMDEs, which are produced using macroeconometric models, accounting frameworks to ensure national account identities and global consistency, estimates of spillovers from major economies, and high-frequency indicators. These forecasts are then evaluated to ensure consistency of treatment across similar EMDEs. This is followed by extensive discussions with World Bank country teams, who conduct continuous macroeconomic monitoring and dialogue with country authorities and finalize growth forecasts for EMDEs. The Prospects Group prepares advanced-economy and commodity price forecasts. Throughout the forecasting process, staff use macroeconometric models that allow the combination of judgement and consistency with model-based insights.

# Global Economic Prospects: Selected Topics, 2015-24

# Global Economic Prospects: Selected Topics, 2015-24

## Growth and business cycles

**Productivity**

| | |
|---|---|
| How do disasters affect productivity? | June 2020, box 3.2 |
| Fading promise: How to rekindle productivity growth | January 2020, chapter 3 |
| EMDE regional productivity trends and bottlenecks | January 2020, box 3.1 |
| Sectoral sources of productivity growth | January 2020, box 3.2 |
| Patterns of total factor productivity: A firm perspective | January 2020, box 3.3 |
| Debt, financial crises, and productivity | January 2020, box 3.4 |

**Investment**

| | |
|---|---|
| The magic of investment accelerations | January 2024, chapter 3 |
| Sparking investment accelerations: Lessons from country case studies | January 2024, box 3.1 |
| Investment growth after the pandemic | January 2023, chapter 3 |
| Investment: Subdued prospects, strong needs | June 2019, special focus 1.1 |
| Weak investment in uncertain times: Causes, implications, and policy responses | January 2017, chapter 3 |
| Investment-less credit booms | January 2017, box 3.1 |
| Implications of rising uncertainty for investment in EMDEs | January 2017, box 3.2 |
| Investment slowdown in China | January 2017, box 3.3 |
| Interactions between public and private investment | January 2017, box 3.4 |

**Forecast uncertainty**

| | |
|---|---|
| Scenarios of possible global growth outcomes | June 2020, box 1.3 |
| Quantifying uncertainties in global growth forecasts | June 2016, special focus 2 |

**Fiscal space**

| | |
|---|---|
| Having space and using it: Fiscal policy challenges and developing economies | January 2015, chapter 3 |
| Fiscal policy in low-income countries | January 2015, box 3.1 |
| What affects the size of fiscal multipliers? | January 2015, box 3.2 |
| Chile's fiscal rule—an example of success | January 2015, box 3.3 |
| Narrow fiscal space and the risk of a debt crisis | January 2015, box 3.4 |
| Revenue mobilization in South Asia: Policy challenges and recommendations | January 2015, box 2.3 |

**Other topics**

| | |
|---|---|
| Education demographics and global inequality | January 2018, special focus 2 |
| Recent developments in emerging and developing country labor markets | June 2015, box 1.3 |
| Linkages between China and Sub-Saharan Africa | June 2015, box 2.1 |
| What does weak growth mean for poverty in the future? | January 2015, box 1.1 |
| What does a slowdown in China mean for Latin America and the Caribbean? | January 2015, box 2.2 |

## Monetary and exchange rate policies

| | |
|---|---|
| Financial spillovers of rising U.S. interest rates | June 2023, chapter 3 |
| Asset purchases in emerging markets: Unconventional policies, unconventional times | January 2021, chapter 4 |
| The fourth wave: Rapid debt buildup | January 2020, chapter 4 |
| Price controls: Good intentions, bad outcomes | January 2020, special focus 1 |
| Low for how much longer? Inflation in low-income countries | January 2020, special focus 2 |
| Currency depreciation, inflation, and central bank independence | June 2019, special focus 1.2 |
| The great disinflation | January 2019, box 1.1 |
| Corporate debt: Financial stability and investment implications | June 2018, special focus 2 |
| Recent credit surge in historical context | June 2016, special focus 1 |
| Peg and control? The links between exchange rate regimes and capital account policies | January 2016, chapter 4 |
| Negative interest rates in Europe: A glance at their causes and implications | June 2015, box 1.1 |
| Hoping for the best, preparing for the worst: Risks around U.S. rate liftoff and policy options | June 2015, special focus 1 |
| Countercyclical monetary policy in emerging markets: Review and evidence | January 2015, box 1.2 |

# Global Economic Prospects: Selected Topics, 2015-24

| Fiscal policies | |
|---|---|
| Fiscal policy in commodity exporters: An enduring challenge | January 2024, chapter 4 |
| How does procyclical fiscal policy affect output growth? | January 2024, box 4.1 |
| Do fiscal rules and sovereign wealth funds make a difference? Lessons from country case studies | January 2024, box 4.2 |
| Fiscal policy challenges in low-income countries | June 2023, chapter 4 |
| Resolving high debt after the pandemic: lessons from past episodes of debt relief | January 2022, special focus |
| How has the pandemic made the fourth wave of debt more dangerous? | January 2021, box 1.1 |
| The fourth wave: Rapid debt buildup | January 2020, chapter 4 |
| Debt: No free lunch | June 2019, box 1.1 |
| Debt in low-income countries: Evolution, implications, and remedies | January 2019, chapter 4 |
| Debt dynamics in emerging market and developing economies: Time to act? | June 2017, special focus 1 |
| Having fiscal space and using it: Fiscal challenges in developing economies | January 2015, chapter 3 |
| Revenue mobilization in South Asia: Policy challenges and recommendations | January 2015, box 2.3 |
| Fiscal policy in low-income countries | January 2015, box 3.1 |
| What affects the size of fiscal multipliers? | January 2015, box 3.2 |
| Chile's fiscal rule—an example of success | January 2015, box 3.3 |
| Narrow fiscal space and the risk of a debt crisis | January 2015, box 3.4 |

| Commodity markets | |
|---|---|
| Russia's invasion of Ukraine: Implications for energy markets and activity | June 2022, special focus 2 |
| Commodity price cycles: Underlying drivers and policy options | January 2022, chapter 3 |
| Reforms after the 2014-16 oil price plunge | June 2020, box 4.1 |
| Adding fuel to the fire: Cheap oil in the pandemic | June 2020, chapter 4 |
| The role of major emerging markets in global commodity demand | June 2018, special focus 1 |
| The role of the EM7 in commodity production | June 2018, SF1, box SF1.1 |
| Commodity consumption: Implications of government policies | June 2018, SF1, box SF1.2 |
| With the benefit of hindsight: The impact of the 2014–16 oil price collapse | January 2018, special focus 1 |
| From commodity discovery to production: Vulnerabilities and policies in LICs | January 2016, special focus |
| After the commodities boom: What next for low-income countries? | June 2015, special focus 2 |
| Low oil prices in perspective | June 2015, box 1.2 |
| Understanding the plunge in oil prices: Sources and implications | January 2015, chapter 4 |
| What do we know about the impact of oil prices on output and inflation? A brief survey | January 2015, box 4.1 |

| Globalization of trade and financial flows | |
|---|---|
| High trade costs: causes and remedies | June 2021, chapter 3 |
| The impact of COVID-19 on global value chains | June 2020, box SF1 |
| Poverty impact of food price shocks and policies | January 2019, chapter 4 |
| Arm's-length trade: A source of post-crisis trade weakness | June 2017, Special Focus 2 |
| The U.S. economy and the world | January 2017, Special Focus |
| Potential macroeconomic implications of the Trans-Pacific Partnership Agreement | January 2016, chapter 4 |
| Regulatory convergence in mega-regional trade agreements | January 2016, box 4.1.1 |
| China's integration in global supply chains: Review and implications | January 2015, box 2.1 |
| Can remittances help promote consumption stability? | January 2015, chapter 4 |
| What lies behind the global trade slowdown? | January 2015, chapter 4 |

# Prospects Group:
# Selected Other Publications on the Global Economy, 2015-24

| Commodity Markets Outlook | |
|---|---|
| Potential near-term implications of the conflict in the Middle East for commodity markets: A preliminary assessment | October 2023 |
| Forecasting industrial commodity prices | April 2023 |
| Pandemic, war, recession: Drivers of aluminum and copper prices | October 2022 |
| The impact of the war in Ukraine on commodity markets | April 2022 |
| Urbanization and commodity demand | October 2021 |
| Causes and consequences of metal price shocks | April 2021 |
| Persistence of commodity shocks | October 2020 |
| Food price shocks: Channels and implications | April 2019 |
| The implications of tariffs for commodity markets | October 2018, box |
| The changing of the guard: Shifts in industrial commodity demand | October 2018 |
| Oil exporters: Policies and challenges | April 2018 |
| Investment weakness in commodity exporters | January 2017 |
| OPEC in historical context: Commodity agreements and market fundamentals | October 2016 |
| From energy prices to food prices: Moving in tandem? | July 2016 |
| Resource development in an era of cheap commodities | April 2016 |
| Weak growth in emerging market economies: What does it imply for commodity markets? | January 2016 |
| Understanding El Niño: What does it mean for commodity markets? | October 2015 |
| How important are China and India in global commodity consumption? | July 2015 |
| Anatomy of the last four oil price crashes | April 2015 |
| Putting the recent plunge in oil prices in perspective | January 2015 |

| Inflation in Emerging and Developing Economies: Evolution, Drivers, and Policies | |
|---|---|
| Inflation: Concepts, evolution, and correlates | Chapter 1 |
| Understanding global inflation synchronization | Chapter 2 |
| Sources of inflation: Global and domestic drivers | Chapter 3 |
| Inflation expectations: Review and evidence | Chapter 4 |
| Inflation and exchange rate pass-through | Chapter 5 |
| Inflation in low-income countries | Chapter 6 |
| Poverty impact of food price shocks and policies | Chapter 7 |

| A Decade After the Global Recession: Lessons and Challenges for Emerging and Developing Economies | |
|---|---|
| A decade after the global recession: Lessons and challenges | Chapter 1 |
| What happens during global recessions? | Chapter 2 |
| Macroeconomic developments | Chapter 3 |
| Financial market developments | Chapter 4 |
| Macroeconomic and financial sector policies | Chapter 5 |
| Prospects, risks, and vulnerabilities | Chapter 6 |
| Policy challenges | Chapter 7 |
| The role of the World Bank Group | Chapter 8 |

| Global Waves of Debt: Causes and Consequences | |
|---|---|
| Debt: Evolution, causes, and consequences | Chapter 1 |
| Benefits and costs of debt: The dose makes the poison | Chapter 2 |
| Global waves of debt: What goes up must come down? | Chapter 3 |
| The fourth wave: Ripple or tsunami? | Chapter 4 |
| Debt and financial crises: From euphoria to distress | Chapter 5 |
| Policies: Turning mistakes into experience | Chapter 6 |

# Prospects Group:
# Selected Other Publications on the Global Economy, 2015-24

| Global Productivity: Trends, Drivers, and Policies | |
|---|---|
| Global productivity trends | Chapter 1 |
| What explains productivity growth | Chapter 2 |
| What happens to productivity during major adverse events? | Chapter 3 |
| Productivity convergence: Is anyone catching up? | Chapter 4 |
| Regional dimensions of productivity: Trends, explanations, and policies | Chapter 5 |
| Productivity: Technology, demand, and employment trade-offs | Chapter 6 |
| Sectoral sources of productivity growth | Chapter 7 |

| The Long Shadow of Informality: Challenges and Policies | |
|---|---|
| Overview | Chapter 1 |
| Understanding the informal economy: Concepts and trends | Chapter 2 |
| Growing apart or moving together? Synchronization of informal- and formal-economy business cycles | Chapter 3 |
| Lagging behind: informality and development | Chapter 4 |
| Informality in emerging market and developing economies: Regional dimensions | Chapter 5 |
| Tackling informality: Policy options | Chapter 6 |

| Commodity Markets: Evolution, Challenges and Policies | |
|---|---|
| The evolution of commodity markets over the past century | Chapter 1 |
| Commodity demand: Drivers, outlook, and implications | Chapter 2 |
| The nature and drivers of commodity price cycles | Chapter 3 |
| Causes and consequences of industrial commodity price shocks | Chapter 4 |

| Falling Long-Term Growth Prospects | |
|---|---|
| Potential not realized: An international database of potential growth | Chapter 1 |
| Regional dimensions of potential growth: Hopes and realities | Chapter 2 |
| The global investment slowdown: Challenges and policies | Chapter 3 |
| Regional dimensions of investment: Moving in the right direction? | Chapter 4 |
| Potential growth prospects: Risks, rewards and policies | Chapter 5 |
| Trade as an engine of growth: Sputtering but fixable | Chapter 6 |
| Services-led growth: Better prospects after the pandemic? | Chapter 7 |

| High-frequency monitoring | |
|---|---|
| *Global Monthly* newsletter | |

## ECO-AUDIT

### Environmental Benefits Statement

The World Bank Group is committed to reducing its environmental footprint. In support of this commitment, we leverage electronic publishing options and print-on-demand technology, which is located in regional hubs worldwide. Together, these initiatives enable print runs to be lowered and shipping distances decreased, resulting in reduced paper consumption, chemical use, greenhouse gas emissions, and waste.

We follow the recommended standards for paper use set by the Green Press Initiative. The majority of our books are printed on Forest Stewardship Council (FSC)-certified paper, with nearly all containing 50-100 percent recycled content. The recycled fiber in our book paper is either unbleached or bleached using totally chlorine-free (TCF), processed chlorine-free (PCF), or enhanced elemental chlorine-free (EECF) processes.

More information about the Bank's environmental philosophy can be found at http://www.worldbank.org/corporateresponsibility.